**The Methuen**
**Plays by Black** and Asian Writers

# The Methuen Drama Book of Plays by Black British Writers

## Welcome Home Jacko
Mustapha Matura

## Chiaroscuro
Jackie Kay

## Talking in Tongues
Winsome Pinnock

## Sing Yer Heart Out for the Lads
Roy Williams

## Fix Up
Kwame Kwei-Armah

## Gone Too Far!
Bola Agbaje

*edited and with an introduction by*
Lynette Goddard

B L O O M S B U R Y
LONDON · NEW DELHI · NEW YORK · SYDNEY

**Bloomsbury Methuen Drama**

An imprint of Bloomsbury Publishing Plc

| | |
|---|---|
| 50 Bedford Square | 1385 Broadway |
| London | New York |
| WC1B 3DP | NY 10018 |
| UK | USA |

www.bloomsbury.com

**Bloomsbury is a registered trade mark of Bloomsbury Publishing Plc**

This collection first published in Great Britain by Methuen Drama 2011

*Welcome Home Jacko* first published by Eyre Methuen Limited in 1980.
© 1980 by Mustapha Matura
*Chiaroscuro* first published in *Lesbian Plays* by Methuen London Ltd in 1987.
© 1987 by Jackie Kay
*Talking in Tongues* first published by Methuen Drama in 1995.
© 1995 by Winsome Pinnock
*Sing Yer Heart Out for the Lads* first published by Methuen Publishing Ltd in 2002.
© 2002 by Roy Williams
*Fix Up* first published by Methuen Publishing Ltd in 2004, revised edition
published in *Kwame Kwei-Armah Plays: 1* by Methuen Drama 2009.
© 2004, 2009 by Kwame Kwei-Armah
*Gone Too Far!* first published in Great Britain in 2007 by Methuen Drama.
© 2007 by Bola Agbaje
Introduction © Methuen Drama 2011

**British Library Cataloguing-in-Publication Data**
A catalogue record for this book is available from the British Library.

| ISBN: PB: | 978-1-4081-3124-4 |
|---|---|
| EPDF: | 978-1-4081-3098-8 |
| EPUB: | 978-1-4081-4571-5 |

**Library of Congress Cataloging-in-Publication Data**
A catalog record for this book is available from the Library of Congress.

# Contents

# Introduction

*The Methuen Drama Book of Plays by Black British Writers* is an
anthology of six plays from some of Britain's most prominent
black playwrights from the late 1970s to the early twenty-
first century. These four decades saw black writers emerge as
new voices in the 1970s, flourish through the work of black
and women's theatre companies in the 1980s and 1990s,
and achieve visibility in London's mainstream theatres in
the early 2000s. Identity politics has remained a key theme
in black British writing and the six plays in this collection
all place issues of black British identity at their heart,
highlighting some of the main concerns of each respective
era. Mustapha Matura's *Welcome Home Jacko* examines the
aspirations of black teenage boys in the racially hostile 1970s;
Jackie Kay's *Chiaroscuro* and Winsome Pinnock's *Talking in
Tongues* focus on black women's concerns within a 1980s and
1990s feminist context; and Roy Williams's *Sing Yer Heart Out
for the Lads*, Kwame Kwei-Armah's *Fix Up* and Bola Agbaje's
*Gone Too Far!* explore topical tensions of race, racism and
national identity in the early twenty-first century.

Mustapha Matura is the only playwright in this anthology
who is from the first generation of black Caribbean
immigrants in Britain. He came to London from Trinidad
in 1961, establishing a high-profile playwriting career that
included productions for the Royal Court Theatre (*As Time
Goes By* (1971) and *Play Mas* (1974)), the Bush Theatre
(*Independence* (1979)), Black Theatre Co-operative (*Welcome
Home Jacko* (1979) and *Meetings* (1982)), the Tricycle Theatre
(*Playboy of the West Indies* (1984, 1994 and 2004) and *Trinidad
Sisters* (1988)), and the National Theatre (*The Coup* (1991)).
Recognition of his achievements include winning the George
Devine Award and the John Whiting Award in 1971 for
*As Time Goes By,* and the *Evening Standard* Most Promising
Playwright Award in 1974 for *Play Mas*, and his plays are
regularly revived in the UK, USA and West Indies.

Matura writes with warmth, humanity and humour, celebrating his Caribbean cultural heritage and broadening British theatre aesthetics by representing West Indian characters speaking in their own accents and articulating their own styles and customs as a political resistance to the dominant conventions of the English stage.[1] His renowned adaptations have relocated classic plays to Caribbean contexts, transposing J. M. Synge's *Playboy of the Western World* to *Playboy of the West Indies* and Anton Chekhov's *Three Sisters* to *Trinidad Sisters*. His new writing has examined the detrimental political and economic effects of colonialism on his native Trinidad, mapping how the post-independence country continues to be affected by its pre-independent past and reflecting on the loss of old traditions to new values.[2]

*Welcome Home Jacko* offers a unique snapshot of issues faced by second-generation black British boys in the late 1970s, many of which remain topical today. After failing to secure any interest from London's fringe theatre companies, Matura co-founded Black Theatre Co-operative with Charlie Hanson to produce the play at The Factory in Paddington, the Riverside Studios in Hammersmith and Theatre Royal Stratford East. He wrote the play after visiting a youth centre in Sheffield that he describes as 'so desolate and hopeless and seemed to [. . .] be just a terminus for young black men moving in and out of prison and struggling to discover some kind of Black identity'.[3] Matura questions ideas of youth centres as safe havens that protect young black men from the racial hostilities of the world outside, demonstrating how they might also sometimes act as a breeding ground for aimlessness, apathy, disenchantment and disillusionment.

The boredom of the four black boys (Marcus, Zippy, Fret and Dole, aged seventeen to twenty-one) is symptomatic of a late 1970s era in which rising unemployment was to become worse following the election of Margaret Thatcher's Conservative government in June 1979, and was compounded by racism that saw black boys and men at risk of attack from the National Front and routinely subjected to increased police surveillance and harassment

exercised under the 'Sus' stop and search laws. With little
else to aspire to, their misguided competitions for status
and supremacy revolve around who will be the champion
of a table football game where the winner stays on and the
loser has to buy the next round of cokes. The boys articulate
their separatism through identification with the Afrocentric
religion of Rastafarianism, which Marcus in particular sees
as an authentic expression of black identity that uniquely
distinguishes him from white British people. Posters of
Ethiopia and Haile Selassie line the walls, reggae music plays
on the jukebox, and they speak with Jamaican accents and
wear 'authentic' Rasta robes sewn by their well-meaning
white youth worker Sandy. Her belief in the youth club
as a space that keeps them out of trouble, protects them
from the hostilities of the world outside and enables them
to articulate their identity on their own terms is contrasted
with Gail, a young black woman who arrives for her first day
working as a volunteer and thinks that they would benefit
from developing outside interests and going on outings to
learn more about black cultural traditions. Neither woman's
approach to dealing with youth disaffection is ideal – Sandy's
hands-off attitude fails to instil ambition or respect in the
teenagers, while Gail's suggestions of going on trips to the
zoo or a recording studio are naïve about the reality of their
lives and the lack of resources in an under-funded youth
centre.

  The youth club also fails to be a safe environment for girls,
who are scared off by the boys' displays of sexually predatory
machismo, and when Marcus violently attacks Gail and
threatens to rape her, a moral concern is raised about
whether the incident should be reported to the police, which
could lead to him being sent to prison. Audiences are invited
to question whether Sandy's refusal to report the incident
protects Marcus from the arms of the law or problematically
condones his misbehaviour. Jacko's return to the youth club
after being released from serving five years in prison for
rape also provokes questions about the boys' identity politics.
They celebrate his misdemeanour and refusal to inform on

co-defendants as the ultimate expression of macho solidarity, but he returns with stories of the reality of life in prison, which show how the illusion of status they experience within the confines of the youth club amounts to nothing in a man's world outside.

Jackie Kay is a poet and novelist of Nigerian and Scottish heritage, whose work draws from her experiences as a mixed race lesbian who was adopted by white Scottish parents, notably *The Adoption Papers* (1991), which is written from the multiple perspectives of the daughter, the adoptive mother and the birth mother. Kay's other publications include *Other Lovers* (1993), *Off Colour* (1998), *Trumpet* (1998), *Why Don't You Stop Talking* (2002), *Strawgirl* (2002), *Life Mask* (2005), *Wish I Was Here* (2006), *Darling* (2007), *The Lamplighter* (2008) and *Red Dust Road* (2010). Numerous awards for her poetry and novels include being made a MBE (Member of the Order of the British Empire) in 2006. Kay's brief foray into playwriting in the late 1980s brought rarely seen lesbian experiences to the British stage in an era that marked a high point in black and women's theatre in Britain. *Chiaroscuro* (1986) examined identity politics at the intersection of race and sexuality and *Twice Over* (1988) contrasted the stories of older lesbians against the experience of teenage schoolgirls.

*Chiaroscuro* (Italian for light (chiaro) and dark (scuro)) was commissioned by the Theatre of Black Women and first shown as a rehearsed reading in the Gay Sweatshop x 10 Festival in 1985, before being developed for a full production at the Drill Hall in 1986, directed by Joan Ann Maynard. Kay's political play centres on issues of naming, belonging and self-definition, particularly in relation to the labels 'black' and 'lesbian'. The four black women characters (Aisha, Beth, Opal and Yomi) explore how the politics of race and sexuality impact on ideas of a collective black female identity, how their diverse African and Asian heritages inform their identities in contemporary Britain, and how black lesbians are affected by racism, sexism and homophobia. A feminist politics of representation is embedded into the form of the play, a loose and symbolic choreo-poem that merges poetry, music, song, storytelling and physical theatre, creating an improvisatory feel to accommodate an ensemble performance where all four actresses remain on stage throughout.

Kay examines how identities are negotiated in a culture premised on ideas of fixed differences between races, genders and sexualities. She interrogates how the politicisation of black, women's and lesbian and gay identities in 1980s Britain were premised on an often unhelpful policing of boundaries between people in various groups, and she touches upon how mixed race people and lesbians unsettle such notions of pure race and/or gender categories. The play was workshopped for four weeks and went through several different versions between the rehearsed reading and the full production, but Kay remained concerned with the issue of naming and ideas about how perceptions of identity are shaped by labels inherited from previous generations. The women's identities are constructed in relation to assumptions, myths, memories and politics of black, women's and/or lesbian identity. Each woman evocatively describes her naming at the start of the play, carrying an object that resonates with her personal story and the issues that she needs to resolve in her (re)naming. Aisha's cushion was made by her grandmother and passed down with the story of her birth; Beth's photo album alludes to her mixed race and lesbian identity, containing pictures of white childhood friends and old boyfriends; Opal's mirror reflects her image back to her, forcing her to accept herself as black; and Yomi has a black doll which she was teased about when young, and upon which she projects her internalised racial hatred.

Their debates about identification and labelling come to a head at the dinner party where Yomi controversially condemns mixed race people as confused about their identity and lesbians as stereotypically butch women. Her outburst could mark the breakdown of communication, but instead is the hopeful start of reconciliation in which the women acknowledge their homophobic and racist internalised programming. They begin a process of reinventing themselves by identifying ways of understanding each other that move beyond the kinds of fixed definitions of race, gender and sexuality that are typically used to oppress black people, homosexuals and women. Critics commended Kay for refusing to romanticise black women within ideas of a shared and uncontested sisterhood. As Barney Bardsley observed: 'Discarding the superficial notion of harmonious sisterhood, Jackie Kay examines the complexities and contradictions of each woman – how she moves with, and against, her friends; how she comes to terms with her race, her sexuality, her history and her destiny.'[4] Kay shows that reinventing and renaming black womanhood comes with recognition of both the similarities and the differences between them, enabling complex perspectives to emerge.

Winsome Pinnock is undoubtedly Britain's leading black woman playwright of the 1980s and 1990s, whose career included writing for theatre, television and radio. Pinnock won the 1991 George Devine Award for *Leave Taking* (1987), which secured two revivals at the Lyric Hammersmith in 1990 and the National Theatre in 1995. The Royal Court hosted productions of *A Hero's Welcome* (1989), *A Rock in Water* (1989), *Talking in Tongues* (1991) and *Mules* (1996). Her other plays include *Water* (2000) and *One Under* (2005). Pinnock depicts black women's experiences of migration from the West Indies to England and consequent experiences of alienation, culture clashes, displacement, hybridity and lack of belonging while negotiating identity in multiracial Britain. Critics applauded the 'universal' humanity of her plays, manifest particularly in a move away from the stridently angry agit-prop plays of the 1970s and early 1980s towards a form of black social realism that resonated with British new writing styles.

*Talking in Tongues* was first produced at the Royal Court Theatre in September 1991, directed by Hettie Macdonald, and focuses on black women's cultural identity in early 1990s Britain. Pinnock takes inspiration from Shakespeare's *Othello* to examine contemporary black women's responses to the contentious issue of interracial relationships, their fears and anxieties that black men prefer white women, and the impact on their self-esteem. Two clearly distinguished acts move from a monochrome coat room at a New Year's Eve party in London, where Leela secretly witnesses her partner Bentley having illicit sex with a white woman (Fran), to a vibrantly colourful beach in Jamaica where she escapes with her friend Claudette to recuperate from the relationship break-up. But the idea that they will no longer feel marginalised in the Caribbean is countered by a trip fraught with conflicts, contradictions and complexities that demonstrate how diasporic migrations have ruptured ideas of a simplistically unified black identity. They are treated as 'English' tourists in Jamaica, and after Claudette embarks on a typical holiday romance with Jamaican Mikie she is upset to discover that a white woman (Kate) has emigrated there and is also having an affair with him. Claudette's extreme racial politics are epitomised by an 'us and them' perspective that rejects interracial relationships as a form of racial betrayal, and her anger is eventually unleashed in a spiteful act of revenge towards Kate. When Leela and Claudette vindictively cut off Kate's long blonde ponytail while she sleeps in the sun, they are lashing out at years of discrimination in which hair is one symbol of the beauty of white women in Eurocentric discourses in opposition to notions of 'nappy' black hair as unruly, unmanageable and ugly.

Nonetheless, the trip abroad enables Leela to find a voice to express herself freely and 'talking in tongues' near the end of the play eventually empowers her to release years of rage and anger that she has suppressed beneath a veneer of polite communication and small-talk in England. Leela finds a language beyond the restrictions of English, which marginalises her as the negative term black/woman in a binary structure in which white/man is the norm. Her coming to voice is pre-empted by a prologue telling the story of Dum Dum, a woman who never speaks, who finds a voice while washing clothes in the gully in the company of other black women, away from the male world she usually inhabits.

*Talking in Tongues* boldly dramatises controversial and provocative issues, opening up pertinent debates about sensitive ideas of race and racism. The play was largely well received as a 'delicate yet tough minded exploration of sexual ethics [. . .] measured and ambitious',[5] although some critics felt that it was 'narrow and angry',[6] portraying crude and pessimistic divisions between black and white people. There is hope at the end of the play, however, as the humiliation of Kate becomes a basis from which the women start to tentatively talk to each other, beginning a process of healing rifts caused by historical traumas and learning how to communicate and understand each other across perceived differences of race. Caroline Donald recognised that the 'complexities of characterization go beyond shallow issues of black and white'.[7]

Roy Williams is one of the most significant black playwrights in contemporary British theatre, whose work is highly commended by the mainstream. His illustrious career includes plays at the Theatre Royal Stratford East (*No Boys Cricket Club* (1996)), the Tricycle Theatre (*Starstruck* (1998), *The Gift* (2000) and *Category B* (2009)), the Royal Court Theatre (*Lift Off* (1999), *Clubland* (2001), *Fallout* (2003) and *Sucker Punch* (2010)) and the Lyric Hammersmith (*Absolute Beginners* (2007)), as well as commissions for the National Theatre (*Sing Yer Heart Out for the Lads* (2002 and 2004) and *Baby Girl* (2007)) and the Royal Shakespeare Company (*Days of Significance* (2007)). His other plays include *Local Boy* (2000), *Little Sweet Thing* (2005) and *Joe Guy* (2007). Williams has won numerous awards, including the George Devine Award in 2000, the *Evening Standard* Charles Wintour Most Promising Playwright Award in 2001 and the South Bank Show Arts Council Decibel Award in 2003, and he was honoured with an OBE (Officer of the Order of the British Empire) for services to drama in 2008.

Williams has developed a niche for raw and uncompromising accounts of multiracial Britain, exposing the fissures of race, class and nation. He explores urgent themes of belonging for urban youth, with a particular focus

on articulations of masculinity that question how black boys
and young men negotiate their sexual and cultural identities
in multiracial contexts and how their identities reflect
changing notions of Britishness.

*Sing Yer Heart Out for the Lads* was first produced at the
National Theatre in 2002, directed by Simon Usher, and
revived with a new cast for a larger-scale production in the
Cottesloe in 2004, directed by Paul Miller. The play has also
since been toured by Pilot Theatre in 2006–7, directed by
Marcus Romer. Usher's original production launched the
National Theatre's 'Transformation' season, a five-month
run premiering thirteen new plays, which also included an
adaptation of Jeanette Winterson's novel *The Powerbook*, Sean
O' Brien's adaptation of Aristophanes' *The Birds*, Matthew
Bourne's *Play Without Words*, Richard Bean's *The Mentalists*
and Tanika Gupta's *Sanctuary*. 'Transformation' aimed to
attract younger spectators to diversify the usual audience
demographic of the National Theatre, and *Sing Yer Heart
Out for the Lads* was produced in the newly created Loft
Theatre, a conversion of the upstairs bar of the Lyttleton
into a 100-seater space with a bar and chill-out lounge area.
Williams's state-of-the-nation play was welcomed by critics
as 'an important bulletin about London today',[8] addressing
precisely the kinds of questions about race and nation
that a national theatre in multicultural Britain ought to be
representing.

Williams is an avid football fan and drew inspiration
from his experience of being in a pub watching England's
defeat to Germany in a World Cup qualifier in 2000, the last
match played at the original Wembley Stadium before it was
demolished and rebuilt, which was also renowned for Kevin
Keegan's immediate resignation as England manager. The
xenophobic responses of English fans to German players
prompted Williams to write the play. *Sing Yer Heart Out for
the Lads* is set in the King George pub on the afternoon of 7
October 2000 as a group of England supporters gather to
watch the match. Action and dialogue are carefully tied to
the real time of the ninety-minute football match which is

being played on a giant television screen, responding to key moments – Beckham's free-kick, Hamman's goal, and Kevin Keegan's post-match interview and resignation.

The first year of a new millennium is an opportune moment to ask urgent questions about racism, national identity and belonging in an increasingly diversified England. Williams examines how the current generation of black Londoners fit into the landscape of Britain, and considers whether attitudes about race have changed since the post-war era or if racist values are simply remodelled slightly for each new epoch. As the first-generation *Windrush* migrants are beginning to die out, the experiences of the subsequent generations become increasingly important to engaging with what it means to negotiate cultural identity in Britain today. How do black and white Britons negotiate the landscape of multiracial Britain? Williams raises debates about race and national identity that are hardly tackled in British theatre, provocatively confronting complex issues in an unapologetic way. He exposes the tribal and nationalistic emotions that are often evoked by international sports matches, commenting on strands of racism ranging from liberal tolerance, nationalistic patriotism and seemingly innocuous prejudice, to blatantly racist violence. Miller's 2004 production re-created the environment of a full pub on the night of an England match, implicating audience members in the offensive racism and violence by seating them in among the action at tables and barstools.

With fourteen characters, it was Williams's biggest and most ambitious play, described in reviews as a 'disturbing meditation on the meaning of Englishness and racial equality'[9] and 'colourful, intense, [and] viscerally affecting'.[10] A range of white and black British working-class characters discuss complex issues of racism, nationalism and Britishness, illustrating how attitudes about race are filtered down through generations. They are united in their support of England, but divisions of race and generation become more apparent throughout the game; as England's fortunes

wane and the men become more frustrated, they begin to
expose their latent racisms.

Every character in the play makes a prejudiced comment
at some point, highlighting the contradictions and
complexities of race and national identity in contemporary
London. Black characters are victims of white racism and
perpetrators of prejudice towards Asians. Jimmy (white,
fifties) welcomes the regular black clientele, yet makes
bigoted remarks about immigrants swamping Britain that
emanate from Enoch Powell's era. His daughter Gina,
the pub landlady, believes in integration and has had an
interracial relationship with black customer Mark, but she
would prefer her son Glen not to hang around with the
local black kids who get him into trouble and when one of
them 'borrows' his jacket and mobile phone a more blatantly
racist voice comes to the fore. Lawrie is an old-fashioned
racist who celebrates violence towards black people, while
his brother Lee is a placid liberal policeman living in a post-
Macpherson era in which he is afraid to openly express his
personal views about race following the Macpherson report's
damning indictment of racism within the Metropolitan
police force following an inquiry into the racist murder of
teenager Stephen Lawrence. The most controversial brand
of racism is articulated by far right extremist Alan, who
justifies his ideas about white supremacy with educated and
rational explanations. Williams is careful not to demonise
Alan, however, illustrating how the popularity of the BNP
can be built upon careful rhetoric that seeks to protect
'Englishness' from the effects of new waves of immigration.

However, it is the representations of the younger
generation who were brought up in an integrated England
that best illustrate how racist and nationalist values are
imbibed and perpetuated. Barry is black and in his early
twenties, an ardent supporter of England who proves
his allegiance by painting the St George flag on his face,
tattooing the British bulldog on his lower back and getting
involved in racist football violence abroad. In one of the
most uncomfortable moments of the play, he is the first to

shout xenophobic comments about the German players while watching the match. As the lead scorer in the pub football team's match earlier in the day, Barry is given a hero's welcome upon his return. Yet we cannot help but notice that he arrives last having walked back alone while his white team-mates shared cars. Barry's older brother Mark has left the army with a sceptical view of race relations in England that verges on being oversensitive by interpreting everything in racial terms. Gina's fourteen-year-old son Glen is the youngest character in the play and initially seems to be a product of a well-integrated multiracial society. He hangs around with the local black children, listens to rap music and speaks a generational 'urban patois',[11] a street talk incorporating African-Caribbean dialects that his mother cannot understand. But Glen and Barry's oblivion to England's racial complexities have serious repercussions at the end of the play, culminating in Glen stabbing Mark to death, and Barry renouncing his allegiance to England by wiping the painted flag from his face. This powerful ending makes a strong impact about the state of race relations in Britain today, reminding audiences that any discussions of contemporary notions of Englishness lead to the inevitable question, 'What form of English culture are we talking about?'[12] Yet, some critics found the ending pessimistic, suggesting that the younger generations' resort to angry racism 'paints a future of danger and despair',[13] which carries an air of hopelessness about the potential for a peaceful multicultural society. On the whole, critics praised Williams for a 'bold and brutal exposé of racism and what it means to be English in contemporary Britain',[14] exemplified in Carole Woddis's comment, 'I can't remember a more upsetting or important night in the theatre.'[15]

Kwame Kwei-Armah is one of Britain's leading black playwrights of the early twenty-first century who also has a thriving career as an actor, director, TV presenter and media pundit. He first became well known as an actor in BBC TV drama series *Casualty* and as a contestant on *Comic Relief Does Fame Academy*, and has also appeared as a panellist on

*Newsnight Review*, *The Culture Show* and *Question Time*, and
presented the documentary *Christianity: A History* (Channel
4) and the short series *On Tour with the Queen* (Channel 4).
Kwei-Armah made his London playwriting debut in 2003
when Jack Bradley (then literary manager for the National
Theatre) invited him to write a play for the National Theatre
Studio. *Elmina's Kitchen* (2003), set in a West Indian takeaway
in Hackney's 'Murder Mile', became the first part of Kwei-
Armah's National Theatre triptych, three plays set in black
British habitats, which also included *Fix Up* (2004), set in
a black political bookshop in Tottenham, and *Statement of
Regret* (2007), set in a black political think tank in London.
*Elmina's Kitchen* was shortlisted for an Olivier Award for
Best New Play, and the television version was nominated for
a BAFTA. Kwei-Armah won the *Evening Standard* Charles
Wintour Most Promising Playwright Award in 2004, and
became the first British-born black playwright to have a play
staged in the West End when *Elmina's Kitchen* transferred to
the Garrick Theatre in 2005. His other plays include *A Bitter
Herb* (1998), *Big Nose* (1999) and *Hold On* (previously *Blues
Brother, Soul Sister*) (2001), *Let There Be Love* (2008) and *Seize
the Day* (2009).

Kwame Kwei-Armah is an openly political playwright
who writes as a 'catalyst for debate around themes that
are pertinent to our communities and to our nation'.[16] His
highly naturalistic plays are written through his cultural
lens as a black British man, provocatively discussing topical
social issues drawn from media concerns such as 'black on
black violence', post-traumatic slave syndrome, immigration
and citizenship, and the possibility of electing a black
mayor for London. Kwei-Armah challenges simplistic
notions of contemporary black identity by placing diverse
characters into conflict with each other about pertinent
issues of race, culture and heritage and allowing a range of
complex and contradictory perspectives to surface. He is
especially mindful of the impact of the past on the present,
how legacies of slavery affect contemporary black lives as
each generation inherits from their predecessors, and the

fundamental question about the need to understand history and heal past traumas in order to secure better futures.

*Fix Up* was first produced in the National Theatre's Cottesloe in December 2004, directed by Angus Jackson. A range of black British characters debate contrasting opinions on race, identity and the routes of progress for contemporary black British people. Kwei-Armah examines how notions of black identity might need to adjust to accommodate an increasingly diversified society, with particular reference to how the growth of mixed race communities in Britain impacts on contemporary race politics and activism and how sticking to outdated political principles can impede possibilities for progress. Bunny Christie's realistic set design transported audiences to 'Fix Up', a small political bookshop in Tottenham, north London, where the dusty old shelves are teeming with books, African statues and carvings that reflect the Afrocentric politics of owner Brother Kiyi. A father figure in the community, Kiyi's 'black conscious' politics are heavily informed by the speeches, lectures and manifestos of prominent black nationalist thinkers and political activists, such as James Baldwin, Marcus Garvey and Claude McKay whose tapes he listens to in the shop. He believes in books as a way of remembering black history, following Marcus Garvey's notion 'There is no future for a people that deny their past', but despite that fact that it is black history month the shop is lacking customers and is under threat of being closed down and converted into a potentially more lucrative venture of luxury flats over a black hair-care shop. The revelation that political activist Kwesi is behind these plans is used to raise questions about how the quest for black liberation might need to adapt to the changing demands of a contemporary world. Audiences laughed at Kiyi's exclamation 'You can't replace history with hair gel!', but Kwesi presents a rational argument for a lucrative business venture that empowers black revolutionary activity through fiscal means. Indeed, Kiyi's comment in Scene Four that 'in the first months of trading no doubt more black folk

will have passed through here than I'd have seen in my
whole fifteen years' is an indictment of the possibility that
'black people today would rather have their roots done
by a hairdresser than examined by a historian', as Patrick
Marmion's astute review puts it.[17]

Hair is a prominent motif in the play, and the most
mentioned theme, underlining the commercial potential
for converting the bookshop into a hair-product store.
Kiyi's best friend Norma wears a different wig in each of
her appearances, and her first concern on deciding to get
involved in local politics is about where she can buy a new
wig to wear to her inaugural election-campaign meeting.
Kiyi's full head of 'greying, unkempt locks' signify his
Afrocentric political allegiance, and sitting centre-stage
cutting them off while the bookstore is being dismantled
around him at the end of the play symbolises a final break
with the past, the end of an era for his radical black-centred
politics and the beginnings of new possibilities that reflect
the current times.

The political debates at the heart of *Fix Up* are refracted
through the personal story of Kiyi's relationship to mixed
race character Alice who turns up in the first scene searching
for knowledge of black history that she felt denied while
growing up with a white adoptive family in Shropshire.
Secrets, lies and past indiscretions are a key motif of Kwei-
Armah's plays, captured here in Alice's determination to
reveal Kiyi as the father who killed her mother and left her
to be brought up in care. Alice's presence impacts on all
of the male characters and she forces Kiyi to see how his
attitude towards mixed race people is outmoded for the
context of contemporary Britain, described in one review as
'flawed by nostalgia, arrogance and a limited view of what
"black" is in a Babylon where mixed race or (the PC term)
"dual heritage" is the norm'.[18]

Kwei-Armah raises important questions about the
current state of black British identity politics and his writing
was praised for being 'full of provocative ideas about
the relationship between political ideals and economic

pressures',[19] 'tough and ebullient'[20] and 'sharp and funny'.[21] Some of the more critical reviews suggested that the weight of the ideas undermined the dramatic potential of the play, leading to contrived characterisation, melodramatic plotting and unbelievable twists. However, John Nathan ranked it as 'the best new work I have seen this year'[22] and Helena Thompson observed 'To his credit, Armah's understanding of traditional structure underpins a script that broaches issues rarely seen at the National. It is a combination that makes his message all the harder to ignore.'[23]

In just three years since her first play was produced, Bola Agbaje has rapidly established herself as an important new voice in contemporary black British playwriting. *Gone Too Far!* (2007) was her first play, written and first produced as part of the Royal Court Young Writers' Festival in 2007, directed by Bijan Sheibani in the Theatre Upstairs, and revived for a mainhouse production downstairs in 2008 when it also toured to the Albany in Deptford and the Hackney Empire. Agbaje won the Laurence Olivier Award for Outstanding Achievement in 2008 and was also nominated for the *Evening Standard* Charles Wintour Most Promising Playwright Award. Her other plays include *Detaining Justice* (2009), *Playing the Game* (2010) and *Off the Endz* (2010).

*Gone Too Far!* was praised as 'an odyssey that gets right under the skin of multicultural Britain',[24] immediately establishing Agbaje's potential to become a new force in dramatising contemporary black Britain. Critics likened her representations of urban London with those found in Kwame Kwei-Armah and Roy Williams's plays, seeing promise in her unique female stance ('joyous irreverent energy, [. . .] fresh, winning playfulness')[25] and particular insight into the perspectives of the younger generation. Agbaje draws from her own experiences of being a teenager to add an air of authenticity to her comic portrayal of a group of young people on a south London council housing estate. Language is a key motif of their identities, reflecting a diversity of influences in which Jamaican, Nigerian, formal

English and street jargon all merge to form the complex identities of young multicultural Britain. James Cotterill's limited décor design created the effect of a bleak urban wasteland, using a few simple props to symbolise the various locations, seating the audience on hard grey-slab benches, and leaving ample space for Bijan Sheibani's high-energy production in which the actors performed choreographed dance routines to loud 'urban' music between the scenes and a memorable strobe-lit, stylised slow-motion street fight that theatricalised the violence.

*Gone Too Far!* uses the story of two brothers with contrasting ideas about their identities to examine the tensions, divisions and prejudices within a group of black teenagers in contemporary London. Yemi has grown up in Britain and rejects his Nigerian culture and heritage in favour of identifying with 'cool' West Indian identity to try to fit in with his friends. His older brother Ikudayisi has just arrived from Nigeria and although he tends to slip into a faux American accent to impress the girls is fundamentally proud of his Nigerian roots. Their sibling rivalry becomes a symbol for the wider conflicts between the African and Caribbean youth in the play. The brothers go on a simple errand to the local shops to buy a pint of milk, getting to know more about each other and the world that they inhabit on their way. They have a number of racist encounters with a Bangladeshi shopkeeper, an elderly white lady and two ignorant white police officers, but it is their equally prejudiced encounters with other black teenagers that accentuate how racial tensions have reached boiling point in contemporary London.

Mouthy mixed race character Armani stands out the most as highlighting the contradictions and complexities of British black identity. She is comically mocked for embracing the Jamaican identity of her father and claiming to be 'from Yard', even though she has never met him or visited the Caribbean and has acquired all of her knowledge about black culture (in terms of hairstyling, food, music and dancing) from her friend Paris. Armani's

offensive statements about dark-skinned people and
her vitriol towards Africans highlight her ignorance of a
cultural lineage that links West Indians to Africa through
the triangular slave trade, while also drawing attention
to reasons why Yemi is ashamed of his cultural heritage
and over-invests in 'Caribbean cool' as a survival strategy
on London's streets. Agbaje gives credit to young people,
however, adamant that they themselves have the best insight
into their disaffection and the answers for improving their
lives. Blazer is an important character who goes some way to
countering Armani's anti-African rhetoric. He is the top man
on the estate who commands respect from the others. Blazer
is a thinker who has read books about black history and is
able to place identity politics within an historical context.
His pride for his Nigerian heritage links an honouring of
cultural traditions of respect that he learnt in the home to
the status that he earns on the street.

A further context of the play is the issue of knife crime
among teenagers in Britain's urban communities, which
reached epidemic proportions in 2008. Agbaji even wrote
to then Prime Minister Gordon Brown inviting him to come
to see the play to learn about the issues affecting young
people in London. She shows how such petty conflicts as
those between African and Caribbean youth can escalate into
violence and even murder. When Ikudayisi is accidentally
stabbed and falls to the ground in the penultimate scene, a
blackout leaves audiences wondering whether he is another
black male victim dying on London's streets. But Agbaje
prefers a happy ending and the final scene sees the brothers
safely back at home, Yemi now wearing his traditional
Nigerian attire with a baseball cap and trainers, finally
proud of his complex identity as a British Nigerian. The
two brothers' final acceptance of each other is a message of
hope for better communications across racial and cultural
divisions in the UK, for an increased awareness of the
cultural contexts that shape our identities and relationships
with each other.

Black British playwriting is thriving at the beginning of the twenty-first century, benefiting from initiatives to address institutional racism in the British theatre sector that have started to make the industry more culturally diverse and closer to truly reflecting the demographic of a multiracial society. The plays in *The Methuen Drama Book of Plays by Black British Writers* show that each generation builds on the stories of its predecessors to reflect the changing concerns of black Britain over the past four decades. Each of these playwrights has made pertinent contributions to developing a narrative of black British identity from the late 1970s to the present day, representing some of the urgent issues of their times and demonstrating diverse black perspectives on race and racism. Their stories play a crucial role in constructing ideas and perceptions of cultural identity in a rapidly changing Britain.

Lynette Goddard

August 2010

## Notes

[1] Michael McMillan, 'Ter Speak in Yer Mudder Tongue: An Interview with Playwright Mustapha Matura', in Kwesi Owusu (ed.), *Black British Culture and Society* (London: Routledge, 2000), 255–64.

[2] D. Keith Peacock, 'Home Thoughts from Abroad: Mustapha Matura', in Mary Luckhurst (ed.), *A Companion to Modern British and Irish Drama: 1880–2005,* (Oxford: Blackwells, 2005), 188–97.

[3] Mustapha Matura, *Six Plays* (London: Methuen, 1992), x.

[4] Barney Bardsley, *Tribune*, 28 March 1986.

[5] Harry Eyres, *The Times*, 4 September 1991.

[6] Milton Shulman, *Evening Standard*, 30 August 1991.

[7] Caroline Donald, *Independent*, 4 September 1991.

[8] Nicholas de Jongh, *Evening Standard*, 3 May 2002.

[9] Nicholas de Jongh, *Evening Standard*, 4 May 2004.

[10] Alastair Macaulay, *Financial Times*, 7 May 2002.

[11] Miranda Sawyer, *Observer,* 10 February 2008.

[12] Roy Williams, NT Platform, National Theatre, London, 17 May 2004.

[13] Autolycus, *Financial Times*, 11 May 2002.

[14] Georgina Brown, *Mail on Sunday*, 9 May 2004.

[15] Carole Woddis, *Herald,* 4 May 2004.

[16] http://www.guardian.co.uk/media/2010/jul/12/kwame-kwei-armah-mediaguardian-100–2010 (visited 13 July 2010).

[17] Patrick Marmion, *Daily Mail*, 7 January 2005.

[18] Benedict Nightingale, *The Times*, 18 December 2004.

[19] Aleks Sierz, *Tribune*, 7 January 2005.

[20] John Peter, *Sunday Times*, 26 December 2004.

[21] Benedict Nightingale, *The Times*, 18 December 2004.

[22] John Nathan, *Jewish Chronicle*, 24 December 2004.

[23] Helena Thompson, *Ham and High Express*, 7 January 2005.

[24] Lyn Gardner, *Guardian,* 9 February 2007.

[25] Sam Marlowe, *The Times*, 8 February 2007.

**Mustapha Matura**

# Welcome Home Jacko

**Mustapha Matura** was born in Trinidad and came to England in 1961. He co-founded the Black Theatre Co-operative with the director Charlie Hanson in 1978 under which he wrote the highly successful *No Problem!*. His plays include: *Rum an' Coca Cola* (Royal Court Theatre and off-Broadway, 1976); *Another Tuesday* and *More, More* (the Factory, London, 1978); *A Dying Business* (Riverside Studios, 1980); *One Rule* (Riverside Studios, 1981); *The Playboy of the West Indies* (Oxford Playhouse, 1984, and produced for BBC television, 1985); *Trinidad Sisters* (Tricycle Theatre, 1988) and *The Coup* (Royal National Theatre, 1991). In 1991, Mustapha received the Trinidad and Tobago Government Scarlet Ibis Award for achievement.

*Welcome Home Jacko* was first presented at The Factory, Paddington, London, on 12 June 1979. The cast was as follows:

| | |
|---|---|
| **Jacko** | Gordon Case |
| **Marcus** | Victor Evans |
| **Zippy** | Trevor Laird |
| **Fret** | Alrick Riley |
| **Sandy** | Maggie Shevlin |
| **Gail** | Dorrett Thompson |
| **Dole** | Chris Tummings |

*Director*   Charlie Hanson

## Act One

*Scene: a Youth Club.*

*Time: afternoon.*

*A bar counter on the side with stools, also tables and chairs against the wall. Posters of Africa, Ethiopia, Haile Selassie, Youth Employment, a Police PR poster. Across the ceiling a larger banner saying:* WELCOME HOME JACKO. *The rear stairs leading to an office upstairs. In the corner a Juke Box/Football machine.*

*Four black boys (seventeen to twenty-one),* **Zippy**, **Marcus**, **Dole** *and* **Fret**, *are playing a football machine.*

**Zippy**   Ras Clart me a beat yer.

**Marcus**   Bet what you a miss ter Ras Clart, you a hit one ball you a call dat beat.

**Zippy**   Aright, make we play one more game, Dole yer ready?

**Dole**   Me no want te play no mor Man, him a make ter much Ras Clart noise make we play some Dominoes.

**Zippy**   Cha Man, I we play.

**Marcus**   Me an Fret go clart yer ras, eh Fret?

**Fret**   Yea, yea, make we play, en last round, first five win.

**Marcus**   Wha yer say?

**Zippy**   Me ready Dole.

**Dole**   Aright, make we play, him a make ter much noise make we shut him Ras Clart mouth.

**Marcus**   Wait, wait, wha we a play for?

**Zippy**   Wha him mean?

**Marcus**   Coke, make we play fer Coke, who a lose him have ter buy, wha yer a say?

**Zippy**   Cha why not you no win.

**Dole**   Yea.

**Marcus**   Make we see.

**Zippy**   Aright.

*They play.* **Zippy** *and* **Dole**, **Marcus** *and* **Fret**.

**Zippy**   Move dey, yer Ras shift, eh.

**Dole**   Block him Ras.

**Marcus**   Go way Block yer Bomba, dat . . . go in, go in.

**Zippy**   Block him Cha.

**Marcus**   Move Fret, block im Fret.

**Zippy**   Goal.

**Marcus**   Cha Fret you a let de Ras Clart Man score him a get easy goal, me no why him a score me no had me sounds wit me punch me a dub, Fret.

**Fret**   Him a lucky, him a lucky.

*Goes, punches Juke Box (Reggae). Throughout the later games music is played.*

**Zippy**   Lucky me Ras Clart dat a skill, skill from above, skill from Jah.

**Marcus**   Jah, me Ras, wha you no bout Jah, dat a luck.

**Zippy**   Me no Jah, me talk ter Jah, him talk ter me, me an him communicate him a tell me hit de Ras Clart ball square, me hit it square it a go in square.

**Marcus**   Cha.

**Zippy**   Me an Dole, we hand guided wha yer say Dole?

**Dole**   Cha, him a seek him revenge.

**Marcus**   Him a right me a hit yer Ras wid de Rod a Correction come Fret, block him Ras.

*They play.*

**Dole**    Go way, go way yer Ras.

**Zippy**    Block him, block him Ras Clart.

**Marcus**    Go in, go in, go, go.

**Zippy**    Block in, cha him gone.

**Marcus**    Block him break Fret, Fret, block him, cross.

**Fret**    We have him de Fret ter Ras.

**Marcus**    Good him Ras worry now, go in, go in.

**Zippy**    Dole.

**Marcus**    Goal, goal ter Ras.

**Zippy**    Dole you let de Ras Clart Man jinx yer.

**Marcus**    Whey yer communicate wid Jah gone me just cut yer wires. Jah do' want ter know you, him a have better Ras Clart ting ter do.

**Zippy**    Aright one all.

**Marcus**    Dat goal was scored by de Lion of Judea, de warrior of Redemption ter Ras Clart, me no me should have me dub.

**Zippy**    Make we play. Make we play.

**Marcus**    Fret like him in a hurry ter buy Coke, him feeling rich come, Resurrection is at hand all Hypocrites I will shed blood come to Canaan.

*They play.*

**Zippy**    Block him Ras.

**Dole**    Me block im.

**Zippy**    Up, up.

**Marcus**    Me have it, me have it.

**Zippy**   Have me Ras, dey.

**Marcus**   Me have it.

**Zippy**   Take him Dole.

**Dole**   Me have im, him gone.

**Marcus**   Fret him coming.

**Fret**   Me have im.

**Zippy**   Have dat yer Ras.

**Marcus**   Fret.

**Zippy**   Goal, goal, fer Ras.

**Marcus**   Cha Fret you let de Man walk round yer.

**Fret**   Me stop him.

**Marcus**   Him score Man.

**Zippy**   Two one, yer see Jah will guide him servant to Paradise him will guide him Warrior ter wreck vengeance on dose who face Judgement, de Sword of Jah is sharp and swift, wit love on one side an blood on de odder.

**Marcus**   Judgement me Ras we have two more ter come we a go see who have Judgement.

**Zippy**   Righteousness is mine to give said Jah, you a get him punishment him wrath.

**Marcus**   Shut yer Bomba.

**Dole**   Make we play him, don't believe him have ter see yer him ter believe, him a unbeliever, him one a dem who have ter feel him pain.

*They play.*

**Marcus**   Watch im Fret.

**Fret**   Me see im.

**Zippy**  See, im, yer could see Lightning yer could see de Desert Wind, see dat.

**Marcus**  Good Fret.

**Fret**  Me see him Ras me read him like Genesis, Chapter One.

**Zippy**  Block him Dole.

**Marcus**  Judgement come to him deserving.

**Dole**  Me have him.

**Marcus**  Have Ras.

**Zippy**  Watch im Dole, him wait.

**Dole**  Me have im Ras covered.

**Marcus**  Cover dat yer Heathen.

**Dole**  Me have im.

**Marcus**  Cover dat yer Hypocrite.

**Dole**  Me cover im.

**Marcus**  Cover dat yer Pagan.

**Dole**  Me . . .

**Marcus**  Goal, goal.

**Zippy**  Dole, him . . .

**Marcus**  Him what him cover dats what him do, him conquer all Jericho is dats what him do, eh Fret?

**Fret**  Cha.

**Marcus**  Make we show one unbelievers who take de road ter greed an vanity dat rudeness do' pay, Cha me could taste de Ras Clart Coke already.

**Zippy**  Last game, two all.

**Dole**  Him a make himself, Ras lose make him see.

**Marcus**   Me a want one large glass ter Ras Clart, wid big ice an a straw, eh Fret?

**Fret**   Cha, dem a miss, dem goal.

**Zippy**   Aright make we see.

*They play.*

Watch im Dole.

**Dole**   Me have him.

**Marcus**   Have . . . Fret him come.

**Fret**   Me have him.

**Zippy**   Have Bomba, him come Dole.

**Marcus**   Dole a sleep ter Ras, me a shepherd. Me a once walk round him.

**Dole**   Me have him.

**Zippy**   Him a want ter sneak in, like Judas.

**Marcus**   Judas me Ras, me a son of Jah, yer Hypocrite, take im Fret.

**Fret**   Me have im Ras.

**Zippy**   Have dat yer Ras.

**Fret**   Me tell yer me have him him path block im power miss.

**Marcus**   Give him Judgement ter Ras.

**Zippy**   Dole im . . .

**Marcus**   Judgement come.

**Zippy**   Him try Dole, block him.

**Marcus**   Goal, goal, in yer Ras Clart, yer Bomba Clart, yer tink yer could escape de Sword of Correction you Hypocrite, Jah a say all will succumb, an him word is law.

**Zippy**    Dole you let dis Ras Clart beat we, Cha.

**Dole**    Him lucky, Man.

**Marcus**    Me no beat yer me righteousness beat yer, Cha Fret, dem a Ras Clart, en know de Warriors of Haile Selassie de Lion of Judah, de Lord of Lords de King of Kings, wen dem see him.

*He beats his chest.*

**Fret**    Whey de Coke dem, me a tirsty, all yer a deal Coke.

**Marcus**    Cha yea, me a hot too, me a want me nice cool down make me gather me wisdom, ter confront dem Hypocrites, get dem Cokes.

**Zippy**    Make we wait till Sandy a come.

**Marcus**    De Coke behind de Bar Man.

**Zippy**    Sandy have de keys Man.

**Marcus**    Cha go behind de Bar and break him Ras, Man, me want me Coke.

**Zippy**    Nar Man.

**Marcus**    Whey Sandy?

**Zippy**    She upstairs in de office.

**Marcus**    Well call she down ter Ras, like yer want me break de Ras Clart lock or yer do' want ter pay fer yer sins.

**Zippy**    Me a pay, me a pay, Dole give Sandy a call.

**Dole**    Cha make dem call, she na drink dem, Jah say, 'Make men toil fer him rewards', me do' like asking she Ras fer notting.

**Zippy**    Call de Ras Clart woman nar.

**Marcus**    Cha me go call she nar fraid no Hypocrite me power stronger dan dem. (*He goes to the bottom of the stairs, shouts.*) Hey Sandy.

**Sandy** (*from upstairs*)   What?

**Marcus**   Come an open de Bar. Zippy want some Coke.

**Sandy**   I'm on the phone, hang on a minute.

**Marcus** (*to the boys*)   She a on de phone. (*To* **Sandy**.) Phone me Ras, dis place suppose ter be fer we, ter keep we outa danger, an you suppose ter be running dis place ter look after we, so come an do yer Ras Clart job. Wha de Ras Clart yer doing on de phone, making date for.

**Sandy**   I'm not making dates, give me a minute.

**Marcus**   Me give you more den a Ras Clart minute, me box yer Ras Clart head. Cha if yer do' want ter interrupt yer romantic conversation trow down dem keys den, we go open up take four Cokes an send back dem keys.

**Dole**   Yea.

*The others laugh.*

**Sandy**   No.

**Marcus**   Well come down or else me break him Ras Clart.

**Sandy**   Coming.

**Marcus**   She a come, a know what a bring she, Ras.

*They laugh.* **Sandy** *comes downstairs. She is white, thirty to thirty-five, plump. She wears glasses, a long Indian skirt and a T-shirt and keys and a crucifix on a chain round her neck.*

**Sandy**   What's all the fuss about? I told you I was on the phone. It wouldn't of killed you to wait a minute, just for a few Cokes, which are only going to rot your guts anyway. I told you.

**Marcus**   We like Coke.

**Sandy**   You boys have no consideration. I was on the phone trying to find out what time Jacko's train gets in.

**Dole**   Yer coulda fling down dem keys.

**Sandy**    You know that's not allowed, I'm responsible for them.

**Dole**    Cha.

**Sandy**    You can Cha all you like, but what's the point in locking something if you don't keep the keys for it.

**Zippy**    Locks could get break.

**Sandy**    Yes, I know locks could be broken, so could doors and chairs and tables, and windows and I can go on for a month, but you know, don't you, so I won't but the whole purpose of having a lock is to make sure someone is responsible for the key, and that is why I have it. If the lock is broken that is not my responsibility.

**Marcus**    So we could break the lock.

**Sandy**    I did not say that, you know, you all know that. That is the last lock I am replacing. I've told you if that lock gets broken, you will have to go to the corner for your Cokes. I mean it. I'm not going to keep up this farce.

**Dole**    But dis a Youth Club, suppose ter have Coke, I know some Youth Club have not only Coke but orange, and food.

**Zippy**    Yes.

**Marcus**    Me know an dat have Billiards an even machine fer French Letter.

**Sandy**    Yes, I'm sure you do, I know of some that even have sensible boys who take part in activities and protect their centre and do repairs and paint also.

*They laugh.*

Yes, crazy as it may sound, they even feel proud of the centre so don't you start telling me about orange and Johnny machines. We've had all that and what happened? Someone was always putting money in and the machine was always jamming and someone always had to have a refund.

**Zippy**   De machine did jam.

**Sandy**   And who had to hand out the refund? Me.

**Marcus**   Well you responsible.

**Sandy**   And when the engineers came, could we find the jammed coins, no they disappeared.

**Zippy**   It jammed.

**Sandy**   And what happened when someone broke open the machine? Did you all go and put those packets to some use to the good use they were designed specifically for? No. I wish to god you had.

**Zippy**   You leave Jah out of dis kind a talk.

**Sandy**   Oh I see I'm not allowed to have my god am I? Why? OK, don't tell me I know. I am white, and we white people don't have a god, we don't believe in a god, we are devils. Is that right?

**Marcus**   Cha, yer right, all a believe in money an greed an oppression, all yer oppress people.

**Sandy**   I see, and we are not oppressed as well. Look at me. I am as oppressed as you, more I think. I've got to worry about this place, to make sure it's run and keep it open, and clean and keep writing letters begging for money so that you harmless creatures have a quiet life, so that you good little boys keep out of trouble and so that I don't have to spend all my life in court saying 'Your Lordship he's never been in trouble before. I have found him responsible and sensible, and no I cannot put up the bail for him but I'm sure if you give him a suspended sentence he will have learned his lesson.' That is my oppression and I feel it so don't you tell me about oppression. Back to the Johnnies, those Johnnies you wanted. What did you do with them? You blew them up and strung them up on the ceiling didn't . . .

**Zippy**   We . . .

**Sandy**    Yes, you did, and you thought it was a big joke, when the girls came in didn't you?

**Marcus**    Dem know what Johnny look like.

*The boys laugh.*

**Sandy**    Yes, yes very funny they were upset and insulted I know that. You know what it told them, it told them you did not respect them, that they, black women, had not earned the respect of you their men. They didn't say it, but I saw their faces, and I also was insulted, me a white woman, I was also insulted. Are you surprised they don't want to come back? How many discos have we had?

**Dole**    Two.

**Sandy**    And how many girls came?

**Dole**    Not much.

**Sandy**    You see.

**Dole**    But dem do' like heavy music, dem want soul, and all that funky business, dem en want Rasta music.

**Sandy**    The music has nothing to do with it, it's this place. We have got the worst name as far as centres go and that's saying something.

**Marcus**    Dat en true you is a hypocrite me know places wid worse name den here, where wen one crowd inside de rest have ter pay dem money fer dem ter get inside.

**Sandy**    Yes all right we are perfect, one bright peaceful, little family.

**Zippy**    Hey Sandy, yer like dem Johnnies.

*The boys laugh.*

**Sandy**    No love they're for little boys like you to try an inflate.

**Marcus**    Cha she call him little boy.

*The boys laugh. Not* **Zippy**.

**Dole**   Sandy, what inflate mean?

**Sandy**   It means to try to make yourself larger than you are.

**Dole**   I tought dat was erection.

*The boys laugh.*

**Sandy**   No love, that is trying to make yourself smaller than you are. All right now how many Cokes and who's paying?

**Zippy**   Marcus.

**Marcus**   Nar Zippy.

**Zippy**   Nar Marcus.

**Marcus**   Zippy Ras him lost me but, him carry him lost so him pay, ask Fret.

**Fret**   Him right.

**Sandy**   Now look, I don't care who's paying but I'm not unlocking that door until I see some money. I haven't got all day to waste here whilst you decide . . .

**Zippy**   All right here.

*He gives her a pound.*

Wha happen yer no joke?

**Sandy**   I'm sorry Zippy. Yes I joke. How many?

**Zippy**   Four. Make it five if ye want one.

**Sandy**   Thanks.

**Marcus**   Watch im Sandy, he a try ter catch yer.

**Zippy**   Do' mind him. Catch what? Me like Sandy, she know dat.

**Marcus**   Yer see.

**Sandy**    I see, I'll watch him. I think he's a nice boy. He's the only one of you who's offered to buy me a Coke, that's for sure.

**Marcus**    Is him lose, him have ter pay.

**Sandy** (*taking the Cokes to the table*)    Nevertheless thanks all the same for the drink Zippy. I'm sure you would have bought even if you had won. Who beat who then?

**Marcus**    Me an Fret lick dem Ras.

**Sandy**    Ah I didn't know you played Fret.

**Marcus**    Me teach him, once an we lick dem me could teach anybody ter lick dem, dem no good.

**Sandy**    I see, so you're our champion.

**Zippy**    Champion what, him is champion.

**Marcus**    Me lick dem me an Fret.

**Dole**    Do' mind he Sandy, he a make one set a noise him put me off.

**Zippy**    Yes, him just lucky.

**Marcus**    Luck, me Ras, me give dem all me powers of righteousness, Rasta man en depend on luck, all him a have is him righteousness. Right Sandy?

**Sandy**    Right, you'll have to play against Jacko when he comes to see who is the real champ.

**Marcus**    Him good?

**Sandy**    He was our champion.

**Zippy**    Whey him is?

**Sandy**    He was inside and he's coming out today.

*She looks at her watch.*

He's out. He's on the way home and I've got to meet him at the station at half-three.

**Marcus**   What him went in fer?

**Sandy**   He's a nice guy you guys will like him and yes, that's something I wanted to say. When he comes he's going to be feeling a bit strange so no aggro.

**Marcus**   We do' give aggro.

**Sandy**   You know what I mean.

**Marcus**   No.

**Sandy**   Come on.

**Marcus**   Cha all right. What him like, him a Rasta?

**Sandy**   No, I don't think so. I don't know. He's been inside for . . .

**Dole**   How long him get.

**Sandy**   Five years.

**Dole**   Dat long?

**Sandy**   Yes.

**Dole**   Dem barstard. Wen dem lock up blackman dem make sure him lock up long.

**Zippy**   What him get lock fer?

**Sandy**   Rape; he and three boys.

**Zippy**   An him get catch, him en rape good.

*The boys laugh.*

**Sandy**   Very funny.

**Zippy**   Me never rape, but if me rape me go rape so good no girl en go get Police, she a go want more an more.

*The boys laugh.*

**Sandy**   Now stop that. That is not funny. That's what you and a lot of men think. That's why so many women are raped and so many men and boys – boys like you and Jacko

– are sent to prison. No, it is not funny, I'm sorry, no man has any right to rape a woman, no matter what his reasons are or what he thinks she wants, you hear, and it's not funny. Jacko took part or the girl said he took part.

**Marcus**   Dem girl tell lie, dem is hypocrite.

**Sandy**   All right and she recognised him, she knew him.

**Zippy**   An she inform on him?

**Sandy**   Yes.

**Zippy**   Him no rape good me say.

*The boys laugh.*

**Sandy**   I said it wasn't funny.

**Zippy**   Me bet yer it was one white girl, dem Ras Clart, always want ter pretend dem good.

**Sandy**   How much?

**Zippy**   What?

**Sandy**   How much you'd like to bet?

**Zippy**   Why?

**Sandy**   How much you want to bet it was a white girl, because I'd bet you.

**Marcus**   It was a black girl.

**Sandy**   That's right. Why do you think it was a white girl?

**Marcus**   I didn't say it was a white girl, it's him.

**Sandy**   It's him I'm talking to. Eh Zippy why, you don't think black girls are sexy too?

**Zippy**   No, black girls sexy, me like black girls.

**Sandy**   So you think white girls should get raped.

**Zippy**   No, me never say dat, but dem like boys ter gang dem an wen dem finish an dem realise what happen, dem start ter feel ashamed and say it happen widout dem consent, me see dem in de back a disco, plenty, if me wanted to me coulda just walk up an . . .

**Sandy**   All right Zippy and you know why? It's because young girls go there, and they have something to drink. Something like whisky which they can't or shouldn't drink and that's what happens.

**Zippy**   Dem like it.

**Sandy**   Would you like –

**Zippy**   No, me tell yer, me never do it.

**Sandy**   No, I mean would you like five men to . . .

**Zippy**   Me like five women.

*The boys laugh.*

**Sandy**   All right, very funny.

**Marcus**   Do' mind dat Zippy, Sandy. Tell me beat dis champion, me want ter know all bout him, him strategy, how me go lick him, him does flick or him does stroke.

**Sandy**   Both, sorry Marcus I don't know much about it, but he was always winning.

**Marcus**   All him games?

**Sandy**   Yes, he used to teach . . .

**Marcus**   Cha, him a cheat.

**Sandy**   No, Marcus.

**Marcus**   No man car win all him games, you a miss . . . so him a warrior me go have ter watch him.

**Sandy**   Yes, Marcus.

**Dole**   Him lost one game an him get five.

**Marcus**   If him so cool Sandy how come him get catch ter Ras.

**Sandy**   He didn't get caught, I told you the girl remembered him and told the Police, and he refused to give the other boys' names so . . .

**Marcus**   Cha.

**Dole**   Yes.

**Marcus**   Cha him a genuine warrior ter Ras.

**Sandy**   Call him what you like, just try and be nice to him. When he comes he's bound to feel a bit . . . just try.

**Marcus**   All right Cha.

**Sandy** *looks at her watch.*

**Sandy**   I better leave now or else I'll miss him.

**Marcus**   Sandy what about dem robes yer was making fer me.

**Sandy**   You want them now?

**Marcus**   Yes, we must look like proper Rasta, to greet de warrior.

**Sandy**   All right, they're in my office on the floor behind the cabinet. Now look, I'm leaving you in charge Marcus.

**Marcus**   Wid de keys.

**Sandy**   Oh – no, you don't need them.

**Marcus**   We might need some Cokes.

**Sandy**   I won't be that long. Christ I almost forgot.

**Marcus**   Leave Jah out of dis.

**Sandy**   Listen, there's a girl coming here, she was meant to be here by two but she's late so tell her I won't be long, will you.

**Marcus**   Who's she?

**Sandy**   My new helper or warden, whichever you like, and don't give her a hard time, practise being nice on her so that when Jacko comes you'll be perfect, we don't want her to get the right impression on her first day do we?

**Marcus**   What?

**Sandy**   Never mind just be nice to her for my sake. Right, keys yes, gloves in the car, yes, right, I'm off. Be good.

*She smiles and goes.*

**Marcus**   Cha, me in charge a what dis Ras Clart place, en worth notting she no give me no keys so how me a in charge, she a hypocrite man genuine hypocrite dat.

**Zippy**   Marcus make me get dem robes nar.

**Marcus**   Cha why yer ask me?

**Zippy**   You are General.

**Marcus**   Cha me no General if yer want robes go find dem yerself, come Fret make me get some practice, before me face dis Goliath.

**Fret** *and* **Marcus** *go to the football machine. They play.*

**Zippy**   Dole make we go upstairs get we robes.

**Dole**   Cha me do' want no robes man, me a stay here, fight ya.

**Zippy**   Cha.

*He goes upstairs.*

**Dole**   Hey Marcus, you a practise yer Ras you still en go beat nobody.

**Marcus**   Shut yer Ras, me beat you, me beat you an Zippy, yer no hear what Sandy a say? She say me champion.

**Dole**   Champion what? Champion caretaker? She a left you in charge a de broom ter Ras.

**Marcus**    Shut yer mouth, Bomba hypocrite, you a interfere wid de working a Jah.

**Dole**    Jah me Ras, you a scheming to beat one guy, de guy out a practice, him been put away for five year, you a want to outnumber de poor guy you en no genuine warrior you a Herod ter Ras.

**Marcus**    Shut yer mouth before me box yer Ras.

**Zippy** *comes down in an African robe.*

**Zippy**    Cha, me a genuine Ethiopian now me a warrior of de Lion, ter Ras Clart, all yer a see Rasta ter Ras Heavy Cloth.

**Marcus**    Cha you look good boy.

**Zippy**    Me look genuine no hypocrite ting dis a genuine robe.

**Marcus**    Whey we own?

**Zippy**    Dem a upstairs.

**Marcus**    Cha.

*He runs upstairs followed by* **Dole**. **Fret** *walks. Sounds from upstairs.*

Cha, give me dat.

**Zippy** (*jumping, sings*)    By de waters of Babylon . . . Cha.

*A girl,* **Gail**, *enters. She is black, attractive (twenty to twenty-five) and is wearing a jacket, skirt and jumper.*

**Gail**    Hello.

**Zippy**    Yes?

**Gail**    I came to see Sandy.

**Zippy**    Yes, she a gone out but she left a message she say she en go be long ter wait fer she.

**Gail**    Yes, I'm a bit late, I couldn't find the place.

**Zippy**   Yes, Cha take a seat, she a come soon.

**Gail** (*sits*)   Thank you, it looks nice.

**Zippy**   It aright, it have office upstairs you ar want to see it?

**Gail**   No, I better wait till Sandy comes.

**Zippy**   Yea, you a come ter work?

**Gail**   I hope so, it's up to Sandy if she likes me.

**Zippy**   Cha, Sandy cool she a like you she a like everybody, you en help she out.

**Gail**   Yes.

**Zippy**   What you a do?

**Gail**   I . . . Lots of things, try to keep you busy most of all. Are you the only one here?

**Zippy**   No de rest a guys upstairs dey look fer dem robes, you like it? (*Stands.*) It a genuine Ethiopian robe.

**Gail**   Yes, it's very nice.

**Zippy**   Sandy a make dem fer we. She a cool, you a ask she, she make you one.

**Gail**   Yes, I'll ask her, so what other rooms do you have?

**Zippy**   Cha, not much, we a have office an phone upstairs, toilet over dey.

**Gail**   One?

**Zippy**   Nar two, one for de girls.

**Gail**   Yes.

**Zippy**   An in de back dey it a have a room for discos.

**Gail**   Ah, I like dancing, how often do you . . .?

**Zippy**   Cha, not too often, it a some time one week, some time two weeks, not steady. Whey you from?

**Gail**   London.

**Zippy**   But yer people black.

**Gail**   Yes.

**Zippy**   Cha, me know dat me take one look at yer me know yer people a dem black. You is a Rastafarian?

**Gail**   No, I don't think so, not that I have anything against it, I just don't know anything about it.

**Zippy**   Me tell yer, me explain everything not Marcus him a hypocrite.

**Gail**   Who's Marcus?

**Zippy**   Him a upstairs. Yer see Rastafarian is a man who believe in de Bible, all peace an love an him a believe in Emperor Haile Selassie to be de Lion a Judah, de King of Kings and Lord of Lords.

**Gail**   Yes?

**Zippy**   Dat is something eh, dat is Rasta man, him belief. Yes, an all white people all a dem, dem a genuine hypocrite dem.

**Gail**   Yes I see.

**Zippy**   See dat what Rasta man believe.

**Gail**   And you're a Rasta man?

**Zippy**   Cha all a we a Rasta an all Rasta man believe in him dread locks.

**Gail**   Yes, the hair.

**Zippy**   Dat not him hair, dat him dread locks.

**Gail**   I see, so tell me what sort of things you do here?

**Zippy**   Cha me nar do much, we a play some dominoes, some football, some sounds.

**Gail**   You have a team?

**Zippy**   Nar, over dey.

**Gail**   Yes. What else?

**Zippy**   Fool around, talk.

**Gail**   Ah, what do you talk about?

**Zippy**   All kinda ting, Rastafarian tings, an Ethiopia.

**Gail**   Would you all like to go to Africa?

**Zippy**   Sure all a we want go dey some day.

**Gail**   Good, well maybe we could go on a trip to see some exhibits from Africa.

**Zippy**   Where?

**Gail**   In London, there's always something going on concerning Africa, you'd be surprised.

**Zippy**   But dat not Africa, dat a white man ting, dem a hypocrite, dem not genuine Africa, is Africa we want ter see, we want ter see real lion not dem circus ting.

**Gail**   I see, but it would give you some idea, of what life is really like in Africa.

**Zippy**   Cha, but not Africa, we want ter know we in Africa dats what we want ter know, you a see.

**Gail**   Yes, where are you from?

**Zippy**   Me from Jamaica.

**Gail**   You were born in Jamaica?

**Zippy**   No, we born in London, but me people from Jamaica.

**Gail**   But you speak with a Jamaican . . .

**Zippy**   Cha, me could talk London if me wanted to but me is a Rastafarian so me talk Ja.

**Gail**   I see.

**Zippy**  Yer all genuine Rasta man him a talk Jamaican or else him not genuine.

**Gail**  Yes, and all the other boys they were born in London?

**Zippy**  Some a dem born in Jamaica some born in London me do' know.

**Gail**  Are they allowed to be upstairs so long?

**Zippy**  Cha Sandy she a cool, she left Marcus in charge. Him upstairs. You a want to see him we call im fer you.

**Gail**  No. (*She gets up.*) I'll just look around. (*She looks at a poster.*)

**Zippy**  Dat is de Emperor Haile Selassie.

**Gail**  Yes.

**Zippy**  You know him face?

**Gail**  Yes.

**Zippy**  Cha, you is Rastafarian.

**Gail**  Are women allowed to be Rastafarian?

**Zippy**  Cha yes man all black people is Rastafarian. Is what dem believe.

**Gail**  I see you have a bar.

**Zippy**  Yes.

**Gail**  Do you run it yourselves?

**Zippy**  Nar Sandy, it a only keep Coke.

**Gail**  Would you like to run it yourselves?

**Zippy**  Cha what for, it en make no profit, it fer someting ter drink, it do' need no running.

**Marcus**, **Dole** and **Fret** *come down in robes.*

**Marcus**  Cha Zippy, a pick up chick.

**Zippy**   Me no pick up no chick Ras dis Gail come to help out Sandy.

**Gail**   Hello, I'm Gail.

**Marcus**   Yes me know, Gail Roberts.

**Gail**   How did you know, have we met?

**Marcus**   No me know yer name, Sandy a tell me yer come an ter take care a you, she left me in charge, me name is Marcus, me was named after de great black warrior Marcus Garvey.

**Gail**   Yes . . .

**Marcus**   Dis is Dole, cause since him born him a draw dole an dis is Fret, him is my warrior an him do Fret.

**Gail**   I see. Hello. Your friend was telling me all the good things you do here.

**Marcus**   Who Zippy? Him do' know notting, me is in charge, me running ting, Sandy say fer me ter look after you not Zippy.

**Gail**   Well he was the one I met first and –

**Marcus**   Cha, yer shoulda wait fer me, me in charge.

**Zippy**   Do' take no notice a he, yer know him just want ter prove him point, him didn't want to be in no command.

**Marcus**   Cha shut yer Ras mouth.

**Gail**   It's OK, I'm fine. How long is Sandy going to be?

**Marcus**   She a back soon, she gone to get a guy, him Jacko.

**Gail**   Oh yes, who's Jacko? I see you're having a party for him.

**Marcus**   It no party, him a coming out today dat all, him a Sandy friend.

**Gail**   I see.

**Marcus**  You a work here?

**Gail**  I hope so. I was saying to Zippy, I hope I can organise some outings and get you guys to come along.

**Marcus**  What kind a outing? Ter museum an ting?

**Gail**  No, I thought maybe we could visit a Safari Park, and see the animals they have. Lions and tigers.

**Marcus**  Me do' want ter see no Sarfari Park, Sarfari is a white man ting dat a fer white people, in dem car to visit.

**Gail**  I just thought maybe you might like to see some lions.

**Marcus**  Cha me know what lions look like.

**Gail**  Or maybe a factory or something.

**Marcus**  Factory what, what kinda factory?

**Gail**  Any kind of factory where they make things. We could see how it's done.

**Marcus**  What?

**Gail**  Anything. I have a friend who works for a record studio. We could maybe go and see how they make records, see how it's done. You like music?

**Marcus**  Me like Reggae. Heavy Dub. Who him a cut?

**Gail**  They cut all kind of records there. Maybe we could go when they are doing some Reggae.

**Marcus** (*calls out*)  Hey all yer hear dat, dis girl know people who make Reggae record.

**Gail**  A friend.

**Dole**  Cha, dat good.

**Marcus**  She a take we ter see.

**Gail**  I could try and arrange it.

**Marcus**  Cha you cool, me dig dat.

**Gail**   What other sort of things do you like? Sports?

**Marcus**   Yer mean running in dem shorts.

**Gail**   Yes.

**Marcus**   Nar, cha, dem a school boy ting. Me like chick and me disco.

**Gail**   I see.

**Marcus**   Me like Rasta man ting.

**Gail**   Yes Zippy was explaining to me.

**Marcus**   Him no explain notting. Him no genuine Rasta man. Him is real hypocrite. Is me de Rasta man here. Anyting you want to know bout Rasta man you ask me. Me know all bout Ethiopia.

**Gail**   And Haile Selassie.

**Marcus**   Him to him is de King of Kings, Lord of –

**Gail**   Lords.

**Marcus**   You know him?

**Gail**   Yes.

**Marcus**   Dis friend wit him record studio, him yer boyfriend?

**Gail**   How did you know it was a him?

**Marcus**   Me know, me know dem tings, me is a righteous man, an me righteousness tell me dem ting, it tell me all kinda ting, me know yer name was Roberts before anybody.

**Gail**   He's a friend, yes.

**Marcus**   Boyfriend.

**Gail**   Friend.

**Marcus**   What kinda friend?

**Gail**   A sort of friend.

**Marcus**   A sort of boyfriend?

**Gail**   A sort of friend.

**Marcus**   What sort?

**Gail**   A sort, any sort really. You have friends.

**Marcus**   You mean like me an Fret?

**Gail**   Is Fret your boyfriend?

**Marcus**   Cha shut yer Ras Clart mouth.

**Gail**   I'm sorry.

**Marcus**   Me is genuine Rasta man, Rasta man do have no boyfriend dat is white man ting.

**Gail**   I said I was sorry, it was a joke.

**Marcus**   Cha, me nearly box yer face if Sandy did ask me look after you, me box. Rasta man don't do dem kinda tings, da is hypocrite ting.

**Gail**   I'm sorry. (*She takes out a cigarette.*) Would you like a cigarette?

**Marcus**   Me no smoke tobacco, me smoke ganja, Rasta man he smoke no tobacco.

**Gail**   Look I'm really sorry, it was a joke right? OK, a bad one, OK . . .?

**Marcus**   Cha.

*He walks off and joins the others. He says something. They laugh.* **Zippy** *comes over to* **Gail**.

**Gail**   Hi.

**Zippy**   Hi.

**Gail**   I think I upset your friend.

**Zippy**   Who, Marcus? Do' mind him him a have a big mouth dats all him have.

**Gail**   Yes, but all the same I think maybe I shouldn't have.

**Zippy**   Do' mind him, him just want to prove him is big man dats him problem.

**Gail**   Yes a lot of men have that problem. I think I'll go upstairs and wait in the office.

**Zippy**   Yer want me show yer?

**Gail**   No thanks.

**Zippy**   It right at de top a de stairs, make yerself at home.

**Gail**   Thanks.

*She goes.* **Marcus** *comes to* **Zippy**. *Music.*

**Marcus**   Cha, punch me a dub dey . . . Cha whey she a gone?

**Zippy**   She gone upstairs ter wait for Sandy.

**Marcus**   Me do' know if she fer wait in office.

**Zippy**   Cha shut yer mouth, Sandy say look after she, you a give she one get a heavy sound. Wha rang wit yer? Yer brainy, or what? De chick is a nice chick, man.

**Marcus**   She a hypocrite, me nearly box she face.

**Zippy**   Box me Ras, you not boxing nobody face.

**Marcus**   Who go stop me?

**Zippy**   Me, me and de lion of Ethiopia to stop yer cha, you like ter go en wit dis Ras Clart ting too long, me vex now, me vex, me spirit go an get vex now Ras Clart, me no heavy guy yer know but wen me get vex, me vex, Cha, go way duck me ter Ras –

**Zippy** *walks off, goes in the corner and sits.*

**Marcus**   All right, brother man me duck yer.

**Marcus** *goes to the boys.*

**Sandy** *enters with* **Jacko**.

**Jacko** *is tall* (*twenty to twenty-five*). *He is wearing a suit and tie.*

**Sandy**   Hi everybody, this is Jacko, come and say hello.

**Zippy** *goes and shakes his hand.*

**Zippy**   Hi man.

**Dole** (*slaps his hand*)   Hi.

**Marcus**   Hey brother how yer is?

**Fret** *comes.*

**Fret**   Hi.

**Sandy**   His train was late and I got held up, so how's things? What's been happening? I see everything's still in one piece.

**Marcus**   We had some Cokes.

**Sandy** *goes to the bar.*

**Sandy**   Oh no, I warned you, I warned . . . (*Looks.*) Shit Marcus I must be stupid, you get me every time, don't you? I never learn, it's my trusting nature. OK, you guys relax. Take a seat Jacko, you're no stranger.

**Jacko**   Tanks.

**Sandy**   And the place hasn't changed that much, some paint here and there that's all, so make yourself at home.

**Jacko**   It feels good.

**Sandy**   That's because it's home.

**Zippy**   Sandy that girl come.

**Sandy**   Christ and what happened?

**Zippy**   She upstairs, waiting.

**Sandy**   Christ, OK, I'll go and see her. You, look. (*Gives the keys to* **Zippy**.) Open the box, let's all have some Cokes, I'll get her.

*She goes upstairs.*

**Zippy** *goes behind the bar and brings out some Cokes.*

**Marcus**   Hey look Zippy, nar him is now barman in hotel.

**Zippy** *opens Coke and gives one to* **Jacko**.

**Zippy**   Here brother man try dis.

**Jacko**   Tanks.

**Zippy**   All yer help all yer Ras.

**Sandy** *and* **Gail** *come down.*

**Sandy**   Have you met everybody?

**Gail**   Yes.

**Sandy**   But you haven't met Jacko. This is Jacko.

**Gail**   Hello Jacko.

**Jacko**   Hello.

**Sandy**   Oh I'm sorry Gail, it is Gail isn't it?

**Gail**   Yes.

**Sandy**   Let's have a Coke then, I'm paying for the damn things.

*She takes one for* **Gail**, *gives it to her. She looks at* **Jacko**.

Oh you've got one. All right everybody, to Jacko, welcome home Jacko.

*They all repeat this. They drink.* **Sandy** *sits.*

Right let's relax now, I needed this. (*The Coke.*) I've been rushing all day. First it was you and I had to get Jacko, and I haven't stopped. So come on then tell me what you think of us.

**Gail**    I think you're all nice, great.

**Sandy**    Well I wouldn't go that far, but we're all right. Let's say we're not as bad as we appear.

**Gail**    OK.

**Sandy**    So what do you think? You think you'd like to work with us?

**Gail**    Yes, I think so.

**Sandy**    Great, hey everybody, Gail is going to work with us.

**Zippy** *goes and shakes* **Gail**'s *hand.*

**Zippy**    Yea, welcome sister.

**Sandy**    That's the spirit. Anybody else?

**Marcus**    Cha.

*The others wave.*

**Sandy**    Take no notice, they're all rushing to welcome you. Let's drink to Gail.

*They drink to* **Gail***.*

**Gail**    Thank you. What do I have to do?

**Sandy**    We'll talk about it, it's not much. Things like answer the phone, take messages, be in charge here when I go out, which is going to be more often I hope. Those sort of things, oh yes, and any bright ideas you have for keeping these guys occupied, except dominoes, the Juke Box or football; we've got those.

**Gail**    I noticed.

**Sandy**    Yes. Now, we're not much of a candidate for Youth Club of the year.

**Gail**    We'll make it better. When can I start?

**Sandy**    Right now. Come upstairs, I'll show you what's what and what goes where.

**Gail**   Great.

**Sandy**   OK, you guys look after Jacko, and don't let them cheek you Jacko.

**Jacko**   I'm all right.

**Sandy**   Come on then.

**Sandy** *is on the stairs.*

**Zippy**   Hey Sandy, how yer like dem robes?

**Sandy**   Great, they look genuine.

**Sandy** *and* **Gail** *go up.*

**Zippy**   Cha, hey brother how yer like dem robes?

**Jacko**   Dey look nice.

**Zippy**   If yer ask Sandy she a make yer one too.

**Jacko**   What dey for? All yer doing a show or what?

**Zippy**   Show, no man, Ras dis is genuine Ethiopian robes, we is Rasta man, genuine Rasta man yer do know bout Rastafarian?

**Jacko**   No, not much.

**Zippy**   Cha me forget you been lock up for long time, well Rastafarian is black man ting now we discover we identity is Rastafarian dats it.

**Jacko**   I hear bout it in Jamaica long time.

**Zippy**   Well it a come ter Britain now, we call it Babylon da is Britain so tell me brother man what it like inside de man place, fer how long?

**Jacko**   Five years.

**Zippy**   What is a like?

**Jacko**   It's not bad, as long as you follow de rules.

**Zippy**   Follow dem rules, me no follow nobody rules.

**Jacko**  Well when yer inside dere yer have ter or else . . .

**Zippy**  Or else what?

**Jacko**  Or else, dey make yer pay.

**Zippy**  Cha nobody car make me a do what me do' want ter do.

**Jacko**  Well inside dey do, a only hope you don't have ter go in.

**Zippy**  Cha me nar go inside dem never catch me, me smarter dem all dem Ras.

**Jacko**  OK.

**Zippy**  But you is a warrior ter Ras.

**Jacko**  How yer mean?

**Zippy**  Sandy she tell we. Sandy tell we how yer en give dem Babylon yer friend en dem names how yer no tell dem notting.

**Jacko**  Yes.

**Zippy**  Dats heroic ting man, dats what genuine Rasta man go do man.

**Jacko**  Yes.

**Zippy**  Genuine hero man even Sandy a call yer hero.

**Jacko**  Tanks, so what you guys do all dey just come here?

**Zippy**  Cha yes is a good place man. Dis is de only place in dis town whey we could come an relax an en get no harrassment. We could do we own ting here, an dey en have nobody ter tell we what ter do or asking we what we doing. If we go by de corner, is Panda Car come up, ter ask we question, Ras Clart, dem do' like ter see we doing notting. Everybody must be doing someting, working or going somewhere or coming from somewhere. If dem see people relaxing dem tink dem up ter someting. Dem people do' relax so dem do' like ter see people relax. Dem like ter have heart attack an give people dem heart attack.

**Jacko**   Yes.

**Zippy**   Cha brother, me like you me could make you genuine Rasta man.

**Jacko**   I do' know, I do' know.

**Zippy**   Cha it no sweat you a catch yer spirit.

**Marcus** *comes over.*

**Marcus**   Hey brother man yer know how ter play dat game?

**Jacko**   Yes, ah used ter . . .

**Marcus**   Come den nar, me give yer a game, make we play.

**Jacko**   All right.

*He goes.*

**Marcus**   Hey Zippy you a come watch.

**Zippy**   Nar, Cha, go long.

**Jacko** *and* **Marcus** *go to the football game.*

**Marcus**   Make we toss fer kick off.

**Jacko**   All right.

*Puts his hand in his pocket.*

**Marcus**   Me have coin, me have coin. (*Tosses.*) Head nor tail?

**Jacko**   Head.

**Marcus**   Head a win, make we punch me tune . . .

*Music.*

**Jacko** *kicks off. They play.* **Dole** *and* **Fret** *go to watch.*

**Marcus**   Cha go in.

**Dole**   Him block yer Marcus.

**Marcus**   Shut yer Ras. Cha go in dat Ras.

**Dole**   Him cover yer Ras Marcus.

**Jacko**   All yer take dis game serious.

**Marcus**   Serious Ras it a warfare ter Ras go in.

**Dole**   You know about him Ras Marcus him block all yer Ras Clart move. Look how him cool, him a real warrior, him worry yer Ras.

**Marcus**   Worry who Ras, me a righteous man. Righteous man no lose no contest.

**Dole**   Win it den nar.

**Marcus**   Cha go in, go in.

**Jacko**   Yer good man.

**Marcus**   Cha course me a good, goodness breed goodness, go in.

**Dole**   Him a block yer Ras.

**Marcus**   Block . . . goal, cha me win, me win.

**Jacko**   Good goal.

**Marcus**   Goal ter Ras me is now champion warrior, me win, all yer a see how righteousness does triumph over evil.

**Jacko**   Good game, da was a good goal. Yer want ter play another game?

**Marcus**   Nar, nar me no play no more me win.

**Dole**   But Marcus yer only win one game ter Ras Clart de rules . . .

**Marcus**   De rules what rules? Who makes rules? Me Ras Clart me win da is all. We no play.

**Dole**   Dat en justice man, de man rusty ter Ras, him a just come out, him not proficient, him just a warm up.

**Jacko**   I do' mind.

**Zippy**   No him right.

**Marcus**   Cha me do' defend no title, right away me get me crown first.

**Zippy**   Cha. (*Goes and* sits. *To* **Dole**.) Leave him Ras.

**Marcus**   Me champ ter Ras.

**Jacko**   All right, but a hope yer go give me another game.

**Marcus**   Cha sure, sure me give yer plenty game ter Ras, all a dem go be like dat ter Ras.

**Dole**   Marcus you is not a righteous man, me say dat now, an me never change it, you is not righteous.

**Marcus**   Cha, ne warrior you a Ras Clart hypocrite, what you know, me have de blood of Haile Selassie an all dem great warrior a pumping in a veins, blood a true warrior cha. (*Sits with* **Fret**.)

**Dole** *goes and* sits with **Zippy**.

**Dole**   Dat man is a . . .

**Zippy**   Cha, left him Ras.

**Dole**   Brother man de mind dat Ras, him profess ter be genuine, but him crooked, him a take de wrong path, but him go learn some heavy wisdom wen him come ter me him maker. Do' let him attitude distort yer destiny, ter Ras.

**Jacko**   Nar is all right. I know guys like him, dey have guys like him inside, dey have ter be big, bigger dan everybody or have more dan everybody else.

**Dole**   Him a Lazarus man, is him sores him want ter spread.

**Jacko**  If he went inside, he see how big he really was, one night a would give him.

**Dole**  What it like inside brother man, it tough?

**Jacko**  Yes it tough, if you tink tings tough outside a prison, it ten time more tough inside, de white screws . . .

**Dole**  De is de guards?

**Jacko**  Yes dem do' like yer at all an if yer black den is worse. Dey do' give yer a chance. Yer have ter ask dem fer everyting, everyting. An de white cons dem come next, dem higher dan yer, dem have tings under control an yer have ter ask dem fer favours too. An every favour yer get yer have ter pay back wid interest, an yer car miss no excuse or yer pay more an more an den everyting yer do have a rule an regulations ter cover it. So all yer guys tink outside hard eh all yer do' know how easy it is . . . take my word fer it, I en going back inside. I make dat pledge de first night I spend, notting go get me inside again. I en care if a man killing me modder I go let him . . .

**Dole**  Yer hear dat Zippy.

**Zippy**  Me hear.

**Dole**  Like what kinda tings dem do . . . ?

**Zippy**  Cha rest de man nar, yer en see de man en want ter talk . . .

**Jacko**  Nar is all right, I do' mind, I en mind talking bout it, is . . .

**Dole**  Me hear dat is man does fock man.

**Jacko**  Yes.

**Dole**  Me would never let no man get me.

**Zippy**  Cha.

**Dole**  Me would kill him first.

**Jacko**    How much people yer could kill, ten, five, three?

**Dole**    All a dem.

**Zippy**    Cha rest yer Ras nar.

**Dole**    Me kill all a dem, Ras, me poison dem, me choke dem, me.

**Zippy**    Cha man go way wid dat Ras nar.

**Jacko**    Yes.

**Dole**    Aright, me stop.

**Sandy** *and* **Gail** *come downstairs.*

**Sandy**    All right who missed me?

**Marcus**    Me win Sandy, me win, me is now de reigning champion me beat yer Jacko licks.

**Sandy**    I see.

**Marcus**    Me beat him.

**Sandy**    Is that true?

**Jacko**    Yes.

**Marcus**    Me say it true yer no have ter ask, you now have ter put up one sign saying Marcus is reigning champion pon wall.

**Sandy**    All right Marcus, but I still don't believe it. Why don't you write the sign yourself? You'll find some card and the felt-tips upstairs.

**Marcus**    Cha champion shouldn't have ter write his own sign.

**Sandy**    Yes Marcus, but you know exactly what you want to say and how it should look. Make it pretty, use lots of colours.

**Marcus**    Cha yes, me use de colours of Ethiopia, de red, de gold an de green ter Ras.

**Sandy**  Yes.

**Marcus**  All right, Cha all yer hypocrite do' know how ter say glorious ting.

**Sandy**  Why not do it now.

**Marcus**  Cha.

**Sandy**  Dole run upstairs and get the card and pens for me.

**Dole**  Me en going Cha, make him go an get him.

**Sandy**  For me.

**Dole**  Cha.

**Gail**  I'll go. (*She moves.*)

**Sandy**  Thanks Gail.

**Sandy** *calls out to* **Gail**.

**Sandy**  You'll find some in the cupboard.

**Marcus**  Cha, dat is power of righteousness.

**Sandy**  That is downright laziness. I don't know why I put up with it. I must be stupid.

**Marcus**  Cha, you is a maiden at de Palace of Kings Marcus ter Ras.

**Sandy** *goes to* **Jacko** *and* **Zippy**.

**Sandy** (*to* **Jacko**)  How are we then, you OK?

**Jacko**  I'm cool.

**Sandy**  Zippy's looking after you then.

**Zippy**  Cha, me do' have ter look after nobody him a big man, him look after himself.

**Gail** (*at the top of the stairs*)  Sandy should I bring all the pens?

**Sandy**  Christ. (*Calls out.*) Yes bring them.

**Gail** *comes down. She gives pens and card to* **Marcus**.

**Gail**    Here you are.

**Marcus**    Tanks sister me go make you second hand maiden to me court.

**Gail**    Do you want me to give you some ideas?

**Marcus**    No tanks sister, me is one heavy designer wen we start ter use me righteous hand me goodness does come out, me do' need no hypocrite to guide me hand.

**Gail**    I only . . .

**Marcus**    Cha, me know yer went ter Art School an ting but me is a natural.

**Gail**    How do you know, I did . .

**Marcus**    Me know everyting bout you sister, me know yer background yer foreground yer cricket ground and yer football ground, me know all bout you, me know yer people an dey respectable, an yer come from posh school.

**Gail**    Not really.

**Marcus**    Cha, yes really you a one English black woman, you a not one a we, you look genuine but me know bout you, every ting . . .

**Gail**    Really?

**Marcus** *starts to draw*.

**Marcus**    Yes, me ask me guardian spirit bout you an him tell me everyting cha.

**Gail**    Okay, but it's better if you do an outline sketch first.

*She goes to* **Zippy**, **Sandy** *and* **Jacko**. *She sits*.

**Gail**    That guy is crazy.

**Sandy**    Who Marcus? No he's not, he's sweet and tender and kind and understanding and totally unselfish, but he's a lazy infuriating bastard. He'll tease the life out of you if you let him.

**Gail**    He's doing it already. He knows so many things about me, I can't understand how he . . .

**Sandy**    He's got you worried has he?

**Gail**    Yes, he . . . he makes me feel as though we've met before, but I know we haven't.

**Sandy**    That's Marcus, he's a cunning bastard. That's his best trick. He tries to undermine you and . . .

**Gail**    Yes, that's what he does and he's so good at it.

**Sandy**    You'll get used to it.

**Gail**    I hope I don't, it's so scary.

**Sandy**    He's harmless, a bastard, but harmless.

**Zippy**    Cha him a want somebody put a stop ter his life, dat what.

**Jacko**    No man, do' say dem ting, dat is trouble, guys like he always run away but dey leave you to answer for dem actions.

**Sandy**    Marcus is one of life's crosses that's all. We all have to bear him that's all. So (*To* **Gail**.) you think you're ready to take over for a little while?

**Gail**    Yes, sure.

**Sandy**    I've got to run Jacko over to his place.

**Gail**    I'll be fine.

**Sandy**    Good. I won't be long but you never know. Come on Jacko let's go. (*Rises*.) Now listen everybody, I'm going to take Jacko to his place and see him settled in, so I'm leaving Gail in charge. I won't be long, so if you need anything see Gail, OK? Be good.

**Marcus**    Cha, yer leaving she dem keys me bet.

**Sandy**   Thank you Marcus, I almost forgot. (*She takes the keys off her neck and gives them to* **Gail**.) Don't let him eat you.

**Gail** (*laughs*)   Go on I'll be fine.

**Sandy** (*to all*)   OK, enjoy yourselves. Come on Jacko.

**Jacko** (*to all*)   See you guys.

**Zippy**   Right, take care.

**Dole**   Cool.

**Marcus**   Cha.

**Jacko** *and* **Sandy** *leave.*

**Gail**   OK. I'll be upstairs if you need me.

*She goes upstairs.*

**Marcus**   Cha me do' need she Ras. Hey Dole how dis a sound in nineteen-seventy-nine in dis place me de warrior of de Lion of Judea, Emperor Haile Selassie, Lord of Lords, King of Kings, defeated no conquered a fellow call Jacko who was de champion at football. Cha how yer like it?

**Dole**   Like me Ras, it a bomba.

**Marcus**   Me know yer would like it ter Ras, signed, who a go sign it, Dole?

**Dole**   Sign it yer Ras self.

**Marcus**   Nar, me have ter have impartial judge come beat witness, come nar Dole.

**Dole**   Go way yer Ras, ask Zippy.

**Zippy**   Cha.

**Marcus**   Nar, Fret, nar nar Fret, Sandy me go get Sandy, me do' want no Corporal me go get General, me go get Sandy she a respectable, yes or me could get what she name upstairs, Madame Roberts ter sign, wha yer a say ter dat eh Zippy?

**Zippy**   Cha why you do a rest de girl, de girl come here ter do she ting, yer keep up one set a Ras, what wrong wit yer man, yer keep up. Keep up dis Ras so long.

**Marcus**   Dis is part a she job, dis is what she a here for yer tink is like me like she Cha. Man is you a like she, you afraid me power a righteousness capture she eh?

**Zippy**   Yes, me like she know what.

**Marcus**   Me do' care, man. Me know dat dat is clear vision me get. Cha, pon she say if we a need she ter come, fer she me need she now, eh me a need yer baby.

**Zippy**   Cha, you a Ras Clart satan, you a want tempt somebody into some wilderness but you en go tempt me, you go tempt you Ras self go dey, yer dey already cha.

**Dole**   Whatap, good, blow Zippy, him never go recover dat spirit blow, him get him Rod of Correction. Cross him back ter Ras.

**Marcus**   Cha all yer a miss all all yer a blow miss because me is a genuine Rasta, no stone car touch me, me have de protection of Daniel, cha, all yer not even Lion. Fret go ask she fer me.

**Fret**   What?

**Marcus**   Go ask she ter sign me record.

**Fret**   Nar me no go up dem stairs.

**Dole**   Cha, even his own man a left him.

**Zippy**   Cha, him get wise.

**Marcus**   Hey Mister Zippy you fer want ter go me know yer need one excuse ter need she.

**Zippy**   Excuse me Ras, you a look in mirror ter Ras.

**Marcus**   All right me going, me en want see she Ras but she come fer dis.

**Marcus** *goes upstairs.*

**Dole**   Cha.

**Zippy**   Dat Ras cha make me a take a walk round de corner.

**Dole**   Yer do' want for stay.

**Zippy**   Cha what for him (*Going to the door.*) a go just come down wit him Ras, talk.

**Dole**   Yer a come Fret.

**Fret**   Yea.

*They all leave.*

## Act Two

*The centre*

**Marcus**'s *board in a prominent position. A large football on top.*
**Marcus** *is at the Juke Box dancing.*

**Zippy**, **Dole** *and* **Fret** *run in.*

**Marcus**   Cha, whey all yer a go. Me tought all a get lock up.

**Dole**   We was up de road.

**Fret** *pulls out a pair of jeans from under his robe.*

**Marcus**   Cha. Jeans a hippy ting. Wha happening up dey?

**Dole**   Notting much. Some chick a walk about.

**Marcus**   Any a know?

**Dole**   Julie en she friend.

**Marcus**   Cha, dem a make some style.

**Dole**   Dem say dem was coming down, but wen dem hear
you was here dem change dem mind.

**Marcus**   Cha yer Ras Clart mouth lie.

**Dole**   It a true dem say you a too weird, dem say you a
favour Frankenstein monster, ter Ras Clart.

**Marcus**   Tell dem me a favour Casanova ter Ras, me d'
want dem, me have me own chick.

**Dole**   Yer a pull a new chick?

**Marcus**   Yes nar.

**Dole**   Who?

**Marcus**   De new chick, what she name, Gail.

**Dole**   You pull she?

**Marcus**    Cha, wha so had in dat? It was a easy, me do' let dem night class chick frighten me. Dem brains do' distract me, me cope wid all a dem have ter trew at me.

**Dole**    Yer hear dat Zippy?

**Zippy**    Me hear, what dat have ter do wit me? Dat him Ras Clart business what him do.

**Dole**    Whey she is?

**Marcus**    You want it, it a upstairs resting.

**Dole**    It good?

**Marcus**    Cha it en bad, me make it good.

**Dole**    Cha man yer a quick ter Ras.

**Marcus**    Cha me give she me power, me make she tink me is wise man, an she car keep no secret from me. Me make she believe me know everyting bout she dat me know all she dark secret, an make she a beg me tell she how me know. But what she en a know is me a read she application letter to Sandy an me know all about she, she believe me have power man, wisdom ter Ras Clart me is she saviour ter Ras.

**Dole**    Cha, you is champion now.

**Marcus**    Cha, who want one game? Me feeling strong.

**Marcus** *punches the Juke Box.*

**Dole**    Me play yer ter Ras.

**Dole** *goes to the game. They play.* **Sandy** *and* **Jacko** *enter.*

**Sandy**    Well I see everything's still normal, football and noise. How's everything?

**Dole**    All right. Cha.

**Sandy**    Zippy?

**Zippy**    All right.

**Sandy**    Fret?

**Fret**  Easy.

**Sandy**  Good then. How's Gail?

**Marcus**  She a OK, take me word for it.

*He laughs.*

**Sandy**  Yes?

**Dole**  Him know.

**Sandy**  I see. Well Marcus, Jacko wants a return match.

**Marcus**  Cha me beat him Ras already. Look pon wall we put up me award. Me is champion.

**Sandy**  Go on, give him a game.

**Marcus**  Cha all right make me finish beat Dole first.

**Sandy**  All right I'll just go and see how Gail is coping.

**Marcus**  Cha she coping fine.

**Sandy**  That's what I'm worried about.

**Sandy** *goes.* **Jacko** *sits next to* **Zippy**.

**Zippy**  So how yer fine tings, it change?

**Jacko**  A bit, a just have ter get use ter some new . . .

**Sandy** *brings* **Gail** *downstairs.* **Gail**'*s face is bloodied.*

**Sandy**  For Christ sake Marcus what did you do this for?

**Marcus**  Me no do notting.

**Jacko**  What happen?

**Sandy**  Marcus you did this. Why for Christ sake did you hit the girl? You had no right to.

**Marcus**  Me no hit she.

**Sandy**  She said you did, look at her, why should she lie?

**Gail**  He hit me, he came.

**Marcus**   Me no hit you, you fall down, me no hit she, she a fall down, me try an pick she up.

**Sandy**   Shut up for Christ sake, shut up. What happened Gail?

**Gail**   He came upstairs, and started to play his game and tried to get me going putting me in a corner, and wanting to touch me and putting his hands . . .

**Sandy**   Did he . . . No OK, all right OK, all right, all right, don't cry, don't . . .

**Marcus**   Me never touch she.

**Sandy**   You're a wicked, dirty, vicious bastard that's what you are, I always knew one day . .

**Marcus**   What?

*A beat.*

Go en take she word for it, just because she's a woman, an better educated you tink dem people do' lie.

**Sandy**   What's that got to do with it? Look at her. (*A beat.*) Zippy go upstairs and get the First Aid Box, you know where it is.

**Zippy**   Yea. (*He runs upstairs.*)

**Dole**   So Marcus you a pull she eh, you a one focking mad Ras Clart.

**Marcus**   Me no try a touch she, me box she Ras Clart. She a tink cause she a educated she a better dan me, but me have 'O' levels just like she, me do' show off da is all an try an talk like de Englishman, and beg him for job in him office. She a black just like me how come she get a job in dis place? She no better, me proud just like she, cha she a Ras Clart hypocrite black woman.

**Zippy** *returns with the box.*

**Sandy** (*takes the box*)   Thanks.

*She takes out cotton wool and a small bottle.*

This won't sting. I'll just clean off the blood. There, there, how does that feel, is that better?

**Gail**    Yes – Sandy he –

**Sandy**    Don't worry, it's all right.

**Gail**    He's a liar.

**Sandy**    Yes, yes I know.

**Marcus**    Dats right believe she, me know you like woman, you always take woman side in tings.

**Sandy**    What do you mean by that?

**Marcus**    Me know you do' like man, all dem young girls who come here you always nice ter dem always want ter touch dem an get dem ter like you, but dem do' come no more, dem know yer, dem know yer secret, yer do see dem no come.

**Sandy**    Marcus, you're nasty and dirty and vicious, they don't come because you frighten them away, they know you better than I did. I – I – now go away and take your dirty mind with you.

**Marcus** *moves. He sits. The boys go to the football game and play.*

**Sandy** (*to* **Gail**)    What do you want to do now? Do you want to go home?

**Gail**    No, I want to go to the Police Station.

**Sandy**    What?

**Gail**    I want to report it.

**Sandy**    Gail, you don't . . .

**Gail**    I want to report that nasty vicious thing. I want to report what he did to me.

**Sandy**    You don't know what will happen.

**Gail**   It will show him. He's got to realise he cannot hit a woman, an get away with it.

*She gets up.*

**Sandy**   Gail, please – (*She sits her down.*) If you go to the Police you know what they'll do? They will come here and take him away, he's already on suspended sentences. He'll go in for sure and what will that prove?

**Gail**   It will show him he can't treat people like this and get away with it.

**Sandy**   He's an animal that's what he is that's how he's been made, that's how he's been treated.

**Gail**   Sandy, you . . .

**Sandy**   I know he's a liar, and vicious. What did you think you were doing when you came here? Did you think you were coming a kindergarten? These boys are all vicious, not as bad as Marcus but, that's why they're here, that's why society pays us, to keep them away from good clean society, out of trouble, out of prison. That's why this place is open. You know how I had to fight to get you here? If you go to the Police, they'll close us down. We're meant to be qualified to do it, to do their dirty work for them.

**Gail**   Sandy.

**Sandy**   Jacko, you tell her, tell her what it's like . . . tell her what will happen if he goes in.

**Jacko**   I en involved in dis, I en know what happening.

**Sandy**   Can't you see what's happened?

**Jacko**   I en know, I en know.

**Sandy**   You want him to go inside, you want him to go through what you went through?

**Jacko**   Why yer asking me? I do' know, me en no judge or jury, do' ask me.

**Sandy**   Well I'm asking you Gail, I'm begging you. I'll
ban him from here. I'll do anything, but don't report him.
Believe me that's the worst.

**Gail**   I'm going.

*She goes to leave.*

**Sandy**   Gail, I know Marcus lied, you think I don't? I know
what he's like, you think I haven't been jammed in a corner
before and had hands all over me? But when I looked in
their eyes they were as puzzled as I was and as frightened.
They do it, they don't even know why they . . .

**Gail**   He hit me, Sandy, he . . .

**Sandy**   I was just like you when I started here, full of bright
ideas. I was going to make it happen. I knew exactly what
was needed, but there is a world outside that I can't change.
They haven't got a chance, the moment they walk on the
street they're guilty, that's why we're here to occupy them, to
contain them because society doesn't want to know, not even
their parents . . .

**Jacko**   Dat en true.

**Sandy**   You went inside right?

**Jacko**   Yes.

**Sandy**   Did your mother visit you?

**Jacko**   No.

**Sandy**   Did any of your family visit?

**Jacko**   No.

**Sandy**   You told me how nice it would be if your father
came. I have the letters to prove . . .

**Jacko**   Dat was foolishness. I was too soft. I believe in your
fairy story.

**Sandy** (*to* **Gail**)   Yes, I let them dress up and fool around and dream about Africa. What else is there? That's all they've got.

**Jacko**   All dat is foolishness too. Ethiopia is a Marxist country an Haile Selassie is dead an he exploit he own people more dan anybody. Dat en true blackness, blackness is seeing tings de way it is nothing more. Inside, inside prison. I was in prison, but me en know whey all yer was. I read all de time I in dey, everyting, I read about how de National Front an dem terrorising black people an nobody en doing notting, an how dis Rasta man ting saying peace and love an smoking dope an dreaming bout Africa an de Bible, an de National Front attacking people. I car understand all yer. Wha happen, all yer car see, all yer blind? I say wen I come out I go meet de youth fighting back, because de paper en go print dem ting, an I go join dem. But de paper right. Wen I went in people eye was opening, now I come out it close. Wha happen, wha happen ter all yer? We fight de racist in prison. All yer outside, wha all yer do?

**Marcus**   What all yer listen ter he for? He en no genuine black man.

**Jacko** *approaches* **Marcus**.

**Jacko**   So you're going to Ethiopia den?

**Marcus**   Sure.

**Jacko**   What you going ter to do wen you get dere?

**Marcus**   Me go do my ting. (*He backs off*.)

**Jacko**   So you believe in peace an love, eh?

**Marcus**   Yes, dat's what de Bible good book say.

**Jacko**   You love me? (*He pushes* **Marcus**.)

**Marcus**   Me do' want know . . .

**Jacko**   Give me some peace and love.

**Marcus**   Me do' want no fight man, Sandy, tell him.

**Sandy**   Jacko . . .

**Marcus**   Sandy, tell him. (*He pulls out a blade.*)

**Sandy**   Marcus, don't.

**Jacko**   Where your peace an love? Give me a kiss you black bastard.

**Marcus**   Me warn you.

*He lunges at* **Jacko**. **Jacko** *overpowers* **Marcus**, *grabs the knife and holds it against his throat. Then he lets* **Marcus** *go.*

**Sandy**   Oh my god.

**Marcus** *runs out. Music.* **Zippy** *walks out. They all follow* **Zippy**, *one by one leaving* **Sandy** *alone on stage.*

**Jackie Kay**

# Chiaroscuro

**Jackie Kay** was born in Edinburgh. She is a poet, playwright, novelist and writer of short stories and has enjoyed great acclaim for her work for both adults and children. Her novel *Trumpet* won the *Guardian* Fiction Prize. She lives in Manchester. Her most recent work is *Red Dust Road* (2010).

*Chiaroscuro* was written for Theatre of Black Women and was first presented at the Soho Poly, London, on 19 March 1986. The cast was as follows:

| | |
|---|---|
| **Aisha** | Vinny Dhillon |
| **Beth** | Bernardine Evaristo |
| **Opal** | Jacqueline de Peza |
| **Yomi** | Ella Wilder |

*Director*   Joan Ann Maynard
*Designer*   Helena Roden
*Choreographer*   Pamela Lofton
*Music*   Gail Ann Dorsey

Author's Note, 2011
*The costumes and costume changes specified in the play's stage directions should be regarded by readers and performers only as suggestions.*

Lighting - like Inspector Calls
        - clear truths


Singing - unrestricted




Time:                           human - life + death          makes a point - subjective
Chronological (BL) - long time    - cyclical                        - SOS
Political evolution (progression)   No sense of time in
Psychoanalysis - flashback / memory   Chiaroscuro
                    BL - Prague

Relationship with past + present


Beth + Opal v Chanu + Nazneen
- speed in passion
- romance (C+N + friendship)

Nazneen sees ice skater - Butterfly Effect = Cause + Effect

Fate - Nazneen is controlled          ↓
Chiaroscuro - has no control
        over audience          Chiaroscuro - also B+O
        - B+O                  Audience realisation
                               link to cyclic structure

## Act One

*On the floor is a grey cloth. There are two high-backed chairs painted black and two stools painted white. These are at the back of the stage unless being used. At the front left is an old wooden chest. The stage should be as free from clutter as possible. It should have the appearance of an almost empty yard. The backdrop is a montage of landscapes and odd photographs. Its main colour is pale grey.*

*The four women are all wearing the same outfit: an all-in-one jumpsuit made from stretchy material.* **Aisha** *and* **Beth**'s *are red.* **Yomi** *and* **Opal**'s *are black. They will wear these throughout, sometimes adding something naturalistic. The suits should look stylised rather than fashionable.*

*When the audience enters,* **Aisha** *opens the chest.* **Yomi** *and* **Opal** *stand and chat to each other.* **Beth** *scrutinises the audience.*

*On the floor facing north, south, east and west lie a photograph album, a cushion, an oval-shaped mirror and a black doll.*

*The four women listen to each other as if they have heard it all before.*

*The lights go down.*

**Aisha** *looks at her watch and decides it's time to begin.* **Opal** *and* **Yomi** *continue chatting to each other as she talks.*

**Aisha**   This is how we got to where we were.

**Opal** *signals to* **Yomi**. *They rush to* **Aisha** *and sweep her into the middle of the stage.* **Beth** *approaches the three* MUSICIANS *and asks them for instruments. They hand* **Beth** *four percussion instruments.* **Beth** *distributes them to* **Aisha**, **Yomi** *and* **Opal**. *The music starts. It is soft and haunting. The four women dance, playing their percussion instruments.*

**All** (*sing*)   Time changes light
light changes time
here we are with the dawn in the dark
the dark in the dawn
trying to find the words
trying to find the words.

*wn in the middle of the objects on the floor with their backs  
.. each other.* **Aisha** *sits by the cushion,* **Beth** *by the album,* **Opal** *by the mirror and* **Yomi** *by the doll.* **Aisha** *puts the cushion between her legs.*

**Aisha**  All this has happened before.

**Beth**  How often have you heard it told though?

**Aisha**  Last night and the night before that.

**Opal**  Let's get on with it.

An "alive women

**Aisha**  Okay. I was called after my grandmother on my mother's side. It is a long, long story that can be told so short; people don't realise the years that went, nor the pain, and trying to find a precise beginning is always tough. So much is hard to place. A little hearsay goes a long way. But I heard say that my grandmother was born in the Himalayas at dawn. Her mother shrieked as she pushed her out of herself . . . (*She pushes the cushion out from between her legs.*) . . . and cried and cried. They called her Aisha.

*They turn in a circle till* **Beth** *faces the audience.*

God is my oath / God is bountiful

**Beth**  I was called after my great-great-great-great-grandmother on my father's side who was taken from Africa to slavery in America and raped often; who had children that were each taken from her. But, Beth was one strong woman; she was like Sojourner Truth or Harriet Tubman – a woman who made change, who was Change herself. She helped some other slaves escape to the free country that was North America.

**Yomi** *laughs loudly.*

**Beth**  The black people have been dispossessed, my daddy used to tell me. I only knew what possess meant; did dispossess mean not to own? My daddy told me he called me Beth because my grandmother's African name was whipped out of her. This was the name the white people gave her

with welts in her black skin. He said *that* history had to be
remembered too.

**Aisha**, **Opal**, **Yomi** (*chanting*)   For we have to remember it
all, For we have to remember it all . . .

*They turn again till* **Opal** *faces the audience. She picks up the
mirror and looks at it sideways.*

Jewel - Gem Stone

**Opal**   They had no one to name me after, so they called me
after a stone. A gemstone, at least they thought me special!
A stone that was both jewel and rock, that was a rainbow,
changing with the light. Each time you looked at it you
would see something different. They had no one to name
me after so they called me Opal. At school the children
teased me singing . . .

**Aisha**, **Yomi**, **Beth** (*sing*)   . . . Opal fruit made to make your
mouth water.

**Opal**   They all liked those sweet insults like . . .

**Aisha**, **Yomi**, **Beth** (*sing*)   . . . Nuts oh hazelnuts. Cadbury's
take them and they cover them in chocolate.

**Opal**   These were the white kids' songs. I don't really know
how I got my name. Somebody in the home said it was after
a very old nurse who wore opal earrings all the time. It was
her idea. Call her Opal. So they say, anyway, but for all I
know that could be hearsay.

*The circle turns till* **Yomi** *faces the audience. She puts the doll on
her stomach.*

**Yomi**   My mother had a time of it with me. I just wouldn't
come out! Her womb must have been too cosy for me
to want to leave! She just got bigger and bigger and it
seemed, she said, she would never have me, like she would
be carrying me around inside her for the rest of her life.
What a thought! Finally they cut her open and out I came,
all six and a half pounds of me. (*She pushes the doll up in the
air.*) At midnight. A midnight baby. She called me Abayomi.

My enemies tried to mock me
but God did not allow them

Apparently I never cried when they spanked me. My name is Abayomi. My mother was afraid I would never arrive. But here I am. Here I am. I surprised the lot of them.

*They all rise. They follow* **Opal** *carrying their objects. They dance to the chest. A walking dance. As they go there,* **Opal** *speaks.*

**Opal**   And so it was that names were also chance things like an old woman's fancy or a mother's dream names relating to nothing specific except desire names with no heavy weight like Aphrodite or Persephone Gauri-Sankar or Tara – names hinged casually onto some instant liking. Name the nameless ones. Name the nameless ones.

*They stop at the chest and peer in as if it is a wishing well.*

**Aisha**   My grandmother Aisha gave me this. She made it. Beautiful, isn't it? I remember lots of the stories she told me whilst I sat on this cushion. It was a magic cushion. Her stories made me travel. Once she told me a true story and I stayed still.

**Yomi**   I remember. (**Yomi** *changes to* **Aisha**'s *grandmother.*) 'Your great-grandmother was so bossy. She bossed me around terrible. I promised myself I would never do that to my children . . .'

**Aisha**   Yeah well, bossiness must skip a generation, 'cos your daughter bosses me around something chronic. (She don't anymore. I think that was during the terrible teens.)

**Yomi**   'Life is too short, Aisha. You must just not bother with it. Get on and do what you want to do. It's hard enough for girls. Too many people wanting to hold them back. Sometimes I think if I could replay my life back again, which bits would I want to edit out and which would stay in, or better still, Aisha, which new bits . . . When you get to the end . . .'

**Aisha** (*interrupting her*)   Please, Gran.

**Yomi**  'Don't be silly. Death is as ordinary as life. When you get to the end you really wish you hadn't been such a coward. Take the risk, Aisha.'

**Aisha**  I didn't really know what she was on about then. But I remembered it and now the words make sense. Good sense.

*She hugs the cushion and drops it into the chest, reluctantly.*

**Yomi** (*hugging her doll*)    I called this doll Amanda. Once . . .

**Aisha**  . . . she was walking down the street she lived in and some kids shouted . . .

**Opal**  . . . Just because you're a darky doesn't mean you have to have a darky doll.

**Aisha**  So when she got home, she took it out of her pram and put Amanda in the airing cupboard. Every so often she guiltily pulled her out and called her names . . .

**Opal** (*vindictively*)   Nigger. Wog. Sambo. Dirty doll.

**Yomi**  Poor Amanda.

**Yomi** *puts the doll into the chest.*

**Opal**  When I was little glass haunted me.

**Beth**  Everywhere she went it would be – in shops, in cars, all over the place.

**Aisha**  Once when she was eight she broke a small round mirror. She was so superstitious. She counted on her fingers how old she would be before she could be happy. Fifteen. It seemed *old*.

**Beth**  Whenever she looked in the glass she saw ghosts of old reflections. A face behind her face. Her face was a shock to itself.

**Opal** *looks in the mirror once more, pulling a face. Then she puts it in the chest. She grabs the album out of* **Beth**'s *hands.*

**Beth**   No. I don't want to.

**Opal**   Come on Beth. We said *all* of us.

**Beth**   It's stupid anyway.

**Yomi**   Too late. All her old boyfriends are in here, the ones she pretends she never had. Yeah look. Photo-booth smooches and slurps. *convince herself she is straight*

**Yomi** *flicks through the album teasing* **Beth**. *suppressed emotion*

**Aisha**   Let's just get on with it.

*Awkward misfit*

**Opal**   Don't forget all her childhood friends – all white. And her mother pale and frightened-looking. As if her whole life is a surprise to her. *Does not git in - Outcast*

*Not stereotypically correct - ALIENATED*

**Beth** *takes the album off* **Yomi** *and puts it in the chest. She throws off her mood and suddenly switches, turning around in a swirl. The light brightens. Innocence of romance heightened by oppression of scene before*

**Beth**   And don't we need surprises!

**Aisha**   All depends on which sort, doesn't it?

**Beth**   Like this one.

**Opal** *picks up one of the stools and carries it to the front of the stage. She sits down.* **Beth** *waits till she is comfortable and picks up the other stool.* **Aisha** *closes the chest and she and* **Yomi** *sit on it watching* **Beth** *and* **Opal**.

**Beth**   Do you mind if I join you? (You with the changing eyes?)

*Thought tracking*
*↓*
*Insecurity*
*Anxiety*

**Opal** *is reading.*

**Opal**   No.

**Opal** *continues to read.* **Beth** *stares at her.*

**Beth** (*to imaginary waitress*)   I'll have a coffee, please. (Her eyes are amazing.) (*To* **Opal**.) It's a lovely day isn't it? (And you are too.)

**Opal** (*reluctantly*)   Yeah. Pity to have wasted it shopping.

**Beth**   What did you buy?

**Opal**   Oh just some earrings for a friend.

**Beth** *takes coffee from imaginary waitress.*

**Beth**   Thank you. (She's like a stranger that I know very well.) Do you work?

**Opal**   (What is this?) Yeah, I'm a nurse.

**Beth**   Oh. (*Pause.*) That's demanding work.

**Opal**   Yeah, you're telling me.

**Beth**   And hospital structures are so hierarchical, aren't they?

**Opal**   Mmmnn (Listen to her! She seems to know more about them than me.) (*Pause.*) Are you a student?

**Beth** (*put out*)   No. I was once. Not that it counts for much these days.

**Opal**   (Thought so.) Well you can only say that if you've got a degree under your belt, can't you?

**Beth**   Suppose so. (She is interesting. I wonder where she comes from.) Where are your parents from?

**Opal**   I haven't got any. (I've had this conversation before.)

**Beth**   Oh. But don't you know anything about them?

**Opal**   Nothing. I was brought up in a home in Hampshire. (I wonder if she always does this.) So what do you do now your student days are over?

**Beth**   I'm an outreach worker for a community centre in Haringey.

**Opal**   Oh. Interesting.

**Beth**   (This is crazy. I don't even know . . .)

**Opal**   Do you always do this then?

**Beth** (*vacantly*)   What?

**Opal**   Talk to strangers.

**Beth**   No. (*Laughing.*) Never, would you believe. It was just; well, I don't know how to put it . . .

**Opal** (*interrupting her*)   You remind me of someone I used to know.

**Beth** (*pleased*)   Really?

**Opal**   Yeah. I'm Opal.

**Beth**   I'm Beth. Opal? That's an interesting name.

**Opal**   Yeah it is, isn't it? It's after the stone, you know, Opal.

**Beth** (*giggling*)   Oh.

**Opal**   Well! People are called after flowers. Anyhow, you think Opal's funny – I know someone called Turquoise.

**Beth** (*laughing*)   Next it'll be Onyx!

**Opal** (*suddenly*)   Well it's getting on. I have to rush.

**Opal** *gathers herself together.* **Beth** *is agitated.*

**Opal**   It was nice talking to you.

**Beth**   You too. Listen. (I must ask her before she goes.) Maybe we could go out for a drink sometime or something. (There, I've said it.)

**Opal** *doesn't know what to say.*

**Beth**   Are you on the phone?

**Opal** (*hesitantly*)   Yes . . .

**Beth**   That's good.

**Opal** *scrambles around for paper. Doesn't find anything.*

**Beth**   I'll write it on my hand.

**Opal**   800-2454.

**Beth**   Thanks. Okay, I'll ring you.

**Opal**   Yeah do.

**Beth**   Maybe I'll ring tomorrow.

**Opal**   (So soon?) Anytime.

*Lights go down and then up again. They are softer.* **Opal** *picks up her stool and sits at the other end of the stage.* **Beth** *stays where she is, smiling.* **Opal** *peers into an imaginary mirror.* **Beth** *watches* **Aisha** *and* **Yomi**. **Aisha** *takes a quilt out of the chest and hands it to* **Yomi**. **Yomi** *dances with it as* **Aisha** *talks.*

**Aisha**   You see they decided it was time, right. Time to get out of the rut. Time to grab a chance. In the beginning there was the dream of decency and opportunity and education. My parents came here in 1953 to work and save and work and one day return home. They were the invited guests who soon found out they'd be treated like gatecrashers . . .

**Yomi** *interrupts her, holding up the quilt.*

**Yomi**
   Whose were the hands that stitched these stitches?
   In what language are these threads
   Did the imagination of some strong woman
   hold this thing together
   has each piece belonged to a different child?
   whose were the hands that stitched these stitches?
   in what language are these threads?

**Aisha**   My mum was a factory machinist. She was constantly sewing. Even when she didn't need to. It was like she couldn't stop. Making ends meet. Sometimes she downed the shirts and the dresses and made quilts – beautiful, angry quilts glorious with colour and pattern. All the words she never spoke stitched intricately. Sometimes when I look into her eyes, I think I see the dead dream in them. When I look at the quilts I hear her laughing – laughing at them that treat her like a child, laughing at her own boldness, laughing like she laughed at home. It makes me want to laugh when I hear them talking about *us* taking over. What do they think they've done? They've even taken over my tongue. Yet sometimes I worry, Yomi, that I'd never fit in back home. That I'd stick out a mile, or worse they'd call me English!

**Yomi** *takes* **Aisha**'s *hand and leads her to the* MUSICIANS *as she talks.*   *Poetry = warmth + connection with audience*

**Yomi**
> The country of origin
> the original country
> back home, the place you came from
> where roots still grow
> out under moon and sun   *Natural - not tied down by*
> the soil on which the past lies   *nation/religion but elements*
> *OWNED* the place which might attach itself to you   *of the world.*
> like a belonging   *juxtaposition of 'logic'*

*intrinsicly linked to*
*past* **Aisha** *and* **Yomi** *take a percussion instrument from the*   *we are attached to the location*
MUSICIANS. **Yomi** *harmonises as* **Aisha** *sings.*

**Aisha** (*sings*)   *More socially aware - accepting*
> *but conforming*
> My dreams are in another language
> my heart is overseas   *COMFORT*
> a need is stretching like the water   *i.e. do not talk of*
> to meet and meet and meet   *sexuality*
> I want to put it all together
> these different bits of me
> show them to my mother and
> all my family my family

> My dreams are deep as dangerous waters
> my heart is beating at the rocks
> a longing is spinning like a whirlpool
> round and round and round
> I want to travel over there
> and join my past to now   *Dual-identity = struggle with*
> be welcomed, not a stranger   *the relationship with heritage*
> for who I am and feel at home.

*The music fades. The lights change.* **Aisha** *and* **Yomi** *stay where they are and watch* **Beth** *and* **Opal.** *Spotlight on* **Beth.**

**Beth**    I feel like I've met her before, you know. There's something about her that made me feel so at home. I just can't get her out of my head. She's left a warm glow all over me. (*Pause.*) I decided I was going to be celibate for two years. (*Pause.*) Maybe I should just give her a ring now. (*She picks up an imaginary receiver and replaces it.*) This is ridiculous! It's too soon. I could always ring her tomorrow. Oh, I just don't know what to do. 'Hello Opal, Beth here. I fancy you, would you like to get to know me better?' Can you imagine! She'd hang up probably. I could phone and a man might answer. I don't even know if she's got a boyfriend. I could phone and listen to the endless ring and my heart beat saying, *Answer-Opal-pick-it-up*!, and finally watch my hand slowly put the phone back in its cradle. My head is spinning. (*Pause.*) I should have given her my number. No, that'd be worse; I'd just be sitting here like a prize ass waiting for the phone to ring.

*Lights go down and up with spot on* **Opal.**

**Opal**    I can't believe I'm feeling like this. It's crazy. I've only seen her three times and seen three very good films into the bargain! Not the sort I'd usually go and see, but when I'm with her it doesn't seem to matter what we do. It is so strange. She's a woman! This attraction is so physical. At first I thought, this isn't real. I must just admire her or something. But, last night I wanted to lean over and kiss her! I wonder if she feels like that for me? Maybe she just wants to be good friends. Wouldn't that be a laugh! Me melting away for her and her just wanting to be good mates. What would we do anyway? We'd go and see another film, maybe that *Desert Hearts* she's been telling me about. I'd go back to her place and . . . oh, I just can't imagine it. Sometimes, you just meet someone like that (*She snaps her fingers.*) and you feel like you've known them all of your life. I feel that way with Beth. Somewhere I believe I was meant to meet

her that day in that café before the sun went down and the
summer slipped away.

*Lights down.* **Aisha** *and* **Yomi** *take the stools from* **Beth** *and* **Opal**
*and place them opposite each other in the middle of the stage.* **Beth**
*and* **Opal** *stand at either end of the stage and do the movements of a
train.* The MUSICIANS *make train sound effects. Lights up.*

**Yomi**   It is one of those summer days that make you want to
live in a country that knows how to be hot!

**Aisha**   Yeah right.

**Yomi**   Do you know, Aisha, I don't think I've seen any
countryside for at least a year. It's Fabayo I feel sorry for. I
don't think it's good for kids to be trapped in cities.

**Aisha**   She'll be all right.

**Yomi**   I've never left her before, you know.

**Aisha**   I know.

*They look out into the audience.*

I hope it's going to be all right.

**Yomi**   So do I. I hope she doesn't wet the bed.

**Aisha**   I wasn't talking about Fabayo, I meant the weekend.

**Yomi**   Well, it'll make a change. (*Pause.*) Actually, I haven't
got a clue what to expect from it. Yet I'm looking forward to
it. If it's disappointing, I can always blame you!

**Aisha**   Thanks, mate.

**Yomi**   I tell you what will be nice though, just having the
time to choose what I want to do. Luxury.

**Aisha**   Do you think you'll go to the social?

**Yomi**   I might. It's women-only, isn't it? You've been to that
kind of disco before, haven't you?

**Aisha**   Only once.

**Yomi**   What was it like?

**Aisha**   It was all right. Made a change not to be hassled to dance by some bloke who reckons you owe it to him 'cos he's bought you a drink!

**Yomi**   Wole would go mad. I can just hear him: 'an *All-Women's disco*?'

*They laugh.*

**Aisha**   Are you seeing much of him at the moment?

**Yomi**   Oh, you know, about every two weeks. It's enough for me! (*Pause.*) I think I'll try silk-screening. I've always fancied trying that.

**Aisha**   I wish I wasn't running this carpentry workshop, then I'd get a chance to go to the others.

**Yomi**   Aisha?

**Aisha**   Uh huh.

**Yomi**   At the social tonight?

**Aisha**   Yeah?

**Yomi**   You won't piss off and leave me alone will you?

**Aisha**   'Course not. You know me.

*Lights down.* **Beth** *and* **Opal** *sit on the chest and pretend to be watching a film. In the middle of* **Yomi**'s *monologue,* **Opal** *takes* **Beth**'s *hand.* **Aisha** *picks up the stool and takes it to the other end of the stage. She sits down and listens to* **Yomi**. **Yomi** *stays where she is. Spot on* **Yomi**.

**Yomi**   I must hoover the carpet! This place looks like a tip. Honestly, you'd think a whole family lived here, not just the two of us. (*Pause.*) We are a whole family, I suppose, me and her. She took ages getting to sleep tonight. Maybe I shouldn't have gone away for that weekend. She's punishing me! (*Laughs softly.*) That was some weekend though! Mind you, some of those women were too angry for my liking.

There's no need to make such a fuss! You'd think, from the way some of them talked, that they hated all men! Well, there's no point in that at all. I've known some pretty nasty women in my time. I felt so out of it, some of the time. Well, it was nice. That bit of time for myself. I surprised myself; I was good at that silk-screening lark. I think there were a lot of . . . lesbians there. That woman teaching silk-screening said some strange things. Half of them didn't even make sense. I think she was one. Judging by that disco, there are more than we know about. God. Was I shocked! I felt so naive. I've never seen two women kissing before. Long ones! Honestly! If they want to do that sort of thing they should do it behind closed doors. And black women at that! I didn't think we produced them. (*Pause.*) Aisha didn't seem too bothered. (*She is irritated with her house again.*) I should have never let Wole paint these walls. The edges are all wonky. God! And that woman asking me if I was going to the sexuality workshop. I said to her – either you enjoy sex or you don't, what is there to talk about?

*Lights down.* **Aisha** *and* **Yomi** *start to mime a game of pool.* **Beth** *watches them nearby.* **Opal** *stands at the opposite end of the stage peering into an imaginary mirror. Lights up. The lights should follow the imaginary pool balls.*

**Beth** (*appraisingly*)　Not bad, Aisha.

**Aisha**　Yeah. I've just about thrashed her.

**Yomi**　Not quite.

**Beth**　I used to play pool in this pub down Dalston. The men in there used to get on my nerves.

**Yomi**　Why was that?

**Beth**　Well, they couldn't stand it if you beat them. They just couldn't take it, you know.

**Aisha** *is awkward and concentrates on the game.*

**Aisha**　Okay Yomi, let's see how you'll get out of this one.

**Yomi**   You're so kind.

**Beth**   Trouble with men is, they're really competitive. Women learn how to behave differently.

**Yomi** *pushes* **Beth** *out of her way to make her move.*

**Yomi**   Oh, I don't know about that. The women I work with are always competing with each other.

**Beth**   For male approval probably.

**Yomi**   For what?

**Aisha** *is exasperated.*

**Beth**   You've got a daughter haven't you, Yomi?

**Yomi**   Yes.

**Beth**   What's her name?

**Yomi**   Fabayo.

**Beth**   What age is she?

**Yomi**   Seven.   *most comfortable in who she is*

**Beth**   I'd like to have a child someday.   *Sig – Lesbian relationship*

**Yomi**   Really? Well they're a handful, change the whole of your life. But I would never be without mine, though. Shot! Oh no. Just the black to go.

**Aisha**   What did I tell you?

**Aisha** *pots the black.*

Sorry old bean.

**Yomi**   Too bad, eh. Do you want to play the winner, Beth?

**Beth**   Okay. I'm a bit rusty.

**Aisha**   Do you want to break?

**Beth** *breaks.* **Yomi** *watches her critically.*

**Yomi**   Where are you from?

Chiaroscuro

*move on Yomi then Beth* (handwritten)

**Beth**   My father's from St Vincent. My mother's English.

**Yomi**   Oh.   *looking for commonality* (handwritten)
            *straight heritage* (handwritten)

**Beth**   And you?

**Yomi**   Nigeria.

**Aisha** (*interrupting her*)   Oh come on, I must have told you both where the other was from.

**Yomi**   No. I don't think that was one of the things you told me about Beth.

**Beth** *is suspicious.*

**Aisha**   She's trying to wind you up.

**Beth** *concentrates on the game and pots several balls in succession.*

**Beth** (*pleased*)   Not bad eh, considering I haven't played for ages. Mind you, the last time was enough to put me off pool for life.

**Yomi**   Why was that?

**Beth**   These jerks started hassling us and one of them poured a beer all over me.

**Yomi**   Oh dear. That must have been a bit of a shock.

**Beth** *pots the black. They freeze. Spot on* **Opal**.

**Opal**   My face was a shock to itself. The brain in my head thought my skin white and my nose straight. It imagined my hair was this curly from twiddling it. Every so often, I saw me: milky coffee skin, dark searching eyes, flat nose. *Some voice from that mirror would whisper: nobody wants you, no wonder. You think you're white till you look in me. I surprised you, didn't I?* I'd stop and will the glass to change me. *Where did you get that nose?*   *Psyche judges her - Internalised Racism* (handwritten)

**Aisha**, **Yomi** and **Beth** *unfreeze.* **Beth** *goes up to* **Opal**. **Aisha** *stands near them.* **Yomi** *sits on the chest, watching.*

**Beth**   Do you still feel alone when you look in there?

**Opal**   No.

**Beth**   I don't feel alone any more, either. When I first met you, you were so familiar, a dream I never expected to come true. Like seeing my own reflection. I used to feel that I was the only black lesbian in the world, you know. Serious. Just me on my tod.

**Opal**   I don't like that word – lesbian.

**Beth**   It's a name.

**Opal**   We don't need a name. What about this?

**Opal** *motions to* **Aisha**. **Aisha** *starts to dance, holding imaginary earphones.* **Beth** *and* **Opal** *watch her, laughing.*

**Aisha**   This is the twilight radio station. The station of this nation. Here's the wonderful smoochy song especially for Margaret, Annie sends you all her love, says she's sorry and still mad about you. (*Sings.*) 'You make my love come down.' Oooh she does.

**Aisha** *stops dancing, switches moods. She turns* **Beth** *around so that she has her back to the audience.* **Beth**'*s body tenses and freezes.*

**Aisha**   (*to* **Opal**)   She first thought she might be a lesbian at school. She was terrified. None of the textbooks mentioned her name. She searched for boyfriends to cover her terror. To play at the stories in all of the school books. She was in love with her female English teacher. Once she looked up lesbian in the medical dictionary. She worried about her hormones. When she was older she discovered the hidden world – the clubs and the pubs. She was still alone. She repeated to herself like a prayer.

**Beth**   It's just a phase; it will pass.

**Aisha**   But it didn't.

**Beth** *turns around. The lights brighten.*

**Beth**   No, thank God.

**Opal**   Well I don't know if it's God you should be thanking!

**Opal** *turns her back to them.*

**Beth** (*to* **Aisha**)   How do you know all those things?

**Aisha**   I told you, I'm psychic.

**Beth**   You don't give away much.

**Aisha**   I'm not charity.

**Aisha** *tries to laugh and stops at the expression on* **Beth**'s *face.*

**Beth**   Okay, I'll ask you straight . . .

**Aisha** (*interrupting her*)   You never asked a straight question in your life.

**Beth** (*smiles*)   How about this: do you fancy anybody?

**Aisha** (*nonchalantly*)   Yeah.

**Beth**   Really? Who is it?

**Aisha**   You said it. I don't give much away.

**Beth**   Oh go on. I tell you things.

**Aisha**   What do you see in Opal? You two don't seem well suited.

**Opal** is *indignant.*

**Beth**   Oh. We are.

**Aisha**   You want to know if 'it's a man or a woman, don't you?

**Beth**   Yes.

**Aisha**   Guess.

**Beth**   A woman.

**Aisha**   Nah. I told you. It's not for me. Too risky.

**Beth**   Oh come off it, Aisha, you've always taken risks. Look at you being a carpenter. Opal? Have you heard this before?

**Opal** *turns around and listens, unimpressed.*

**Beth**    When she was eleven she sat on one of her mum's new chipboard shelves and broke it.

**Aisha** (*to* **Opal**)    I was a bit of a podge then.

**Beth**    She felt so bad 'cos her mum didn't have an awful lot of money. She tried to fix it with superglue. She wished she could make them herself – fine pine shelves. Strong. Unbreakable. She looked at the table that wobbled on its shaky leg; she thought about making a cosy home for the gramophone. She decided then she was going to be somebody. Somebody who made things from wood. She started sketching distinguished desks, tremendous tables . . . Her imagination had a little setback when her father came home and saw the superglued shelf. He wasn't impressed was he when she told him – 'Never mind. One day I'm gonna be a carpenter.'

**Opal** *laughs.*

**Aisha**    Like I said, it's too risky.

**Aisha** *goes to the chest. The lights soften.* **Yomi** *and* **Aisha** *take masks from the chest and put them on.*

**Opal**    Did you mean it when you said we are suited?

**Beth**    Yes.

**Opal**    Why?

**Beth**    You make me feel I can be myself and . . .

**Opal** (*interrupting her*)    How long do you think we'll last?

**Beth**    How do I know? I don't like speculating.

**Opal**    I'm scared of losing you. I can't imagine my life without you now.

**Beth**    Opal, you're a real drama queen sometimes. You were living before you met me and you'll keep living if we split.

**Opal** (*hurt*)    You must know what I mean. I want to imagine growing old with you.

**Beth** (*incredulous*)    Old?

**Opal**    Well if you're not there, who will be? You're the only family I have, Beth, the only one I can call home. That's what freaks me out – what happens when you go?

**Beth**    Why are we having this conversation? I'm not going anywhere. Do you see me heading for the door? But I can't promise any forevers either. I don't believe in always. Always is a lie like till death do us part. Look at the divorce rates amongst the straights.

**Opal**    I'm not talking of marriage.

**Beth**    You are, Opal. (*Pause.*) Look should we ever split up, and we might, we'll leave each other stronger than we were when we first met. Strong enough to continue, Opal. Our love is filling me up today. Tomorrow is something I can't plan. Anyhow, I'm not the only woman in the world, you know.

**Opal**    Yes you are. Oh Beth. I love you so much it's frightening. I don't trust happiness. Why can't I say always?

**Beth** (*impatiently*)    Because there is nothing worse than shattered promises. I love you too. I don't want to hurt you.

**Opal**    I understand. Promises used to hurt so much – the foster parents that never arrived. I used to feel so unwanted. That's what terrifies me. I feel wanted by you.

**Beth**    You are, honey. You're a wanted woman.

*Chorus would wear mask – Greek Mythology Theatre*
*They start to dance close. The lights go dim. As* **Aisha** *and* **Yomi** *approach wearing masks and walking like robots, the lights flash madly. The* MUSICIANS *play intense, frightening music.* **Aisha** *and* **Yomi** *break up the dance; their movements are violent but stylised.*

*Masks – hides identity to captivate a majority*
*link to time    Reflections of society*
*past + present    Robotic – internalised to follow others*

*Naznoor's psyche* [handwritten annotation]

*morally incorrect p* [handwritten annotation]

*Yomi: is dehumanised - lack of emotion* [handwritten annotation]

Act One

**Yomi**  Wanted for murder! For killing off the race. God
says it isn't natural. God says it isn't natural. AIDS is God's
vengeance on the men. On the men. Punishment for their
sins. Their sins. Man and woman. Adam and Eve. That's the
way it was meant to be. Meant to be.  *Link to religion (BL)* [handwritten]

*Short, quick sentences.*  *= excuse (Bible verse)* [handwritten]

**Aisha**  It is sick. But it can be treated. There is hope for
them yet. Psychiatrists are God's disciples. Aversion therapy.  *biblical* [handwritten]
Special diets. Electric shocks. A screw. A screw.  *misogyny not just* [handwritten]
*homosexuality* [handwritten]

**Yomi**  What do they do what do they do these les-bi-ans? It
is easy to imagine what men do – but women, women. The
thought turns the national stomach, stomach.  *Repetition*  *heterosexuality* [handwritten]

*The robots walk off.*  *NF - minority v majority* [handwritten]

*Internalised view* [handwritten, right margin]

*Interrobation* [handwritten]

**Beth**  Is that your nightmare?

**Opal**  Some of it.

**Opal** *walks to the front of the stage.* **Beth** *goes to the other side at
the back, so that she is diagonally opposite.* **Aisha** *and* **Yomi** *return.
During* **Opal** *and* **Beth**'s *poems,* **Aisha** *and* **Yomi** *match the words
with symbolic movement.*

**Opal**
    If I could tear it up
    this fear that wears no soft gloves
    could just banish all the *what ifs*
    and twenty years from now
    where will I be – how do dykes grow old?
    I have this picture of Beth and I
    loving all the finds
    maturing like good wine
    love keeping us warm
    whenever I see it
    love stretched over years
    with plenty left to spread
    I butcher the picture with my carving knife
    and she is suddenly dead
    I am at her funeral

and no one there knows what we meant to each other
and all her remaining relatives wonder –
who is the sobbing woman in the dark coat
at the back with a pew to herself?

The picture makes me want to say now
and for ever my name
tell them all where my loving lies
allowing them no weapon
for there is no bullet-proof protection
for the likes of us
and even though I have no family
I still turn my insides out
when I imagine what they would say
the old school friends, the old home friends
the nurses the doctors and all the anonymous
who should mean
Nothing
but might carry a knife
might follow me home
might write graffiti on my wall.

I want to banish it all
the dread that keeps all hours
and let me live my life
and let me live my love
and let me love my life.

*Spotlight on* **Beth** *who smiles at* **Opal**.

**Beth**

Yesterday the sky was white bright white
I couldn't see anything not even outlines
then, without warning, splashes of black and red
fire flies in the sky
inside me was a glow-worm glowing
the sky darkened to grey.

I never expected to be anything other
than alone – I am a wishing well

*somewhere at the very bottom*
*I echo when touched*
*but I am hollow and it's a long way down*

*her need sucks like mosquitoes*
*my need is camouflaged*
*I am all green and brown*
*inside my leaves laugh and whisper:*
*you call yourself a risker?*

*Then I see another picture*
*we lie close talking tongues*
*she is under my skin*
*we are each other's dream*
*she and her opalescent eyes*
*me and my fire flies*
*we are dawn and dusk together*

*she is the first woman*
*to see all of me*
*and keep holding, holding.*

**Beth** *and* **Opal** *dance towards each other and twirl each other*
*around. They join in* **Aisha** *and* **Yomi***'s dance. The four dance*
*together in a dance of conflict and happiness. Wild carefree music*
*accompanies them. Suddenly they separate.* **Yomi** *dances to the front*
*of the stage and sits down, she tucks her imaginary child into bed.*
**Aisha** *and* **Beth** *and* **Opal** *continue dancing through* **Yomi***'s story.*
*The lights soften.*

**Yomi** (*to her child*)    My mother told me, and her
grandmother told her, that old Yomi was born with her
tongue missing. People had never heard of such a thing. At
first they were terrified, thinking that someone had done
something wrong and this was the revenge. They spurned
her: if it wasn't their fault, she must have brought it on
herself.

But. When as a child old Yomi started to draw and paint,
people suddenly realised they were mistaken. She had a gift.
They saw themselves in her pictures. They saw their grand-

parents; they saw people they had not yet met. They saw people she could never have seen. She had powers. She was special.

**Yomi** *closes the imaginary door quietly and walks to the edge of the stage. She talks confidentially to the audience.*

When I gave birth to Fabayo, I had the most incredible experience. My waters broke and she just slid out without any problems. But, she never cried when they spanked her. She didn't talk till she was three. I thought old Yomi was trying to pass something down and not quite making it! The other day I came home and Fabayo was drawing a picture of someone who in a funny way looks like Beth! That was what reminded me of the woman my mother called me after.

*Lights go down and then up again.* **Yomi** *motions to the others who begin to walk around the stage in different directions frantically. They repeat.*

**All**   I really hope it's going to be all right.

**Opal** *and* **Yomi** *open the chest.* **Yomi** *gives* **Aisha** *a loose black shirt.* **Opal** *gives* **Beth** *some colourful wraps.* **Opal** *takes out a red belt and ties it round herself.* **Yomi** *takes out a yellow skirt and puts it on.* **Aisha** *and* **Beth** *dress opposite each other to music in a stylised fashion; they are laughing nervously.* **Yomi** *and* **Opal** *put some lipstick on each other. They separate.* **Aisha** *starts to move the chairs to the middle of the stage.* **Yomi** *and* **Opal** *sit down on the chest, watching her.* **Beth** *walks round the stage, carrying an imaginary bottle of wine. She stops and presses an imaginary bell.* (*The* MUSICIANS *do the ding-dong!*) **Aisha** *opens the door.*

**Beth**   Hello, Aisha. I'm a bit early.

**Aisha**   That's all right – you can help me set things up.

**Beth** *gives* **Aisha** *the bottle of wine. They move the chairs.*

**Aisha**   Thanks. Where's Opal, then?

**Beth**   She's coming along a bit later. She's still at the hospital.

*Dinner party setting – stereotypes (do not bring politics to tab*
*Applicable setting stages the issues of society*

**Aisha**  Oh good. For a minute, I thought she wasn't coming. Yomi should be here in a bit.

**Beth**  How is she?

**Aisha**  All right. (*Pause.*) Listen, Beth, I was going to ask you if you could tone it about the lesbian bit, 'cos Yomi doesn't know and . . .

**Beth** (*interrupting her*)  Why didn't you tell her then?

**Aisha**  Well I didn't think that . . .

**Beth**  What?

**Aisha**  That you'd want me to.

**Beth**  Oh come off it, Aisha, since when have I kept it a secret?

**Aisha**  You look nice.

**Beth**  Thanks. Oh, I don't know; sometimes I just get really fed up with having to hide it from certain people in order to get on with them. I mean if they can't deal with it, it's their problem, not . . .

**Yomi** *walks to the 'door' She pushes the bell.*

**Aisha**  That'll be Yomi, probably.

**Yomi**  Hello, Aisha.

**Aisha**  Yomi! How are you doing?

**Yomi**  Not bad, not bad at all.

*They walk to* **Beth**. **Yomi** *eyes* **Beth**'s wrap *with suspicion.* **Beth** *is upset. She lights a cigarette.*

**Beth**  Hi Yomi, how are you?

**Yomi**  Well, thanks, and you?

**Beth**  Knackered. Too much work, you know.

**Aisha**  I've just got some bits to attend to, won't be long.

**Aisha** *walks to the other end of the stage and stands still watching them.*   [handwritten: Yomi is Nigerian (identifies)]

**Yomi**   I like your wraps. Where are they from?

[handwritten: Takes offence - cultural appropriation]

**Beth**   This friend of mine brought them from Nairobi. She went to the international women's conference there a few summers ago.

**Yomi**   Oh. (*Shouts.*) Aisha? Do you need a hand?

**Aisha**   No, I'm all right.

[handwritten: non - naturalistic set (i.e. no door/good)]

**Opal** *walks to the 'door' and pushes the bell.*

**Beth**   Shall I get it?

[handwritten: Society = superficial goes on people not objects (audience influenced by individuals)]

**Aisha**   Go ahead.

**Beth** *lets* **Opal** *in. They kiss.*

[handwritten: Yomi uses solid object to attack in defence of homosexuality]

**Opal**   Hello everybody.

**Aisha** *walks back carrying 'food'.*

**Aisha**   Hiya Opal, how's things?

**Opal**   Oh all right.

**Yomi**   Fabayo's been asking when you're going to come and see us, ever since we bumped into you that day.

**Opal**   Soon as I get an invite.

**Aisha**   Are you all ready to eat then?

**Beth**   Sure.

*They concentrate on the 'food'.*

A friend of mine is getting married tomorrow.

**Aisha** *is surprised.*

**Opal**   Oh, who is that?

**Beth**   You don't know her.

**Yomi**   Are you going to the wedding?

**Beth**    Have to, really.

**Yomi**    You don't sound too enthusiastic.

**Beth** (*to* **Aisha**)    Well, I really don't want to go on my own, and I couldn't take Opal with me. She's an old school friend. My mum knows her mum. My mum will be there too. I haven't seen her for a while. That'll be nice.

**Aisha** (*uncomfortable*)    So . . . what have you been up to, Opal?

**Opal**    Just work, work and more work. It seems to take up the whole of my life. I had a day of it today.

**Aisha**    Why, what happened?

**Opal**    Well, I was telling one of my patients that it was curry for lunch and she said, 'It's not us that like that, but you coloured!' I didn't know what to say, so I just told her that I didn't like the word coloured, and she asked me what I'd call myself then. I told her black. She laughed and said, 'But you're a half-caste.'

**Beth**    Shit.

**Aisha**    What a cheek.

**Yomi**    What's wrong with half-caste?

**Aisha**    Come off it, Yomi!

**Yomi** (*angry*)    Well. Tell me then! I've said it all of my life.

**Beth**    It's derogatory – it's just like all those other horrible descriptions: half-breed, mulatto, the lot. It really gets to me when people insist on saying that I'm half and half.

**Yomi**    But it's true, isn't it?

**Beth**    What do you mean?

**Yomi**    Well, you are half and half; you can't just pretend that you don't have a white parent. You can't say that you're not half white even if you don't . . .

**Beth** (*interrupting her*)   Half white!

**Yomi**   Well, are you denying that your mother is white?

**Beth**   Of course not. That's not the point, is it? I mean . . .

**Yomi**   What is the point, then? You like theories, don't you? Theories aren't life.

**Aisha**   Yomi, what are you saying?

**Yomi**   I'm saying that Beth can't change what she is with theories.

*National Front – link to BL*

**Beth**   Look, when I walk down the street and some NF thug wants to beat me up – what does he see, white or black? Is that a theory too?

**Yomi**   He won't want to beat you up as much as he'd want to beat me up.

*Who is more racially abused*
*Stems from colourism*

**Beth**   Nonsense.

**Aisha**   This is getting too ridiculous for words. Competing to see who the NF wants to beat up the most! Honestly.

**Yomi**   You know, I still think there's some truth in that saying: if you're white, you're all right, if you're brown stick around, but if . . .

*Nasty Rhyme – privilege with whiter skin*

**Beth** (*interrupting her*)   Why are you so suspicious of light-skinned women, Yomi?

*Internalised racism*

**Yomi**   What? I'm not suspicious. Actually, if anything, I feel sorry for them. I don't envy the dilemma. I've always felt sorry for children of mixed marriages.

*host grasp by her point*
*Prevailing insecurities*
*DOLL = object*

**Beth**   Thanks. I don't feel sorry for myself. I know where I belong.

**Yomi**   Good for you. Where is that?

**Aisha**   Yomi! You're just focusing on colour. Beth's talking about using the word black as a political statement.

**Yomi**   Exactly – a theory.

**Aisha**   You don't understand.

**Yomi**   Don't tell me I don't understand.

**Aisha**   You should never put anybody in the position of having to justify why they call themselves black. It pisses me off when Afro-Caribbean women tell me I have no right . . .

**Yomi**   I wasn't talking about that. Look, all I was trying to say (*To* **Beth**.) is that you needn't be ashamed of being half-caste. I mean, it's not as if you are illegitimate, is it?

**Opal**   Meaning, I have got something to be ashamed of.

**Yomi**   Oops. Sorry. No. No, I don't think that at all. It's just that some people do. They're daft though. What was I saying, oh yes, Beth, don't try and cover up the fact that your blood is mixed, it's nothing to be . . .

**Aisha**   You still haven't got it, Yomi.

**Beth**   I am not denying my mother. I choose to call myself black. All this pure blood stuff is really dangerous.

**Yomi**   Really! Is this another theory? I came to eat food, not ideas.

**Aisha**   Can we talk about something else?

**Beth**   No.

**Opal**   Let's forget it. God, I didn't realise what I was starting. Let me see, what else happened in my day . . .

**Beth**   Very funny.

**Opal**   Well, Beth. I just think people ought to be able to say what they think without being afraid of someone jumping down your throat.

**Yomi**   Look I'm sorry if I've caused offence, it really wasn't intentional.

**Opal**   That's okay. This food is delicious, Aisha. You've done a great job.

*They concentrate on the food.*

**Beth**    You were talking in your sleep last night, Opal.

**Yomi** is *shocked,* **Aisha** *is embarrassed.* **Opal** is *terrified.*

**Opal**    Was I?

**Aisha** (*quickly*)    I've always wondered if I ever talk in my sleep. Nobody's ever told me, I suppose that's because . . .

**Beth** (*interrupting her*)    It was funny. I kept wondering what you were dreaming. You just repeated, 'I'll do it, that's all right.'

**Yomi** *gets up.*

**Yomi**    Excuse me. I have to go to the bathroom.

**Yomi** *walks off and stands watching them.*

**Aisha**    What are you up to, Beth?

**Beth**    What do you mean?

**Aisha**    Oh come on. Look, I will not have my house used like this as some sort of fighting ring.

**Beth**    Tell that to your friend.

**Aisha**    This is wonderful this is.

**Opal**    I think that was below the belt, Beth.

**Beth**    I have this strange feeling that I'm being ganged up upon. Must be another one of my theories.

**Aisha**    Beth!

**Yomi** *walks back to them.*

**Yomi**    Beth, I was thinking, you make things difficult for yourself, love. Life would be a lot easier if you didn't . . .

**Beth**    Tell me more!

**Yomi**    Well if you didn't go at everything with a hammer and chisel.

**Beth**    You're getting mixed up. Aisha's the carpenter.

**Yomi**    Every time I've met you, you've gone on the offensive about one thing or the other. Last time it was men. In fact you often go on about men. Why pay them all that attention, if you think they're so . . .

**Beth**    Rubbish! I hardly ever talk about men. I'm not interested . . .

**Yomi**    Well, that in itself . . .

**Opal**    I think what Beth means . . .

**Beth**    I can talk for myself thank you, Opal.

**Aisha**    This is great, isn't it? I must have been mad to think we could all get on together. I invite you . . .

**Beth**    Wait a minute, Aisha. Yomi has just implied that . . .

**Opal**    Forget it, Beth. Why are you getting so upset?

**Beth**    Well if you don't know that . . .

**Yomi**    I didn't imply anything. I only said that you are always on the offensive.

**Beth**    Have you ever thought about who puts me there? I just don't like pretence, that's all.

**Opal**    Look, Beth, we have all come round to Aisha's place. She has cooked us a lovely meal. We only wanted to have a good time.

**Beth**    Good time!

**Yomi**    There is no need to be contemptuous about having a good time. There are enough bad times without cooking them up deliberately.

**Beth**    You must be the No. 1 chef then. It's not me that's made all this happen. You've been trying to wind me up all evening. I don't know what your problem is.

**Yomi**   Go on. Invent a theory. Honestly! You don't know how to relax, do you? It's a pity.

**Beth**   Look, if you want to come out with those things – go ahead, but don't expect me not to react to them. I can't live like that. (*To* **Opal**.) You see, this is what I mean; it's not easy being . . .

**Aisha** (*interrupting her*)   None of us have it easy, Beth. We all know that.

**Beth** (*close to tears*)   I'm sorry, Aisha. I have to go. I can't take any more of this. I am not made of metal.

**Yomi**   Nobody said you were. Oh dear. Well, I'll be off too, Aisha. The food was wonderful, but . . .

**Aisha**   Great. Off you all go. Leave me the dishes and this horrible air. Oh I really wish I hadn't bothered.

**Opal** (*goes over to* **Aisha** *and hugs her*)   Oh Aisha, it's not your fault. We have to have arguments sometimes. Maybe they're even good for us.

**Aisha**   Oh yeah? Well you can count me out of the next one. I'd rather do something positively bad for me.

*The lights go down and up again. They all change mood suddenly.*

**Aisha**   Well that bit is over. It was too near the bone.

**Beth** *goes to the* MUSICIANS *and gets percussion instruments from them. She hands one to each woman. The music starts. They all sing.*

**All**
> Yesterday was so strange a day
> we each had to go our separate way
> we believed the mirror held only one face
> and it seemed like the world was empty of others.
> Finding each other we have to find a place to say
> those words we need to utter out loud
> those words we need to hear

because there is nothing like fear.
Alone in it all – the black solo
searching for it in the rain
we were looking for
that meeting place
and we needed it bad
show us we are not the only ones
show us we are not the only ones.

Yesterday was so strange a day
it was not so easy as we thought it would be
we have to find that meeting place
or separate or separate again
and it will seem like the world is empty of others
and it will seem like the world is empty of others.

## Act Two

*The stage is the same as before. The two chairs and the stools make a bed in the middle. The lights are dim. There is a vague threatening music playing in the background.* **Opal** *stands at one end of the stage peering into her imaginary mirror (the audience).* **Beth** *lies on the bed.* **Aisha** *and* **Yomi** *stand watching everything, next to the* MUSICIANS. **Opal** *is wearing a long white T-shirt over her all-in-one-suit.*

**Opal**    It's you again. I might have known you wouldn't be gone for long. So what do you want me to do, welcome you back? I had a good break without you. Didn't miss seeing your ugly features one bit. Nor those funny eyes. The opals. Some precious stone you are. I could die and no one would notice. Beth would, I suppose. I'm not sure.

**Beth** (*looking through an imaginary photo album*)    Here they all are; all different bits of past. All the various Beths. Here I am at six. A little black girl amongst the little white girls wearing bobbles in my hair, as if that would make me the same. I could never grow a ponytail. Opal reminds me. She reminds me of so much.

**Opal**    I'll admit it. I was stupid to think I'm all right just 'cos some crazy black queer tells me so. Is that it? Why do I do this to myself? Maybe I am crazy after all. Maybe they should have just moved me from one institution to another. That's what you think, isn't it? It's strange, even although Beth is next door, I feel as if I have this house all to myself. Me and my ghosts. *You will always be alone.*

**Beth**    Someday I'd like to be able to be all of myself to all of those close to me. To have my mother love my lover. Sometimes I feel such a sham. When I was eighteen I rushed out and bought the black records that had never sat on my shelves, the blues, funk, jazz and soul I'd been missing. I bought books too. It was a whole new world. James Baldwin. Toni Morrison. C.L.R. James. I was

excited. I dumped Dostoevsky, Dire Straits and Simon
and Garfunkel. I pretended I'd never sang Joni Mitchell's
'Blue-oo-oo-oo-oo-oo-oo' to myself in the mirror.

**Opal**    What would they say if they all knew? Opal, sweet
friendly Opal is a pervert! What does a pervert look like? Do
you know, can you tell at a glance walking down the street?
When I first met Beth I was swimming in purple oceans,
dancing on dangerous waters. I could let time go. I could let
you go. Now you've come back, my boomerang reflection.
You will always return, won't you. *Of course. Depend upon it.*

Yes. Smiling Opal is a mess. That's what you want to hear,
isn't it? Beth is wrong. You were right all along. I was a fool
to think any different. *Dry your nose will you? It's running. Your
eyes look pathetic.* I don't want to know. Fuck you. I don't want
to know.

*The lights go down and up. They are flickering and flashing.* **Aisha**
*and* **Yomi** *take cymbals from the* MUSICIANS *and play them to*
**Opal**'s *song.* **Beth** *is sleeping. The music starts. It is soft and scary.*

**Opal** (*sings*)
    And I am waiting for
    discovery to come
    one night that will have no tomorrow
    one day that will come with no dawn
    and fear hangs up doubts
    a knowledge that sometime
    would come this dusk –
    soft and silent soft and silent

*The lights go down.* **Opal** *is rushing around the stage. She combs
her hair and puts on a turquoise beret.* **Yomi** *gives her cymbal back
to the* MUSICIANS. *She approaches* **Opal**.

**Opal**    Yomi!

**Yomi**    Can't stop now. Got to rush.

**Beth** *gets out of the bed slowly.* **Aisha** *walks towards* **Beth** *clanging
the cymbal in a humorous manner.* **Yomi** *walks to the other end of*

*the stage.* **Aisha** *passes* **Beth** *touching her lightly and then walks to the front of the stage. They form a triangle.* **Opal** *is caught inside it.*

**Yomi**    Hiya Opal.

*She waves.* **Opal** *rushes to* **Yomi**.

Come here, darling.

**Opal** *stands in front of* **Yomi** *who looks right through her.*

**Aisha** (*laughing*)    Fool.

**Opal**    Why are you laughing at me? Stop mocking me.

**Yomi** (*to* **Beth**)    Tut. She has such a large ego, doesn't she? Thinks we can't laugh unless it's about her.

**Aisha**    Well, it's self-indulgence, isn't it?

**Opal**    What are you all talking about?

**Beth**    Oh come on, Opal, you know. No good pretending now.

**Opal**    *Beth!* Beth! Don't do this to me.

**Yomi**    Shit. She needs attention. Her adam's apple's jumping.

**Aisha**    Lost her rag.

*The lights flash more, the music intensifies.* **Beth** *runs to the bed and lies down on it.*

**Beth**    Nurse! Nurse! Nurse!

**Opal** (*switches moods*)    Yes. Yes Beth. I'll be with you in a minute.

**Beth**    Nurse!

**Opal**    Coming. (*Going up to her.*) Okay. What's the problem? I get the feeling you like to keep me on my feet, Beth.

**Beth** (*whispers*)    I know what you do on your back.

**Opal** (*shocked*)    Pardon?

**Beth**     I said I've got a sore back.

**Opal** (*relieved*)     Oh.

**Beth** (*mocking*)     Oh you say Oh-*oh-oh-oh*.

**Opal** (*takes her temperature*)     You're very hot.

**Beth** (*whispers*)     Not as hot as you.

**Opal**     Pardon?

**Beth**     Get your hands off me.

**Opal**     What did you say?

**Beth**     My hands hurt me.

**Opal** *takes her pulse.* **Beth** *shoves* **Opal**'s *hands up her nightdress.*

**Beth**     Why don't you feel here? That's what you want.

**Opal** *pulls her hands out, shocked.*

**Opal**     I'm going to get . . .

**Beth** (*shouts*)     Help, *help, help.*

**Yomi** *rushes up.*

**Yomi**     Did she touch you?

**Beth** (*smiling*)     Yes.

**Yomi**     Oh dear. Doctor.

**Opal**     Wait a minute. It's *her.* She's practically delirious. Feel her temperature.

**Yomi**     Now, now. We've had quite enough feeling for the one evening, Nurse Black.

**Aisha** *goes up to* **Opal**, *clanging her cymbal. She leads* **Opal** *to the back of the stage, gently.*

**Aisha** (*whispers*)     It's all over now. It's better this way.

**Opal** (*screams*)     *I'm a good nurse.*

**Aisha** *and* **Yomi** *force* **Opal** *to stand on the chest.* **Beth** *gets out of the bed. The music deepens.* **Opal** *stands in a crucifixion position.* **Aisha**, **Yomi** *and* **Beth** *fire these questions like bullets.*

**Yomi**    Have you ever wanted to be a man?

**Opal**    No.

**Yomi**    Were you ever raped?

*Psychoanalysis*

**Opal**    No.

**Beth**    Is it because you are too ugly to get a man?

**Opal** (*turns around and stares at* **Beth**)    *Beth Beth Beth.*

*Lights down. Music stops abruptly.* **Beth** *and* **Opal** *lie on the chairs together.* **Aisha** *and* **Yomi** *sit down on the chest and watch them.* **Beth** *shakes* **Opal**. *Lights up.*

**Beth**    You have to face it, Opal.

**Opal**    Face my face, face my face.

**Beth**    Whatever it is you're afraid of. Stop running.

**Opal**    My face is up like a big balloon. My eyes are swimming pools. My nose is an ape's nose. My lips are rubber. My face is dark and smooth. My cheeks are high and mellow. My eyes are deep and knowing. My nose sniffs new scents. My lips are soft and gentle. Which is me?

**Beth**    Both.

**Opal**    I'm afraid I'll lose face.

**Beth**    With who?

**Opal**    You, Yomi, lose face with myself. I have a string of boyfriends. I liked the feeling of a penis inside me!

**Beth**    So?

**Opal**    So does that mean I'm not a real lesbian?

**Beth**    No of course it doesn't mean that.

**Opal**    I can't take myself seriously. I've gone through my life taking on new things. Now all of a sudden I'm a black lesbian? What is that? It's a joke.

**Beth** (*furious*)    It is not a joke.

**Opal**    You make me sick. You go about all self-righteous, pretending you know the answers. I've seen into your dreams. They are not clean.

**Beth**    What rubbish are you talking? I think you need some sleep.

**Opal**    You mean you need some sleep. I'm getting too much for you now. Why don't you just get rid of me then?

**Beth**    Oh Opal! Please.

**Beth** (*mimicking*)    Opal! Please.

**Beth**    Stop it.

**Opal**    Why?

**Beth**    You know why. You're just being destructive. I don't want to get into it.

**Opal**    Oh nice choice. That's your choice. I wish I had the fucking choice.

**Beth**    You do.

**Opal**    See! There you go again. Self-righteous. You think you know everything about me. Well you don't know fuck all.

**Beth**    Believe that if it makes it easier.

**Opal**    Don't patronise me.

**Beth**    I can't say anything right can I? (*Softly.*) Tell me, Opal, what did I do to you in your dream?

**Opal** (*shocked*)    So you do know me.

**Beth**    A little.

*Lights down.* **Beth** *and* **Opal** *hug each other. Lights up.* **Opal** *goes to* **Yomi**. **Aisha** *goes to* **Beth**. **Yomi** *and* **Opal** *are painting.* **Aisha** *is making a cabinet.* **Beth** *watches* **Aisha**.

**Yomi**   I just keep noticing more and more bumps. I suppose I'm a perfectionist. Nobody will notice but me.

**Opal** *is very nervous. She can't relax. She is building up to talking.*

**Yomi**   Fabayo wanted to help us today, but she's with her father. Just as well. (*Laughs.*) She'd have made a proper mess. Well, children need to see their father, don't they? I mean; it's not natural and I don't want to be the one . . .

**Opal**   Yomi, do you think it's unnatural to be . . .

**Yomi** *looks at her strangely, waiting.*

**Opal**   Well, to have no father whatsoever?

**Yomi**   Oh dear. Have I put my foot in it again?

**Opal**   No. No. Don't be silly. I just meant . . .

**Yomi**   Thank goodness for that. At least you're not as touchy as your friend.

**Opal** (*ignoring that*)   No I just meant if you were to choose to bring up a child on your own . . .

**Yomi**   Well if you're thinking about having kids, I tend to think, go ahead, why not, as long as it's loved . . .

**Opal**   No I'm not. Beth wants kids though.

**Yomi**   Really? Has she got a boyfriend, then? Oh, I suppose it's none of my business.

**Opal**   No she hasn't. Actually that's what I was wanting to talk to you about.

**Yomi** *is very wary. She doesn't want to hear what* **Opal** *has to say. Whilst* **Beth** *and* **Aisha** *talk,* **Opal** *and* **Yomi** *continue to paint, furious and concentrated.*

**Aisha**    Look, Beth, it's no good. We have to talk about it.
I'm sorry, right, if you felt let down, but Yomi matters to me
and I know some of her ideas are crap but she's been a good
mate to me . . .

**Beth**    Aisha, you don't have to justify it all. I understand. I
just wished you'd told me she was so homophobic.

**Aisha**    Homophobic. Listen to yourself. Yomi probably
thinks that means queer. Anyhow she doesn't even know,
so . . .

**Beth**    Oh she knows all right.

**Aisha**    I'm just pissed off with the lot of you. That's all.

**Beth**    Why?

**Aisha**    You don't know a lot, do you?

**Beth**    I don't want to assume.

**Aisha**    Opal's welcome to you.

**Beth** (*shocked*)    What do you mean?

**Aisha**    Ah forget it.

**Aisha** *concentrates on the cabinet. She is furious.* **Beth** *is upset and
doesn't understand what's going on.*

**Opal**    I've been telling myself I want to tell you and then
thinking I should forget it.

**Yomi** (*ignoring her*)    So. How would Beth get this baby?

**Opal**    A donor probably.

**Yomi**    You're not serious! Ugh. Syringes and sperm, who
could ask more from life?

**Opal**    Well how else?

**Yomi**    Oh dear, did nobody tell you?

**Opal**    You are so sarcastic sometimes.

**Yomi**    Do you think so? Really? I don't mean to be.

**Opal**    Do you know then? After all. Beth was right.

**Yomi**    Know what?

**Opal**    About me and Beth.

**Yomi**    Oh that!

**Opal** (*starts to smile*)    And it's all right with you? It doesn't bother you?

**Yomi**    Have you ever thought of getting married?

**Opal**    What?

**Yomi**    Marriage. You know, ding-dong, paper . . . confetti.

**Opal** (*giggling*)    To tell you it straight. When I was a kid I used to have these fantasies of me and my lovely middle-class white husband and our children. I even had names for my children – Pauline, Graham and Amanda. I could even picture the little concrete garage for our car. Pathetic, isn't it?

**Yomi**    No.

**Opal**    It's a myth. A big candy-floss lie.

**Yomi**    Speak for yourself. There are some that are happily married.

**Opal**    So. It really doesn't bother you?

**Yomi**    Do you want it to? No. I just think it's a waste, that's all. But you must know that. I can't imagine what on earth you can . . . but it takes all types. I suppose I should have guessed sooner about Beth. But you. If it hadn't been for all that the other night, I would have never guessed about you. Not in a month of Sundays. I didn't want to believe it. Not about you.

**Yomi** *is sad and then she brightens.*

Anyway, maybe it's just . . .

**Opal**  A phase?

**Yomi** *is surprised.*

**Yomi**  Well, you don't know, do you, what might happen. Never say never, that's my motto.

**Opal** (*angry*)  So you'd never say never to having a relationship with a woman?

**Yomi** (*shocked*)  That's different.

**Opal**  Why?

**Yomi**  It just is.

**Opal**  And you said you weren't bothered.

**Yomi**  I'm not. It doesn't stop me thinking it unnatural, I mean . . .

**Opal**  I've heard enough.

**Yomi**  How do you expect me to react?

**Opal**  I don't know. I hoped that knowing me . . . I'm not suddenly a different person, you know, Yomi.

**Yomi**  Yes you are to me. I'm sorry, but that's how it is. It's not my fault.

**Opal**  I wish you could hear yourself. I really do.

**Yomi**  Look. Don't look at me like that! As if I'm the one that's saying something terrible to you. You're the lesbian.

**Opal**  I've heard enough. I really wanted to be friends but I just can't . . .

**Yomi**  Neither could I. Too many things to think about. What about Fabayo?

**Opal**  What do you mean what about Fabayo?

**Yomi**  Well.

**Opal** (*angry and hurt*)   Yomi! You don't mean what you're saying.

**Yomi**   Oh, so you read minds too?

**Opal**   This is the waste.

**Opal** *and* **Yomi** *continue to paint.*

**Beth**   Aisha, we can't throw it all away.

**Aisha**   There's not a lot to throw, is there?

**Beth**   Don't be like that.

**Aisha**   You've got a nerve, Beth.

**Beth** (*angry*)   You've got none, Aisha. I'm not crawling any more. Give me . . .

**Aisha**   Yeah, yeah, when I'm ready and all that sensitive shit. Why don't you shout or something? Feminists don't shout?

**Beth** (*exasperated*)   Aisha. I don't understand. What did I do?

**Aisha**   Open your eyes then!

**Beth**   If it's . . . (**Aisha** *has turned her back to her.*) Oh . . . never mind.

*Lights down. All four women freeze.* **Opal** *sits down on the chest and watches* **Aisha** *and* **Yomi**. **Beth** *sits and watches them from the other side of the stage.*

(*To* **Aisha**.) That's one of the worst bits.

**Aisha**   Are you kidding? Mine's to come.

**Aisha** *walks towards* **Yomi**, *who is still painting.* **Yomi** *turns around, furious.*

**Yomi**   You knew all along, didn't you?

**Aisha**   Knew what?

**Yomi**    Don't play games, Aisha. I'm not in the mood.

**Aisha**    Neither am I. If you've got something to say, say it.

**Yomi**    You knew about those two.

**Aisha** *stares at* **Yomi**.

**Yomi**    Oh come on, Aisha. They're a couple of lezzies, aren't they?

**Aisha**    That's not a word I'd use.

**Yomi**    I've made a complete fool of myself!

**Aisha**    How come?

**Yomi**    You could have told me.

**Aisha**    I thought you'd find out in your own time. It wasn't for me to tell. Anyhow, what difference does it make?

**Yomi**    If it doesn't make any difference, why did you hide it?

**Aisha**    I didn't hide anything. You are the one who was hiding.

**Yomi** *stares at* **Aisha**.

**Aisha**    You picked it up, but you didn't want to believe it 'cos you liked Opal and so you just pretended to yourself that you hadn't seen what you saw.

**Yomi**    Nonsense, though I might have guessed about Beth. (*Pause.*) Anyhow they can't even keep lasting relationships with each other. I don't imagine Beth and Opal will be together long.

**Beth** *and* **Opal** *pull faces at each other across the stage.*

**Aisha**    You and your husband lasted ages of course.

**Yomi**    At least we were in a natural relationship.

**Aisha**    Oh yeah?

**Yomi**    Yeah. If we were all meant to be like that, no one would exist, would they? . . .

**Aisha** (*interrupting her*)    If you want to worry about generations, why don't you worry about the neutron bomb?

*[handwritten: more to worry then of someones potential happiness]*

**Yomi**    She really wanted to shock me too. Well I wasn't giving her that. I wasn't handing it to her on a plate.

**Aisha**    Who are you talking about?

**Yomi**    I liked her too.

**Aisha**    Past tense? Yomi! I would have thought you could have done better than this.

**Yomi**    Why are you defending them so ardently? Don't tell me . . .

**Aisha**    What if I am?

*[handwritten: monosyllabic - can hear her answers]*
*[handwritten: PASSIVITY]*

**Yomi**    Don't, Aisha. I can't take jokes at the moment.

**Aisha**    Suit yourself.

*[handwritten: Dehumanises - Others]*

**Yomi** (*bewildered*)    You're not, are you? I would definitely know if you were one. (*Pause.*) Well. If you think you're a lesbian, I'm really sorry.

**Aisha**    What are you sorry about?

*[handwritten: Power in requiring pity - NORMALITY accepting but uncomfortable]*

**Yomi**    Aisha, stop messing around.

*[handwritten: closed book]*

*The lights go down.* **Beth** *and* **Opal** *start to dance slowly matching each other's movements like an echo. They are still at opposite ends of the stage.* **Aisha** *and* **Yomi** *look at each other during their poems as if they are still continuing their conversation.*

**Aisha**

It is just the wondering
the small frail maybe
the pushing away
before it can settle –
I am like they are
terrified of plunging

into that unknown country
the landscapes with no familiar trees or flowers
the vastness of the moors
the never endingness of the earth rolling
fear can stop a dream beginning
and wondering is wandering in the dark
stranger's voice echoing
yearning for that other woman
to hold me close –
could I sink into her depth?

**Beth** and **Opal**'s *dance becomes more brittle. They jar with their
bodies. The light goes blue.*

**Yomi**

I just pictured it blue
not the blue of the sea
but the blue of the blues
and bruises, how could anyone
be happy that way
touching the very core of
anti creation; how could
someone love unnatural
like the last rays of sunshine
how could she feel hot for she
and want the heat on her back
like the pounding midday sun
opening the pores for the sweat to run

*The lights soften.* **Aisha** *takes a step forward.*

**Aisha**

It is the terror of beginnings
where the end cannot be envisaged
malicious words sitting on the edge
of my tongue, where *I want* is smothered,
the terror of endings.
And the family, the family
what would they say
and knowing anyway that I could say nothing

*Handwritten annotations:*
- vague + ambiguous language – sense of confusion
- sexuality
- Physical location of culture
- moves foreward to new country
- romance / love — morphes into each other
- Symbolism – found connection
- trans / sadness
- AESTHETIC of dance
- "brittle" – broken by societal views
- creatio ex nihilo – manipulate religion
- Reproduction – man + woman purpose
- To be homosexual will be alienated further
- Yomi feels dehumanised enough by being a black woman
- scared of uncertainty
- worried of others opinion
- lack of support – ?
- Italicised – emphasises society not permitting the desires/happiness of others
- Q's her options – TRAPPED "in the closet"
- Colonised by Society
- Suppression – no voice

the emptiness of the unspoken years
how long could I live a lie?                    (bottom of 109)
how long would the air stifle me in that closet?
Yet the smell of an unwanted husband's breath
in the morning would make me        untamed lust
long for those uncertain moors.   Free, sexual liberation

*The lights glare.* **Beth** *and* **Opal** *dance facing outward, not looking at each other. Their movements are hard.*

**Yomi**

And I pictured it ugly
like the ugliness of something
you don't want to look at
imagining one might accost me
in the Ladies' restroom
as soon as I heard lesbian
I saw ugly and blue
and lonely and not being able to get
THE REAL THING
and a tall angular looking woman
white with men's things on,
too much hair around the mouth
and always on the prowl
she was so lonely
would die lonely
never knowing any kind of love
because lesbian and love
could not come together
like man and woman.

*The lights soften.* **Beth** *turns around and starts to dance towards* **Opal** *who dances on the spot, with confident steps.*

**Aisha**

And my landscape
is coloured in browns and reds:
she walks firm steps over it
I envy her
the way she's making history

whilst she walks, the implications of the
foot steps left behind
I follow them, sink into shapes
a wood pigeon calls at dawn
lights uncertainty creates morning shadows
I watch her go
that sturdy black woman walking
can just see her dark hair swing
I want to go with her.
I want to go with her.

*The lights stay soft.* **Opal** *and* **Beth** *start to dance closely together,
happy. They whirl and twirl each other around.* **Yomi** *watches them.
At the end of her poem, they freeze into an album photograph.*

**Yomi**
I pictured ugly and lonely
that was my only bit of sympathy
and I couldn't see anyone
or smiles and softness and need
like Beth and Opal
looking good together
dark eyes lit by the fire in her
dark eyes sparkling at the woman in her
dark eyes dancing
out the need of time
I looked at Beth and Opal
and I looked at my old pictures
I had to get out those albums
and go over the years.

*The lights go down and up again.* **Opal** *approaches* **Yomi** *and
takes her hand.* **Beth** *smiles at* **Aisha.**

**Opal**    We are still going over the years.

**Aisha**    We are running out of time.

**Beth** (*to* **Yomi**)    Are you going to?

*[handwritten annotations in margins:]*
*Impact of mothers on characters (B, L + C)*
*Religious upbringing → dif. of mother saying to explore sexuality or not — homophobic mothers*
*Mothers Job - act of care (peace/protection) — fairytale*

**112 Chiaroscuro**

*avoiding reality*

**Yomi**

*causes divide* — I don't want to run anymore. *FEAR - scared for her friend*
I was remembering something my mother told me. She said there were *Links to homosexuality* these women she used to know in *to Nigeria - not apart of* Nigeria who lived with their husbands *society related to past* but loved each other. She said, God it surprised me so much, that it was a *internalised sympathy* pity they had to hide, a pity they *Related to Beth/Aisha* couldn't just live together out in the open, if that's what they wanted. *the relation to her mother* *brushing comment* *- diff perspective*

**Aisha** (*looks at her watch*)  This is the one I remember the best. The first time I heard Opal sing it, it made me cry.

**Opal**  Don't cry this time, Aisha. Sing!

**Beth** *goes to the* MUSICIANS *and gets percussion instruments. She distributes them.*

**Aisha** (*to* **Opal**)  Are you ready?

**Opal**  Are you?

**Aisha**  Yeah. All right.

**Aisha** *starts to play her instrument. They all start to dance. The others harmonise as* **Opal** *sings.* *not attached to name superficial - adop...*

**Opal** (*sings*) *Identity - IRONIC*
They had no one to name me after *game of oppression*
in so many different ways *through names*
so tell me what do you call her
a woman who loves another like her *Searching for label*
what do you call her
*no role model - not in public sphere* where are her people *History manipulated by*
who are her ancestors *white heterosexual men*
tell me what is her name *King calls for adjustment*
tell me what is her name
*King believes only black homosexual in world*
I want to find it all now
know our names know the others in history

so many women have been lost at sea
so many of our stories have been swept away
I want to find the woman
who in Dahomey 1900
loved another woman
tell me what did they call her
did they know her name
in Ashanti, do they know it in
Yoruba do they know it in patois
do they know it in Punjabi
do they know it in Arabic
do they know it in Hindi
do they know it in Cantonese
do they know it in English

do you think my mother is still living
and would she like to have a daughter
who is a lesbian, would she call my name
tell me would she know my name?

*The lights go down. They hand back their instruments.* **Aisha** *hugs* **Opal**.

**Aisha**   You are brave. Do you think you'll try and trace her?

**Opal**   I might. Some day. I'm not in a hurry anymore.

**Yomi** (*to* **Beth**)   I'm sorry.

**Beth**   Don't say sorry.

**Yomi**   But I am.

**Beth**   Sorries are never going to get us anywhere.

**Aisha**   Oh come on. They're a start.

**Beth**   They're a stop.

**Opal** (*laughing*)   We can't even agree on sorry. (*To* **Beth**.)
You have to change too. Change isn't compromise.

**Beth**   Oh no?

*Handwritten annotations:*
*Female solidarity*
*Taught to perceive through male gaze.*

**Opal** (*firmly*)   No.

**Beth**   What is it then?

**Opal** *goes to the chest. She takes the mirror out.*

**Opal**   It is all this.   *Yomi: gains CONTROL*

*She gives* **Yomi** *the mirror.*

*Personified*

Yesterday I looked in her and she said to me: it's not me
that's changed – it's you. I liked myself!   *Vanity*

*Product of society = identities perception*

**Yomi** (*defensively*)   It doesn't happen overnight, you know.
A lifetime under these eyes. Seeing the way I saw. You want
to get me some new eyes? I banished so much from my sight.
Sometimes that's bliss.   *Ignorance is bliss*

*Reality = hindrance*

*She looks critically at herself in the mirror.*   *Judgement*

(*To* **Beth**.) It's true, isn't it? I mean sometimes you don't want
to look at yourself.   *Fear + anxiety of reflection*

**Beth**   Or out. You know I used to pride myself in being
so active politically. Maybe it was a secret alternative way of
getting to Heaven. But so much of me was still hiding. At
least some of my desires. And I locked the past that gave me
no kudos away.

**Beth** *goes to the chest and takes out the album. She gives it to*
**Aisha**, *who is surprised.*

**Aisha**   It's not the same.

**Beth**   I know. I'm not pretending it is.

**Aisha** (*angrily*)   Pretence was always a murderer.

**Beth**   All I'm saying is, don't chop yourself into little bits. Be
it all.

**Aisha**   How can I? It's luxury.

**Beth**   No, it's necessity. I know now, Aisha. I'm sorry I
couldn't see for looking.

**Aisha** *is embarrassed.* **Yomi** *goes to the chest and takes the doll. She gives it to* **Beth**, *who is shocked.* _Accepts Beth's future_

It's all come round.

**Yomi**    You've not come round.

**Beth**    Now it's a game.

**Yomi**    Oh no. It was never a game. It was serious. See this baby you want to have?

**Beth** (*defensively*)    Yeah?

**Yomi**    Give this to her. Give her a name if you like. I could never give her to Fabayo.

**Beth** (*takes the doll appreciatively and laughs*)    I've made up so much. This is all make-believe. Now I want it to be real. Stop acting, will you?

**Opal**    We can't. We are real. Feel.

**Aisha**    Here we go again. Do you think by the next time we'll have stepped forward?

**Yomi**    Certainly.

**Aisha** *goes to the chest and takes the cushion out. She gives it to* **Opal**.

**Aisha**    We're moving on. You can make your own tales of generations after generations. Invent yourself.

**Opal**    That's what we're all doing, isn't it?

**Aisha**    I'm working at it. It's lonely sometimes.

**Beth** *takes* **Aisha**'s *hand.*

**Yomi**    That's funny. I remember you standing exactly there and saying those lines, and Beth . . . _Feel like experiencing something again_

**Opal** (*laughing*)    Yeah, yeah, yeah. Déjà vu vu vu. Okay, Aisha, it's down to you. _Fate - hope but feel they will experience again_

**Beth**    Wait a minute. You forgot the song.

_Yomi's change of character on sexuality UNREALISTIC - Kay wants to show evolved outlook_

**Opal**   Oh yeah.

*She motions to the* MUSICIANS. *They start playing.*

**All** (*sing*)
>   If we should die in the wilderness
>   let the child that finds us   *Impressionable + Innocent*
>   *(new gen)*
>   know our name and story
>   know our name and story
>   let us never forget to remember
>   all our heres and theres   *Poetic - elements*
>   let a hot sun shine on our wishes
>   let the rain fall without our tears
>
>   and we will look for our landscapes   *Geographical image*
>   listening to the river running
>   knowing we are different from each other
>   but we still have something to share
>   scraping at the skies together
>   scraping at the skies together.
>
>   If we should die in the wilderness
>   let the child that finds us
>   know our names and stories
>   know our names and stories
>   we cannot afford to fall apart
>   we can create out of chaos
>   rubble and dust can build a dream for us.
>
>   If we should die in the wilderness
>   let us go down singing our forbidden songs
>   for life
>   let us go down remembering
>   old Yomi could not talk but she could tell stories
>   old Yomi could not talk but she could tell stories.

*They all start to dance. The music changes to the same tune as in the beginning.*

*[handwritten top margin: Light + Dark - enlightenment / have to see play repetitively for this to form]*

## All

Time changes light
light changes time *[handwritten: chiaroscuro - only will 'become in repetition]*
there we were with the dawn in the dark
the dark in the dawn
trying to find the words
trying to find the words. *[handwritten: ↗ Form + Structure]*

*These lines overlap.* *[handwritten: Cyclical narrative]*

*[handwritten: Development / change in characters but not society (audience)]*

**Aisha**   This is how we got to where we are. My name is
Aisha, remember, I was called after my grandmother on my
mother's side. *[handwritten: Breaks down 4th wall]*

**Beth**   My name is Beth. I was called after my great-great-
great-great-grandmother on my father's side.

**Opal**   My name is Opal. I was called after some old
woman's earrings. *[handwritten: Key - dramatic effect / negative - audience haven't learnt anything]*

**Yomi**   My name is Yomi. I was called after old Yomi.
Remember her? *[handwritten: Have to perform play repetitively / Nothing changed.]*

*Lights down. They exit, leaving the doll, the album, the cushion and* *[handwritten left margin: on to Beth]*
*the mirror in the same position as they were in the beginning. They*
*re-enter.* **Beth** *watches the audience.* **Aisha** *opens the chest.* **Opal** *[handwritten: Clarity in characters (acceptance)]*
*and* **Yomi** *stand and chat to each other about the performance.*
*Lights out.*

*[handwritten:
who are the audience?
Usually open minded but not the people who need to watch
Reputation around theatre - 'not for everyone'
↓
educated / prestige]*

*[handwritten:
BL's Ending:
"Do whatever you like"
- oppression in diss way to Eastern culture
- sari + ice skating (liberal + free)]*

# Winsome Pinnock

# Talking in Tongues

**Winsome Pinnock** was born in London. Her award-winning plays include *The Wind of Change* (Half Moon Theatre, 1987), *Leave Taking* (Liverpool Playhouse Studio and National Theatre, 1988), *Picture Palace* (Women's Theatre Group, 1988), *A Hero's Welcome* (Women's Playhouse Trust at the Royal Court Theatre Upstairs, 1989), *A Rock in Water* (Royal Court Young People's Theatre at the Theatre Upstairs, 1989), *Talking in Tongues* (Royal Court Theatre Upstairs, 1991), *Mules* (Clean Break Theatre Company, 1996) and *One Under* (Tricycle Theatre, 2005). She has also written for radio and television. She is Senior Lecturer in Creative Writing at London Metropolitan University and is currently writing a new play for Clean Break Theatre Company.

*Talking in Tongues* was first presented at the Royal Court, Theatre Upstairs, London, on 28 August 1991. The cast was as follows:

| | |
|---|---|
| **Sugar** | Cecilia Noble |
| **Leela** | Joanne Campbell |
| **Claudette** | Pamela Nomvete |
| **Curly** | Cecilia Noble |
| **Jeff** | Neil Dudgeon |
| **Bentley** | Nicholas Monu |
| **Fran** | Lizzie McInnerny |
| **Irma** | Ella Wilder |
| **Mikie** | Nicholas Monu |
| **Kate** | Lizzie McInnerny |
| **David** | Neil Dudgeon |
| **Diamond** | Ella Wilder |

*Director*   Hettie Macdonald
*Decor*   Ian McNeil
*Lighting*   Johanna Town
*Sound*   Bryan Bowen


**Irma** can be played by either a male or female performer.

# Prologue

*Very bright light.* **Leela** *is lying on her tummy on a towel while Sugar crouches over her. Sugar pours ointment on to her hands, rubs them together, then starts to massage* **Leela***'s back.*

**Sugar**   Them used to say them was going down a gully fe go wash clothes, but the way them women leave dragging themself like them have rock tie to them foot, then come back skipping like children make everybody suspec' them have some business a gully that have nothing to do with dirty washing. Sometimes them man would try to follow back a dem, but they would only reach so far before something bad happen: one a them get lost in a bush, grow round him while he was walking; another man get bite up by a snake and haffe quick hop home and bind up him foot, an' a nex' one suck up inna hurricane lie dizzy ina bed for a week. No man ever find them.

There were three of them: Jo-Jo, a big, mighty woman who everybody used to say batter her husband; Dum-Dum, a woman who never speak; and Mary, a good, gentle woman who would give you her last penny even if she was starving. These women were a mystery to me. Every day them like every other woman, cooking and cleaning for them husband, except this one afternoon when them bundle up them clothes and go off by themself. I couldn't wait to grow up to discover the mystery of womanness for meself. I used to sit and stare at them to see if I could see it on them, but I couldn't. So one day I follow them. I was nine years old.

I wait for them to leave, pretending like I wasn't taking any notice a them, then after a few minutes I went after them. Me have to run hard to keep up with them. It look like they was walking slowly, them hip a swing from side to side under them frock, but they was moving further and further away from me, so I run as fast as my little leg would go and still they would be ahead of me. Then they come to a gully I never see before – a huge waterfall falling over great white rock. I hide meself behind a rockstone and watch.

Them take them clothes out a the basket and start to wash them in the water, slapping them against rock, then rub them under the water and slap them against rock, lie them out to dry in the sun. Then they start again, slap clothes against rock, rinse them under running water and lie them out to dry. Slap, rinse, slap slap, rinse dry. Them never say anything to one another, never even look at one another, for musse half an hour or more.

I was so disappointed I could cry. I thought I was going to see a woman fly. I thought woman was a mystery – click her fingers and fire would fly out – but woman was just washing clothes. Woman was washing clothes then going home and cooking food for man. I had tears in my eyes. Me ready fe run till one a them start to hum. It seem like everything stop and listen to that humming, the breeze still, the water hush up. Then the other women join in, singing together like in one voice. You couldn't move when you hear them singing. Then them start to sway. Dum-Dum, the silent woman, was in the middle, she start to sway and rise up on her toes like there was something inside her, pulling her up. The other women start to sway too and rise up, and I tell you I see the spirit rise in them women. Them start to tremble and make little jump till they was jumping around like them didn't know where them was. Then all of a sudden the silent woman stand very still like her body seize up and lift her head to the sky and start to call out. She was shouting – a woman I never hear say a word in my life – was shouting to the sky loud loud and saying words very fast in a language you never hear before. A woman who couldn't even talk, filling the sky with words in a language must be not spoken in a million years, a language that go back before race. She lift her fist and strike out one more time. After, she collapse, but the other women catch her before she fall. She just lie there, like she sleeping, and the other women finish washing her clothes for her. When she wake up they give

her something to drink and they all go home like nothing
happen. I always wonder what madness them release when
they shout out like that. (*Slight pause*.) But all that finish now,
them women dead off long time. Me, I just go walk down
by the beach, lift weight, jog, take aerobic exercise. No need
now to go down to gully, eh?

## Act One

*The entire act takes place in London. Throughout the act there is the constant sound of party music.*

### Scene One

*A house in London. A room with lots of coats in it.* **Claudette,** *a young black woman, enters. She's hurt her foot. She sits down and takes her shoes and tights off, examines her foot.* **Curly** *enters.*

**Curly**   Why did you run off like that?

**Claudette**   My foot.

**Curly**   I thought there was something wrong with you.

**Claudette**   There is. He trod on my toe. He's crushed it. It's hanging off on its cord, look.

**Curly**   Calm down and let Curly have a look at it. It can't be that bad.

**Claudette**   Trust me to get caught in the stampede . . .

**Curly**   A man stands on your toe –

**Claudette**   One minute I see all their heads turn toward me, next thing I know I'm flat on my back with footmarks all over me.

**Curly**   It was an accident.

**Claudette**   It's always the same when a white woman comes in the room.

**Curly**   Don't start, Claudette.

**Claudette**   Our men are straining at the leash like hunting dogs on the scent of the fox. Ow. Careful.

**Curly**   There's only two black men here. That's hardly a
pack of hounds, is it? Anyway, Bentley's a good bloke.

**Claudette**   Why do you think they invited us here? Do you
think it's to get the party going? We're supposed to be good
for a party, aren't we?

**Curly**   Leela invited us.

**Claudette**   So why did they invite Leela?

**Curly**   Because they're friends of Bentley's.

**Claudette**   Hours we've been here and we're the only ones
dancing.

**Curly**   The fun won't start till after midnight, then you'll
think you're in a madhouse.

**Claudette**   It takes these people a long time to warm up.

**Curly**   Stop complaining. Least you got asked to dance.

**Claudette**   While he's dancing with me he's looking over
my shoulder at her. I might as well be a burst blow-up
rubber doll he's dragging around.

**Curly**   We can always dance with each other.

**Claudette**   What is it with our men?

**Curly**   I read a good book about it. I'll lend it to you.

**Claudette**   I don't give a toss about the science of it. What I
want to know is where the next fuck's coming from.

**Curly**   Sit still or this'll hurt.

**Claudette**   Careful. One man told me he thought black
women were too aggressive.

**Curly**   I'm not aggressive.

**Claudette**   Aggressive my arse. Pride. That's what it is.

**Curly**   People do sometimes fall in love, Claudette.

**Claudette**   What do they feel when they're holding her? Have you watched their faces when they're holding a white woman? They look as though they're in a seventh heaven. Makes you feel like the invisible woman. It's not as if you can escape from it. She's everywhere you go. And every blown-up picture of her diminishes us.

**Curly**   For God's sake, Claudette, sit still.

**Claudette**   It's not as if they want to be your friend. The only time one of them wants your friendship is when she's trying to get her hands on one of our men, and once she's done that they're both off without a backward glance: she never rated us in the first place and he doesn't want to be reminded of the detritus he left behind on his way to the top.

**Curly**   Stand up.

**Claudette** *stands.*

**Curly**   Does it still hurt?

**Claudette** *practises putting weight on the injured foot.*

**Curly**   Can you walk on it?

**Claudette** *walks up and down.*

**Claudette**   What I really hate is the way they have to get off the tube before you do, as though you were some maid following on behind. Or they'll sit beside you brushing their hair out like Rapunzel, thinking they're making you jealous. Many's the time I've missed my stop because I've had my mouth full of some white woman's hair.

**Curly**   We're supposed to be welcoming in the New Year, not griping about the one just gone.

**Claudette**   Touchy.

**Curly**   It's the same old record, Claudette, every time we meet. I don't blame Leela for not coming out with us any more.

**Claudette**   What's she been saying?

**Curly**   Nothing.

**Claudette**   She's been talking to you about me.

**Curly**   I told you. She hasn't said a word. (*Slight pause.*) I used to like Friday nights. It was fun, wasn't it? Giggling at the pictures, getting drunk and having a good bitch. I haven't had a good bitch for ages. Why don't we start Friday nights again?

**Claudette**   Friday nights have been cancelled due to lack of interest. Times I've left messages and neither you or Leela got back to me. God knows what you've been up to, and as for Leela, well you only have to look in her eyes to see she's too far gone for intelligent conversation.

**Curly**   I'm happy for her.

**Claudette**   So am I. I'm also just a bit concerned. Did you see the look in Bentley's eye when he caught sight of the living Barbie doll?

**Curly**   Leave them alone, Claudette. They're doing all right.

**Claudette**   She's flying high as a kite all right. Basking in this aura of cosy coupleness. She hasn't got time for us any more.

**Curly**   You two used to be such good friends.

**Claudette**   If you've been single more than six months, coupled women shun you, as though singleness were some kind of curse.

**Curly**   You'd be the same. I know I would.

**Claudette**   She's high on love all right. I want to be there when she comes crashing down.

**Curly**   You sound as though you might enjoy it.

**Claudette**   I didn't mean it like that.

**Curly**    I wonder about you sometimes. I can't see why you have to be so angry all the time.

**Claudette**    But then you wouldn't, would you?

**Curly**    What does that mean?

**Claudette**    Nothing.

**Curly**    Starting on me now, are you?

**Claudette**    Should I start on you?

**Curly**    What gives you the right to tell people how to live?

**Claudette**    When did I tell anyone how to live?

**Curly** (*referring to* **Claudette**'s *foot*)    That should be all right now, as long as you don't stand in the way of any rampant male egos. (*Starts to go.*)

**Claudette**    Where you going, Curly?

**Curly**    I fancy a dance and a drink.

**Claudette**    You know how you get after a few drinks.

**Curly**    What's wrong with forgetting myself for a while?

**Claudette**    Me, I don't want to forget, I want to remember.

**Curly**    See you outside then.

**Claudette**    What's up, Curly?

**Curly**    Nothing.

**Claudette**    I've known you long enough to know when something's wrong. Why don't you tell your Auntie Claudette?

**Curly**    I can't.

**Claudette**    I'm not such a heartless bitch, am I? Come on, Curls, you know how I feel about my friends. Is it that white guy?

**Curly** (*nods*)    It finished. (*Slight pause.*) It was just one of those things. Happens to everyone, doesn't it? It was nobody's fault. I mean, we got on well enough. We got on really well. He even took me to meet his parents.

**Claudette**    He must have liked you, Curls, if he took you to meet his parents.

**Curly**    Nice people. Very simple life, you know the type. Nice. When we got there, they'd bought me a present. They'd bought me this expensive make-up set. Mirror, brushes, eyeshadows, lipstick, the lot.

**Claudette**    You don't wear it much, do you?

**Curly**    Just as well because it was the English rose collection, wasn't it? English rose they were expecting.

**Claudette**    Guess who's coming to dinner.

**Curly**    We're all just standing there. He's saying nothing. They're saying nothing. I'm holding the English rose collection, not knowing whether to laugh or cry. Then we had dinner. (*Slight pause.*) You're thinking it serves me right, aren't you? You're thinking I'm always setting myself up to get hurt like this.

**Claudette**    It's not your fault, Curls.

**Curly**    You've got to keep trying, haven't you? Why didn't he tell them?

**Claudette**    You're too good for him.

**Curly**    It wouldn't have happened to you.

**Claudette**    Fuck that. Let's dance. I thought we were supposed to be welcoming in the New Year, not whingeing about the old one. Come on, Curls, my feet are itching.

**Curly** *stands*.

**Claudette**    Teach them how to dance, eh?

*They go.*

**Scene Two**

**Jeff** *and* **Bentley** *are in the room.* **Jeff** *is holding a bottle and two glasses.*

**Jeff** (*filling glasses*)    That is what you call a well-cut suit, Bentley.

**Bentley**    Come on, Jeff.

**Jeff**    Bet your shoes are Italian, handmade.

**Bentley**    Come on, man, stop taking the piss.

**Jeff**    I'll bet you've brought your portable phone with you. Just in case.

**Bentley**    You've got the wrong man, Jeff. I know when to stop working.

**Jeff**    Success suits you. That your car outside?

**Bentley**    Which car?

**Jeff**    You did drive here, right? Very nice. BMW. When I saw it parked outside I knew straight off it was yours. You've got style, Bentley.

**Bentley**    What you talking about, style? I don't even know cars. A car's a car to me. I drive a Ford Scorpio. We took a taxi.

**Jeff** (*raises his glass*)    To Bentley. Congratulations and continued success.

**Bentley**    Thanks, Jeff.

**Jeff**    I'm proud of you. When we were at college you said you'd be a partner by the time you were thirty-five.

**Bentley**    Did I?

**Jeff**    But then you always had drive.

**Bentley**    You've got drive.

**Jeff**  Oh, yes? Who was always being chased up for his essays? Who never attended lectures if he could help it? Nothing's changed, only now I'm not as actively lazy, things just sort of wash over me these days.

**Bentley**  Don't put yourself down. You always put yourself down.

**Jeff**  Now you, you worked your arse off for that partnership.

**Bentley**  Ignorance. If I'd known what hard work it was I'd never have bothered.

**Jeff**  That's what I'm saying. You always had that fight in you. What fight I ever had is gone now, vanished. (*He fills their glasses again.*)

**Bentley**  About that letter . . .

**Jeff**  It's all right about the letter, honest.

**Bentley**  I meant to bring it with me tonight, but we were running late and it went right out of my head.

**Jeff**  I don't need it right this minute, do I? It can wait.

**Bentley**  First thing Monday morning I'll get my secretary to type something up and get it posted.

**Jeff**  That's brilliant. I got Richard to write a reference for me as well.

**Bentley**  How is Richard?

**Jeff**  He's got kids.

**Bentley**  Yeah?

**Jeff**  Two.

**Bentley**  Kids, eh?

**Jeff**  I've got to move on, Bentley. I'm stuck where I am now. I said I was lazy. I'm not lazy.

**Bentley**   That's what I said.

**Jeff**   But my boss, now she's got drive – but she gives me far too much to do. By the end of the day I'm so stressed I can't move. Somehow, God knows how, I manage to get myself home, but I spend the rest of the night in front of the TV. I can barely get up to go to bed. Ask Fran.

**Bentley**   It gets you like that sometimes.

**Jeff**   You get like that?

**Bentley**   We all do.

**Jeff**   I thought it was just me.

**Bentley**   It's normal.

**Jeff**   We're thinking about leaving London.

**Bentley**   Are you?

**Jeff**   Well, I am. Fran won't leave without a fight. She loves it, she's happy with her work, but I can't breathe here. I don't feel at home. Of course it's home, I was born here, but it doesn't feel like a home, more like a place you rest at overnight on your way to somewhere else.

**Bentley**   It's something you've got to think about carefully. You might end up feeling even more stuck than you are now.

**Jeff**   I know you're right, but what else can I do? We want kids. I do. I don't want them to grow up here.

**Bentley**   I'm sorry you're feeling down.

**Jeff**   Forget it, it's nothing.

*Pause. The record changes.*

**Jeff**   Do you remember this?

**Bentley** (*trying to remember*)   A blonde.

**Jeff** *shakes his head.*

**Bentley**   Dark hair. Of course I remember.

**Jeff**    Ginger hair.

**Bentley**    Oh yes, yes.

*Slight pause. They both laugh.*

**Jeff**    Sometimes I think about when we were at college, don't you?

**Bentley**    Hardly at all, life moves on, Jeff.

**Jeff**    Just sometimes, because it was – we were free then, weren't we?

**Bentley**    Yes, I suppose we were. Can you still dance to this?

**Jeff**    Ginger bush.

*They both laugh.* **Leela** *and* **Fran** *enter.*

**Leela**    Here they are. They're in here.

**Fran**    There you are. We thought you'd gone off. What are you laughing at? I don't trust it when men are laughing alone together. It's bound to be some woman they're making fun of. It'd better not be me, that's all.

**Jeff**    We were talking.

**Leela**    About old times.

**Fran**    You get that as well, do you? It's all he ever talks about.

**Jeff**    What's wrong with talking about the past?

**Bentley**    Best years of your life.

**Jeff**    We were a team.

**Bentley**    The two-tone twins.

**Leela**    The what?

**Bentley**    We used to tell women that we were unidentical twins, one of us a throwback baby.

**Fran**    Which one?

**Jeff**    Worked every time.

**Bentley**    The novelty, you see.

**Leela**    You men are such deceivers.

**Fran**    I don't think I'd have been taken in by it. Would you?

**Leela**    I don't know.

**Jeff**    Come on. Twins? Every woman's dream.

**Fran**    It's not like that for women.

**Jeff**    What? Not even the novelty value?

**Fran**    I tell you, it's different for women. Sex is different.

**Jeff** *snorts loudly.*

**Leela**    I'm not sure I believe they really thought you were twins.

**Bentley**    They wanted to believe us because –

**Jeff**    They wanted to have sex with the two-tone twins.

**Fran**    I don't think I want to hear any more of this. Come on, we need you two outside. They've all stopped dancing again. Why don't you get out there and get the thing going again?

**Jeff**    Why don't you get them going? I can't dance.

**Fran**    I thought you were always going to discos when you were at college.

**Jeff**    That was different.

**Fran**    Why?

**Bentley**    We were kids.

**Fran**    And now you're stodgy old men.

**Bentley**    Not exactly.

**Fran**    Looks like it's down to you and me, Leela.

**Leela**    I don't want to. I mean, I can't.

**Fran**    I'll bet that's not true. I'll bet you're a great dancer, isn't she, Bentley?

**Bentley**    She's all right. You dance all right.

**Fran**    See.

**Leela**    Honestly. I'm not very good. I bump into people. It takes all my effort to keep myself upright.

**Fran**    I don't believe you.

**Jeff**    They don't want to dance, Fran. She's so bossy, she thinks everyone should do what she wants.

**Fran**    I love dancing. I love letting go and forgetting myself, don't you?

**Leela**    I never forget my body. That's the trouble.

**Jeff**    Why don't you just go in and dance?

**Fran**    On my own?

**Bentley**    Can't you dance on your own?

**Jeff**    Fran believes in people dancing together. She's romantic that way.

**Fran**    What's wrong with people dancing together properly? People don't dance together any more and when they do it's always this sex thing. I'd like to have been around in the tea dance era when you had to know all the different steps. Don't you think it would be a good thing to know all the rules of the dance? It would be a sexual thing, of course, dancing close to each other and everything, but then the music would end and there'd be no mess, no emotional complication or guilt, just on to the next dance.

**Jeff**    Do us a favour, Bentley – dance with her.

**Bentley**    I'd love to dance with you.

**Jeff**    There you go.

**Bentley**    Later on.

**Fran**    Oh.

**Leela**    Why don't you dance with her?

**Bentley**    I don't feel like it just now.

**Fran**    Well, that's put me in my place, hasn't it?

**Jeff**    I remember you liked dancing at college.

**Fran**    He doesn't want to dance. No one wants to dance. Fine. I think I'll go and get myself another drink.

**Jeff**    Fran –

**Fran**    I'm trying to make things good and all you can do is just stand there and leave everything to me. As per usual. You're not even trying. It wasn't my idea to have a stupid fucking party in the first place. (*She goes.*)

**Bentley**    Did I upset her?

**Leela**    She seemed upset.

**Bentley**    I wouldn't want to upset her.

**Jeff**    I better get out there. She's right. What's the point in having a party if everyone goes off for chats in other rooms? Let's all go, shall we? All you have to do is shake one leg then shake the other and you're dancing, aren't you? (*He goes.*)

**Leela**    Why don't you dance with her?

**Bentley**    I don't want to dance.

**Leela**    You like to dance.

**Bentley**    I said I don't feel like it.

**Leela**    You're always telling me to relax and enjoy myself.

**Bentley**    I am enjoying myself.

**Leela**    Does she frighten you?

**Bentley**    Why would she frighten me?

**Leela**   Women like that frighten me. They're a strange couple.

**Bentley**   How, strange?

**Leela**   They don't hide anything. Don't you think they're strange?

**Bentley**   No.

**Leela**   I can't imagine you being friends with him.

**Bentley**   We were good friends.

**Leela**   Still, people change. What time shall we leave?

**Bentley**   We only just got here.

**Leela**   It looks as though it's going to be one of those parties. We could go on somewhere else.

**Bentley**   You brought your friends with you, you can't just abandon them. At least stay till midnight.

**Leela**   I don't feel very well, flu or something. It's the weather, the way it keeps changing. It's a kind of phobia, my fear of parties, like claustrophobia. I'd love to be able to enjoy myself like other people. But I just get nervous. When I'm in a room and I don't know anyone . . . even my friends seem like strangers.

**Bentley** (*gentle*)   We'll leave just after midnight.

**Leela**   All right.

**Bentley**   So let's go out and shake a leg.

**Leela**   I wanted to ask you something.

**Bentley**   What?

*Slight pause.*

**Leela**   Nothing.

**Bentley**   Okay.

**Leela**    All of a sudden I feel like dancing.

**Bentley**    Fran'll be pleased.

**Leela**    Yes, she will, won't she?


**Scene Three**

**Leela**, **Claudette** *and* **Curly** *are hiding under coats.*

**Curly**    We'll miss the countdown.

**Claudette**    Who cares? This party is so dry. I can't stand the thought of watching those people trying to enjoy themselves.

**Curly**    We should have brought a bottle up with us. I'll go and get a bottle, shall I? You've got to toast the New Year in, haven't you?

**Leela**    I've never liked parties. People get so desperate at parties, don't they?

**Curly**    You like parties. We used to go to a party every Saturday when we were younger.

**Leela**    I never liked those either. I only went because there was nothing else to do. What else do you do on a Saturday night when you're sixteen?

**Curly**    I thought you enjoyed them. We were the bee's knees, weren't we? I loved getting dolled up, trotting around on high heels – we wore high heels!

**Leela**    Getting stuck with your nose up the armpit of some bloke you never fancied.

**Claudette**    Or doing something stupid like this just so that you had something to tell your mates on Monday morning.

**Curly**    I'll get those drinks, shall I?

**Leela**    We don't need drinks.

**Curly**   It's bad luck to be without a drink when the clock strikes twelve. What do you fancy? I don't suppose we'll have much choice, anyway. I'll just get what I can find.

**Claudette**   Don't let anyone see you coming up, Curls. Before you know it they'll be up here getting us to join them in the bloody conga.

**Curly** *goes.*

**Claudette**   What a lot of coats. I'll dream coats. (*Picks one up, tries it on.*) Suit me?

**Leela**   It's not your colour.

**Claudette**   How much do you think a coat like this costs?

**Leela**   Enough.

**Claudette**   You and Bentley know some smart people.

**Leela**   Take it off, Claudette.

**Claudette**   I think I'll keep it on. It suits me.

**Leela**   Do what you like.

**Claudette**   You can't slouch in a coat like this. You've got to walk upright, haven't you? Did you have a nice Christmas?

**Leela**   All right. You?

**Claudette**   What did you do?

**Leela**   We stayed at home.

**Claudette**   Just the two of you?

**Leela**   We wanted it quiet.

**Claudette**   That's nice. Exchanged presents in the morning?

**Leela**   Yes.

**Claudette**   What did he get you?

**Leela**   I can't remember.

**Claudette**   It was only last week.

**Leela**   A chain – a necklace, some perfume.

**Claudette**   What kind of perfume?

**Leela**   Claudette –

**Claudette**   I tried to get in touch with you, left messages on your answering machine.

**Leela**   Yes, thanks, it was good to hear from you. The song 'Jingle Bells' – it made me laugh.

**Claudette**   I thought you might ring me back.

**Leela**   I meant to. I was busy. I write the message down on a bit of paper and it gets lost.

**Claudette**   Things have been happening. I needed to talk.

**Leela**   I'm here now.

**Claudette**   It passed.

**Leela**   People have to get on with their lives.

**Claudette**   Their men.

**Leela**   I don't have to apologise, Claudette.

**Claudette**   I was always around for you.

**Leela**   Curly lives near you.

**Claudette**   Curly doesn't know me. You know me inside out.

*Pause. They hear the countdown to the New Year, then cheers, whistles and people singing.*

**Claudette**   Watching's becoming a habit with me. I can't walk down a street at night without stopping to look through someone's window. I'm becoming obsessed. Honestly, I don't care whether they're in there or not. I stop in the middle of the road to listen to couples quarrelling and listen in on people's conversations in restaurants. The other day I was listening to this couple arguing about whether she ought to go away or not. I must have been staring at them without realising it. He turns to me and says 'Do you mind?' It's becoming embarrassing.

**Leela**   Poor Claudette.

**Claudette**   I can cope.

*There's a knock on the door.* **Claudette** *puts her fingers to her lips. They both sit still.*

**Curly** (*off*)   Quick, it's me. Curly.

**Claudette** *goes to the door and lets* **Curly** *in, helping her with bottles and cups.*

**Curly**   They're going mad down there. Streamers everywhere. I got caught up in the conga. Did I miss anything?

**Claudette**   You didn't miss anything.

**Leela**   We were talking about Christmas.

**Curly**   I'd rather put Christmas behind me, wouldn't you? All I could find was Babycham.

**Claudette**   Which cheapskate brought Babycham to a party?

**Curly**   We used to have a lot of laughs, though, didn't we? We were always giggling, remember? We didn't even need a reason, just laughed for the sake of laughing. I reckon we should all make a New Year's resolution to see more of each other.

**Claudette**   I'm all for that.

**Leela**   Me too.

**Curly**   Let's drink to it.

*They raise their cups. There's the sound of someone approaching.*

**Man** (*off*)   I don't understand what's wrong with you.

**Woman** (*off, bitter laugh*)   You wouldn't, would you?

**Claudette**   Under the coats.

*They hide under the coats.*

**Curly**   It's just like being back at school.

**Leela** *and* **Claudette** *Sssh.*

*Silence.* **Fran** *and* **Bentley** *enter.* **Bentley** *tries to hold* **Fran**, *but she moves away and locks the door.*

**Fran**   I can see why you chose her. She has a certain charm, a certain passive charm.

**Bentley**   Come on, Fran.

**Fran**   Though I'd always pictured you with someone a bit more dynamic. A real go-getter. Like you.

**Bentley** *tries to take her hand. She pulls it away.*

**Fran**   No. (*Slight pause.*) Do you want to end it?

**Bentley**   Why would I want to end it?

**Fran**   You might be bored.

**Bentley**   No. Are you?

**Fran**   What do you think?

**Bentley** *kisses* **Fran**. *They lie on the floor.* **Fran** *traces her finger along* **Bentley**'s *face. He strokes her shoulders, removes her panties. They make love. It's tender, noiseless, furtive. They look at each other all the time. Afterwards, they lie still. Then* **Fran** *sits up on her elbows.* **Bentley** *stands, adjusting his clothes.*

**Bentley**   Happy New Year.

*They laugh.*

**Fran**   Close your eyes.

**Bentley**   What for?

**Fran**   Go on. Don't you trust me?

**Bentley** *closes his eyes. A moment passes.* **Bentley** *opens his eyes again.*

**Bentley**    What?

**Fran**    I just wanted to look at you.

**Bentley**    Crazy woman. (*He kisses* **Fran**'s *cheek.*)

**Fran**    Let's make love again.

**Bentley**    What if someone comes in?

**Fran**    Good. Let them come in.

**Bentley**    Crazy.

**Fran**    She's your guilty conscience, isn't she?

**Bentley**    What?

**Fran**    This is hardly politically correct, is it?

**Bentley**    Come on. Let's get dressed.

**Fran**    I am dressed. Is it?

**Bentley**    Politics doesn't come into it.

**Fran**    Politics comes into everything.

**Bentley**    Even fucking?

**Fran**    Especially fucking.

**Bentley**    Get dressed.

**Fran**    I agree politics shouldn't come into it. Whatever happened to *amor omnia vincit* and all that stuff?

**Bentley**    What do you want me to do?

**Fran**    A little honesty would be nice.

**Bentley**    I'm always straight with you.

**Fran**    I'd leave Jeff tomorrow, you know that. We're finished anyway.

**Bentley**    It's not that easy, Fran. You know that.

**Fran**    Tell me, do all black men let their heads rule their hearts?

**Bentley**    Every evening she comes home she needs to talk. I mean really talk. She never does, though. She just potters around, makes pleasant conversation: 'had a nice day at the office dear?' Underneath it all you can hear this, like a grating sound, you can hear what she really wants to say struggling to get out. But she won't let it out.

**Fran**    Let what out?

**Bentley**    You wouldn't understand.

**Fran**    I see. It's a black thing.

**Bentley**    No. (*Slight pause.*) Yes. She's fighting to make something of herself. I know how hard that is even though I do believe that it's up to the individual to rise above all the shit. That's all that matters. Work hard and you can achieve anything. You're judged by what you do these days, aren't you? Not that she doesn't work hard. Do a good job and no one can touch you. (*Slight pause.*) So the small talk goes on and on. Worse thing is you stop listening and she knows you've stopped listening and she can't help resenting that. So there's that between you. Sometimes you – I can't bring myself to look at her, say I've got a lot of work to do. So it gets worse. You can't rest. You're so busy trying . . . to cope with it, deal with it. To be decent. You can't rest. I owe it to her find the right time . . . explain . . . or . . . (*He shrugs hopelessly.*)

**Fran**    (*rolls over on to her tummy*)    I don't want to make trouble, but I don't want to be hemmed in. I want to be free. I think people should be free.

**Bentley**    (*takes her hands, pulls her up*)    And we will be. Soon.

*They go. After a short while* **Leela**, **Claudette** *and* **Curly** *come out from underneath the coats. Silence.*

**Curly**    Sorry, Leela.

**Leela**    What for? It's not your fault.

**Claudette**    The bastard.

**Curly**    Claudette.

**Claudette**    Fucking bastard.

**Curly**    What do you want us to do?

**Leela**    I want us to go downstairs, that's all.

**Claudette**    Let's go downstairs then.

**Leela**    I'll follow you down.

**Claudette**    We'll wait for you.

*Slight pause.* **Curly** *nudges* **Claudette**.

**Claudette**    All right.

**Curly** *and* **Claudette** *go.*


**Scene Four**

*Later.* **Curly** *and* **Jeff** *are in the room, getting dressed.*

**Curly**    Of course, I knew the minute I set eyes on them together. It takes an outsider, doesn't it? It could have gone on for years and you and Leela wouldn't have guessed. It was watching them dance together that confirmed it. You could see it even in the dark. They fit together perfectly. None of the usual little bumps and knocks that embarrass people dancing together for the first time. And the way they didn't make small talk, not even look at each other, as though they'd give something away if they did. Elementary, my dear Watson. It won't last.

**Jeff** *yawns.*

**Curly**    Tired? I'm not surprised. You're a bad boy. And to think they used to kill the bearer of bad news.

**Jeff**    You've got a good body.

**Curly**    What?

**Jeff**    Your body, it's . . .

**Curly**    I suppose they had to. To restore the balance of power. It was bad enough that the messenger knew all his master's secrets, but can you imagine him struggling to keep a straight face as he told his tale? Overstepping the mark. Aren't you getting dressed?

**Jeff**    I am dressed.

**Curly**    You'd look a picture if anyone were to burst in here, wouldn't you?

**Jeff** *stands up and tucks his shirt in.* **Curly** *takes out a small eye-shadow box and applies make-up.*

**Jeff**    You don't need that. You've got a lovely face.

**Curly**    I don't usually bother but, well, it's a party, isn't it? I suppose we'd better get out of here, hadn't we?

**Jeff**    What about the wine? Let's have some wine.

**Curly**    I don't feel like it. (*Slight pause.*) You have some. (*Puts eye-shadow away.*) I'll see you downstairs then.

**Jeff** *holds* **Curly** *by the shoulders, then strokes her face, her hair.*

**Jeff**    Why did you tell me?

**Curly**    Don't you want to know?

**Jeff**    No.

**Curly**    You should know the truth.

**Jeff**    Why?

**Curly**    If you don't know what's going on, you're living in a fantasy, aren't you? Perhaps you'd prefer that.

**Jeff**   Perhaps I would. (*Gulps wine.*)

**Curly**   Steady.

**Jeff**   Why did you tell me?

**Curly**   Because I thought you should know.

**Jeff**   Why?

**Curly**   You'd have found out sooner or later, bumped into them in the street or something.

**Jeff**   I wouldn't have let them see me.

**Curly**   You are in a bad way. But that's life, isn't it? It happens. You shouldn't take it so hard. These days lots of people I know have open relationships.

**Jeff**   Do you remember that perfume ad where the woman's running through the street at night?

**Curly**   Which perfume ad?

**Jeff**   It's very striking. There aren't any words. Just this image of a woman running. She just keeps running but doesn't arrive anywhere.

**Curly**   They're like art films these days.

**Jeff**   You're left wondering what she's running to.

**Curly**   Or, more to the point, what she's running away from.

**Jeff**   I'll call you a cab, then, shall I?

**Curly**   Oh.

**Jeff**   We got a number here somewhere. (*Slight pause.*) I'm sorry.

**Curly**   Yes, I'd better be off.

**Jeff**   I'll call you a cab then?

**Curly**   Thanks.

**Jeff** *goes out.* **Curly** *takes a gulp of wine, stands.* **Jeff** *comes back.*

**Jeff**  It's on its way.

**Curly**  Thanks.

**Jeff**  You don't mind leaving, do you?

**Curly**  'Course not. Why should I mind? I'm a big girl.

**Jeff**  I don't want you to take offence.

**Curly**  Honestly, no offence taken.

**Jeff**  I can see that you have.

**Curly**  Because you want me to.

**Jeff**  Listen . . . tonight . . . it was nothing . . . I mean, it was something, it was good, I enjoyed it I mean, but it wasn't . . .

**Curly**  What?

**Jeff**  You know.

**Curly**  Yes, I know.

**Jeff**  Not that it wasn't, you know.

**Curly**  Don't go on about it. I know.

**Jeff**  Stay if you want to. You can stay.

**Curly**  You just called a cab.

**Jeff**  I can cancel it.

**Curly**  You said you wanted me to go.

**Jeff**  I didn't say that.

**Curly**  It's what you meant.

**Jeff**  Look, stay. Why don't you stay?

**Curly**  Do you want me to?

**Jeff**  Stay if you want to.

**Curly**  But you want me to go?

**Jeff**  I want you to stay. I'll cancel the cab.

**Curly**    You said it was on its way.

**Jeff**    I'll call them. They'll put a call through to him and say not to bother.

**Curly**    They'll charge you.

**Jeff**    So let them charge me. (*He gets up and puts the cork back in the bottle as much because it gives him something to do in this uncomfortable atmosphere as anything else.*) Why don't you have some wine?

**Curly** *takes the bottle.*

**Jeff**    What happened was just between us. You and me. No one else comes into it.

**Curly**    Why would I think they did?

**Jeff**    Just in case you did.

**Curly**    I didn't.

**Jeff**    Good. I'll cancel that cab. (*Slight pause.*) Just between us, eh?

### Scene Five

*Lights change. Alone,* **Leela** *pours herself a drink, then another and another. She starts to sob quietly, rocking herself. Sound of gentle laughter. Lights up on* **Irma**, *who's sitting on the floor in a corner of the room, cross-legged. She's wearing a multicoloured jump suit and trainers, large gold earrings and has a bald head. As* **Leela** *sobs, she laughs softly. As* **Leela**'s *crying gets louder, she can't control her laughter and has to hold her stomach. Hearing her,* **Leela** *looks up and her sobs subside. She walks towards* **Irma**.

**Irma** (*wiping her eyes*)    I'm sorry. I hope you're not offended. I laugh at everything.

**Leela** *stares at* **Irma**.

**Irma**   You know, it's rude to stare. It's a power thing, an
expression of hostility. Though I myself have never had a
problem with people looking at me. It's being ignored I can't
stand.

**Leela**   Have we met?

**Irma**   I doubt it. I just got here. I'm always late. My friends
get used to it. (*Holds her hand out.*) Irma.

**Leela** (*taking* **Irma***'s hand*)   Leela.

**Irma**   You were crying. It always ends in tears. Either
that or the china gets broken. (*Pause.*) You don't say much,
do you? Not that it matters. I can talk the hind legs off
an armchair. (*Pause.*) I was born in south London thirty
years ago. My birth was the occasion of great trauma for
my mother who, prior to going into labour, had witnessed
the strange couplings of common or garden slugs on her
kitchen floor at midnight. It wasn't the bizarreness of their
copulation that struck her but the realisation that each
partner had both projectile and receptacle – she was very
fastidious – which, in effect, made the sex act redundant
as a particularly flexible slug could impregnate itself. That
such a phenomenon existed on God's earth – she was also
very superstitious – undermined the very tenets by which
she'd thus far kept her life together. She felt cheated. If God
had seen fit to bestow this gift upon human beings then she
would not have had to undergo the ritual Friday Night Fuck,
a particularly vigorous, not to mention careless, session of
which had resulted in my conception. She was overwhelmed
by the depth of her anger, and the shock of it propelled
her into labour. The doctors didn't know how to tell her at
first. It doesn't happen very often, but sometimes a child is
born with both receptacle and projectile nestling between
its legs. I was such a child and the doctors told my mother
that she had to make a choice, or I would be plagued by
severe mental confusion and distress for the rest of my life.
Of course she didn't know which way to turn. In the end
she settled on getting rid of the male appendage, not least

because she held the things in contempt but also because she felt that black men were too often in the limelight, and that a woman might quietly get things done while those who undermined her were looking the other way. However, she hadn't reckoned with the fact that she had already become attached to me and found me perfect the way I was. So even while the surgeon was sharpening his knives my mother had wrapped me in an old shawl, woven by her own grandmother, and taken me home. I hope I'm not boring you.

**Leela**    No. (*Blinks and sways on her feet.*)

**Irma**    You're drunk.

**Leela**    Am I?

**Irma**    You don't know whether you're coming or going, do you? I've an itch. Would you mind?

**Leela**    Where?

**Irma**    My head. Go on. Don't be scared.

**Leela** *touches* **Irma**'s *head nervously.*

**Irma**    Give it a good rub, go on. It happened while I was undergoing one of those torturous hair treatments – you know the kind where they put some foul-smelling cream on your head and tell you to shout when it starts to burn. Only when you shout out they can't hear you because they're off on their tea break. So by the time they come back they've got to call the firemen out to administer the final rinse. Not that I'm complaining. I've always been in the vanguard of fashion. You watch. In the future all black women will sport bald heads. And those who haven't had their hair ruined by hairdresser chemicals will go bald in sympathy with those who have.

**Leela** (*smiles*)    That's a lovely thought.

**Irma**    It is, isn't it?

**Leela**   I wouldn't have the guts to shave all my hair off. It wouldn't suit me.

**Irma**   Oh, I don't know.

**Leela** *looks away.*

**Irma**   Why were you crying? Distance. That's what I'd do. I'd go away. Of course our mothers had religion.

**Leela**   For all the good it's done them.

**Irma**   I wouldn't knock it.

**Leela**   It frightened me watching my mother surrendering to the spirit every Sunday afternoon. When she fell to the ground you'd pull back her eyelid and it was like looking into the eyes of the dead. That total surrendering up of the will frightens me.

**Irma**   You're not telling me you watched that and didn't yourself feel a tingling in your extremities?

**Leela**   Mass hysteria.

**Irma**   Never felt the spirit stirring inside you?

**Leela**   Sometimes I felt I wanted to get up and whirl around the room with them, yes.

**Irma**   Why didn't you?

**Leela**   It would have been dishonest. Deep down I didn't feel anything. I wish I did.

**Irma**   The point is that our mothers found a way of releasing the pain, they never let themselves become victims of it.

*Pause.*

**Leela**   I've always felt really self-conscious about the way I speak. No one else seems to notice it. At least they've never said anything, but, well, words are sometimes like lumps of cold porridge sticking in my mouth. I always have to think before saying anything in case I get things wrong. I mispronounce words. Or sometimes when there's a choice of two words that sound similar I'll use the wrong one. Not all the time. Sometimes I forget and surprise myself with my eloquence, the precision of my grammar. It's because this isn't my first language, you see. Not that I do have any real first language, but sometimes I imagine that there must have been, at some time. You can feel that sometimes, can't you? If you don't feel you belong to a language then you're only half alive aren't you, because you haven't the words to bring yourself into existence. You might as well be invisible. Other people seem very real. Like you, now, at this moment, seem very real to me. Sometimes it feels as though there's something stuck down here (*Holds her tummy.*) and I want to stick my fingers down my throat and spew it all up. (*Slight pause.*) We've only just met and I'm telling you everything.

**Irma**   There's nothing wrong with that.

**Leela**   I've got to find my friends.

**Irma**   Distance.

**Leela**   It's not that easy.

**Irma**   Did I say it was?

**Leela**   They'll be wondering what happened to me. (*She goes.*)

**Scene Six**

*A room.* **Fran** *picks up a coat and is about to leave the room when she's stopped by* **Jeff,** *who hides a bottle behind his back.*

**Jeff**   People leaving already?

**Fran**   It is very late.

**Jeff**   We haven't spoken to each other all evening. I've been ignoring you.

**Fran**   You know what it's like when you're playing hostess, you don't notice things like that.

**Jeff** *takes the bottle and two paper cups from behind his back.*

**Fran**   That's nice.

**Jeff**   Thought you might like something to drink.

**Fran**   I think I've had too much to drink. Don't look at me like that.

**Jeff**   Can't I even look at you?

**Fran**   You're looking right through me, I don't like it.

**Jeff**   Sorry.

**Fran**   I must look a mess, anyway. Can you remember which is Karen's coat?

**Jeff**   The green one.

**Fran**   You're good at things like that.

**Jeff**   I wish they'd all go home.

**Fran**   Didn't you enjoy yourself?

**Jeff**   I just wish now that they'd all go home and leave us alone. We haven't been alone together for a long time.

**Fran**   Don't be silly. We're alone all the time. Get fed up of each other.

**Jeff**   Are you?

**Fran**   Sometimes. Everyone gets like that. You get ratty with me all the time.

**Jeff**   The first time I saw you I thought you looked like the girl in that perfume ad.

**Fran**   Which perfume ad?

**Jeff**   The one where she's running through the street in her bare feet.

**Fran** (*laughing*)    Oh, that one. She's running through the street in her bare feet and her knickers, in the pouring rain. I don't look a bit like her. Men.

**Jeff**    I think you do. (*He is staring.*)

**Fran**    I'd better give Karen her coat.

**Jeff**    She's still saying goodbye to people. She'll wait. Have a drink. (*He fills the cups.*)

**Fran**    I'll be sick if I drink any more.

**Jeff**    Go on.

**Fran** *takes a cup.* **Jeff** *looks out of a window.*

**Jeff**    Black night. Black black night. I love night-time.

**Fran**    You used to be scared of the dark.

**Jeff**    Still am. (*Drinks.*)

**Fran**    You'll be ill.

**Jeff**    I won't be ill.

**Fran**    You know what you're like.

**Jeff**    For God's sake, I can drink.

**Fran**    I'm not clearing up after you, that's all.

**Jeff**    I fixed our radio.

**Fran**    I thought it was beyond repair. What was wrong with it?

**Jeff**    Nothing much.

**Fran**    I didn't know you could do things like that.

**Jeff**    My dad used to say that you should always keep something in reserve.

**Fran**    Full of good advice, your dad.

**Jeff**    I think we should go away.

**Fran**   Oh.

**Jeff**   We need a holiday. We could go to the Lakes.

**Fran**   Why this sudden desire to get away?

**Jeff**   I just fancy getting out of London.

**Fran**   Is something wrong?

**Jeff**   Breathe the fresh air.

**Fran**   You love London.

**Jeff**   Why don't we both take some time off work and just take off?

**Fran**   I don't want to go to the Lake District.

**Jeff**   Why not?

**Fran**   Because it's all pensioners and babies and rain.

**Jeff**   All right, pick somewhere else.

**Fran**   I've got too much work to do.

**Jeff**   You'll feel better for getting away.

**Fran**   You always do that. I don't need you to tell me what will make me feel better.

**Jeff**   I'm not trying to tell you what to do.

**Fran**   What was all that about then? Let's go to the Lakes. You always do that. I don't have to go with you. We're not joined at the hip. Why don't you go on your own?

**Jeff**   I just thought it would be nice.

**Fran**   I've said I don't want to go.

**Jeff**   All right. I don't want to fight.

**Fran**   If I wanted to go away, I'd say.

**Jeff**   All right. All right.

**Fran**   Look, I don't want to go away. If there's some reason why you want to go away, if there's something bothering you, then we can talk about that here.

**Jeff**   Like what? What could be bothering me?

**Fran**   You tell me.

**Jeff**   There's nothing. Honest. It was just an idea.

*Pause while* **Fran** *looks for coat and finds it.*

**Fran**   You used to get angry about things, but it's all gone. You've fallen asleep. You don't care what's going on in the world, can't see beyond your own front doorstep, can you? Wake up, Jeff. (*Slight pause.*) Sorry. I didn't mean that. (*Slight pause.*)

**Jeff**   You're right. Even my parents had something to fight for. Their one dream was to own their own home. It kept them going, the thought that one day they'd get out. They worked themselves into the ground to achieve that dream. Okay, it's not the most admirable of dreams, but it was something to believe in, wasn't it? And they achieved it. All right, so they're still in the same council flat, but at least they own it.

**Fran**   Karen'll think I've run away with her coat. Thanks for the drink.

**Jeff**   Fran?

**Fran**   Yes?

**Jeff**   I fixed your radio.

**Fran**   Yes, you said.

**Jeff**   It's still very fragile, so you've got to be careful with it, make sure you don't drop it or bang it or anything.

**Fran**   Okay. (*Slight pause.*) I don't listen to it any more anyway. (*She goes.*)

**Scene Seven**

*For the first time in this act there is no music.* **Leela** *sits on the floor.* **Curly,** *ill, has her head in* **Leela's** *lap.* **Jeff, Bentley** *and* **Claudette** *are standing.* **Fran** *enters with coats.*

**Fran**   Taxis will be here in a minute.

**Jeff**   Everybody hated Othello because he was black.

**Claudette**   In which sense do you mean black? In the biblical sense?

**Jeff**   I'm not talking platitudes now, about darkness within, original sin and all that shit. It's about putting yourself in the other man's shoes, isn't it? I mean, look at the world through Othello's eyes: surrounded by racists, neurotic about his age and appearance, worried about losing his job, his hair. No wonder he ran off with Desdemona.

**Claudette**   I thought they were supposed to be in love with each other.

**Jeff**   He ran off with Desdemona in order to fit into the white world and she ran away with him in order to escape from it. I suppose you could call that a sort of love, if you define love as a mutual need to fulfil each other's fantasies: he wanted to be white and she wanted to be black, or to have conferred on her what she saw as blackness, a certain mystique – all those references to voodoo. In other words, his difference turned her on.

**Claudette**   Why would he need to fit in?

**Jeff**   Everybody needs to fit in.

**Claudette**   Not Othello.

**Jeff**   He needed to fit in more than most.

**Claudette**   Why? Why would he need to fit in? He was the boss. The one who hired and fired, told them what to do, wrote references for them. They had to fit in with him, more like.

**Fran**    Does anybody want another drink?

**Leela** (*cradling* **Curly**'*s head*)    I think we've all had enough, don't you?

**Claudette**    Fitting in. That's crap.

**Curly** *groans.*

**Bentley**    You all right, Curly? (*To* **Leela**.) She all right?

**Leela**    Her tummy's upset, that's all.

**Claudette** (*to* **Jeff**)    Did you give her something?

**Jeff**    Why would I . . .?

**Claudette**    To eat, I mean. It must have been something she ate. I'm always telling her to be careful about what she puts in her mouth. Of course, she never listens.

**Leela** (*to* **Curly**)    Are you going to be sick, Curls?

**Curly**    No.

**Leela**    Tell me if you want to be, won't you?

**Fran** *and* **Bentley** *are standing over* **Curly**, *looking down at her.*

**Fran**    She looks in a bad way. Do you think she wants a coffee?

**Bentley** (*reaching his hand out to* **Curly**'*s forehead*)    Has she got a temperature?

**Leela**    Don't touch her. Can't you see she's hot enough as it is? The poor girl's ill. She can't breathe with you standing over her. Can't you see you're stifling her?

**Bentley**    Sorry.

**Bentley** *and* **Fran** *are more cautious, standing back a bit.*

**Fran**    Shall I get her an aspirin or something?

**Leela**    She'll be all right.

**Bentley**    Go on, let Fran get her something.

**Fran**   It's no trouble.

**Leela**   I said she doesn't want an aspirin. If she wants one of your aspirins I'll ask you to get her one, won't I?

**Bentley**   Leela –

**Leela**   What? (*Slight pause.*) What?

**Bentley**   Too much to drink.

**Leela**   That's what you think.

**Curly** *groans.*

**Leela**   Sssh. That's what he thinks.

**Fran**   I'll get that coffee. Make myself useful.

**Claudette**   Of course, I reckon that what really got Iago's goat, what really made him jealous, was the size of Othello's penis. Are you telling me they didn't get drunk occasionally in the officers' mess and have spunk-shooting contests? Believe me, they got drunk one evening and Iago offered to do the honours with the old tape measure. Big mistake. He spent the rest of the evening crying into his beer.

**Jeff**   No, no. That's quite valid. It's just another way of looking at it, isn't it? Of course, you could look at it another way . . .

**Fran**   Shut up, Jeff.

**Jeff**   Why? We're just having a harmless post-party discussion. What the hell's wrong with that?

**Fran**   You're talking shit, that's what's wrong with it.

**Jeff**   Of course we're talking shit, we're pissed, aren't we? Though, in our defence, it has to be said that the argument has had its moments of subtlety. You've missed the finer points, that's all.

**Fran**   I don't want to hear any more points – fine, coarse or otherwise.

**Jeff**    What's bothering you, Fran?

**Fran**    Nothing's bothering me.

**Jeff**    I want to know what's wrong.

**Fran** (*to the others*)    Your taxis will be here soon.

**Bentley** (*to* **Leela**)    Are you all right?

**Claudette**    Why shouldn't she be all right?

**Bentley**    You're acting weird.

**Jeff**    Must be the full moon, Bentley. You know what women are like.

**Claudette**    Go on, tell him what's wrong with you.

**Fran**    We're all drunk. I'll get that coffee.

**Bentley**    Eh, Leela?

**Claudette**    I'll tell you what's wrong with her.

**Bentley**    I was talking to Leela, not the fucking ventriloquist's dummy.

**Leela**    Leave her alone.

**Bentley**    I asked you a question, Leela.

**Leela** (*shrugging him off*)    How dare you? After touching her, how dare you come and put your hands on me?

**Fran**    God.

**Claudette**    *Amor. Omnia. Vincit.*

*Pause. Sound of car horn honking.*

**Jeff**    Its all right, Fran. I've been stupid. Now we can talk.

**Fran** (*to* **Bentley**)    So they know. It's good. It's good they know.

**Bentley** (*to* **Leela**)    We've got to talk.

**Claudette**    Bit late for that now.

**Bentley**    I'm sorry, Leela.

**Claudette**    You'll be more than sorry in a minute.

**Bentley**    I sincerely didn't want it to be like this.

**Claudette**    Because, like all men, you wanted the best of both worlds, didn't you? To have your cake and eat eat eat.

**Leela**    For God's sake, Claudette, I can speak for myself.

**Claudette**    Why don't you, then? Go on, speak.

*Pause. Sound of taxi horn honking outside.*

**Jeff**    You've got your coats, have you? Right, thank you all very much for coming. Happy New Year.

**Claudette**    Charming.

**Jeff**    Not that I'm rushing you or anything but, you know, the party's got to end sometime and now me and Fran want to be alone together.

**Fran**    Stop it.

**Jeff**    Don't we?

**Bentley**    Cool it, Jeff.

**Jeff**    That's funny, after everything you've . . . Are you telling me, in my own house, you come into my house . . .

**Bentley**    I know how you must feel.

**Claudette**    Hark at Mr Sensitive.

**Jeff**    You don't know. Nobody knows. This is my house, Bentley. Get out of my house.

*Front doorbell rings.*

**Bentley**    Come on, let's go home.

**Fran**    You can't leave now.

**Jeff**    Why didn't we talk? If you'd told me what you wanted . . .

**Fran**    You could never be what I wanted. Bentley –

**Claudette**    I'm not getting into any taxi with you. You go if you want to, Leela, but I'm going to try for another cab.

**Bentley**    Coming, Leela?

**Leela**    No.

**Bentley**    All right. (*Slight pause.*) All right.

*Persistent ringing at front doorbell.*

**Fran**    I think we should go. We might as well go. We can't stay here. (*Shouting through door.*) We're coming! Hold on! I'm going, anyway. You can stay if you want. (*To* **Jeff.**) My things . . . I'll call round for them . . . sometime.

**Jeff** *is on his knees.*

**Fran**    Stop it, Jeff.

**Jeff**    I don't want you to go.

**Fran**    Get up, you look stupid. (*She goes to the door.*) I'm going anyway, Bentley.

**Bentley** *walks over to* **Fran,** *and they go.*

**Claudette** (*as they leave*)    That's right, why don't you just fuck off with your white woman? I hope you'll be very happy together. Leela's too good for you, but you've been so brainwashed you can't see it. Go on, run away. You'll get a shock when you wake up in the morning and the face staring back at you in the mirror is still a black one. She can't make you white, black boy.

*Pause. Sound of door slamming shut and car driving away. Pause.*

**Claudette**    That's that then?

*Silence.* **Jeff** *pulls the string on a party popper. Streamers fly out. He zips up his jacket and leaves.*

**Claudette**    How're you feeling?

**Leela** (*after a short while*)    Frozen.

**Claudette**    We let them off too easily.

**Curly** *sits up, holding her stomach.*

**Claudette**    Aye aye. First sign of life she's shown. Slept right through it, didn't you, Curls?

**Curly**    I feel sick.

**Claudette**    That doesn't surprise me. Do you know what she's been up to?

**Leela**    We'd better walk down to the cab office.

**Claudette**    You've got to admire Curly's indomitable faith in mankind, haven't you?

**Leela**    Leave her alone, Claudette. This has got nothing to do with Curly.

**Curly** (*sitting up*)    No, let her carry on. After all, it's just Claudette, isn't it, that's the way she is. Besides, she's right. She is right, though, isn't she? Claudette always is. I deserve her contempt. (*Stands*) After all, she's so high and mighty squeaky clean. (*To* **Claudette**.) Life would be so much simpler if we were all like you. We wouldn't have to question ourselves . . . we'd always be right. We could all feel good about ourselves all the time because we'd be so pure, like little girls who can't risk dirty puddles because they're wearing white socks. The shouting's got to stop some time. Why can't we just live together, why can't we just have some peace? (*She turns, is sick, and then leaves the room.*)

**Leela**    I'd better see she's all right.

**Claudette**    She'll be all right. She'll have forgotten half of this in the morning. Curly always does. (*Slight pause.*) What does she know?

**Leela**    Curly's not stupid.

**Claudette**    Curly's got no self-respect.

**Leela**   Fuck self-respect, at least she's honest with herself.

**Claudette**   What does she know? I'm shaking, look. (*She touches* **Leela**'s *shoulder.*)

**Leela**   I can feel you're shaking.

**Claudette**   Why am I shaking? I can't stop. I hate what that bastard's done to you. (*Almost laughing at herself.*) Look, I'm nearly in tears, I'm so angry.

**Leela**   Poor Claudette.

**Claudette** (*surprised*)   What?

**Leela**   Poor poor Claudette.

## Act Two

*This entire act takes place in Jamaica.*

### Scene One

*A beach. Dusk.* **Leela** *is drying herself with a towel while* **Claudette** *stands, drink in hand, watching her.*

**Leela**    I was scared at first. Then one of them made a clicking noise in its throat and gave me a sort of gentle nudge. We swam out together. I've never swum out so far.

**Claudette**    You don't want to swim too far out. You know what they say about dolphins.

**Leela**    I've never even seen a dolphin before. Not in the wild. The water's so clear. It's another world. (*Smiles.*) Like a wildlife film.

**Claudette**    Fucking Jacques Cousteau.

**Leela**    You should come with me.

**Claudette**    I do all the communing with nature I want right here on the beach.

**Leela**    I'd get bored sitting around on a beach all day long. You haven't moved from this spot since we got here.

**Claudette**    Two weeks' time and you'll be back in that office and I'll be back on the road: rain by the bucketful and sexual austerity. I intend to rest, eat, drink, soak up as much sun as I can stand and fuck everything that moves. Yesterday I had three men dancing attendance on me. All the rich young American women on the beach and they're swarming around me. You should have seen Mikie's face.

**Leela**    Jealous, was he?

**Claudette**   Serves him right for chatting up the tourists. He was all over me. Fetching me this, bringing me that. If I didn't fancy him I'd've found it nauseating. As it was . . .

**Leela**   You kissed and made up.

**Claudette**   We made love on the beach. The sea nibbled my toes and the sky seemed so low you could pluck the moon out and eat it like a ripe mango.

**Mikie** *enters.*

**Claudette**   Talk of the devil.

**Mikie**   I can't stay on this side of the beach too long. That damn Diamond been on my tail all the morning, say I have to walk up and down selling peanuts.

**Claudette**   Who buys them? Nobody wants to eat peanuts on a beach.

**Mikie**   You tell Diamond. Diamond think that people would buy anything if you force it on them long enough. That woman get crazier every day.

**Claudette**   You've got to admire her.

**Mikie**   I don't have much time. I have to talk quick.

**Claudette**   What is it?

**Mikie**   Tonight.

**Claudette**   You can't make it.

**Mikie** *nods.*

**Claudette**   Why, Mikie?

**Mikie**   Sugar.

**Leela**   I think I'd better go.

**Mikie**   I'm in big trouble . . . Sugar believe in one man, one woman.

**Claudette**   Why did you tell her, stupid?

**Mikie**    *I ain't tell her nothing. She say she can smell it on me. That woman have nose like a dog. After I bath and everything.*

**Claudette**    I suppose we are both in trouble.

**Mikie**    Not you. She won't say anything to you. Diamond wouldn't allow her to mess with the tourists. Is me she beating up on. I got to stay in for the next few nights.

**Claudette**    Why? She doesn't own you. Mikie, we're only here for two more weeks, this week's almost finished.

**Mikie**    Maybe, but it's better to keep Sugar sweet. You don't know how much grief she can give a man.

**Claudette**    I can imagine. Under that obsequious demeanour she looks like a spitfire.

**Mikie**    Spitfire. Thas Sugar. Spitfire. Yes. Sugar really know how to hit a man where it hurt.

**Claudette**    So I won't be seeing you for a few nights.

**Mikie** *shakes his head.*

**Claudette**    I'll just have to find someone else to take me out on the sea.

**Mikie**    Two nights. That's all I need to keep Sugar sweet, just two nights. Wait for me for two nights.

*They kiss.*

**Mikie**    Pull you shirt down.

**Claudette**    Why?

**Mikie**    You can't see that old American watching you? Watching like a man ain't eaten for months. A so them does like to watch we woman. Sugar always telling me how American invite her to them room. But Sugar know how to cuss them. Is Diamond fault for setting Sugar on the beach to give massage to tourist. Chuh. Two nights.

**Claudette**    Make sure it is just two nights.

**Mikie** *goes.*

**Leela**   Be careful, Claudette.

**Claudette**   Aren't I always?

**Leela**   I was thinking about Sugar.

**Claudette**   Sugar doesn't own him. Nobody owns Mikie.
Look along the beach, Leel. Everybody knows what the
score is. You don't begrudge me a little holiday fling, do
you? We all use each other. Everyone goes home happy. No
one gets hurt. (*She stretches out lazily.*) Even the sea smells of
sex. Forget the dolphins, Leel. Dougie is besotted with you. I
tell you, the man's in love. He keeps talking about you. He'll
be at Diamond's barbecue.

**Leela**   Which one's Dougie?

**Claudette**   Mikie's friend.

**Leela**   The one who takes his teeth out in the middle of a
conversation?

**Claudette**   Life and soul of the party, our Dougie.

**Leela**   I think I'll stick with the dolphins.

**Claudette**   I wouldn't mind if you were enjoying yourself.

**Leela**   I am enjoying myself.

**Claudette**   We don't even get to see each other during the
day. You're either off swimming or walking before I've even
opened my eyes.

**Leela**   You should come with me.

**Claudette**   I can't think what you get out of it. It's not as if
you meet anyone.

**Leela**   I don't want to meet anyone.

**Claudette**   I worry about you.

**Leela**   Don't you wonder what lies beyond the beach? It's
more beautiful than I imagined. You can be alone yet not

alone. There's a vastness about the place. It doesn't seem like an island at all. The people . . . they seem so at ease with themselves. They have that confidence that comes from belonging. Everyone's got a story to tell. I could listen to them all day. London seems like a figment of my imagination.

**Claudette** (*gets up, pours wine into a glass for* **Leela**)   Now you're talking. Young women like us should be free. We shouldn't walk around with our heads bowed, apologising for ourselves. We should walk tall. We're young, healthy, beautiful girls. We were born to live like this, Leel. Sod the angst, the wretchedness –

**Leela**   and the rain and the boredom –

**Claudette**   To two girls from London –

**Leela**   two black girls –

**Claudette**   To hot days and balmy, passionate nights –

**Leela**   To dolphins –

**Claudette**   and boys who flex their biceps on the beach just for us –

**Leela**   To mosquito bites –

**Claudette**   love bites –

**Leela**   long walks, coconut milk and mango. To the magnificent silence of the sea –

**Claudette**   and things that go bump in the night. (*Slight pause.*) To Freedom.

*They clink glasses.*


**Scene Two**

**Kate** *and* **David** *are on the beach.* **David** *is scratching his legs.*

**Kate**   Scratching makes it worse.

**David**   How come you haven't been bitten?

**Kate**   They like foreign blood.

**David**   By foreign you mean . . .?

**Kate**   Tourists.

**David**   Oh, of course. You're a bona fide exile now, right? Sorry, I forgot.

**Kate**   I thought you were going scuba-diving.

**David**   See me scuba-diving? That was Mikie's idea. He's got it into his head that I'm some sort of action man. He keeps suggesting water-skiing and wind gliding. Perhaps he's trying to kill me. He's promised to take me on a guided rum tour of the island.

**Kate**   He's a nice guy.

**David**   He hasn't got a chip on his shoulder like some of the others. Like that waitress, Sugar. She deliberately keeps getting my order wrong – brings me rum punch when I ask for Coke, chicken when I ask for fish.

**Kate**   Do you blame her? All you tourists care about is sex and cocktails.

**David**   What's wrong with that?

**Kate**   You deserve all the contempt you get.

**David**   It's a long way from home.

**Kate**   Thank God.

**David**   How long are you planning on staying here?

**Kate**   God, it's the Spanish Inquisition again. I don't know how long I'll be staying out here.

**David**   Part of the new lifestyle, eh? Take each day as it comes?

**Kate**   Something like that.

**David**   Isn't everyone looking for their island in the sun? I mean, gardening on a tropical island.

**Kate**   It's a living. I fit in here.

**David**   You?

**Kate**   Okay, so they think I'm a bit strange, but they leave me alone. You sound just like Dad.

**David**   I don't.

**Kate**   You do.

**David**   Sorry.

**Kate**   Wouldn't you stay?

**David**   I don't know. Though I can see why you might want to. (*Slight pause.*) Poor Mum and Dad. Pretty unfortunate to have produced two drop-outs.

**Kate**   You want me to conform so that you can go off and do what you like.

**David**   Yes, why not?

**Kate**   I paid my dues to conformity, David. Now it's your turn. Did they send you out to come and get me?

**David**   No. It was my decision.

**Kate**   Bet they did. You always were a sneak.

**David**   I just wanted to see you were all right. I couldn't live in that strange vacuum of belonging neither here nor there. Wanting here when you're there and there when you're here.

**Kate**   I hardly ever want there.

**David**   Don't you get homesick?

**Kate**   Never. The great thing is feeling yourself disappearing. A little part of you dissolves every day, but you hang on to those things that distinguish you: an accent, the way you walk. You don't give in to the lazy hip-swaying that the other women have. You walk very straight, very fast. People think I'm mad. But the best times are when I feel myself stateless, colourless as a jellyfish.

**David**    Do you think you'll stay here for the rest of your life?

**Kate**    How can I know that?

**David**    Oh yes, sorry, I forgot, nowadays you live moment by moment.

**Kate**    And right at this moment it suits me. It suits me fine.

### Scene Three

*The beach. Dusk.* **David** *and* **Kate** *at one table and* **Leela** *and* **Claudette** *at another. They've just eaten.* **Diamond** *is cutting up tissue-paper to make paper flowers. While* **Diamond** *talks,* **Mikie** *wipes down the tables while* **Sugar** *sets down drinks. Music plays from a radio cassette.*

**Diamond**    I got fed up. I was working my arse out – excuse the French – working my fingers to the bone for those people. I was on my feet for hours in some filthy café. Treated like a dog, worse than a dog. And for what? I had to get out. Back there I was nothing. Here I'm a lady. You can live like a lady here.

**David**    Was it that bad?

**Diamond**    I just couldn't stand it any more. If I had an education, now, like these girls, it would have been fine.

**Claudette**    I wouldn't count on it.

**Diamond**    But as it was . . . I had to get out.

**David**    That's a shame.

**Diamond**    I don't feel bad about it. It was my life. And now this is my life. I don't regret a bit of it.

**David** (*takes a sip of his drink*)    I asked for banana, this is strawberry.

**Diamond**    Mikie, go and tell Sugar to change this.

**David**    Please, don't bother, strawberry's fine.

**Diamond**    That girl must have something on her mind make her forget things so. Look at me. If you let me I would talk all night.

**David**    We wouldn't mind, would we?

**Diamond**    You don't want to listen to me rambling on. I only came out here to try to move you people further down the beach. I'm worried about you all stuck up this side of the beach every evening.

**Leela**    It's more private down here.

**Diamond**    But you missing all the fun. Tell them what they missing, Mikie.

**Mikie**    Jerk pork, jerk chicken. Lobster.

**Diamond**    Cool drinks, swimming in the midnight sea.

**Mikie**    My friend Dougie blowing fire and dancing limbo under a flaming stick. He's very good. Teach himself at home outa book. Nearly burn up him grandmother.

**Diamond**    Get away with you. He think that funny.

**Mikie**    She only get a little burn on she hand, you can't even see it.

**Diamond**    Well, is up to you all what you do, but try to come down. I know sure you would enjoy yourself. See you later. (*She goes.*)

**David**    Diamond's one of those people you could listen to all day.

**Mikie**    If you let her she would talk all day, all night, all year. Diamond have a lot of stories.

**Claudette**    Did you see that? All the beautiful flowers and she was making paper ones.

**Mikie**    She use them as table decorations. She learn it at night school in England.

**Claudette**    I'm glad her time wasn't entirely wasted, then.

**Sugar** *enters, wearing a cardigan. She's embarrassed talking in front of the hotel guests.*

**Sugar**    Mikie, Mikie. I going barbecue now.

**Mikie**    See you later.

**Sugar**    You coming?

**Mikie**    I follow you later. Diamond want me to stay here a little.

**Sugar** *wants to say something, but with the others there she can't.*

**Sugar**    All right, see you later. (*She turns and goes.*)

**Mikie**    Sugar, wait one minute. Sugar. (*He goes after her.*)

*Pause.*

**Leela** (*fanning herself*)    You'd think it'd cool down in the evening.

**David**    I've found that the coolest time is early morning.

**Leela**    You want to strip off, don't you? But then you'd have no protection at all against the heat.

**David**    The other day – (*Nervous laughter.*) I'm embarrassed to say. But the other day I just rolled in the dew, wet my back, my torso, buried my face in the wet grass.

**Leela**    Yesterday it was so hot I got in the shower with my dress on and let it dry, sticking to me like paper and the dye running off down my legs like blood.

**David**    It's cooler in the early morning.

**Leela**    We'll miss it when we get back to England and it's raining. It is hot.

**Mikie** *enters.*

**Mikie**    English people always talk about the weather. You go anywhere in the island and find English people, that's what they talking about.

**Kate**    That's because it's the only thing that unites us. Even in the blazing sun every day, they're talking about the weather.

**Mikie** *picks a stick up from the ground. While he talks, he makes* **Kate** *and* **David** *stand and each take an end of the stick.*

**Mikie**    Limbo have a tradition, you know. When people dead, limbo mark the crossing from this world into the other world. The gates of heaven rolling down, people running across quick before the gates of heaven fall on them, then the space between heaven and earth getting smaller and smaller, people so desperate they limboing under the gates so that they can escape from this world.

**David**    What happened to those people who didn't make it?

**Claudette**    That's not the point of the story.

**Mikie** *limbos under the stick. The others – not* **Claudette** *– cheer.*

**Mikie** (*to* **Kate**)    Now you.

**Kate**    Me?

**Mikie**    Go on.

**Mikie** *takes end of stick.* **Kate** *tentatively limbos under stick. She does it.* **Mikie** *and* **David** *cheer. Then it's* **David**'s *turn. The stick goes lower and lower. They all take turns until it's too low and* **David** *falls over. Then they all stand dusting themselves off and laughing. The ice broken.*

*Scene between* **Claudette** *and* **Leela** *overlaps.* **Leela** *watches* **Mikie** *and the others fooling around, smiling.* **Claudette***'s not so pleased.*

**Claudette**    I'm going to that barbecue. Coming?

**Leela**    In a minute.

**Leela** *watches,* **Claudette** *won't.*

**Claudette**    I hate it when he plays the nigger minstrel.

**Leela**    He's just having a laugh, Claud.

**Claudette**    They can't enjoy themselves unless they've taken drugs or drink or got some black to entertain them.

**Leela**    You're jealous, you want him to yourself.

**Claudette**    I'm not that stupid. I'm not that stupid, Leel. Me and Mikie speak the same language. When he's kissing me under the stars and telling me he loves me, I know exactly what he means. I say yes darling, yes, and guide his hand up between my legs. It's a cattle market. You sell, I buy. All relationships are some sort of business transaction.

**Leela**    You weren't always this hard.

**Claudette**    If I'm a hard bitch it's because I've found that it's the only way to survive.

**Leela**    Nothing's black and white the way you say.

**Claudette**    Look at you, aren't they black and white for you? Wandering around the island barefoot like some nun who's just been visited by the Virgin Mary, pretending you can transcend pain through beauty. Mikie and his friends laugh at you. They call you the mad woman of the roadside. Nothing's black and white. What about you and Bentley?

**Leela**    I'm going to join in.

**Claudette**    Yes, making fools of ourselves always was a way of evading the issue. Don't expect me to join in, will you? See you at the barbecue. (*She goes.*)

*The limbo over, the others collapse into loungers, laughing.*

**Mikie**    You all staying here all night?

**Kate**    I fancy a quiet night on the beach. We've had a hectic day.

**David**    We drove right round the island.

**Kate**    Not quite round the island.

**Mikie**    You don't want to eat Diamond jerk pork? After I kill that pig with my own hands? Yes. I bring that pig up like it was my own. We was good friends. I used to tell it all my troubles.

**Kate**    Before you killed it? Poor pig.

**Leela**    I couldn't kill something I'd reared.

**Mikie**    Why? Is just a pig.

**Kate**    You see, that's the difference between men and women. A woman could never see it as just a pig.

**Leela**    Certainly not if it was a pig you'd told all your troubles to.

**David**    Pigs bleed a lot, don't they?

**Kate**    David.

**Mikie**    Yes, it have a lot of blood. I think that that pig did know when I come in with scraps for it that something was wrong. I didn't talk to it, just throw down the food and watch it eat. Then quiet quiet I get up behind it. You get up behind it, straddle it and hang on. It start to buck like bull then. So you got to hold on tighter. You holding on so tight, you can feel the pig, inside and out, churning about, you can feel fear churning around inside it, trying to throw you off. You have to keep away from it face because pig does like to bite. Pig ready to fight. It would kill you if it could. You holding on tight so that you can smell the pig smell on you stink, feel something beating between you like one animal.

Then you feel for the knife, but the knife slip off over him skin in the pig sweat, so you have to get a grip on youself, focus, then slip the knife in. You can feel the last of the life rumbling against you leg. (*Slight pause.*) It have a lot of blood. You soak up with blood.

**David**  You can almost smell the blood, can't you?

**Leela**  I feel sick.

**Mikie**  Why you feel sick?

**Leela**  I'm going to walk by the sea, get some sea air.

**David**  We'll come with you. Coming, Kate?

**Kate**  Not just yet.

**David**  We promised Diamond we'd go.

**Mikie**  No rush. Diamond barbecue go on all night.

**Kate**  You go. I'll catch up with you.

**Leela**  Coming, Mikie?

**Mikie**  Later. I better put these things away.

**Leela** *and* **David** *exit.* **Mikie** *and* **Kate** *are alone.* **Mikie** *smiles.*

**Kate**  Is your pig story true?

**Mikie**  It have to be true? You soak up with blood. All over you chest, you hands, it drying on you, sticky. But you don't want to wash youself off, you want to smell that blood on you, let it dry on you. You smell like a animal.

**Kate** *laughs.*

**Kate**  I've never met such a cynical people.

**Mikie**  Who cares as long as we do it with a smile?

**Kate**  I suppose that story makes the tourists swoon.

**Mikie**  Some of them even faint.

**Kate**    I feel a bit faint myself and I've heard it before, or at least something very similar.

**Mikie**    It's a true story.

**Kate**    Who were you telling it for?

**Mikie**    You still here.

**Kate**    I suppose I should be flattered.

**Mikie**    You telling me you not flattered?

**Kate**    I'm not a tourist, Mikie. I've heard that story before.

**Mikie**    So if l was to invite you to come out with me on my boat, to take in the ocean air . . .

**Kate**    I'd know exactly what you were talking about.

**Mikie**    You wouldn't come?

**Kate**    What is it that you boys who hang out on the beach want? Money? Another notch on your limbo stick?

**Mikie**    Maybe all those things and more.

**Kate**    You've probably got a bet on with your friends, haven't you?

**Mikie**    Now you flattering yourself.

**Kate**    I'm not one of these foreign women who lie on a beach all day lusting after local boys. You see it in their faces. Young women, there's something aged about them. Harpies ready to tear the flesh off any young man who comes near them. I'm no harpy.

**Mikie**    And I'm no beach boy. (*He kisses his teeth.*) You think you giving off some sort of sweet odour to mad a man? What make you think you special? You know how many woman like you down on that beach?

**Kate**    Plenty more fish washed up gasping on the shore, eh?

**Mikie**    Plenty more ripe mango fallen off the trees, yes. Maybe I shoulda tell you my snake story.

**Kate**    At least it sounds more original.

**Mikie**    We have a lot of snakes round here. In the hills. When the sun get too hot they slide down so that they can be cooled by the sea breeze. Sometimes you wake up in the morning and the beach black with snakes. Many people wake up in the middle a the night, find snake wrap round them like rope.

**Kate**    There aren't any snakes round here.

**Mikie**    How you know?

**Kate**    You're making it up.

**Mikie**    That's what you think.

**Kate** (*tremor in her voice*)    I don't believe you.

**Mikie** *hisses at her like a snake.*

**Mikie**    You scared a snake?

**Kate**    Always have been.

**Mikie**    Some people terrified a snakes. (*He pours **Kate** a glass of water.*)

**Kate**    Thanks. (*Drinks.*)

**Mikie**    So you scared a snakes. Everybody scared a something.

**Kate**    I'm sure there's not much that frightens you.

**Mikie**    I'm scared a many things.

**Kate**    Like what?

**Mikie**    If I tell you, you could use it against me. (*Slight pause.*) It's strange: a woman on her own in a foreign country.

**Kate**    It isn't strange to me.

**Mikie**    I think you're a brave woman.

**Kate**    Not brave. Stupid maybe.

**Mikie**    You must be lonely.

**Kate**    I don't want to talk about this.

**Claudette** *enters, watches.*

**Mikie**    I would miss my family, friends.

**Kate**    Well, I don't.

**Mikie**    Why don't you want to come out with me on my boat?

**Kate**    Because . . . I didn't say I didn't want to.

**Mikie**    So you coming?

**Kate**    Why not? It's a lovely night. Why not?

**Mikie**    I didn't think you would come out with me.

**Kate**    It has to be on my terms. I know what you are, Mikie, and I don't want any games.

**Mikie**    What you see is what you get.

**Claudette** *moves upstage.*

**Claudette**    The water's lovely. Of course, I've only got as far as dipping a toe in.

**Mikie** *and* **Kate** *are embarrassed.*

**Mikie**    Kate want to come out on the boat with me.

**Claudette**    You're going out on the boat?

**Mikie**    Yes.

**Claudette**    I thought Sugar was expecting you.

**Mikie**    Sugar will wait.

**Claudette**    What a good idea. Out on the boat. I hope it isn't too cold.

**Kate**     Why don't you come with us?

**Claudette**     Ask Mikie, I'm terrible on boats.

**Kate**     All right. See you later.

**Claudette**     Later.

**Mikie** *and* **Kate** *leave.* **Claudette** *sits, pours herself a drink.*

### Scene Four

**Claudette** *and* **Leela** *on the beach.* **Kate**, *asleep, close by.*
**Claudette** *gets up, chooses a tape and switches on cassette player,*
*pours herself another drink.*

**Leela**     Alcohol won't cool you down. This is the hottest
its been at night since we got here. There's usually a fresh
breeze off the sea.

**Claudette** *makes swaying movements to the music.*

**Leela**     So clammy. I'm sticking to myself. And that smell.
Can you smell it? The rawness of the sea and something
filthy behind it. Funny how it all seems so big and endless in
the daytime but at night closes in on itself.

**Claudette** *takes* **Leela***'s arm, pulls her up and dances with her.*
**Leela** *places her head on* **Claudette***'s shoulder, her eyes closed.*
**Claudette** *starts to dance faster.*

**Leela**     You're going too fast for the music. Claudette.
(*Giggles.*) Stop it, Claud. Stop it.

**Claudette** *swings her out. She collapses. They both laugh hard.*

**Claudette**     Your face.

**Leela**     Your face.

*They laugh.*

**Leela**     Sssssh. (*Points at* **Kate**.) Asleep.

**Claudette**    Asleep.

**Leela** *and* **Claudette**    Ssssssh!

**Claudette**    Poor love's shagged out.

**Leela**    She's had a rough night.

**Claudette**    It gets pretty rocky on that boat. You need a strong stomach.

**Leela**    And an even stronger back.

**Claudette**    Do you know where they went tonight?

**Leela**    No.

**Claudette**    He took her to a cave on the other side of the island. There's a rock pool in it that looks like dirty water during the day. At night it comes alive with all kinds of tropical fish darting about in it like sparks. It's called the Cave of Ghosts because at night the wind whistles through it like a dead man's whisper. It's so frightening you're glad to feel arms around you. (*Slight pause. Referring to* **Kate**.) Travel halfway across the world and they're still there acting like they own the place.

**Leela**    I didn't think it could get any hotter.

**Claudette** *pours herself another drink and plays with sticks or stones on the ground.*

**Leela**    Alcohol just makes it worse.

**Claudette**    Come halfway round the world –

**Claudette** *buries her head in her hands, weeping silently.* **Leela** *goes to her, puts her arm around her.*

**Claudette**    It's like there's no escape. You can't run away, it follows you. You can't be yourself because you've always got to be ready to defend yourself. I hate, Leel. I can't stop hating. I hate her. I hate her because she's never been my friend, because she thinks there are two different kinds of woman and that I'm the inferior kind, because she takes comfort in the fact that at least she's not bottom of the pile and delights in my oppression. Because she's constantly betrayed me.

*In frustration* **Claudette** *throws something at* **Kate** *who stirs. They watch her anxiously. She doesn't wake up.* **Claudette** *smiles.*

**Claudette**    Stupid. Why don't you shut me up? You should shut me up.

**Leela**    She's dead to the world.

**Claudette**    Dead meat. (*Referring to* **Kate**.) Reminds me of a little girl who used to live next door to us. She'd walk past you with her nose in the air, and if she did deign to play with you she'd have to be the one bossing everybody around. It makes me sick to think about the power she had over me. I'd have done anything she told me to. I envied her power. I used to pose in front of my mum's dressing-table with a yellow polo-neck on my head. I'd swish it around, practise flicking my hair back like she used to.

**Leela**    God. Why didn't anyone tell us we were all right?

**Claudette**    I soon grew out of it, though. One day me and my brother lay in wait. We gave her such a beating. (*Laughs.*) Beat her black.

**Leela** (*laughs*)    Beat her black.

**Claudette**    Its make-up's run. You'd think it'd take more care with its appearance, wouldn't you?

**Leela**    Doesn't seem to be bothered with things like that, does she?

**Claudette** *rummages around in her bag and takes out a lipstick. She goes to* **Kate** *and gently colours* **Kate***'s lips, quickly moving away every time* **Kate** *stirs.*

**Leela** (*laughing*)    Claudette. You smudged it.

**Claudette** (*laughs*)    My hand's shaking.

**Leela**    You've got the DT's. Give it to me, let me do it.

**Claudette** *hands* **Leela** *the lipstick.* **Leela** *draws a line across* **Kate***'s forehead.* **Claudette** *looks* **Kate** *over.*

**Claudette**    Great improvement, I must say, but the hair –

**Leela**    Mmmm. The hair.

**Claudette** *picks up scissors* **Diamond** *had been using earlier. She opens and closes them.*

**Claudette**    Snip snip.

**Leela** *watches* **Claudette***.*

**Claudette** (*approaches* **Kate**)    Snip snip. (*She tries to cut* **Kate***'s plait.*) The scissor's stuck.

**Leela**    Stop it, Claud. She'll wake up. Leave it.

**Claudette**    I can't. They're stuck, Leela.

**Leela** *gets up, takes over. She gently tugs at the plait and, with some difficulty, cuts through it. It falls away in her hands.*

**Leela** (*shakes it in* **Claudette***'s face*)    It's alive.

**Claudette**    Look at those dark roots. She's a fake.

**Leela**    I knew there was something phony about her.

**Claudette**    She slept right through it.

**Leela**    She's had a very tiring night.

**Claudette**    It looks much better short.

**Leela**    Did her a favour, then, didn't we?

**Claudette**    Did her a favour all right.

*The mood has changed.*

**Leela**    I haven't had such a laugh since . . . What shall I do with this?

**Claudette**    Keep it as a souvenir. Snip Snip.

*They try to laugh but can't.*

**Leela**  Snip.

**Claudette**  Snip.

**Leela**  We'd better clear up.

**Claudette**  No we won't. They pay people to do that. Bed.

**Leela** *(drops plait)*  Bed.

**Claudette** *and* **Leela** *exit.* **Kate** *stirs, then wakes up, rubbing her eyes as if unsure of where she is. She stands up, then bends down to put her shoes on. When she does so she notices the plait on the ground. She stands stock-still and then slowly backs away. She tries to cry out, but nothing comes. She stands stock-still.*

**Diamond** *and* **Sugar** *enter.*

**Diamond**  Don't tell me, you haven't gone to bed yet. You English girls. Bet you don't behave like this in your own country, but as soon as you land out here you go mad. It must be the sudden exposure to the sun or something. I don't know. All I do know is that I've got to clean up after you.

**Kate** *(barely whispers)*  Diamond. *(Calls out louder.)* Diamond.

**Diamond**  What is it?

**Kate**  Snake.

**Diamond**  What?

**Kate** *points at the plait.*

**Diamond**  My God. Don't move. Sugar.

**Diamond** *indicates the 'limbo' stick.* **Sugar** *picks it up and passes it to* **Diamond**. **Kate** *stands stock-still, trying to control her nerves.* **Diamond** *prods the 'snake'; it doesn't move. She prods again, then straightens up, reaches down and picks it up.*

**Diamond**  I knew it could never be real. That would be the first time in all the time I live here –

**Sugar** *laughs.* **Kate** *collapses into a sun lounger, all fear and shock being released. She starts to sob.*

**Diamond**   I wonder what they would call a snake like this.

**Diamond** *puts the 'snake' in* **Kate***'s face.* **Kate** *feels her cropped head. As realisation dawns, she cries out.*

**Diamond**   Who would do a thing like this? Mikie! Poor girl. Somebody must see something. Mikie!

**David** *and* **Mikie** *enter.*

**David**   What's going on? Kate?

**Diamond**   She have a little shock, that's all. She thought she saw a snake.

**David**   Snake?

**Diamond**   This was her snake. (*Holds up her plait.*) Somebody from round here playing a trick while she slept.

*On seeing the plait,* **Sugar** *bursts into a fit of giggles.*

**David**   Some trick. (*Puts his arm around* **Kate**.) Are you all right? (*Seeing* **Kate***'s face.*) God. (*Takes tissue out of his pocket, wipes* **Kate***'s face.*) What the fuck's been happening?

**Diamond**   I sorry this have to happen. These people really too jealous. Why can't they just accept the way things are? Her hair will grow again. (*To* **Mikie**.) Go and get her some hot, sweet tea.

**David**   Don't bother. (*Lifting* **Kate** *up.*) Come on, let's get you inside.

**Diamond**   You want me to bring you anything?

**David**   I hope you're going to do something about this.

**Diamond**   What can I do?

**David**   Anything. Call the police.

**Diamond**   Written up on every door in the hotel is a sign which says that the management accept no liability for loss or damage to personal items. I think hair can count as a personal item. Something sweet you, Sugar?

**Sugar**   The way you swinging that rat tail. It look so funny, Miss Diamond.

**Diamond**   You think this funny, Sugar?

**Sugar**   Stop it, Miss Diamond, you going kill me.

**Diamond**   Anybody would think is you do it.

**David**   That wouldn't surprise me.

**Diamond** (*to* **David**)   Go inside. We'll bring you the tea.

**David**   I don't care how many disclaimers you put up on hotel doors. This amounts to assault. Either you do something about this or we get in touch with the British Embassy and it's trouble for you.

**Diamond**   No need for all that. We already have enough excitement round here for one day. (*Turning to* **Sugar**.) Get your things and go, Sugar. I don't need people like you working for me.

**Mikie**   Sugar never do anything. She have alibi. She was with me all night.

**Sugar**   You think I do that, Miss Diamond?

**Diamond**   Don't argue with me, Sugar.

**Mikie**   Miss Diamond, Sugar never . . .

**Diamond**   You want to lose your job as well?

**Mikie**   No, Miss Diamond.

**Diamond**   Well then. Round here we all live together good, have a good time. I don't need people like you to spoil things. We all live good together round here.

**Scene Five**

*Very late, the same day. The beach.* **Mikie** *and* **David** *are playing cards and drinking beer.*

**David**    They could have done anything to her. She was asleep.

**Mikie**    All I know is, it wasn't Sugar. Sugar wouldn't do a thing like that.

**David**    I suppose Diamond was a bit hasty sacking her like that. I can't believe she did it either. That's the awful thing, though, Mikie – not knowing who it was. I don't like to think that it was someone from the hotel, but it's even worse to think that it was someone from outside. You don't have any idea who might have done it?

**Mikie**    Nope.

**David**    Would you tell me if you had? Certainly in England black people don't tell white people anything. Even your best friend won't tell you his secrets. Why?

**Mikie** *deals the cards.*

**David**    She'll be upset, of course, but she won't go home. Too stubborn.

**Mikie**    Mmmmm.

**David**    Diamond's right, it'll grow again. But how can people do this to each other? It's not every day you wake up to find your hair's been chopped off.

**Mikie** *laughs.*

**David**    Are you laughing at me, Mikie?

**Mikie** *pulls himself together.*

**David**    What are you laughing at?

**Mikie**    Snake.

**David**   I suppose that it could seem quite funny, though I must say it doesn't make me laugh.

**Mikie** *hisses like a snake, then laughs.*

**David** (*puts his cards down*)    Rummy. Another game?

**Mikie** (*getting up*)    Time for bed.

**David**   Go on. Another game. I can't sleep, Mikie. I don't feel like sleeping. Go on, stay. You haven't even finished your drink. Finish your drink. (*He deals the cards.*) You wonder what they were thinking while they were doing it. Then you start to wonder what's wrong with these people. Is it some sort of grudge, Mikie? You tell me. You're a man of the world, or should I say a man of the island. Ever been abroad, Mikie?

**Mikie** *shakes his head.*

**David**   Don't you want to?

**Mikie**   I happy here. One day I might go America.

**David**   You should keep in touch. You're welcome to stay if you find yourself in our part of the world. I doubt if I'll be coming back here. Holiday's fucked anyway. (*Puts his cards down on the table.*) I can't concentrate.

**Mikie**   See you in the morning.

**David**   Don't go, Mikie man. I don't know anyone else here. You're the only one I know. (*Shuffles cards.*) Another game. Something else. I know. Come on. (*Puts his arm on the table.*) See if I can beat you. Come on, you're a strong guy.

**Mikie**   Go to bed, man. You can't stay up all night.

**David**   I told you, I can't sleep. Come on, put your arm on the table.

**Mikie** *reluctantly sits and puts his arm on the table. They grip hands.* **David** *wins.*

**David**    Come on, Mikie man, you weren't even trying.
Come on. (*Takes money out of his pocket, throws it on the table.*)
Winner takes all.

*They wrestle again.* **David** *wins.*

**David**    What's the matter? Isn't that enough incentive for
you? That's a surprise. Everybody else here has been quick
enough to take our money from us. You've got to tip them
for every blasted little thing they do for you. You drop
something on the floor and someone picks it up for you,
they stand there holding out their hands for you to give
them something. I mean, do I look like the world bank?
(*Puts some more money on the table.*) That enough? That better?
That should get your blood pulsing, shouldn't it. Come on.

*They wrestle.* **David** *wins.*

**David**    Looks like I've won all my own money back.

*Before* **David** *can pick up his winnings,* **Mikie** *takes some notes out
of his pocket and throws them on the table. He takes* **David**'s *hand.
They wrestle.* **Mikie** *is bending* **David**'s *hand back.*

**Mikie**    You see, now, at this time a night, I not on duty. You
see, now, I don't have to smile. You see, now, I don't have
to pretend that you have something special about you. You
see, what happen out here in the daytime, it's a game, just a
game, understand?

**David** *doesn't reply.*

**Mikie**    Understand?

**David** *nods.* **Mikie** *bends* **David**'s *arm down on to the table and
wins the game.*

**Scene Six**

*Very early morning.* **Sugar** *sits, hugging her knees, staring out to sea.* **Leela** *enters barefoot, her dress torn, mud on her feet.*

**Leela**   Sugar.

**Sugar** *looks up and, seeing* **Leela**, *looks away.*

**Leela**   You can't sleep either. (*No answer.*) My head . . . The sea looks very beautiful. What a night.

*Pause.*

**Sugar**   You have mud all over you foot.

**Leela**   I've been walking.

**Sugar**   At this time a night? Boy, unno tourist . . .

**Leela**   I've walked round the whole island. Virtually.

**Sugar**   You better wash that off in the sea. (*Slight pause.*) Why you don't wear shoes?

**Leela**   It's not always practical, is it, to wear shoes.

**Sugar**   I always wear shoes.

*Pause.*

**Leela**   She'll give you your job back. I'll talk to her, shall I?

**Sugar**   I don't want her filthy job. I tired a people treating me like shit. I tired a fucking tourist.

**Leela**   It won't be easy finding another job.

**Sugar**   I know how to get by.

**Leela**   I feel responsible.

**Sugar**   How could you be responsible? (*Slight pause.*) Diamond must think I have feelings for these people make me want to do a thing like that. I don't feel no way about those people. They coulda dead for all I care.

**Leela**   I know you didn't do it, Sugar.

**Sugar**    How you know?

**Leela** (*after a short pause*)    I did it. (*Slight pause.*) Me and my friend, we had too much to drink . . . things got a bit out of hand . . .

**Sugar** (*laughing*)    You? That too sweet boy. I don't understand you people at all. Mikie right. He say you all sick, say unno come out here because you broken people. (*Laughs.*) Too sweet boy. What you want from me? You come here looking for . . . You tell me what you looking for. Unno tourist think you belong here. But you come out and you don't know where to put youself: one minute you talking sisterhood, the next minute you treating us like dirt. You just the same as all the other tourists them.

**Leela**    Where else can we go?

**Sugar**    I ain't got nothing for you. I can't give you what you looking for because I ain't got it meself. What happen to unno make you so broken?

**Leela** (*as she speaks she becomes more emotional and starts to tremble through this speech*)    Broken, yes. Invisible people. We look all right on the outside, but take our clothes off and you'll find nothing underneath, just thin air. That's what happens to people who have no language – they disappear. Only your feelings tell you that you exist, so you cling on to them even if they're not nice. And they're not nice. I'm angry, Sugar. I can't stop hating. I hate the world that tries to stifle me. I'm angry with myself for not being strong enough to hit out at it. I want revenge. I want to lash out . . .

**Leela**'s speech becomes a garble as she struggles to get the words out, her body trembling out of her control. She's breathing very quickly. She starts to mutter under her breath. **Sugar** stands and watches, not quite sure what to do. **Leela**'s muttering becomes louder and she starts to talk in tongues. **Sugar** is bewildered at first, then frightened as **Leela** releases all the rage and anger that she has repressed for so long.

*Soon the outburst subsides.* **Sugar** *gets behind the exhausted*
**Leela** *and holds her by the waist.* **Leela** *is still in a trance, but her
utterances have subsided into a muttering again. Her body is quite
limp, supported by* **Sugar**, *who rocks her from side to side like a baby.*

**Sugar**   That's right, you relax, you cool down. You rest now.
You safe. Safe now. Sssssssh. Sssssssh. Rest. Rest.

### Scene Seven

*On the beach.* **Leela** *and* **Claudette** *at a table drinking,* **Kate** *on
stage left at a table on her own, wearing sunglasses.*

**Claudette**   Dougie says everyone'll be there. His little
brother's playing. Why don't you come with me?

**Leela**   I can't stand football.

**Claudette**   I suppose you'll be going on another of your
walks?

**Leela**   Maybe.

**Claudette**   He's taking me out on his friend's boat.

**Leela**   Oh yes?

**Claudette** (*defensive*)   Our last night, Leel.

**Leela**   What time's he picking you up?

**Claudette**   Seven. I'd better get ready. Will you be all right
on your own?

**Leela**   'Course I will.

**Claudette**   You can always come with us. He asked me if
you wanted to come.

**Leela**   Did he?

**Claudette**   I said you probably wouldn't want to.

**Leela**   It's nearly seven now.

**Claudette**    Will you be all right on your own?

**Leela**    Of course I will.

**Claudette**    Well, you know where to find me.

**Leela**    Have fun.

**Claudette** *goes.* **Kate** *takes off her sunglasses, goes over to* **Leela**'s *table.*

**Kate**    Can I have some of your water?

**Leela**    Help yourself.

**Kate**    The new girl keeps getting things wrong. I ask her for Coca-Cola and she brings rum punch. (*Slight pause.*) It's getting cooler.

**Leela**    It's always cool in the evening. It's the daytime I find unbearable.

**Kate**    My brother couldn't stand the heat.

**Leela**    It is hot.

**Kate**    Not to mention the mosquito bites, though you haven't been bitten.

**Leela**    Time for my walk.

**Kate**    You're going then?

**Leela**    I always walk around this time.

**Kate**    I know some good walks. Some are so scary you can't go on your own. Rickety little pathways. Look down, you'd have a heart attack. I could show you. Let me put my shoes on.

**Leela**    Actually . . .

**Kate**    You don't want to?

**Leela**    Not right now. Next time.

**Kate**    It's a deal, next time you're here I'll show you.

**Leela**   Sounds like my kind of walk. I've got used to walking here. I'm not so frightened of the pitfalls now. It's the way you displace the weight of your body, isn't it? You've got to be in touch with your body. It soon gets used to sudden challenges. That sounds like my kind of walk.

**Kate**   The next time you're here then.

**Leela**   It's a deal.

Roy Williams

# Sing Yer Heart Out for the Lads

**Roy Williams** worked as an actor before turning to writing full-time in 1990. He graduated from Rose Bruford in 1995 with a first class BA Hons degree in Writing and participated in the 1997 Carlton Television screenwriter's course. *The No Boys Cricket Club* (Theatre Royal, Stratford East, 1996) won him nominations for the TAPS Writer of the Year Award 1996 and for New Writer of the Year Award 1996 by the Writers' Guild of Great Britain. He was the first recipient of the Alfred Fagon Award 1997 for *Starstruck* (Tricycle Theatre, London, 1998), which also won the 31st John Whiting Award and the EMMA Award 1999. *Lift Off* (Royal Court Theatre Upstairs, 1999) was the joint winner of the George Devine Award 2000. His other plays include: *Night and Day* (Theatre Venture, 1996); *Josie's Boys* (Red Ladder Theatre Co., 1996); *Souls* (Theatre Centre, 1999); *Local Boy* (Hampstead Theatre, 2000); *The Gift* (Birmingham Rep/Tricycle Theatre, 2000); *Clubland* (Royal Court, 2001) which won the *Evening Standard* Charles Wintour Award for the Most Promising Playwright; *Fallout* (Royal Court Theatre, 2003) which was made for television by Company Pictures/Channel 4; *Sing Yer Heart Out for the Lads* (National Theatre, 2002, 2004); *Little Sweet Thing* (New Wolsey, Ipswich/Nottingham Playhouse/ Birmingham Rep, 2005); *Slow Time* (National Theatre Education Department tour, 2005); *Days of Significance* (Swan Theatre, Stratford-upon-Avon, 2007); *Absolute Beginners* (Lyric Theatre, Hammersmith, 2007); *Joe Guy* (Tiata Fahodzi/ Soho Theatre, 2007); *Baby Girl* (National Theatre, 2007); *Out of the Fog* (Almeida Theatre, 2007); *There's Only One Wayne Matthews* (Polka Theatre, 2007); *Category B* (part of the Tricycle Theatre's Not Black and White season, 2009); *Sucker Punch* (Royal Court Theatre, 2010); and he contributed to *A Chain Play* (Almeida Theatre, 2007). His screenplays include *Offside*, winner of a BAFTA for Best Schools Drama 2002. His radio plays include *Tell Tale*; *Homeboys*; *Westway*, which was broadcast as part of Radio 4 First Bite Young Writers' Festival; *To Sir with Love*; and *A Choice of Straws* (adapted from E.R. Braithwaite's novel for BBC Radio 4, 2009). He also wrote *Babyfather* for BBC television.

*Sing Yer Heart Out for the Lads* was first presented in the Loft auditorium of the National Theatre, London, on 2 May 2002. The cast was as follows:

| | |
|---|---|
| **Gina** | Jane Hazlegrove |
| **Jimmy, her father** | Gawn Grainger |
| **Glen, her son** | Billy Seymour |
| **Mark** | Kolade Agboke |
| **Duane** | Oladapo Tijani |
| **Bad T** | Marvyn Johnson |
| **Lawrie** | John Marquez |
| **Becks** | Callum Dixon |
| **Lee, Lawrie's brother** | Alex Walkinshaw |
| **Phil** | Gary Oliver |
| **Alan** | Paul Copley |
| **Jason** | Sid Mitchell |
| **Barry, Mark's brother** | Freddie Annobil-Dodoo |
| **Sharon** | Kay Bridgman |

*Director*   Simon Usher
*Designer*   Anthony Lamble
*Lighting Designer*   Steve Barnett
*Sound Designer*   Rich Walsh
*Company Voice Work*   Patsy Rodenburg & Kate Godfrey

## Act One

*Saturday, 7 October 2000, the King George Public House, south-west London. This section of the bar area is decorated with flags of St George. Windows, walls tables, etc. A huge TV screen is draped in the corner.* **Jimmy** *is assembling rows of stools and chairs in front of the TV screen.* **Gina**, *his daughter, is writing names on stickers with a felt-tip pen and sellotaping them on the stools, one by one.*

**Gina**    There had better not be any trouble.

**Jimmy**    Lee will be here.

**Gina**    Lee?

**Jimmy**    He'll sort 'em out.

**Gina**    Lee is juss as bad as they are.

**Jimmy**    He's a copper.

**Gina**    Yer point being?

**Jimmy**    He's a copper, Gina, nuff said.

**Gina**    Get a few pints down him, you'll see. I should know.

*She looks at her dad who has the remote for the telly.*

You awright over there, Dad?

**Jimmy**    Can't get this fuckin thing to work.

**Gina**    Well, I don't want to hear that, do I?

**Jimmy** (*looks at screen*)    Fucking static.

**Gina**    Leave it to me. (*Takes the remote.*) Wat you done?

**Jimmy**    Nuttin, I was . . .

**Gina**    Pissin about.

**Jimmy**    Oi!

**Gina**    *presses the button on the remote. The screen becomes all blue.*

**Jimmy**    Piece of shit.

**Gina**    You finish with the names, I'll do this.

**Jimmy**    You put Lawrie at the front?

**Gina**    Yeah. On second thoughts, stick him near the back. He'll only piss about. (*To TV.*) Come on, come on!

**Jimmy**    Ain't workin.

**Gina**    The satellite signal ain't comin through. Dad, do me a favour, check that the cable for the dish is plugged in.

**Jimmy**    Have already.

**Gina**    What about the dish outside?

**Jimmy**    Done that.

**Gina**    Then what is its fucking problem? Where's the instruction manual?

**Jimmy**    Behind the bar.

**Gina**    Well, giss it. (**Jimmy** *hands over the manual.*) If I said it once, I've said it a hundred times.

**Jimmy**    Oh don't start.

**Gina**    Becks is nuttin but a thievin little git. You should know better.

**Jimmy**    It was a steal.

**Gina**    Here we go. Come on, baby, come on, come on . . . (*A picture comes on.*) Yes!

**Jimmy**    It'll be typical if they called the match off. It's pissing down. We ain't gonna win.

**Gina**    That's patriotic.

**Jimmy**    Kevin Keegan is a fucking muppet. Have you seen his line-up? (*Holds up paper.*) Tosser!

**Gina**    A bit of faith, Dad.

**Jimmy**    Bollocks. He oughta fuck off back to Fulham, be Al Fayed's bleeding lapdog! Never mind manage the national team. A bit of faith, my arse!

**Gina**    What's wrong?

**Jimmy**    Southgate. Keegan has given him the midfield holding position. The midfield holding position, I have trouble even saying it. Look, Southgate is a defender, bloody good one, no argument, but a good passer of the ball, he ain't! I mean Keegan's got Dennis Wise in the frame, why didn't he pick him? Use him? If that ain't torture for the lad, to be picked for the squad, but only to be left on the touchline, whilst some muppet makes a right bollock of the position he's blinding at. I ask you, where's the sense?

**Gina**    Southgate might surprise everyone.

**Jimmy**    Yeah, he'll be more shittier than I thought.

**Gina**    You won't be watchin the match then. You can clear out the backyard at last.

**Jimmy**    Now, I didn't say I weren't gonna watch it. I'm juss stating my opinion, thass all.

**Gina**    Who's up front?

**Jimmy**    Owen and Cole. Andy fucking Cole. Our last game at Wembley an'all. Fucking Keegan.

**Gina**    Does Andy Gray's face look blue to you?

**Jimmy**    Very.

**Gina**    I can't work out anything on this.

**Jimmy**    Let one of the boys do it. Look at his poxy formation.

**Gina**    Dad!

**Jimmy**    3–5–2! Poxy, continental shit!

**Gina**    Let me guess, 4–4–2?

**Jimmy**   Too right, 4–4–2. It's the English way of playing: go with summin the lads are comfortable with, fer crying out loud. 3–5–2!

**Gina**   Dad, yer boring me, shut up! This screen is giving me a headache.

**Jimmy**   Leave it. They'll be here soon.

**Gina**   He had better behave himself.

**Jimmy**   Who?

**Gina**   Lawrie.

*Loud rap music coming from upstairs.*

I don't believe him. (*Shouts.*) Glen! Turn it down. Glen! I tell you, I have had it with that bloody kid, he don't answer me no more!

**Jimmy**   I don't suppose that arsehole of a dad of his has bin to see him.

**Gina**   You taking the piss? Glen, I swear to fucking Christ!

**Jimmy**   Let me go.

**Gina**   What do you think I'm going to do?

**Jimmy**   I've seen the way you two have been at it lately.

**Gina**   Drag his arse down here.

**Jimmy** *goes upstairs to get* **Glen**. **Gina** *lights up a cigarette.* **Jimmy** *returns with* **Glen***, fourteen and with an attitude.*

**Glen**   Yeah, wat?

**Gina**   You deaf ?

**Glen**   No.

**Gina**   Bloody should be, shit you play.

**Glen**   Ain't shit.

**Jimmy**   I can't even understand half the things they're saying.

**Glen**   Ca you ain't wid it guy.

**Gina**   English, Glen, we speak English in here.

**Glen** *sucks his teeth.*

**Gina**   Excuse me, what was that?

**Jimmy**   Just tell me what you get from it.

**Glen**   Loads.

**Gina**   Yeah, like learning to call a woman a bitch.

**Jimmy**   You want to listen to music, Glen, the Kinks, Pink Floyd, the Who!

**Glen**   Who?

**Jimmy**   You taking the mick?

**Glen**   Old man.

**Jimmy**   Oi!

**Gina**   He ain't bin rude, Dad, he ends every sentence on 'man'. And you know why? Because he's been hanging round with them black kids from the estate, when I specifically told him not to.

**Glen**   I don't remember that.

**Gina**   Do not take the piss, Glen.

**Glen**   Dem boys are awright, Mum.

**Gina**   No they are not.

**Jimmy**   Yer mum's right, son, I've seen them, they'll get you in bother.

**Gina**   They have already. I had to go down his school again, him and his black mates were picking on sum little Asian kid.

**Jimmy**    What, him? You sure?

**Gina**    One more strike and he's out.

**Glen**    I weren't picking on him.

**Gina**    Not what the teacher said.

**Jimmy** *clips him on the head*.

**Glen**    Oi! Move, man!

**Jimmy**    Little kid thinks he's a hard man now eh? Picking on sum little Asian kid.

**Glen**    Mum?

**Gina**    Mum what?

**Glen**    Tell him.

**Gina**    You won't always have yer black mates backing you up, you know; one day, those Asian kids are gonna fight back. Prince Naseem was a little Asian kid once, look at him now.

**Jimmy**    Come on, take yer grandad on, if you think yer hard enuff.

**Glen**    Will you move from me please.

**Gina**    All right, Dad.

**Jimmy**    I hardly touched him.

**Gina**    It's enuff.

**Jimmy**    Little girl.

**Gina**    No more trouble, you hearing me?

**Glen** (*sees the fag in the ashtray*)    Was that you? Thought you quit.

**Gina**    I am addressing my addiction.

**Glen**    See her, Grandad, she fuckin goes on about me . . .

**Gina**   Oi, oi, less of the fuckin! If I want to have a smoke, I will have a smoke, so shut yer noise. The best thing you can do with temptation, is give in to it – Oscar Wilde.

**Glen**   Who dat, yer new boyfriend?

**Gina**   I don't even want to think about what they are not teaching you at school, I really don't. This whole area is going nowhere.

**Glen***'s mobile phone rings.*

**Glen**   Who dis? Awright, man, wass up? You joke! Is it! Nuh, man, wat? Yeah, I'm up fer it dread.

**Gina** *takes the phone off him.*

**Glen**   Giss it.

**Gina** *(to phone)*    Hello, this is Glen's mother speaking –

**Glen**   Mum, no.

**Gina**   I am afraid he cannot come to the phone, as he is in an awful lot of trouble, and will not be coming out, for the next twenty-five years, feel free to call back then. *(Hangs up.)*

**Glen**   Yer chat is dry.

**Jimmy**   What was that he was saying?

**Gina**   'Nuh, man!'

**Jimmy**   'Yeah, I'm up fer it dread!' *(Laughs.)*

**Glen**   You don't hang up on T like that.

**Gina**   Who?

**Glen**   T. Bad T.

**Gina**   Is that his name?

**Glen**   His street name.

**Gina**   Wass yer street name?

**Glen**   Ain't got one yet.

**Gina**   Ah! (*Pats his cheek.*)

**Glen**   I won't get it now, yer shamin me.

**Jimmy**   Yer little whiner.

**Glen**   I'm sorry.

**Gina**   Like you mean it!

**Glen**   SORRY!

**Gina**   Good.

*She pops her head round the other bar.*

Dad, go give Kelly a hand.

**Jimmy**   Ware you going?

**Gina**   Cellars.

**Jimmy**   Oi, Glenny boy.

**Glen**   Glen!

**Jimmy**   Don't get arsey with me, you little shit. Put these names on these seats. Some of the boys have reserved seats for the game.

**Glen**   Awright if I have a drink?

**Jimmy**   Yeah of course it is, don't be silly. (**Glen** *strolls to the bar.*) Get out of it! He only believed me. And don't even think about sneaking one away, cos I'll know.

**Glen**   Cool.

**Jimmy** *leaves.* **Glen** *pours himself a shot of whisky.* **Jimmy** *creeps up from behind, clips him round the ear, and takes the glass from him.*

**Jimmy**   Moby. (*Exits.*)

**Glen** *does as he is told, and puts down the stickers.* **Mark** (*black, early thirties*) *comes in.*

**Glen**   Awright, man?

**Mark**   Yeah.

**Glen**   Wass up?

**Mark**   What?

**Glen**   Nuttin.

**Mark**   Where's yer mum?

**Glen**   Cellar. Who are you?

**Mark**   Mark.

**Glen**   Mark who?

**Mark**   Juss Mark.

**Glen**   Awright man, easy guy!

*His phone rings again.*

(*Answers.*) Who dis? Awright, man. It was my mum weren't it. She took it off me, wat was I supposed to do, lick her down or summin? Yeah, so wass up? Wat now? Yeah, well why didn't you, awright come in.

*Two young black kids come in,* **Bad T** *and* **Duane**. *They are the same age as* **Glen**.

**Duane**   Yes, Glen!

**Glen**   Awright, man? T?

**Bad T**   Ware de booze, boy?

**Glen**   You mad?

**Bad T**   Did yu juss call me mad?

**Glen**   No.

**Bad T**   Did the boy juss call me mad, Duane?

**Duane**   Musta done! Cos I heard it.

**Bad T**   Lesson number one, don't ever call T mad, yeah.

**Glen**   Awright, I'm sorry.

**Bad T**   S'right. So pass the booze.

**Glen**   I can't, man.

**Bad T**   Did the boy jus say he can't, Duane?

**Duane**   Musta done, T, cos I heard it.

**Bad T**   Lesson number two, don't ever say you can't, yeah?

**Glen**   Yeah.

**Bad T**   Yeah wat?

**Glen**   Yeah watever, I'm sorry.

**Bad T**   Better.

**Duane**   The boy learnin, T. Awright, Mark?

**Bad T**   Come on, boy, booze! I want a Jack D and Coke.

**Glen**   My mum will go mad.

**Bad T**   Mad bitch. 'bout she chat to me like that on the phone.

**Duane** (*finds a picture of* **Gina** *behind the bar*) Rah, is that her?

**Glen**   Yeah, she won, landlady of the year or summin.

**Bad T**   How much you have in this till?

**Glen**   T, don't man.

**Bad T**   Did the boy juss say don't T, Duane?

**Duane** (*laughing*)   Musta done, cos I heard it.

**Bad T**   Lesson number three, never say T don't man, yeah? Yeah? Come on?

**Glen**   Sorry.

**Bad T**   Good. I was joking anyway yer fool, chill.

**Duane**   Check his mum, man.

**Bad T**   Rah!

**Duane**    Ennit!

**Bad T**    This yer mum, boy? Fer trut?

**Glen**    Yeah.

**Bad T**    Rah!

**Duane**    Definitely.

**Bad T**    Definitely would!

**Duane**    Definitely!

**Bad T**    She like it on top, Glen?

**Glen**    Top of wat?

**Duane** *roars with laughter*.

**Glen**    Wat?

**Bad T**    She turn tricks, Glen? Yer mudda turn tricks? You know wat I mean by tricks don't yer?

**Glen**    Yeah.

**Bad T**    So, does yer mudda turn tricks?

**Glen**    Yeah, you mean like card tricks right?

**Duane** *and* **T** *carry on howling*.

**Glen**    Wat you saying about my mum, T?

**Bad T**    Nuttin, forget it, Glen, yer awright.

**Duane** (*looks at picture of* **Gina** *again*)    Hmmm, oh yes!

**Bad T**    Definitely!

**Glen**    Careful, man.

*The boys glare at him.*

My mum's in the cellar.

**Bad T**    Did the boy juss tell us to be careful?

**Duane**    Musta done, cos I . . .

**Bad T**    Lesson number four, never . . .

**Glen**    . . . Yeah, I'm sorry.

**Bad T**    You gotta learn to relax, bredren.

**Duane**    Ennit.

**Bad T**    So wat you say, Mark?

**Mark**    Nuttin. Yer the one doing all the talkin.

**Duane**    So wass up, Mark, how come you don't come round no more?

**Mark**    Ask yer mum.

**Bad T**    Wass this?

**Duane**    Went out wid my mum ennit.

**Bad T**    Yer mum's had nuff men.

**Mark**    You keeping out of trouble, Tyrone?

**Bad T**    T! Bad T!

**Mark**    Listen, I used to watch yer mudda change yer nappy, so don't even bother coming to me wid this Bad T business.

**Bad T** (*eyes* **Glen** *and* **Duane** *laughing*)    Wat you laughin at?

**Duane**    Nuttin, T.

**Glen**    Sorry, T.

**Duane**    You watchin the game today, T?

**Bad T**    I ain't watchin no rubbish English match. They lose at everyting.

*Someone's phone goes off. All the boys reach for their pockets. But it is* **Mark***'s that is ringing.*

**Mark**    Sorry, boys. (*Answers.*) Hi, Karen, wass up? Nuh, he ain't here yet. I don't know, hold up a minute. (*Walks over to a discreet part of the bar.*) Yeah, go on.

**Bad T**    Rah, Glen, so thass yer phone?

**Glen**    Smart ennit?

**Duane**    Smarter than yours, T.

**Bad T**    Let me see. (*Examines it.*) It's light, wass the reception like?

**Glen**    Sharp.

**Bad T**    You get text yeah?

**Glen**    It's got everything. I can download e-mail, go on Internet and that. Free voicemail.

**Duane** Nice, Glen.

**Glen**    I know.

**Mark** (*to phone*)    No, I'm stayin here till he comes. I'll come back wid him. How am I suppose to know that, I juss got here.

**Bad T**    It's so light.

**Mark**    Cos yer good wid him.

**Bad T**    Fits into my pocket nice.

**Mark**    Karen, please don't start, I beg you. I'll see you later.

**Bad T**    Don't mess up the lining or nuttin.

**Glen**    Told yer.

**Bad T**    Sell it to me.

**Glen** *laughs.*

**Bad T**    Sell it.

**Glen**    Nuh, man.

**Bad T**    Come on.

**Glen**    I don't want to sell it.

**Bad T**    Fifteen.

**Glen**    No.

**Bad T**    Twenty.

**Duane**    For that? It's worth twice that . . .

**Bad T**    You see me talking to you, Duane?

**Glen**    I don't want to sell it, T.

**Bad T**    Wat you gonna do wid a phone like this?

**Glen**    Ring people and that.

**Duane**    Give the boy back his phone, man.

**Bad T**    Yeah, but it's too nice fer a white boy like him to have, best let me have it, someone who appreciates it. Look, the fool ain't even got no numbers in his phone book.

**Glen**    I only bought it the other day.

**Bad T**    Glen, has anyone, anyone at all, rang you on the phone, besides me?

**Glen**    No.

**Bad T**    Anyone ask fer yer number?

**Glen**    No.

**Bad T**    So why you reach for it, when Mark's phone rang then?

**Glen**    I dunno, I juss thought . . .

**Bad T**    You thought wat, Glen?

**Glen**    I dunno, juss thought.

**Bad T**    I'm surprised yer brain can even do that, you thick cunt!

**Duane**    T man!

**Bad T**    So much you sellin it to me, Glen?

**Glen**    Nuttin.

**Bad T**    Nuttin, you giving it to me fer nuttin, cheers.

**Glen**    Hold up.

**Bad T**  Nice.

**Glen**    I don't wanna sell it.

**Bad T**    Twelve quid.

**Glen**    You said twenty a minute ago.

**Bad T**    Every time you say no, the price goes down. You got a nice jacket too.

**Duane**    T?

**Bad T**    Glen?

**Glen**    I ain't sellin it.

**Bad T**    Nine.

**Glen**    I can't.

**Bad T**    Eight.

**Glen**    I saved fer months to get it.

**Bad T**    Six. Keep whining, Glen. You crying now?

**Glen**    No.

**Bad T**    Fucking boy's crying, man.

**Glen**    I ain't.

**Bad T**    White boy love to cry, ennit, Duane?

**Mark**    Give the boy back his phone.

**Bad T**    Excuse me?

**Mark**    No, excuse you, give the boy back his phone Tyrone.

**Bad T**    The name's T, right.

**Mark**    Fuck wat yer name is, give the boy back his phone.

**Bad T**    Here. (*Hands it back*.) Tek yer fuckin phone. (*To* **Duane**.) And you defendin him.

**Duane**    All I said was . . .

**Bad T**   Ca you love the white, man. You want suck him off, ennit? (*To* **Glen**.) It was a joke, Glen, I was jokin wid you. You shouldn't carry on so, someone might juss come and tief up yer life, never mind yer mobile phone.

**Gina** *comes back to find* **Bad T** *and* **Duane** *behind her bar.*

**Gina**   Well, make yerself at home, why don't yer? And you are?

**Glen**   Duane and T.

**Gina**   Oh, so yer Bad T?

**Bad T**   I'm big too. (*He and* **Duane** *laugh.*)

**Gina**   So wat are Duane, and Big T, doing behind my bar? Come on, move, out!

**Bad T**   You mind?

**Gina**   No.

**Bad T**   Don't touch wat you can't afford.

**Gina**   Is that right?

**Bad T**   Ennit.

**Gina**   I will do more than touch, little boy, if you don't shift, never mind ennit.

**Duane** *and* **T** *ogle over her again.*

**Duane**   Oh yeah.

**Bad T**   Definitely.

**Gina**   You wish.

**Bad T**   When you lass have black in you?

**Mark**   Hey!

**Gina**   Is that supposed to make me quiver?

**Mark**   Tek yer friend and go home, Tyrone.

**Bad T**   You my dad?

**Mark**   No, but I can call him. Do you want him chasin you round the estate wid his leather belt again?

**Bad T** (*sees* **Duane** *giggling*)   Wat you laughin at? Come!

**Duane**   Later, Glen.

**Bad T**   Yeah go kiss yer wife goodbye!

**Glen**   Hold up.

**Bad T**   Well come now, if yer comin.

**Gina**   Ware do you think yer going?

**Glen**   Yer shamin me, Mum.

**Gina**   I'll do more than shame yer, if you step one foot out of that door.

**Glen**   I won't be late.

**Gina**   You won't be back at all.

**Glen**   Later. (*Leaves.*)

**Gina**   He don't listen to a word I say. Like I ain't here. Fuckin kids.

**Mark**   That Tyrone come juss like his dad, too much mout.

**Gina**   So?

**Mark**   So?

**Gina**   What about you?

**Mark**   Nuttin.

**Gina**   How you doing, gorgeous?

**Mark**   Awright.

**Gina**   Thought you didn't drink in here no more.

**Mark**   I thought I'd slum it.

**Gina**    Cheeky sod. You on leave?

**Mark**    No I'm out.

**Gina**    Wat, for good?

**Mark**    So that was little Glen?

**Gina**    Little cunt more like. He wants a slap. How's yer dad, Mark?

**Mark**    So-so.

**Gina**    I used to see him all the time down the high street, coming out of the betting shop, he would always call me over, sayin hello and that, askin if I have a boyfriend yet.

**Mark**    Yer still look good, Gina.

**Gina**    Yeah, yeah.

**Mark**    You still love to put yerself down. Didn't you see the way those boys were lookin at yer? Yer fit, gal, deal wid it.

**Gina**    I know someone who will be very pleased to see you.

**Mark**    No don't.

**Gina**    Shut up. (*Calls*.) Dad! In here a minute, I got a surprise.

**Mark**    Oh, look at the time.

**Gina**    Sit! Dad!

**Jimmy**    Wat?

**Gina**    In here. Fuckin 'ell.

**Jimmy** (*approaching*)    Wat?

**Gina**    Look.

**Jimmy**    Marky boy! How you doin, you awright, son? You look it.

**Mark**    Cheers, Jimmy.

**Jimmy**   Still playing footie, I hope. Pub team are playing this mornin.

**Mark**   Yeah?

**Jimmy**   I still remember when you played for us, blindin he was, blindin! Everyone still talks about that goal you got against the Stag's Head: he ran with it, one end of the pitch to the other he was, no lie. He pissed on that goal Ryan Giggs got for Man U against Arsenal, pissed on it, well and truly pissed on it!

**Gina**   Yeah, Dad, cheers. Punters!

**Jimmy**   We'll talk sum more in a minute, son, you watchin the game?

**Mark**   Na.

**Jimmy**   Na!

**Mark**   I dunno.

**Jimmy**   Behave yerself.

**Mark**   We'll see.

**Jimmy**   Gina, buy him a drink on me. (*Leaves*.)

**Gina**   Yes, sir!

**Mark**   He ain't changed.

**Gina**   So, Mark?

**Mark**   Yes, Gina?

**Gina**   We gonna talk about what happened, or are you juss gonna sit there wid yer gob open?

**Mark**   Let's not. I'm juss looking for my brother, I heard he drinks in here now.

**Gina**   I was wondering how long it would be before you came back. You see the door? Well, keep yer eyes on it, our pub team will be back any sec. He plays for them. You know he looks juss like you.

*Doors swing open.* **Lawrie**, **Lee**, *followed by* **Becks** *come in. They do not look happy.*

**Gina**   Oh shit. Well, come on, how bad was it.

**Lawrie**   We stuffed the bastards!

*The lads cheer.*

**Boys** (*singing*)   Cheer up Duke of Yorks, oh what can it mean, to a, fat landlord bastard, and a, shit football team. (*Chants.*) King George, King George . . .

**Gina**   You tellin me you useless bastards won?

**Becks**   3–fuckin–2!

**Gina**   Oi, Dad, they only bloody won!

**Lee**   Set 'em up, Gina.

**Lawrie**   Oh yes, nuttin more sexier than a landlady pouring a smooth top.

**Gina**   Don't get out much, do yer, Lawrie?

**Lawrie**   I'll show yer wat I can get out.

**Lee**   Oi, behave yerself.

**Gina**   Like I'll be able to see it.

**Becks**   Nice one, Gina.

**Lawrie**   Kiss her arse while yer at it.

**Gina**   Well come on then, blow by blow.

**Lawrie**   Played them off the field, Gina, gave 'em a fuckin lesson in football.

**Becks**   Fat cunts.

**Lee**   It's funny how those fat cunts were 2–0 up.

**Lawrie**   Only cos of him, I coulda driven a bus through the amount of space he give 'em. Wants shooting.

**Becks**   Fuck off, Lawrie.

**Lawrie**   Oooh! You shoulda seen the looks on their faces at half-time, Gina, every one of them, looking like their case was about to come up. Right, thass it I thought, time for my pep talk. I rounded them all up, like this see. (*Demonstrates using* **Lee** *and* **Becks**.) I goes, listen to me, listen to me! Passion! I wanna see some passion. We gotta help each other out, this is no good, we gotta learn to pass to each other, keep control of the ball! (*Screams.*) Look at me! Ain't we?

**Lee/Becks**   Yeah!

**Lawrie**   Who are yer?

**Lee/Becks**   The George.

**Lawrie**   Who are yer?

**Lee/Becks**   The George!

**Lawrie**   Thank you! Well, that was it then, second half, different story. I was going, keep back, keep back, chase, chase, keep the ball, keep the ball –

**Lee**   Thought he was gonna lose his voice.

**Becks**   I prayed he would lose his voice.

**Lawrie**   When Lee got the ball, I tell yer, I heard music, Gina. I goes to him.

**Lee**   Screaming down my ear he was.

**Lawrie**   Yer tart! I goes, go on, broth, give it a good spin, he places it right into the back, the goalie didn't know wat day it was. Coulda kissed him.

**Lee**   You did.

**Lawrie** *kisses him again.*

**Gina**   Who got the other two?

**Lawrie**    The black kid, wasshisface?

**Becks**    Barry. Useful, weren't he, Lawrie?

**Lawrie**    Yeah, he was good, the boy done good.

**Becks**    He did more than good, he won the game for us.

**Lee**    Good penalty taker.

**Becks**    Wicked player.

**Lawrie**    Wicked player? Listen to him, trying to sound like a brother.

**Becks**    I'm juss sayin, he won the game for us.

**Lawrie**    Yeah I know wat he did, he's a wicked player, as you so delicately put it. But it was a team effort. He didn't juss win it by himself.

**Becks**    Might as well have.

**Lawrie**    You married to the cunt or wat? The boy did good, no need to break out into a song about it. Worry about yer own football, never mind droolin over wasshisface.

**Becks**    You callin me queer?

**Lawrie**    You got summin to hide, precious?

**Gina**    Ladies?

**Becks**    So wat about you, taking a swing at their captain.

**Lawrie**    Weren't my fault.

**Becks**    Nor was the goal.

**Lee**    Will you two lovebirds shut up.

**Lawrie**    That ref was a knob.

**Becks**    Now thass true.

**Lawrie**    That captain of theirs was committing untold fouls, not once did he get his book out.

**Lee**   Till you opened yer mouth.

**Gina**   What did he say?

**Lawrie**   Only the truth.

**Lee**   Don't tell her.

**Lawrie**   I accused him of not wanting to book one of his own.

**Lee**   Arsehole.

**Lawrie**   Cheers, broth.

**Lee**   I meant you.

**Lawrie**   Don't tell me you weren't thinkin it an'all.

**Becks**   It's true. I saw them havin a right old chat afterwards.

**Lawrie**   They love stickin together them lot.

**Gina**   Let me guess, the ref was black?

**Lawrie**   As soot. Never seen anything so dark.

**Lee**   Hold it down.

**Lawrie**   Awright, Mark? Long time no see. Still giving it large in Paddy Land? He lose his tongue or what?

**Gina**   Behave.

**Lawrie**   Only askin.

**Gina**   You've asked.

**Lawrie**   You know me, Gina, keep the peace.

**Gina**   Yeah.

**Lee**   She knows yer.

**Lawrie**   Got our seats, Gina?

**Gina**   Have a look.

**Lawrie**   Oh wass this, you put us at the back.

**Gina**   Jason asked first.

**Lawrie**   Fuck that. (*He swaps seats.*) You don't mind, do yer?

**Gina**   Any trouble, it's you I'm comin for.

**Lawrie** (*clicks on the remote, picture is blue*)   Gina, wass this, it's all blue.

**Gina**   Ask yer thievin mate over there.

**Lawrie**   Becks! You fuckin . . .

**Becks**   It was workin all right when I sold it to them.

**Lawrie** (*throws the remote at him*)   Fix it!

**Lee**   So how you doing, Mark?

**Mark**   Lee.

**Lee**   You on leave?

**Mark**   I quit.

**Lee**   You joke?

**Mark**   I had enuff.

**Lee**   You!

**Mark**   Yep.

**Lee**   How's yer dad?

**Mark**   Up and down . . . Heard about yours. Sorry, yeah.

**Lee**   S'right. Look, listen, yeah . . .

**Mark**   Don't.

**Lee**   Mark . . .

**Mark**   Don't.

**Lawrie**   Lee, over here a sec.

**Lee**   Wat?

**Lawrie**    Nuttin.

**Lee**    So wat you callin me for?

**Lawrie**    Geezer don't wanna know, mate.

**Gina** (*to* **Becks**)    Wat you fuckin done now?

**Becks**    I'm adjusting.

**Gina**    It's black an'white. Juss give us some colour.

**Becks**    Awright, don't get out of yer pram over it. You reckon we'll win, Lawrie?

**Lawrie**    We better, restore some pride after that fuck-up in Belgium. I mean, how fuckin bad was that? The nation that gave the world football. (*Roars.*) Come on, you England!

**Becks**    Come on, England!

**Lee**    Come on!

**Lawrie**    2002, boys, make it happen.

**Gina**    Becks, Becks, stop!

**Becks**    Wat?

**Gina**    Weren't you watchin? You had it, picture, it was perfect, colour and everything, go back.

**Becks**    *presses the remote.*

**Gina**    It's turned blue again.

**Becks**    Hold up.

*The menu comes up on the screen.*

Wass this?

**Lawrie**    It's the menu. Yer pressin the wrong button, you muppet.

**Lee**    Hold up, Becks?

**Becks**    Wat now?

**Lee**   Don't get arsey, I'm tryin to help you here.

**Becks**   Wat?

**Lee**   Go to services, on yer right.

**Becks**   I know.

**Lee**   Well, go on then.

**Becks**   Right.

**Lee**   Click on that. Now, scroll down to picture settings. Click on that. Contrast. Go up.

**Gina**   Yer going down, he said up.

**Lawrie**   Prat.

**Lee**   Up, up.

**Becks**   I'm going up.

**Lee**   Awright, yeah thass it, stop! That'll do.

**Lawrie**   Finally.

**Gina**   Thank you, Constable.

**Lee**   Pleasure to be of service, Madam.

**Gina**   It's good to have someone here with brains.

**Becks**   Hey, wass keepin them?

**Lawrie**   They'll be here. Alan won't miss the kick-off, trust me.

**Lee**   You invited Alan?

**Lawrie**   Yeah.

**Becks**   I saw yer mate Darren, Lawrie, going into one about not getting a ticket for the game. Geezer's off his head. He reckons he's gonna stand outside Wembley, give the Germans some verbal. Take them on like he did in Charleroi.

**Lawrie**    He shat himself in Charleroi. Ran back to the hotel before it all kicked off. It was me giving them Germans some gyp.

**Lee**    I didn't hear that, did I?

**Lawrie**    Of course not, Constable.

**Becks**    What you do?

**Lawrie**    Wat do you think? We gave them a right spanking. We were in this caff, watching the game. One–nil up right.

**Becks** (*chants*)    Shearer!

**Lawrie**    Right, shut up. There was this couple of Krauts sitting nearby, so juss for a laugh, I goes, I gives the old Nazi salute, going like this I was. Fuckin ages I was at it, till finally I catches one of dem giving me the eyeball, I ask wat his problem was, he goes all menstrual, going on about cos they're Germans, it don't make them Nazis, blah, blah, bloody blah! I goes, awright, mate, calm yerself, you a Jew or wat?

**Becks** *laughs out loud.*

**Lawrie**    Next minute, the cunt's comin at me comin at me wid a beer bottle. Tiny little cunt he was an' all. I goes, give us that, behave yerself. I take the bottle right off him, give him a slap, stamped on his fuckin head, shoulda seen it, I lean down to him, I goes, Do I take it that yer not a Jew then?

**Lee**    I didn't hear that, I am so not here.

**Mark**    You ain't changed.

**Lawrie**    Did he juss say summin?

**Lee**    No.

**Lawrie**    Oi, Mark, you say summin, mate? Mark? You found yer tongue then? Oi?

**Lee**    Lawrie.

**Lawrie**    I heard him say summin.

**Lee**    No you didn't. Let's play.

**Lawrie**    Have a day off, will yer? Yer off duty.

**Gina**    Listen to the policeman, Lawrence.

**Lawrie**    Awright. Well, put the money in.

*The boys head for the table football,* **Lee** *puts fifty pence in, a ball comes out. The brothers play against each other.*

**Becks**    Do you know if Rob got a ticket for the match, Lawrie?

**Lawrie**    He said he'd try. Bastard!

**Lee**    It's all in the wrist!

**Becks**    I thought I juss saw his face in the crowd, one of the cameras whizzed by, I'm sure it was him.

**Lawrie**    Yeah? Give us a shout when you see him next. Oh wat?

**Lee**    Skill, mate.

**Becks**    You want to play doubles?

**Lawrie**    Fuck off, yer worse than me.

**Becks**    Come on.

**Lawrie**    Ask our West Indian friend over there.

**Becks** (*to* **Mark**)    You fancy a game, Mark?

**Lee**    Leave him alone, Becks.

**Mark**    Yeah, come, why not.

**Becks**    I got a partner.

**Lawrie**    Wat do you want me to do, sing? So, Marcus?

**Mark**    Mark.

**Lawrie**    How confident are yer?

**Lee**    Wat you doing?

**Mark** *throws down forty quid.*

**Mark**    This much? Best out of three?

**Lee**    Mark, don't.

**Mark**    You my dad?

**Lawrie**    Exactly, Mark, pay no attention to the old woman. Becks?

**Becks**    I'm short.

**Mark**    Don't worry about it.

**Becks**    Cheers, mate.

**Lawrie**    Let's play ball.

**Mark**    You gonna cover the bet?

**Lawrie**    Lee?

**Lee**    Oh bloody hell, Lawrie.

**Lawrie**    Come on.

**Lee**    Do I look like a cashpoint?

**Lawrie**    All I got is ten.

**Lee**    Yer a pain in the arse.

**Lawrie**    Come on.

**Lee**    Every time I see you, you cost me money.

**Lawrie**    Broth? Brother!

**Lee**    You juss don't listen. (*Gives him thirty.*) You ain't even listening now.

**Lawrie**    Wat? Joke. Come here. (*Kisses him on the head.*)

**Lee**    Get off me. I hate it when you do that.

**Lawrie**    Love yer! Gina, my love, bank this for us, will yer. Let's play ball! Mark, my boy, would you care to kick off.

**Mark**    No you can.

**Lawrie**    No yer awright, go ahead.

**Mark**    I said I'm awright.

**Lawrie**    Come on.

**Mark**    You start.

**Lee**    Will somebody.

**Lawrie**    Yer missin the point here, Mark.

**Mark**    Which is what?

**Lawrie**    You see, this here is my pub, my home from home as it were. You are a guest, I am the host, extending my hospitality.

**Mark**    I don't want it.

**Lee**    Fuck's sake, I'll do it.

**Lee** *drops the ball, they all play.* **Lee** *scores.*

**Lawrie**    Yes!

**Becks**    Shit, sorry.

**Mark**    Don't worry.

**Mark** *plays the ball. He plays like a lunatic, he is too fast for* **Lawrie** *and* **Lee** *and scores.*

**Mark**    Yes!

**Lawrie**    Right, come on, Lee.

**Lee** *drops the ball in,* **Mark** *is just as fast, if not faster, he scores again.*

**Becks**    Yes!

**Lawrie**    Shit. Come on, Lee.

**Lee**   Awright!

**Lee** *drops the ball again.* **Mark** *is playing like a maniac now.* **Becks** *just stops and stands back and watches him.* **Mark** *scores.*

**Mark**   Oh yes!

**Lawrie**   Bollocks!

**Becks**   Does it hurt being that good, Mark?

**Mark**   Torture. Cheers, Gina. (*Collects the money from her.*)

**Lawrie**   You knew he was useful.

**Lee**   I knew you wouldn't listen.

**Mark**   Another please, Gina.

**Gina**   So you still here?

**Mark**   Till I see my brother.

**Gina**   Jimmy will be pleased.

**Lee**   Still practising?

**Mark**   Another time, Lee.

**Lee**   She dumped me as well, you know.

**Mark**   I don't care about that.

**Lee**   Sod yer then.

**Mark**   Right on.

*Door opens.* **Phil**, **Jason** *and* **Alan** *enter, loud cheering, singing, except* **Alan**, *who walks in coolly, standing between them.* **Lawrie**, **Becks** *and* **Lee** *join their mates in the singing.*

**Boys**   We're on our way, we are Kev's twenty-two, hear the roar, of the red, white and blue, this time, more than any other, this time, we're gonna find a way, find a way to get it on, time, to get it on together.

**Gina**   Shall we keep it down, gents? Hi, Phil.

**Phil**    Awright, Gina.

**Gina**    So how's life in Watford?

**Phil**    Sweet as.

**Becks**    He'll be following their team next.

**Phil**    Bollocks.

**Becks**    Giving Elton John a tug.

**Phil**    Shut it, Becks.

**Boys** (*sing*)    Don't sit down, with Elton around, or you might get a penis up yer arse!

**Gina**    Now, now, boys, not in front of the lady.

**Alan**    It's all right, Gina, I'll keep them in line. (*To screen.*) Come on, lads, got a lot of living up to do.

**Phil**    We had 'em in June.

**Alan**    Romania had us in June.

**Boys** (*sing*)    Come on England, come on England, come on England, let's have another win.

**Alan**    Where's yer dad?

**Gina** (*shouts*)    Dad? Like yer haircut, Phil.

**Phil**    Yeah?

**Gina**    Yeah, very David Beckham. Suits yer.

*The boys start teasing* **Phil** *regarding* **Gina**.

**Phil**    Behave yerselves.

**Becks** (*watching the screen*)    Commentary's started.

**Jason** (*roars*)    Come on, lads.

**Phil**    Come on, you England!

**Lawrie** *and* **Lee** *join in the roar.* **Jimmy** *appears to get some crisps.*

**Jimmy**    Wat?

**Gina**    Yer little friend's here.

**Jimmy**    Awright, Alan?

**Alan**    James. Watchin the game?

**Jimmy**    Be right wid yer, juss serving.

**Alan**    Lawrie my boy. Good result today, well played.

**Lawrie**    You remember my kid brother Lee.

**Alan**    The policeman, you all right, son?

**Lee**    Yep.

**Alan**    Spitting image of yer old man, you are. Still a PC?

**Lawrie**    Detective constable now, if you don't mind, movin to Sutton.

**Lee**    Lawrie.

**Lawrie**    Shut up, I don't know why yer keepin it a secret, I'm proud of yer. I kept tellin him it would work out for him, but he never believes me. The state he was in last year.

**Alan**    State?

**Lawrie**    Got stabbed.

**Alan**    Nasty.

**Lawrie**    Yeah, some coon. It happened at a rave, weren't it, Lee?

**Lee**    Will you shut up.

**Lawrie**    He didn't hear, like I care.

**Alan**    Easy, son.

**Boys** (*chant*)    ENGLAND, ENGLAND, ENGLAND . . .

**Becks**    Come on, Rob, ware are yer?

**Jason**    Wat is he there?

**Becks**    He was in the crowd a second ago.

**Phil**   How did he get in? He's banned from every ground in the country.

**Lawrie**   You think that'll stop Rob? They tried to stop us going into France for '98, we were there though, despite all the efforts and a huge operation by the boys in blue to keep us away. Ooops, sorry, Lee, you didn't hear that. We were there though, oh we were so there.

**Jason**   You there when the trouble kicked off?

**Lawrie**   The second Batty missed that penalty, I knew it was gonna kick off. It was fuckin war on the streets. Argies, Krauts, coppers, didn't fuckin matter. We were England!

**Alan**   Thinking went right out of the window.

**Lawrie**   Least we were winnin that one.

**Alan**   You got arrested and thrown in a French cell, you daft sod. Never fight a battle you can't win.

**Jason**   Wat was Batty doin taking a penalty anyhow?

**Mark**   Jase?

**Jason**   Awright, Mark?

**Mark**   Where's my brother? He was playin today?

**Alan**   You're Barry's brother?

**Mark**   Yes.

**Alan**   You should be proud of him, that boy is useful.

**Mark**   He ain't a boy.

**Alan**   Easy.

**Mark**   Where is he?

**Jason**   He walked.

**Mark**   While you all drove?

**Alan**    There wasn't enough room. I had a lot of stuff in the back. I'm a painter and decorator. It was hard getting those two muppets in. We drew straws.

**Mark**    And he got the short one.

**Alan**    Yes, he did. What's his problem?

**Mark**    You can talk to me.

**Alan**    No need to fly off, son.

**Mark**    Where's my brother?

**Barry** *comes in, dancing and singing (New Order's 'World in Motion'); he makes a right show of it, parading himself in front of the lads who are egging him on.* **Barry** *has the flag of St George painted all over his face.*

**Barry** (*singing*)    You've got to hold or kick, and do it at the right time, you can be slow or fast, but you must get to the line, they'll always hit you and hurt you, defend or attack, there's only one way to beat them, get round the back, catch me if you can, cos I'm the England man, wat yer lookin at, is the master plan, we better move with pace, this is a football song, three lions on my chest, I know we can't go wrong! We're singin for England . . .

**Boys**    EN-GER-LAND! We're singin the song, We're singin for England, EN-GER-LAND, Arrivederci, it's one on one! We're singin for England, EN-GER-LAND . . .

**Phil**    Barry, over here!

**Barry** *goes over to the boys. One by one they take turns rubbing or kissing his bald head.*

**Barry**    Anyone else?

**Alan**    Yeah, over here, boy . . . (*Rubs his head.*)

**Phil**    Good boy.

**Jason**    Fuckin won it for us.

**Barry**　Thank you, thank you, thank you – (*Sees* **Mark**.) Awright, broth?

**Mark**　Can I talk to you?

**Barry**　Game's gonna start.

**Mark**　Won't take long.

**Jason**　Got yer seat here, Baz.

**Barry**　Cheers, Jase.

*The teams line up to hear the national anthems. The German one plays first. The lads boo and jeer.*

**Boys** (*to the tune of 'Go West'*)　Stand up, if you won the war! Stand up, if you won the war, stand up, if you won the war . . .

**Gina**　Feet off the seats, if you please.

*The English national anthem is played. The boys sing along. Some jump on the table,* **Gina** *protests. They all cheer at the end. The boys then cheer and applaud as each player is called on the TV screen. They do the same when the German team is read out, only this time they jeer.*

**Boys** (*chant* )　ENGLAND! ENGLAND! ENGLAND!

**Alan**　Come on, lads.

**Lawrie**　Let's fuckin have some!

**Alan**　Lawrence? About wat we spoke about, yer in.

**Lawrie**　Cheers.

**Lee** (*approaching*)　Wat was that?

**Lawrie**　Nosy.

*Game kicks off. Boys cheer and applaud.*

**Mark**　Barry?

**Barry**　Later, Mark, come on, pull up a chair.

**Phil**    You tell him, boy.

**Mark** (*grabs him*)    Come here!

**Barry**    Hey!

**Mark**    Excuse us!

**Mark** *ushers his brother into the Gents where they start to bicker.*

**Becks**    Wass up there?

**Lawrie**    Must be a black thing.

**Becks**    Two black geezers in the Gents, dodgy.

**Lee**    Shut up, Becks.

**Becks**    Joke.

**Phil**    Come on, you England!

*The boys join* **Phil**'s *roar. Lights up on the Gents.*

**Barry**    I'm missin the start here.

**Mark**    Wat was that? Dancin like sum spaz, lettin them rub yer head like a genie's lamp.

**Barry**    They do it at every match, for luck. It's a laugh.

**Mark**    Wipe that shit off yer face.

**Barry**    Don't come down here and start, Mark.

**Mark**    You think I'm here by choice? I feel ill juss bein here. I can't wait to go home so I can have a wash.

**Barry**    Go home then.

**Mark**    All this, 'Leave it out, mate, you know wat I mean, I'm a geezer ain't I' –

**Barry**    Let me watch the match!

**Mark**    Karen said you ain't bin home fer weeks, wass that about? Too busy to see yer own dad?

**Barry**    You come to take me back?

**Mark**   He's askin for yer.

**Barry**   I ain't seein him.

**Mark**   Show sum respect.

**Barry**   For that mess that lies in bed all day? That ain't my dad, why can't he hurry up and die?

**Mark**   Fuckin little . . .

**Barry**   Karen feels the same way, you as well. You love to act high and mighty now yer back; where were you when he was gettin sick?

**Mark**   Look, let's chat when we get home, yeah?

**Barry**   I'm watchin the game.

**Mark**   Ware you get that cut on yer neck?

**Barry**   Romanian fan. Charleroi.

**Mark**   You were at Charleroi? Fuck's sake.

**Barry**   Shoulda seen wat I did to him. (*Demonstrates.*) Glassed him right up.

**Mark**   Why don't you get a tattoo of the Union Jack while yer at it.

**Barry** *rolls up his shirt. He has a tattoo of the British Bulldog on his lower back.*

**Barry**   I didn't even pass out. Almost as good as yours, I reckon.

**Mark**   Wat are you doin to yerself?

**Barry**   Nuttin you wouldn't do, once.

**Mark**   I don't want Dad going thru this shit again.

**Barry**   Fuck off back to the army.

**Mark**   I'm outta the army, little man, for good.

**Barry**   Lose yer bottle again, Mark?

**Mark**    Yer comin home.

**Barry**    No.

**Mark**    I'll follow you all day if I have to.

**Barry**    Do it.

**Mark**    Kid . . .

**Barry**    I ain't a fuckin kid no more! You don't understand!

**Mark**    I don't understand?

**Barry**    I'm missin it.

**Mark**    You think yer a badman now, cos yu've had a couple of rucks, kicked a few heads? You've got no idea, son. When yer all alone with a gang of them, havin to fight 'em off by yourself, getting the shit kicked outta yer for yer trouble, you get back to me. It's bollocks, kid. It's their bollocks.

*The boys stamp on the floor as they chant to the theme tune of* The Great Escape. **Barry** *leaves the loo to watch the match with his mates. He joins in with the chant. The screen turns blue again. The boys protest.*

**Gina**    Becks, you stupid . . .

**Becks**    I'll fix it.

**Gina**    Keep yer bloody hands off.

**Lee**    Giss it.

**Lawrie**    Come on, broth.

**Lee**    Shut up.

**Lee** *sorts out the contrast. The colour picture comes back. The boys applaud.*

**Phil**    Nice.

**Becks**    Juss needs a bit of TLC now and then.

**Gina**    I want my money back.

**Phil**   Come on, England!

**Boys** (*chant*)   ENGLAND! ENGLAND! ENGLAND! . . .

**Beck** (*mocks*)   Southgate in the middle though.

**Phil**   When did Cole score last?

**Mark**   When did he last get a full game?

**Gina** (*approaching*)   Come on, boys, bunch up.

*The boys get all excited by* **Gina** *joining them. Cheers, wolf whistles, etc.*

**Gina**   All barks, no bites. You stayin then, Mark?

**Mark**   Yeah. Might as well.

**Jason**   Lampard should be playing.

**Phil**   An 'ammer playing, behave yerself.

**Jimmy**   Shut yer hole, Philip. You juss bring on yer bloody Chelsea at Upton Park next week, you'll bloody know it then.

*Mobile phone rings. It's* **Becks**'s.

**Becks** (*answers*)   Hello. Awright, Rob!

**Jason** (*shouts*)   Robbie, yer cunt!

**Lawrie**   Yer wanker!

**Becks**   Yer hear that? I said did yer hear that?

**Lawrie**   Ware is he? (*Shouts.*) Ware are yer, yer cunt!

**Becks**   He's there!

**Jason**   Wembley?

**Becks**   Yes, Jase, fuckin Wembley! (*To phone.*) Wat now? He goes, there's a camera comin into view, he's gonna wave at us.

**Phil** He's there, fuckin 'ell!

*They all cheer and wave.*

**Becks**   We see yer, yer there.

*They all see Rob from the screen, the boys scream and cheer louder.*
**Phil** *pulls his trousers down and moons at the screen.*

**Becks**   Rob, Phil is only showin you his arse.

**Gina** (*to* **Jimmy**)   No trouble eh?

**Jimmy**   Philip, no more arse!

*The boys roar with laughter as they see Rob mooning back at them.*

**Lawrie**   He's only moonin back at us!

**Jason**   Yer wanker!

**Becks**   Ring me at half-time, yer nutter!

**Lawrie**   I tell yer, if we lose again, it's gonna kick off in there.

**Kelly** (*off* )   Jimmy?

**Jimmy**   Kelly needs some help, Gina.

**Gina**   You better get back there.

**Jimmy** (*shouts*)   I'll be there in a sec.

**Gina**   Dad?

**Jimmy**   Fuck's sake!

*The boys laugh as* **Jimmy** *has to leave.*

Yeah, yeah, up yours.

**Becks**   Germans playing three at the back?

**Barry**   Looks like it.

**Jason**   Yes, come on, Owen.

**Becks**   Fuck!

**Lee**   Good run though.

**Barry**   He's a fast one.

**Alan**   Yeah, but then he lost it.

**Jason**   Nice one, Adams, make him eat dirt.

**Lawrie**   He's given away a free kick, yer sap.

**Phil**   Watch the post, watch the fuckin post!

**Jason**   Good one, Le Saux.

**Becks**   Doin summin right for once.

**Jason**   Leave him.

**Becks** (*acting camp*)   Oooh! (*Blows* **Jason** *a kiss.*)

**Jason**   Fuck off.

**Gina**   Nice control by Cole eh?

**Lawrie**   Yeah, but he's all mouth, no delivery him.

**Mark**   Cos no one gives him a chance.

**Lawrie**   Cos he never fuckin scores.

**Mark**   Shearer played nine games without scoring for England, nine! Didn't stop Venables pickin him.

**Lawrie**   Cole ain't Shearer.

**Mark**   He's never bin given a chance to be Shearer.

**Barry**   Lawrie's right.

**Mark**   Wat you know?

**Barry**   Watch him. He needs three or four chances to score a goal, Shearer only needed one.

**Mark**   He got forty-one goals in one season when he was with Newcastle, how many's he put in for Man U? War'do you want? Since when is a striker judged on how many chances he gets, leave me alone.

**Phil**   Southgate, you useless piece of shit.

**Jason** *takes out horn and blows on it, everyone jumps.*

**Becks**    Jase!

**Phil**    'kin 'ell.

**Jason**    Juss tryin to whip up a bit of excitement.

**Gina**    I'll whip it up yer arse.

**Alan**    Nice one, Scholes.

**Lawrie**    Come on, Scholes.

**Barry**    Get it up.

*They sigh as Scholes loses the ball to German player Ballack. Scholes tugs him, Ballack falls. Free kick.*

**Becks**    Wat!

**Phil**    Hamman won't score.

**Barry**    He plays for Liverpool ennit.

*Hamman shoots from the free kick. He scores. German fans cheer. The boys are stunned.*

**Phil**    Oh wat!

**Jason**    Nice one, Baz, yer jinxed it.

**Barry**    Move.

**Jason**    He did.

**Lee**    Wat difference it makes, he still scored.

**Lawrie**    Fuck off Voller, you German cunt!

**Boys** (*chant*)    YER DIRTY GERMAN BASTARD! YER DIRTY GERMAN BASTARD!

**Lawrie**    Jase, ring Rob, tell him to give one of them Krauts a slap from me.

**Alan**    There's no point in taking it out on them.

**Lawrie**    Oh come on.

**Alan**   We should have had a red shirt in front of the ball. It weren't a strong kick, Seaman should have got that. A blind man could have got that.

**Barry**   We were well asleep at the back. Hamman saw a chance, he took it.

**Alan**   Too right he took it. The boy's right.

**Phil**   Check Keegan's face.

**Becks**   Yeah, you better be worried.

**Jason**   He was never cut out to be manager.

**Barry**   Ain't wat you said when he got the job, going on about him being the people's choice.

**Jason**   I never said that –

**Barry**   Lie!

**Gina**   Can we not bury them yet please.

*England are awarded a free kick. Beckham lines up to take it.*

**Lee**   Oh yes!

**Lawrie**   Come on, Beckham.

**Phil** Get it in the box, please.

**Jason**   Let's have some more reds in there!

**Barry**   And leave them well exposed at the back, good call, Jase.

**Jason**   Piss off, Barry.

**Barry**   Ooh, handbag.

**Jason**   Scores a couple this mornin, and he thinks he's the dog's bollocks.

*Beckham crosses the ball. It's headed back.*

**Gina**   Get it back. And Philip?

**Philip** Yeah?

**Gina**   Stop lookin at my tits.

*The boys laugh as they tease* **Phil**, *calling him a pervert, etc.*

**Phil**   I weren't.

**Jimmy** (*approaching*)   How goes it?

**Becks**   Phil's bin looking at Gina's tits.

**Phil**   I weren't, Jimmy, I swear to God.

**Jimmy**   You'll be prayin to God for your life, mate, if you step out – (*Sees.*) Oh Jesus. One–nil!

**Mark**   Hamman scored a blinder.

**Lawrie**   You a Kraut-lover now?

**Alan**   Easy, Lawrence.

**Lawrie**   It was a poxy free kick.

**Mark**   Watever.

**Lawrie**   No watever about it, boy.

**Mark**   Shut yer hole.

**Lawrie**   Shut my what, wass he say?

**Lee**   Yer missin the match.

**Gina**   Are we happy over there?

**Lawrie**   Sweet as.

**Gina**   Good.

*Germans are on the attack, Bierhof is passed the ball. He is in an excellent position to score.*

**Becks**   Shit.

**Jason**   Flag's up.

**Barry**   Offside!

**Phil**   Come on, England!

**Jimmy**   They wanna stop playin wid themselves!

*Cole has the ball, he makes a run.*

**Phil**   Come on, Cole.

**Jason**   Yes.

**Barry**   Free kick.

**Jason**   Which cunt got him?

**Gina**   Rehmar. Do you know any other words apart from cunt, Jase?

*Beckham lines up for another free kick.*

**Alan**   Come on, Beckham.

**Gina**   I don't care how he talks, he is gorgeous.

**Jason**   He'll score.

**Barry**   Got a crystal ball, Jase?

*Beckham shoots, he misses.*

You were sayin?

**Jason**   It was on target.

**Barry**   Yeah, look on the bright side.

**Jason**   Wass yer problem?

**Barry**   I'm havin a laugh.

**Jason**   Leave it out.

**Barry**   Or wat?

**Gina**   Girls!

**Lawrie**   Come on, Owen!

**Alan**   Ooh, unlucky, son.

**Phil**   That fuckin coach of theirs looks like Terry McDermott.

**Jimmy**   He was a good player that Voller.

**Alan**    How many goals he got when he was playin, Jimmy?

**Jimmy**    'bout forty-seven. Class player.

**Lawrie**    For a Kraut.

**Alan**    Nothing wrong with admiring the enemy once in a while.

**Phil**    Come on, boys.

**Barry**    England!

**Jason**    They wanna take fucking Cole off.

**Mark**    Why?

**Jason**    Ain't pullin his weight.

**Mark**    He ain't alone.

**Jason**    I'm juss stating my opinion.

**Mark**    Funny how he's the only black player on the pitch.

*The boys protest at that remark.*

**Gina**    Come off it, Mark.

**Mark**    All I said, it was funny.

**Jason**    If thass wat I meant, that's wat I woulda said.

**Mark**    Why him?

**Jason**    He's playin shit.

**Barry**    Yer talkin shit.

**Mark**    Thank you.

**Barry**    Both of yer.

**Mark**    Hey, easy.

**Jason**    Paranoia.

**Mark**    I'm done.

**Mark** *goes to the Gents,* **Lee** *follows.*

**Lawrie**    Ware you going?

**Jason**    Wass yer brother's problem? He sayin I'm a racist?

**Barry**    I don't know wat he's doing.

**Jason**    Wanker.

*Lights on in the Gents.*

**Lee**    You don't even like Andy Cole. You told me once, you can't fart loud enough to describe how much you hate Man U, and anyone who plays for them.

**Mark**    Is it?

**Lee**    So wat gives? Did you hear that the Post Office recalled their Man U treble commemorative stamps, people couldn't figure out which side to spit on? Wat do Man U fans use for birth control? Their personalities. A man meets up with his mate and sees that his car is a total write-off, all covered with leaves, grass, branches, dirt and blood. He asks his mate, wat happened to yer car? The friend replies, well, I ran over David Beckham. Bloke goes, that explains the blood, but what about the leaves, the grass, and branches and dirt. The geezer says . . .

**Mark**    . . . he tried to escape runnin by through the park.

**Mark** *tries hard not to laugh, but gives in a little. He then heads out.*

**Lee**    So wat was that shit wid Jason?

**Mark**    He's a prick.

**Lee**    I know he's a prick, he ain't a racist.

**Mark**    Like you?

**Lee**    Yeah, gwan, Mark, tell half the story.

**Mark**    Wass there to tell, yer Lawrie's brother.

**Lee**    You know I ain't like him.

**Mark**    Wat you gonna do about Alan King?

**Lee**    He ain't committed an offence.

**Mark**    Not yet.

**Lee**    If he does.

**Mark**    When.

**Lee**    I'll have him. So wass this about you quittin the army?

**Mark**    They didn't like the colour of my eyes.

**Lee**    Oh come on.

**Mark**    Don't worry yerself.

**Lee**    I'm gettin married, next month. Her name's Vicky. She's nice, fit.

**Mark**    Nice one.

**Lee**    Come to the wedding. Please.

*Lights up in the bar.*

**Barry**    Don't tell me we don't have players who know how to pass, it's like we're scared of the ball or summin.

**Lawrie** (*aside*)    Them and this 'we'.

**Alan**    You enjoy supporting our boys then, son?

**Barry**    They're my boys too.

**Lawrie**    Armchair supporter.

**Barry**    I bin to Wembley eight times, I never saw you there.

**Alan**    Wat was yer first game?

**Barry**    1990, against Yugoslavia. Mark took me.

**Alan**    Two–one. Bryan Robson, both goals.

**Becks**    Put the fuckin ball away! Unreal. They don't get better than that.

**Lawrie**    Fuck this!

**Lee** (*approaching*)    Where you going? (*Follows.*)

**Lawrie** *heads for the pool table. He wipes off the names from the board.*

**Lee**    You can't do that.

**Lawrie** (*points at his own face*)    Bothered?

**Lee**    We still got the second half.

**Lawrie**    They're gonna walk over us, like everyone else!

**Lee**    Calm down.

**Lawrie**    Fuckin taking it! Same old shit like Belgium.

**Lee**    You give up too easily.

**Lawrie**    So do they. Why do they always do this to us? I wish I was there, give them Kraut bastards summin to laugh about.

**Lee**    Enough.

**Lawrie**    They're got no heart, Lee. We give 'em ours, every single game, and we get fuck all back. If those cunts can't do it on the pitch, we can, we will! We're England!

**Lee**    Yer a prick.

**Lawrie**    Yer not playing?

**Lee**    Fuck off.

**Alan** (*approaching*)    Set 'em up, Lawrie.

**Lee** *blocks* **Alan**'s *path.*

**Alan**    Help you, son?

**Lee**    Leave him alone.

**Alan**    Spittin image of yer old man.

**Lee**    Are you deaf ?

**Alan**   Not at all. You and I should have a drink. (*Goes over to* **Lawrie**.) Tragic ennit?

**Lawrie**   Ninety minutes, Alan, to forget about all the shit out there, and they can't even do that.

**Alan**   Your dad would be spinning.

*They play pool.* **Mark** *is at the bar with* **Gina** *who is pouring him a pint.*

**Gina**   You calm down? Arsehole. You hate Andy Cole.

**Mark**   I know, I'm sorry. Is Barry behavin himself?

**Gina**   Rowdy as the rest of them, nuttin I can't handle. He's all right.

**Mark**   He's stupid. Loves to get led round all the time. The amount of times Mum and Dad had to go to his school, cos of him.

**Gina**   Like you weren't like that as well.

**Mark**   He should listen to wat I'm sayin then ennit?

**Gina**   You and Lee still ain't talkin. I've had blokes fightin over me before, but this is silly.

**Mark**   I knew you'd dump him.

**Gina**   He's gettin married.

**Mark**   He said.

**Gina**   He's brought her in a few times. Posh bit, really nice. Daddy owns a computer company.

**Mark**   You coulda called me.

**Gina**   And get back wid you, yer mad! I hated myself.

**Mark**   Don't.

**Gina**   You two were like that. I got between yer.

**Mark** Writing was on the wall long before. He listens to his brother too much.

**Gina** And yours don't listen at all.

**Mark** *rejoins the boys.* **Glen** *comes into the pub, he has been beaten up. He is not wearing his jacket. He tries to sneak in without being seen.*

**Jimmy** Glenny boy, get yer arse over here, make yourself useful, clear up the glasses from the table.

**Glen** I ain't doin nuttin.

**Jimmy** You'll do as yer told, I ain't soft like yer bleedin mum. (*Clocks his face.*) Watcha you run into?

**Glen** Don't worry yerself.

**Jimmy** Gina?

**Glen** No.

**Jimmy** Over here.

**Gina** Jesus! You bin fighting again? Wass the matter wid you? And ware's yer jacket? Ware's yer fuckin jacket?

**Glen** Gone ennit.

**Gina** Gone where?

**Glen** Juss gone.

**Gina** Well you better find out ware's it gone, and get it back.

**Glen** *winces when* **Gina** *grabs his arm.*

**Jimmy** Oh Christ, she barely touched yer.

**Gina** Glen?

**Glen** He took my jacket and my phone ennit? Cos he liked 'em.

**Gina** Who?

**Glen**    Tyrone. Bad T.

**Gina**    That fuckin little black kid?

**Jimmy**    You let him take it off yer? You didn't even fight back?

**Alan**    All right there, Jimmy?

**Jimmy**    Should be ashamed of yerself.

**Alan**    Jimmy?

**Jimmy**    Some fuckin little black kid has had a pop at my boy.

**Gina**    Little bastard.

**Lawrie**    Who are they?

**Jimmy** (*to* **Glen**)    Stop cryin.

**Glen**    I ain't.

**Jimmy**    Only got a scratch, stand up straight.

**Gina**    Dad?

**Jimmy**    Teach you how to fight, then you can go back, sort 'em out.

**Gina**    Leave him alone. I'm gonna kill the little cunt.

**Mark**    You mean black cunt? (*To* **Barry**.) You gettin this?

**Gina**    Come on, Mark, they were a couple wrong uns you saw 'em yerself, even if I was thinkin it, can you blame me? Wass the matter wid you, look at his face.

**Jimmy**    A poxy scratch.

**Gina**    I call it as I see it.

**Mark**    You all bloody do.

**Gina**    Would they have nicked his stuff if he was black?

**Lawrie**    No.

**Lee**  Ware you goin?

**Lawrie**  Find this kid.

**Lee**  Lawrie!

**Alan**  I'll go.

**Lee**  You stay. (*Leaves.*)

**Becks**  You ever seen a more shittier pass than that?

**Phil**  Come on!

**Barry**  England!

**Jason** *comes back with a round of drinks.*

**Becks**  Wass goin on, Jase?

**Jason**  Gina's boy got into a fight wid sum black kid.

**Phil**  As long as he won.

**Jason**  Only nicked his phone and jacket.

**Phil**  Little bastard. Sorry, Baz.

**Barry**  Wat for? (*Screams.*) Come on, you England!

**Mark** *sits alongside his brother.*

**Barry**  You still here?

**Mark**  Juss watchin the game.

**Barry**  So wat about Dad?

**Mark**  Karen's lookin after him.

**Barry**  You don't want to go back home.

**Lawrie** and **Lee** *come in, they have* **Duane**.

**Duane**  I was comin to give 'em back, right.

**Lawrie**  Yeah.

**Duane**  Move, right!

**Lawrie**    Mouthy little . . .

**Duane**    Glen, tell 'em man, it weren't me, it was T, right.

**Lawrie** (*slaps his head*)    You want another?

**Mark**    Hey, you don't have to hit him.

**Lee** (*stands between them*)    Let's juss chill, yeah.

**Mark**    Let the boy go.

**Lee**    Mark, I swear, I'll arrest yer.

**Mark**    Me?

**Jimmy**    Go on, son, game's still playin.

**Mark**    Fuck the game!

**Lee** (*to* **Duane**)    Ware's the phone?

**Duane** *hands it over.*

**Duane**    I was gonna give it back, I told T, he loves to go too far sometimes, but he don't listen.

**Lee**    You scared of him?

**Duane**    Yeah.

**Lee**    So how come you got the phone and jacket off him?

**Duane**    I dunno. I juss did.

**Lawrie**    Lying.

**Lee**    On yer way.

**Duane**    Glen, I'm sorry yeah.

**Lawrie**    He said out!

**Duane**    Fuck off!

**Lawrie** *grabs the boy and slings him out.*

**Mark**    Fuckin . . .

**Lawrie**    Come on, come on!

**Lee**    It's over. (*To* **Lawrie**.) Cool it, Lawrie.

**Mark**    You big it up now ennit?

**Jimmy** (*to* **Glen**) See wat trouble you've caused? Wouldn't happen if you stick up for yerself.

**Gina**    Dad, if you don't stop goin on at him, I'm gonna shove this beer glass into yer face! (*To* **Mark**.) And you, sit down and watch the game.

**Alan** (*aside*)    Rivers of blood.

**Gina**    Go upstairs, Glen, clean yer face. Alan, I appreciate your trade, it's always nice to see yer, but I've told you before, I don't want to hear that kind of talk in my pub. Leave that England for whites bollocks outside.

**Phil**    Fuck's sake!

**Jason**    Will somebody please score!

**Alan**    Come on, Jimmy, you know what I'm talking about.

**Gina**    It's my name above that door.

**Alan**    I'm sorry, babe, I didn't mean to upset you.

**Gina**    Then don't say it.

**Alan**    It's not just me, darling. I've got nothing against the blacks myself, but even you have to admit we've got a problem here. There are too many different races all trying to fit into the same box, how is that supposed to work? Now they've got our kids, talking like them. It's no wonder you feel the same.

**Gina**    I do not.

**Alan**    But I just heard you call that kid a black cunt.

**Gina**    Cos they beat up my son.

**Becks**    Fuckin chase it!

**Alan**    Not because he's black? Come on, Gina.

**Becks**    Chase it!

**Alan**    It's OK, we are all racists, you know.

**Becks**    Come on!

**Alan**    All white people are racists. I heard this black geezer say it once, dead clever. We are racists. We are white, he says. Our history, our culture, our jobs, people on TV, it's all white, if not predominantly. It's not by coincidence, it's by design. Being white is the norm. It always has been. We are the norm. You should have heard him.

**Gina**    Well, he's wrong.

**Alan**    Is he?

**Jimmy**    You were barely on solids when Enoch said his piece, Gina, they were lining to carve him up.

**Gina**    Good.

**Jimmy**    They booted him out of his party. All he said was the truth.

**Gina**    And you agree, you stupid old git.

**Jimmy**    Look at all the trouble we've got now, it's those fucking black kids from that estate that are causing it all. You know that. I can handle the older blacks, Mark's dad used to drink in here, blindin fella. But these young ones really know how to push it, mouthing off all the time, for no good reason, carryin like the world owes them a favour, bollocks.

*The boys watching the match let out a huge sigh.*

**Jason**    That was so close.

**Phil**    Nice one, Seaman.

**Becks**    Not bad for an Arsenal man.

**Jimmy**    Then there's the immigrants.

**Gina**    Oh Dad.

**Jimmy**   It's in the papers, you can't deny it, they're everywhere.

**Gina**   Where, Dad? Where? Down the high street, in here? Where? I don't see 'em.

**Lawrie**   Tucked away in their nice council homes.

**Gina**   I'm not hearing this, Lee?

**Lee**   Leave me out of it.

**Lawrie**   He knows it's true.

**Lee**   You a mind-reader?

**Lawrie**   I'm yer brother.

**Jimmy**   Papers don't lie, love.

**Gina**   They lie on a regular basis when it comes to the likes of you. Throw in a pair of tits and they've got you hypnotised. Can you not prove their point please.

**Alan**   Gina, love, I don't read papers, I haven't picked one up in years. I read books, and I'm tellin you, it's amazing what you read. Pages of it, reams of it, history, telling you, making valid points that the blacks, the non-whites, have absolutely nothing in common with the Anglo-Saxon Celtic culture.

**Gina**   The what?

**Alan**   If they want to practise their black culture and heritage, then they should be allowed to do it in their own part of their world. By all means.

**Gina**   So whites are superior to blacks?

**Alan**   Yes, if you like.

**Gina**   Bollocks.

**Alan**   Consider this, the blacks lived side by side with the Egyptians for thousands of years, only about twenty miles of sand separated them. When the Egyptians came into contact with them, they hadn't even invented the wheel, which the Egyptians had thousands of years ago, they couldn't even copy it.

**Gina**    Maybe they didn't need it.

**Alan**    They didn't need the wheel? What has the black man done in the world?

**Gina**    Thass it! (*Goes back to watching the game.*)

**Alan**    I'll tell you. When the British and European powers colonised Africa, the colonies had a high standard of civilisation, when the decolonialisation came round, we left these countries economically sound with good administrative government. As soon as the whites left, those blacks are killing each other. Now they've got some of the poorest countries in the world. That's how capable the blacks are of running their own countries and looking after themselves. You look at the rest of the black hemisphere, the Caribbean, rotten with poverty, half of them, now we gave them the means to run their countries efficiently, but we're still pumping aid into these countries to keep them afloat. They can't run themselves; if they can't even live with each other, why should we be expected to live with them as well? We gave them everything they had to carry on, look at us, we won the war militarily, but we lost it in real terms; see the Germans, Japanese, the two strongest economies in the world, because their countries had been so completely destroyed, that money had to be pumped in to rebuild the industries that support these countries. They've managed it, why couldn't the blacks whose countries weren't even destroyed? Why do we always have to keep giving in to their begging bowls? Money which we could do with ourselves, never mind how the poor blacks are suffering around the world.

**Lee** *gives* **Alan** *a sarcastic, slow hand-clap.*

**Alan**   You know, Lee, you remind me of this copper I met once, told me this story. This black geezer is parking his car, music blaring out from his speakers. My mate the copper still has to go over and have a word, asks the geezer to turn the music down, neighbours bin complaining. The geezer says no, carrying on like my mate was putting the chains back on him. Anything like that happen to you, Lee?

**Lawrie**   All the time, par for the course.

**Lee**   Why don't you tell him my whole life, you seem to know it better than me. (*Goes back to the game.*)

**Lawrie** (*follows*)   They got no respect, Lee, you know that.

**Lee**   Yer gonna lecture them about respect, Lawrie?

**Jason**   We're gonna be 2–0 down.

**Becks**   We need a goal.

**Mark**   Doubt it somehow.

**Barry**   No ideas, not one creative mind.

**Jason**   Where's Gazza when you need him.

**Mark**   Gazza of old.

**Sharon**, **Duane**'s *mum, comes bursting in.*

**Sharon**   Which one of you bastards hurt my boy?

**Jimmy**   Gina?

**Sharon**   Which one of you touch him?

**Gina**   You wanna calm down please, love.

**Sharon**   Move!

**Gina**   Do it, or leave my pub.

**Sharon**   Yer lucky I don't bring the police, 'bout you rough up my son!

**Gina**   Yer son nicked my boy's phone.

**Sharon**    Weren't him.

**Gina**    He told you that?

**Sharon**    I said it weren't him. You didn't even give him a chance to explain, you tek one look, see his face, thass it! Hey, don't walk away from me, yer racist bitch!

**Gina**    Wat did you say?

**Sharon**    Yer deaf ?

**Alan**    Yer boy was shoutin the odds.

**Sharon**    You can shut yer mout as well. I bet it was you.

**Lee**    Calm down, love.

**Sharon**    Let go of my arm.

**Lee**    I said calm down.

**Sharon**    You the police?

**Lee**    Yes. Now calm yerself down, before I arrest yer.

**Sharon**    Oi, bitch, I ain't finished wid you. Who did it?

**Gina**    Get her out of my face.

**Lee**    Mark, help us out here.

**Mark**    No.

**Sharon**    Don't look yer nose down on me right!

**Gina**    Get out, you silly cow.

**Sharon**    Come mek me, I'll tear yer fuckin eye out.

**Lee**    Leave it!

**Sharon** *strikes out at* **Lee**. **Lawrie** *screams out his brother's name.* **Lee** *restrains her by twisting her arm behind her back.* **Sharon** *shrieks in pain.*

**Lawrie**    You awright, son?

**Lee**    Yes!

**Lawrie**   Are you sure?

**Mark**   Lee!

**Lee**   You had yer chance, back off.

**Phil**   Wass goin on?

**Becks** (*sees the commotion*)   Jesus! Yer brother, Baz.

**Barry**   So wat?

**Mark**   Lee, get off her, man.

**Lee**   I told you, Mark.

**Sharon**   Bitch!

**Lee**   Jimmy, call the police.

## Act Two

*Same location as Act One.*

**Jason**, **Barry**, **Becks** *are watching the game. It is a few minutes into the second half.* **Phil** *is watching the commotion going on outside the window.*

**Barry**  I'd give Posh Spice a fucking good seeing to I would. Fuck her till she screams. I'd strip off all her clothes, her damp and sticky knickers, I'd lay her down on the floor, frig her pussy with my fingers, rubbing away at her clit, till she had an orgasm. Then I'd give her a fuck, long lingering fuck. And she'll take it cos she's juicy and sexed up. I'll find out if she takes it up the arse. I'll do it. You hear me, Beckham? Thass wat I'm gonna do to yer fucking wife, if you don't score some goals!

**Jason**  Easy, Barry.

**Barry**  He's gettin on my nerves.

**Becks**  Ain't he carryin sum injury?

**Phil**  His left knee, I think.

**Becks**  I bet he's thinkin about Man U. They got a Champions League game soon, he don't want to get injured. Playing for England don't mean nuttin to them any when England play, Man U don't exist. Bloody money they're on.

**Phil**  More police out there, they're tellin that Sharon to shut it.

**Jason**  Wat still? Just cart her off, the mad bitch.

**Phil**  She's got sum mouth.

**Barry** (*chants*)  ENGLAND! ENGLAND!

**Phil**  Now Mark's gettin stuck in, he's gonna get nicked an all, if he ain't careful.

**Barry**  Come on!

**Phil**   Now she's mouthin off at Mark.

**Jason**   Gina?

**Phil**   Sharon! Tellin him she don't need his help. Barry, shouldn't you be out there?

**Barry**   ENGLAND!

**Phil**   Baz!

**Barry**   Wat?

**Phil**   He's your brother, you should be backing him up.

**Barry**   I'm watchin the game.

**Becks**   You ain't gonna miss anything.

**Barry**   So why are you still here then?

**Jason**   Cos we follow England.

**Barry**   Wat you tryin to say, Jase?

**Jason**   Nuttin.

**Barry**   I'm not white enuff for England?

**Jason**   Oh behave yerself.

**Barry**   Is it?

**Jason**   You lot need to chill out.

**Barry**   Black people.

**Jason**   Awright, yeah! Black people. Going off on one all the time. Whenever someone says the slightest thing. All yer doing is pissing people off.

**Barry**   All I'm doing is watching the match.

**Jason**   So watch it! 'kin 'ell.

**Becks**   Awright, boys, come on, let's bring out the peace pipe. Look, Kieron Dyer's on, he might do summin. (*Goes behind the bar*.) Who wants a drink, Phil? Come on, free round.

**Phil** Awright quick, top this up.

**Barry**   Sharon is nuttin but a mouthy cow. She wants to get nicked, thass her problem.

**Becks**   Yes, Baz, watever, mate, calm yerself.

**Barry**   I am calm.

**Becks**   Good.

**Barry** (*chants*)   ENGLAND!

**Jimmy** *and* **Glen** *come back in.*

**Gina**   Crazy bitch.

**Jimmy**   Awright, love.

**Gina**   She's a fuckin loon. (*To* **Jason** *and* **Barry**.) Get yer bloody feet off my seats.

**Jimmy** (*to* **Becks**)   Settling in? Get yer arse out of there. Yer a thievin bastard, Julian, juss like yer old man.

**Becks**   I was gonna pay.

**Jimmy**   Too right you'll pay, how much you had, you little . . . ?

**Jason**   He ain't had much, Jimmy, I swear, come on, whose round, Phil?

**Phil**   Na.

**Jason**   Yer as tight-arsed as Becks, you.

**Barry**   I'll get 'em in. man.

**Phil**   And me.

**Barry** *goes to the bar.*

**Gina**    Sorry for wat I said. That Sharon juss wound me up. You know me, I ain't got a problem with nobody.

**Barry**    It's awright.

**Gina**    Yer brother won't see it that way.

**Barry**    I ain't my brother.

**Gina**    OK.

**Barry**    I ain't losin my rag awright.

**Gina**    OK.

**Barry**    Stop sayin OK. I'm juss sayin, I'm tellin yer, I'm not my brother. I want to watch the match, wat Mark does is up to him. I don't want to be like 'em. Go all mad all the time, like we've all got an attitude. I don't.

**Lee** *comes in followed by* **Lawrie** *and* **Alan**.

**Lawrie**    You soft cunt. I'm talkin to you.

**Becks**    Wat?

**Lawrie**    He only tells his mates to let that Sharon off.

**Lee**    I didn't see the point in taking it through.

**Alan**    The point was made when they put the cuffs on her.

**Lawrie**    She only bit one of them.

**Alan**    You can't change people like that.

**Lee**    And you juss had to stand there, stirring it.

**Lawrie**    Lee, she went for yer, she coulda had a knife.

**Lee**    You see knives everywhere, Lawrie. Whenever we go out, whenever you see a black person, you think they've got a knife.

**Lawrie**    Well, pardon me for caring.

**Lee**    I'm awright.

**Lawrie**    Ungrateful or wat eh? Don't come crying to me when one of them stabs yer again.

**Alan**    You want to be a bit more grateful, son.

**Lee**    Get out of my face.

**Alan**    Comfortable, is it? The fence you're sitting on? Wake up.

**Lawrie**    Oh leave him. I don't know wass the matter wid him.

**Alan**    Don't ever lose your rag like that again.

**Lawrie**    Eh?

**Alan**    You were this much from getting arrested as well. It seems par for the course with you. Is it any wonder no one listens to us?

**Lawrie**    Hold up.

**Alan**    I couldn't believe my eyes when I saw you lot running amok in Belgium this summer. Fighting in the streets, smashing up bars and caffs. What was that?

**Lawrie**    It's about been English. All the things you've said.

**Alan**    That wasn't been English, you were acting like a bunch of savages. You were no better than the coons.

**Lawrie**    It's how I feel.

**Alan**    That's no excuse.

**Lawrie**    There's nuttin that makes me wanna say I'm proud to be English.

**Alan**    No one wants to speak up for you. It's not fashionable.

**Lawrie**    Right.

**Alan**    But they want to speak up for the blacks, queers, Pakis, that's fashionable.

**Lawrie**   Yes!

**Alan**   You just want to run out and beat the shit out of someone. I understand.

**Lawrie**   So wass the problem?

**Alan**   It scares people off.

**Lawrie**   It don't scare me.

**Alan**   You don't speak for the country.

**Lawrie**   So, what?

**Alan**   It's smart-arses who are in control of this country, on every level, and we have to be as clever. Keep this country white, away from the blacks. They're just marginalising them. Don't let them marginalise us. Gina's right, get your head out of crap like the *Sun*, get down the library, read a book, read ten books.

**Lawrie**   I hate books.

**Alan**   Not any more. I'll give you a list. Because knowledge is power. You want to hide something from the black man, put it in a book.

**Lawrie**   I'd rather kill 'em.

**Alan**   Read.

*They continue their game of pool.* **Lee** *is by the bar with* **Gina**. *The lads are still watching the game.*

**Jason**   We should be wearing our home kit. The blue and white.

**Becks**   Why?

**Jason**   We always seem to play worse in our red. Wat do you think?

**Phil**   I think yer talkin shit.

**Jason**   Look.

**Phil**   We wore red in '66, and won.

**Becks**   We wore white and blue in the semis in Italy and lost.

**Barry**   We wore all white against the Argies in '98 and lost.

**Phil**   And in Euro '96, against the fuckin Germans again!

**Barry**   No we didn't.

**Phil**   We did lose.

**Barry**   I mean, we wore all blue for that, yer muppet.

**Phil**   Oh right. I musta bin thinkin about the other game.

**Jason**   I hated that blue kit.

**Becks**   Everyone hated it.

**Barry**   Our home kit then was all right, I like that. I don't know why they changed it. I really liked the touch of light blue it had, on the collars and cuff, and that bit on the shorts.

**Boys** (*agreeing*)   Yeah.

**Barry**   Nice.

**Phil**   I thought the last one we had was awright as well, with the blue and the red stripes down the sides. With a touch of white on the blue shorts.

**Boys** (*agreeing*)   Yeah.

**Phil**   Very nice.

**Gina**   I don't care what colour she is. She deserves to be carted off. Mouthin off like that.

**Lee**   Lawrie didn't help. I'm so sick of this. He won't listen.

**Gina**   He loves his football.

**Lee**   From the day he was born. Thirtieth July, 1966.

**Gina**   And?

**Lee**   Day England won the World Cup.

**Gina**   Shut up.

**Lee**   On my life.

**Gina**   No way!

**Lee**   Dad wanted to name him after Geoff Hurst. (**Gina** *laughs*.) Mum wouldn't have it. You know how many times I've heard Dad going on about that match, describing every goal? When England ruled the world again for four glorious years, when Enoch, best prime minister we never had, spoke the truth. Lawrie loved that shit.

**Gina**   Wait till I tell Dad.

**Lee**   I can't do it, Gina.

**Gina**   Do wat?

**Lee**   The job. He's my brother, he gets on my tits, but I feel like agreeing with him sometimes. Cos thass the bitta Dad rubbing off on me. But that's not the kind of copper I want to be. But then I'm thinkin it's too late. Whenever a black geezer comes up to me now, I'm shakin. I'm angry. All I wanted to do that night, Gina, was calm it all down. All the things they moan about on the telly, all the things police officers don't do, that they hate, what they should be doing, well, I was doing it! All of it! I was treating all those people at that rave like people, not black people, but people! I wanted to understand, I was trying to listen, I wanted to prove that not all coppers are the same.

**Gina**   Lee?

**Lee**   Then he stabbed me. That fuckin black bastard stabbed me. I ain't racist, Gina, but it's how I felt, it's how I still feel, is that so wrong? That bloke tried to kill me, and he got away with it.

**Gina**   I ain't judging yer.

**Lee**   All I wanted to do was help.

**Gina**    There's yer problem. Don't help them. Don't try to understand them. Do yer job. Don't lose yerself in anger, Lee.

**Phil**    Oh come on!

**Jason**    Fuck's sake

**Becks**    They're gettin comfortable again, we gotta keep possession, gotta push 'em back, see how they like it in their own half for once.

**Jason**    Oh yu useless wankers, come on. Please! I'm beggin yer!

*The boys get excited as Le Saux makes a run.*

Yes, yes!

**Phil**    Come on, Le Saux!

**Becks**    Come on, Le Saux!

**Jason**    Fuckin cross it!

*German defender heads it away.*

**Phil**    Shit.

**Jason**    Wass he head that away for? Let us have one, yer greedy cunts!

**Barry** *leaves his seat.*

**Jason**    Ware you goin, Baz? Baz? (*Mimics* **Barry**.) All I'm doing is watchin the watch.

**Barry** *goes to the pool table.*

**Barry**    My name was on the board.

**Alan**    Was it?

**Barry**    I was supposed to be playing next.

**Lawrie**    Yeah?

**Alan**    Lawrie?

**Lawrie** *steps aside as* **Barry** *picks up a cue.*

**Alan**    We are all friends here.

**Barry** *and* **Alan** *play pool together.* **Lawrie** *watches on.*

**Alan**    So, how is it going?

**Barry**    Awright.

**Alan**    That was a splendid couple of goals you got this morning. Did you ever think about turning pro?

**Barry**    Had a trial for Fulham. Didn't cut it.

**Alan**    Their loss. Who do you follow?

**Barry**    Man U.

**Alan**    Man U?

**Barry**    Ain't they good enough?

**Alan**    Comedian.

**Lawrie**    I'd shit on Man U.

**Alan**    Yes, that is very nice, Lawrie, but no one is asking you, are they? (*To* **Barry**.) Follow your local team, what is the matter with you? It's about loyalty. Family even. You don't choose your family, they are just there, from the moment you are born. Through thick and thin. They're with you, you're with them. You are born in the town of your team. They are your family as well, your blood. And every Saturday, you are watching them play, willing them on to score, then another, and another. Final whistle goes. And you all roar and cheer. You can't wait till next Saturday. Starts all over again. And no matter where you go, where you move. You take them with you, in your heart. When was the last time you've been to Old Trafford?

**Barry**    Does it matter? I follow them.

**Alan**    But do you feel them?

**Barry**    Course.

**Alan**   Where were you born?

**Barry**   Shepherds Bush.

**Alan**   Queens Park Rangers.

**Barry**   They're shit.

**Alan**   They're yer blood.

**Barry**   I ain't following them.

**Alan**   Just as you like.

**Barry**   So who do you follow?

**Alan**   Aston Villa. What are you laughing at? My dad followed Villa. I was born in Birmingham. We all moved to London when I was ten. But I took them with me, in my heart.

**Barry**   You still watch them?

**Alan**   Whenever I can. I can still remember my first game. My dad took me when I was nine. 1961 it was. We beat Sheffield Wednesday 4–1. We played them off the Park. And it was John Dixon's last game for Villa.

**Barry**   Who?

**Alan**   One of the best players we ever had. He stayed with the club for seventeen years. He could score goals as well as make them and play all five forward positions as well as his own, left half. He was our captain when we won the cup in '57. What a game. I've still got the programme. Still, Man U, are a blinding side, can't argue with that. Your Andy Cole is doing all right for himself, and the other one, wasshisface.

**Barry**   Dwight Yorke. Used to be one of yours.

**Alan**   Yes all right, don't rub it in. Class player he was.

**Barry**   Still is.

**Alan**   Always smiling. Should have seen the verbal he got from some of the fans though when he came back to Villa, wearing a Man U shirt. Black this, black that! I have never heard anything like it. What was it that them Liverpool fans used to chant at John Barnes when he first started playing for them? Lawrie?

**Lawrie**    Better dead, than a nigger in red.

**Alan**    Right. Must be hard for you as well.

**Barry**    I never get it.

**Alan**    Well, then you are lucky. Isn't he lucky, Lawrie?

**Lawrie**    Yeah, he's lucky.

**Alan**    It's good to hear that. It gives hope to us all. You are a black person who everyone sees as a person first, not their colour.

**Barry**    I am a person.

**Alan**    That is what I said. Never mind the ones who only see you as a black person. Have you ever run into those people, son?

**Barry**    No.

**Alan**    The ones who think being white is the norm?

**Barry**    I said no.

**Alan**    Awright, son. I'm just trying to put myself in your shoes. No need to get jumpy.

**Barry**    I'm not jumpy.

**Alan**    I understand where you are coming from, I really do. You're from this country, you live here, born here, but there are still a few, the minority, that won't accept you.

**Barry**    I am accepted.

**Alan**    Course you are. I mean, you're not like the Asians, are you?

**Barry**    Damn right I ain't.

**Alan**    No. I don't see your lot owning hundreds of shops all lined up next to each other down Southall. Cutting yourselves off from the rest of the country. Not speaking the Queen's English. Your lot ain't like that at all. You're sweet with us now. Two shots. It must get to you though, when you meet the ones who just want to know about the black experience.

**Barry**    That ain't me.

**Alan**    White girls, eyeing you up all the time, because they're curious, about the myth. White guys wanting to be your mates, because they are curious as well. Penis envy, hardly acceptance, is it, Barry?

**Barry**    Wass the matter wid yer?

**Alan**    Right-on liberals, stupid lefties, all lining up, wanting to do you all a favour, they're just scared you'll lose yer tempers, mug them after work, how equal is that? All that talk, understanding, deep down they know, they believe, blacks are inferior, whites are superior. You must feel really small when you meet people like that . . .

**Barry**    . . . Look, juss fuck off, awright!

**Barry** *rejoins the others.*

**Alan**    Barry? Barry son?

**Lawrie**    Wat was that?

**Alan**    Reeling them in, throwing them back. The boy's got no idea who his friends are.

**Phil**    Oh look, he's bringin a sub on.

**Becks**    Oh nice one, Keegan, yer muppet!

**Barry** (*screams*)    Come on, you England!

**Jason**    Baz?

**Barry**   Stand up, if you won the war! Stand up, if you won the war!

**Jason**   Not again.

**Barry**   You dirty German bastard! You dirty German bastard!

**Jason**   Barry!

**Barry**   ENGLAND!

**Jimmy**   Oi, Lionel Ritchie, keep it down yeah.

**Mark** *comes back into the pub.*

**Jimmy**   You going to be nice now?

**Mark**   Leave me alone, Jimmy.

**Jimmy**   I can't do that. Leave the attitude outside, Mark.

**Mark**   I'm juss watching the game.

**Jimmy**   Wat happened to that happy little smilin coloured kid I used to know eh? Good little boy? Go on, sit down.

**Mark** *joins the boys, he sits near* **Lee.**

**Jason**   Wat do you call that?

**Lee**   You go to the station?

**Mark**   They had to drag her in there.

**Lee**   She was resisting arrest, Mark.

**Mark**   Like an animal.

**Lee**   Wat were they supposed to do?

**Mark**   Four coppers, one woman.

**Lee**   You saw how she was.

**Mark**   Four coppers, one woman.

**Lee**   You never listen, it's your point of view or nuttin.

**Jimmy**    Mark?

**Lee**    We're all right, Jimmy. (*To* **Mark**.) I tried to calm the situation as well as I could.

**Mark**    You takin the piss?

**Lee** *goes to the bar.*

**Mark**    Wat you runnin for?

**Lee**    Top it up, Gina.

**Mark**    Wat you runnin for?

**Gina**    Leave it out, Mark.

**Mark**    You really think she deserved to be treated like that?

**Lee**    Why you always pushin me?

**Mark**    Do yer, Lee?

**Gina**    He was doing his job.

**Mark**    Stick together, like old times ennit?

**Gina**    Oh piss off!

**Lee**    Bloody . . .

**Mark**    Say it, Lee, call me a nigger again.

**Lee**    He really wants me to.

**Mark**    It's wat I am!

**Gina**    Will you stop.

**Mark**    You didn't want me havin her cos I was black.

**Gina**    Oh Mark.

**Lee**    White guy steals white girl from black guy, it juss doesn't happen, does it, Mark? It's the other way round.

**Mark**    You wanted to finish wid me cos I was black.

**Gina**   I finished wid you cos you were boring. You were boring in bed, and you were boring to talk to. If you woke up tomorrow as white as I am, you'll still be boring.

**Jimmy** (*approaching*)   I warned you, son, come on.

**Gina**   Leave it alone, Dad.

**Barry**   ENGERLAND! ENGERLAND! ENGERLAND!

**Becks**   Awright, Baz, Jesus!

**Gina**   Will you sort him out please.

**Mark** (*approaching*)   Barry, come on.

**Barry**   Wass up, bro? My brother! He's more English than any of you, he's protected this country. He's protected you! Come on, you England! Stand up if you won the war!

**Gina**   Take him home.

**Barry**   Game ain't finished.

**Mark**   He'll be awright. Come on!

**Becks**   Wat again? They tugging each other's plonkers or wat?

*Lights on* **Barry** *and* **Mark** *in the Gents.*

**Barry**   Fucking bastard! 'bout I ain't English.

**Mark**   Who?

**Barry**   That geezer Alan. Talkin to me like I'm stupid.

**Mark**   You shoulda stayed away from him.

**Barry**   Shoulda told him about Euro '96. Wembley, Holland, the game!

**Mark**   I know.

**Barry**   We killed them, oh man, we killed them! Four goals, class written all over them. The best match since '66. Saw it wid me own eyes. You, me and Lee. Cheering the lads on, singing our hearts out. I backed you and Lee up when those bunch of Dutch fans tried to have a pop, we kicked every bit of shit out of them. Then we roared, right into their faces, England! Shoulda told him that, then give him a fuckin slap.

**Mark**    See? They only pretend to be yer friends.

**Barry**    I don't have problems with the rest of them.

**Mark**    Not yet.

**Barry**    What are we, a couple of Pakis now? Wass happened to you?

**Mark**    I juss saw Sharon dragged by her hair.

**Barry**    So what, she's a loudmouth bitch. You told me yerself, thass why you dumped her.

**Mark**    So, she deserve that?

**Barry**    Stop using her as an excuse.

**Mark**    I ain't.

**Barry**    You are.

**Mark**    Look, yer right, I don't want to go home either. I don't want to see Dad like that. So let's get out of here, check out Daryl and dem, I bet they're watchin the match.

**Barry**    I don't like Daryl and his mates.

**Mark**    You shouldn't be afraid of yer own people.

**Barry**    I ain't afraid of them, I juss don't like some of 'em. I don't fit in. You feel the same, Mark, well, used to. I loved the way you were with them. Them carryin on with their bad attitude, you used to slap them down, they were havin a laugh. Wass the army done to you? (*Takes off his shirt, shows his tattoo.*) Look.

**Mark**    Barry . . .

**Barry**    Thass British, thass us! Don't laugh at me, it's us. Show me yours.

**Mark**   Get off.

**Barry**   You were gonna wear it wid pride, you said. You didn't care who sees your red, white and blue, or who laughs, cos you ain't ending up like some black cunt. We are British, we are here! We kick arse with the best of them. God save the Queen, you told me that.

**Mark**   They don't want us here, Barry.

**Barry**   We were born here.

**Mark**   They don't care.

*Lights up on the bar.*

**Glen** *comes down. The screen turns blue again. Lads groan.*

**Becks**   Oh shut up, yer gettin on my tits now, the lot of yer.

**Gina**   How's my little prince then?

**Glen**   Awright.

**Gina**   Yer still gorgeous. (*Kisses him on the cheek.*)

**Glen** (*embarrassed*)   Mum?

**Jimmy**   You stopped cryin then?

**Gina**   Dad?

*She holds up a beer glass to remind her father of her earlier threat.*

I thought you were going to watch telly?

**Glen**   Nuttin's on.

**Gina**   Watch a video then. (*Gets a fiver from the till.*) Here, go down the video shop.

**Glen**   I don't want to go out.

**Gina**   You can't stay in here for ever, sweetheart. Sooner or later you're going to have to face those boys 'gain.

**Glen**   I know I have to face them again, Mum, but I don't want to do it now.

**Gina**  Calm down, I'm on your side, darlin. Go on, sit with the lads, watch the game. Go on, they don't bite.

**Glen** *joins* **Lee** *and the others. They all greet him warmly.*

**Jason**  Awright, Glen?

**Phil**  How you doing, son?

**Lawrie**  You want a Coke, Glen?

**Glen**  Yeah.

**Gina**  Yeah wat?

**Glen**  Yeah please.

**Gina**  Cheers, Lawrie.

**Lawrie**  Top this up as well, Gina.

**Jason**  Come on, Glen, cheer up.

**Becks**  Wat goes around, comes around, those black kids will get theirs.

**Phil**  This whole area is going down.

**Becks**  See, Glen, wat you have to do, is get a little gang of yer own, you and a few white lads.

**Jason**  Don't let Gina hear yer.

**Lee**  Or me!

**Becks**  There's nuttin wrong wid that?

**Lee**  You sure?

**Becks**  I've seen black gangs, Asian gangs, how can it be racist, if them boys are doing it? Get yerself some white boys, Glen, stick together, show sum pride. (*To screen.*) Unlike these wankers!

**Lee** (*to* **Glen**)    Oi, you ignore every word he said, you hear me?

**Phil**   Glen, come here, got a joke for yer. There's this black geezer right, Winston, nice fella, well thick. Anyway he's feelin a sick one morning, so he rings up his boss at work sayin (*puts on worst West Indian accent*), Ey, boss, I not come work today, I really sick. I got headache, stomach ache, and my legs hurt, I not come work. The boss goes, Oh Winston, you know I really need you today. It's important. Now, when I feel like this, I go to my wife, and tell her to give me sex. That makes me feel better and I can go to work. You should try that. Two hours later, Winston calls back, saying, Boss, boss, I did wat you said and I feel great, man! I be back at work real soon, boss. By the way, you got a nice house!

*The boys roar with laughter.*

Oops, I can see a smile, a smile is coming, he's smiling, he's smiling!

*Boys cheer.*

**Lee**   Is anyone watchin the match here?

**Phil**   What match?

**Jason**   Useless cunts.

**Phil**   Ere, Glen, come here. Yer mum still got that same boyfriend?

**Glen**   No. Why?

**Phil**   Nuttin.

**Barry** *and* **Mark** *come back.*

**Becks**   Barry my man, were you bin?

**Jason**   Have a nice tug, did yer? (*Rubs* **Barry**'s *head.*)

**Barry**   Don't.

**Jason**   Oooh, handbag.

**Gina**   We happy over there?

**Mark**   Sweet as, Gina.

**Alan**    Fancy a game, son?

**Mark**    I'm outta here.

**Alan**    Come on, one game.

**Mark**    Play me like you did my brother?

**Alan**    I have no idea what you mean.

**Mark**    Don't even bother.

**Alan**    All right then, I won't. But I bet you've fantasised about having a debate with someone like me. You want to shoot me down, find flaws in my twisted logic.

**Mark**    I've fantasised about kicking the shit out of someone like you.

**Alan**    That would be too easy. You and I agree on similar things.

**Mark**    Move.

**Alan** (*quotes*)    'They don't want us here, Barry.' I was in one of the cubicles. I overheard.

**Mark**    We got nuttin in common.

**Alan**    Let's see. (*Offers a cue-stick.*) Do you know what the main thing is that I hear people moan about? It's that, they don't think they can talk about it. They can't voice their concerns, how they feel, they're too scared to be called racists by the PC brigade. Now, I don't know about you, Mark, but I think we've got to get through that, because if people can't talk to each other, different communities, being honest, we are not going to get anywhere. So, come on. You and me, let's pave the way. If you want to stop people from being like me, then you had better start listening to people like me.

**Mark** *takes the cue-stick.*

**Alan**    So, army boy . . .

**Mark**    Ex.

**Alan**   What happened?

**Mark**   My CO was a racist wanker, so I smacked him one.

**Alan**   Nasty.

**Mark**   For him.

**Alan**   Do you know what you are going to do now?

**Mark**   You gonna give me a job? Let's get on with it.

**Alan**   Putting me straight. I like that. Do you watch TV, Mark?

**Mark** (*sarcastic*)   Once or twice.

**Alan**   All of those chat shows they have in the morning. *Trisha*, *Kilroy*, Richard & Judy.

**Mark**   Is there a point coming?

**Alan**   Any time they have some big issue to bang on about, they invite the general public, the great working class to have their say. Live debates, phone-ins, big mistake. I shudder when I hear them speak. Cringe. They are so inarticulate, they cannot string two sentences together. They are on live TV, and I'm screaming at the telly, articulate, you stupid sap. And their arguments, their points of view, Jesus Christ! So ignorant, stupid, dumb, deeply flawed, simplistic. It's obvious they have never read a book in their lives. I've seen black people on those programmes as well, son, and no offence, but it seems as though they've been eating retard sandwiches. Have you ever felt that way about them?

**Mark**   No.

**Alan**   Come on, Mark, honesty. Play the game.

**Mark**   Yes.

**Alan**   You hate the way they talk.

**Mark**   Yes.

**Alan**   You want to scream at them, they're letting the side down.

**Mark**   Yes.

**Alan**   Make your point, and make it well.

**Mark**   You gonna make yours?

**Alan**   Like me, you want to be better than that, but, unlike me, you know, wisely I might add, that can never happen. Not here.

**Mark**   Wat?

**Alan**   Look at us, Mark. (*Points at everyone.*) The white working class. You think it was an accident we are all as thick as shit? It's because of the powers that be. I know their game. Britain needs people like Lawrie to do the shit jobs. It can't have everyone bein a doctor or a lawyer, the economy would fall apart. Give them the shit life, shit education, the works. And do you know who we are going to blame for not getting ahead? You. Why? Because you're different, because it's convenient, because it's easier to blame you than it is to think about what's really going on, and the reason why we don't think is because we can't, and the reason we can't is the Hoo-ra-Henrys made sure of it. Spin us a tale, put it in the tabloids, we'll buy it. We'll blame anyone thass different for our own shortcomings. They want us to fight, they want us to fight you. We'll fight, but not the way they think. This is our country, we made it, and we don't belong in the gutter, because they say we do.

**Mark**   But we do, yeah?

**Alan**   You're not dragging us down.

**Mark**   Gimme one good reason why I shouldn't wrap this cue-stick round yer head.

**Alan**   Because I can help you.

**Mark**   By sending me back to ware I come from?

**Alan**    Eventually.

**Mark**    Convincing all my brothers and sisters to do the same, work for you?

**Alan**    It's not as uncommon as you think. Some of our European friends have had black and Jewish branches. We're thinking of setting up our own ethnic liaison committee.

**Mark**    Yer certifiable.

**Alan**    Don't tell me you're happy wid the way yer lot carry on, especially round here. They can't fall out of bed without getting into trouble.

**Mark**    I know how I feel, and yeah they make me sick to be black. All they're doin is provin you and me right. But I don't want to be right, any more, I want to be proved wrong. I'm sick of being angry.

**Alan**    That's soppy talk.

**Mark**    I want to be who I want.

**Alan**    You are telling me you want to spend the rest of your life walking round like an arsehole with your cap in hand, waiting for the great white man to save you? He wants to kill you. Have some respect for yourself, stand up on your own two feet, make your own mark in the world, no one else will do it for you.

**Mark** (*laughs*)    You sound like my old man.

**Alan**    Wise man, was he?

**Mark**    He thought he was.

**Alan**    What did he do?

**Mark**    Bus conductor.

**Alan**    How long?

**Mark**    Thirty-odd years.

**Alan**    And I bet he had to scrimp and save all his life.

**Mark**    Who doesn't?

**Alan**    But that is not what he wanted when he came here, I bet. Or are you telling me he left the sun and sea of the West Indies for the grey skies of London to be a bus conductor? The poor sod probably wanted to party all night, sleep with as many white women as possible, and smoke loads of shit.

**Mark** *bursts out laughing.*

**Alan**    You looked at him, and you thought, no way am I ending up like that. But you are, it's still happening. That is why you should go. Tell this country what to go and do with itself. No one is going to help you.

**Mark**    I don't want help.

**Alan**    You all want it, you're lost without us.

**Mark**    I want a chance.

**Alan**    But it us white people that's pulling all the strings, Mark. We'll decide how many chances you get. We're never going to change, so stop wishing. Show me one white person who has ever treated you as an equal, and I will show you a liar. The minute one of them says they are going to treat you as an equal, they're not. Because, in order to do that, they have to see you differently. It will never come as naturally as when they see another white person. All this multiculturalism. Eating a mango once a year at the Notting Hill Carnival is still a long way from letting your kids go to a school that is overrun with Pakis and blacks.

**Mark**    Wat is it wid you?

**Alan**    We come from different parts of the world, son, we have different ways of living.

**Mark**    I'm English.

**Alan**    No you're not.

**Mark**   I served in Northern Ireland. I swore an oath of allegiance to the flag.

**Alan**   Oh please.

**Mark**   How English are you? Where do you draw the line as to who's English. I was born in this country. And my brother. You're white, your culture comes from northern Europe, Scandinavia, Denmark. Your people moved from there thousands of years ago, long before the Celtic people and the Beeker people, what? You think cos I'm black, I don't read books. Where do you draw the line?

**Alan**   That's exactly the kind of ridiculous question we have to deal with.

**Mark**   Answer me.

**Alan**   The fact is, Mark, that the white British are a majority racial group in this country, therefore it belongs to the white British. If that was the case, what you're asking, we'd all be putting ourselves back into the sea. Because that is where we all originally came from, isn't it?

**Mark**   Yer full of shit.

**Alan**   We say that the people of European, white European descent are entitled to settle in Britain. Or the rest of Europe, where they are. We regard our racial cousins, the Americans, Canadians, as British. They've been implanted there over the centuries, now why should we take a time on it? The fact is the majority of blacks haven't been in this country for centuries, a few yes, maybe, but that's it. You've been here, predominantly, in your own numbers, three generations at most. That gives you squatters' rights. We're taking those squatters' rights away from you. You have given nothing to Britain, and you have never served any purpose in British history.

**Mark**   Oh, so the fact that thousands of black soldiers died during the war is lost on you.

**Alan**    Not as many as the Brits.

**Mark**    Or the fact that in the eighteenth century, there was a thriving black community, living right here?

**Alan**    Not as many as the Brits.

**Mark**    With their own pubs, churches, meeting places. Or the fact that in 1596, there were so many black slaves over here, working for their white owners, putting money in their pockets, doing all the work, that Queen Elizabeth saw them as a threat and wanted them out.

**Alan**    What are you on?

**Mark**    How many black Roman soldiers were here, when they came over and built your roads?

**Alan**    You're losing it.

**Mark**    Were you bullied at school, Alan? Couple of black kids nicked your dinner money? Or did your wife run off with a big black man? And I mean big black man? Or was it your mum?

**Alan**    If you're so smart, son, how come you still haven't caught up with us?

**Mark**    Cos you love pushing us down.

**Alan**    Well, push us back. You've had thousands of years. What are you waiting for, you useless bastards. Always some excuse. Can't you people take account for what you are doing to yourselves, instead of blaming us every five seconds?

**Mark**    You are to blame.

**Alan**    If you cannot hold your own to account for what they are doing, then we will be left to take drastic measures.

**Mark**    Is that right?

**Alan**    Lack of accountability creates anger, Mark, look at all the hate in the world, and it will twist some people's logic, just like Lawrie's, and flavour thought. Bad things are motivated purely by anger. You lot need to feel we will be held to account for what we've done, well, we need to feel it from you first.

**Mark**    You don't have the right.

**Alan**    Why's that?

**Mark**    Because yer white.

**Alan**    Who's the bigot now?

**Mark**    Go fuck yourself.

**Alan**    Face it, son, you're nothing but a ticked box. You will never be equal to us, and you know it.

**Mark**    You won't win. Thass wat I know.

**Alan**    We already have.

**Mark** (*chants*)    We shall not, we shall not be moved!

**Alan**    Mark?

**Mark**    We shall not, we shall not be moved, we shall not, we shall not be moved, we shall not, we shall not be moved, we shall not, we shall not be moved, we shall not, we shall not be moved, we shall not, we shall not be moved, we shall not, we shall not be moved, Baz!

**Barry** (*joins in*)    We shall not, we shall not be moved! We shall not, we shall not be moved –

**Mark/Barry**    We shall not, we shall not be moved! We shall not, we shall not be moved, And we'll go on, to win the great world cup, we shall not be moved!

**Phil**    You two pissed?

**Barry/Mark**    ENGLAND! (*Clap*.) ENGLAND! (*Clap*.) ENGLAND! (*Clap*.) ENGLAND! (*Clap*.) ENGLAND!

**Lawrie** (*approaching*)    You awright, Alan?

**Alan**    They can't even see when someone is doing them a favour. I've got a good mind to set you on him.

**Lawrie**    Why don't yer?

**Alan**    Don't be stupid.

**Lawrie**    I'll be careful.

**Lee** *comes out of the Gents.*

**Lawrie**    No fall-back on you. Say the word and he's dead.

**Lee**    Who's dead?

**Alan**    We are.

**Lee**    Who's dead, Lawrie?

**Lawrie**    No one.

**Lee** (*to* **Alan**)    You, fuck off.

**Alan**    Excuse me?

**Lee**    I'm talking to my brother.

**Alan** (*approaching*)    Another Scotch, Gina.

**Lawrie**    Take a shot.

**Lee** *throws the cue-stick across the table.*

**Lawrie**    Oh thass clever, Jimmy will love you if you break his cue.

**Lee**    You touch Mark, I'll have yer.

**Lawrie**    Easy, tiger.

**Lee**    I've had enuff of yer shit, Lawrie.

**Lawrie**    Oh why are you still sticking up for them?

**Lee**    It weren't Mark that stabbed me.

**Lawrie**    They're scum.

**Lee**    I won't let you.

**Lawrie**   Who looked after yer, held yer hand every night while you had yer nightmares, Lee? Do you still see him when you shut yer eyes? That coon coming at yer with his knife?

**Lee**   It's me he tried to kill.

**Lawrie**   And I want to kill every one of them.

**Lee**   Yer never happy unless yer gettin stuck in on someone's head.

**Lawrie**   Go on, fuck off. Go back to yer posh bird.

**Lee**   If you weren't such a prick, you'd come live with us.

**Lawrie**   I ain't no ponce.

**Lee**   You need looking after.

**Lawrie**   Yer my kid brother, you don't look after me. God, I feel like I want to explode sometimes.

**Lee**   See.

**Lawrie**   I woulda killed someone by now if it weren't for Alan. I really would. I can feel myself wantin to do it sometimes. Every morning when I wake up. I wanna make a bomb or summin, go down Brixton and blow every one of them up.

**Lee** (*slaps his face*)   I'll kill you first. Do you want me to choose, Lawrie?

**Lawrie**   Do wat you want.

**Lee**   I want me brother.

**Lawrie**   I'm here.

**Lee**   Ask Alan about Reading, watch his face drop.

**Lawrie**   Wat about it?

**Lee**   Him and his lot were recruiting teenagers. One of them got a little excited, beat up some Asian kid. Alan, blindin geezer, didn't even wait for the Old Bill to breathe down his neck. He gave up that boy's name so fast, well desperate to save his arse. My new DS comes from Reading. He worked on the case. You want that to be you?

**Lawrie**    That kid was stupid, he got caught.

**Lee**    Why won't you ever listen to me?

**Lawrie**    I ain't you, Lee.

**Lee**    Fucking Dad.

**Lawrie** (*snaps*)    Leave it!

**Lee**    Don't think I won't warn him.

**Lawrie**    You think thass gonna stop me?

*The final whistle blows. The game is finished.*

**Jason**    Wat a load of fuckin bollocks.

*Screen shows Kevin Keegan walking away with his head down. Sound of the crowd booing.*

Yeah, nice one, lads, boo the cunt!

*The boys join in the jeering.*

**Jimmy**    Southgate in midfield!

**Phil**    Cole up front wid Owen!

**Becks**    Lass game at Wembley!

**Phil**    You see that? Hamman's wearing an England sweater.

**Barry**    Who swapped jerseys?

**Phil**    It's a number 4 he's wearin.

**Becks**    Southgate.

**Barry**    Fuckin Kraut lover. We lose 1–0 and he's given him his jersey.

**Becks**'s *phone rings.*

**Becks** (*answers*)    Awright, Rob? Yeah I know, fuckin disgrace ennit? Wat? Rob goes the fans are booing Keegan.

**Jason**    They wanna fuckin lynch him.

**Mark**    Come on, who's drinkin?

**Phil**    Yeah, go on then, with any luck, I might drown the memory of this day away.

**Barry**    Lass game at Wembley.

**Mark**    They're buildin a new one.

**Barry**    Won't be the same.

**Becks**    Awright, see yer in a bit. (*Hangs up.*) Rob's gonna come over. Well, come on, let's have some beer.

**Jason**    Yeah whose round is it, Becks?

**Mark**    Na yer awright, I'll get 'em in.

**Becks**    Cheers, Mark.

**Mark**    Barry?

**Barry** *goes with his brother.*

**Jason**    You are so bleeding tight, Becks. You ain't put yer hand in yer pocket all day, have yer?

**Becks**    Is it my fault our coloured friends over there are so generous? Come on, smile, yer cunts. We can still get to the finals, it's not impossible. We'll beat the Germans next year.

**Phil**    Oh yeah, we're really gonna hammer them on their own turf, ain't we?

**Jason**    Wat do you reckon the score will be, Becks, 5–1 to us?

**Becks**    Sod yer then.

**Lee** *approaches* **Barry** *and* **Mark**.

**Lee**    You gotta get out of here. Both of yer.

**Mark**   Why's that?

**Lee**   Lawrie's on the warpath, I don't know if I can hold him back.

**Mark**   You've never tried.

**Lee**   Come on, not now.

**Barry**   He's gonna have a pop in front of everyone?

**Lee**   He doesn't care. Look, juss go, awright.

**Barry**   Mark?

**Mark**   We're stayin.

**Lee**   He's gonna do some damage.

**Mark**   It's nice to know you care.

**Lee**   Yer my best mate.

**Mark**   Were.

**Lee**   Are!

**Mark**   Then why'd you say it, Lee?

**Lee**   I'm sorry, fer fuck's sake.

**Mark**   If that walrus wants to have a pop, let 'im.

*A brick comes smashing through one of the windows.*

**Phil**   Oh fuck!

**Jason**   Jesus!

**Gina**   Dad!

**Phil**   I'm cut.

**Jimmy** (*sees the window*)   Christ.

**Phil**   Bastards!

**Gina**   You awright, Phil?

**Phil**   Do I look it?

**Gina**    Glen, get me the first-aid box.

**Alan** (*peers out of the window*)    You had better get the police as well. There is a whole army of black kids out there.

**Jason** (*looks out*)    Jesus!

*Another brick comes flying through.*

Oi! You black cunt.

**Lee**    Shut up, Jase.

**Jason**    They're lobbing bricks at us, wat you expect me to say?

**Lee**    I'm going out there.

**Lawrie** (*concerned*)    Lee?

**Lee**    You stay.

**Alan**    Lawrence. (*To* **Lee**.) He'll be all right.

**Mark**    Lee, hold up, mate.

**Lee**    Jimmy, call the police.

**Gina**    Tell them if they step one foot in my pub, they'll be murders.

**Mark** *and* **Lee** *go out.* **Gina** *treats* **Phil**'s *wounds with the first-aid box.*

**Becks** (*looks through the window*)    Thass the little sod who took Glen's phone.

**Glen** *runs behind the bar and goes upstairs.*

**Gina**    Glen, come back here, Glen!

**Phil**    He'll be awright. He's a good kid.

**Gina**    Oi, stop lookin at my tits.

**Phil**    I can't help it. They're lovely.

**Gina**    Excuse me?

**Phil**  Yer lovely.

**Gina**   Am I now?

**Phil**   Yeah.

**Gina**   You don't half pick yer moments, Philip.

**Jimmy** *approaches holding* **Glen** *by his ear.*

**Jimmy**   He was only trying to sneak out through the back door.

**Gina**   Wat you playing at?

**Glen**   It's my problem right, I'm gonna deal wid dem.

**Jimmy**   Listen to him.

**Glen**   Wat you moanin for?

**Jimmy**   There's a whole bleedin tribe out there, you wanna take them on? I've got a good mind to throw you out there myself.

**Gina**   You wanna do summin? Go change the loo rolls in the Gents.

**Glen** *goes to do as he is told.*

**Gina**   You call the police?

**Jimmy**   They're comin.

**Becks**   Might not need 'em now. Lee is doing the business, tellin them to back off.

**Phil** Send one of dem bastards in here, I'll do the business on them.

**Lawrie**   Is Lee awright?

**Becks**   He's doing the business. (*To* **Barry**.) And yer Mark. They make a good team.

**Gina** (*shouts by door*)   Mark? Lee? You find the bastards who broke my winder and tell them they owe me money.

*Some of the crowd shout obscenities at* **Gina**.

Yeah, fuck you an 'all. (*Shuts the door.*)

**Mark** *and* **Lee** *come back in.*

**Barry**   You awright, bruv?

**Mark**   Yeah. Thanks ever so much for helpin out there, Gina, very useful.

**Gina**   I weren't jokin, Mark, I want money for my winders.

**Mark**   It coulda bin worse.

**Lee**   They were well pissed.

**Mark**   Speakin of which. (*Goes to the loo.*)

**Lee**   I don't know how long me and Mark held them off for, they could come back. You call the police?

**Jimmy**   On way.

**Gina**   You sure that will do any good?

**Lee**   I dunno.

*He catches sight of* **Lawrie** *who looks like he's heading for the Gents.*

Lawrie? Lawrie!

**Lawrie** *in fact detours slightly and goes to the cigarette machine. Where he buys a packet of fags.*

**Lawrie** (*as calm as you like*)   Wat? (*Walks back to the pool table.*) *On the screen, Keegan is being interviewed.*

**Jimmy**   Wass he goin on about, Jase?

**Jason**   He's only fuckin quit.

**Phil**   Wat?

**Jason**   Straight up, Keegan's quit!

**Phil**   Muppet.

**Jimmy**   Jesus.

**Becks**    Gotta tell Rob. (*Dials.*) Rob! Yeah, I know, shit game. Listen, Keegan's quit. He bloody has, it's juss come on. Yer bloody booin musta got to him. (*Aside.*) They don't know.

**Jason**    Course they don't know, they won't know till they leave the stadium.

**Becks** (*to phone*)    Well, I won't miss him, dozy sod. Yeah we'll see yer in a bit. (*Hangs up.*) Wass Keegan sayin, wass he moanin about?

**Alan**    He's going on about how he can't do it no more.

**Becks**    Bloody girl.

**Lawrie**    Wat? He said wat?

**Becks**    Summin about him wantin to spend time wid his family.

**Lawrie** *throws his drink. It almost hits the screen.*

**Gina**    Lawrie! Thass our screen.

**Jimmy**    Yer lucky you didn't hit it. Oi, I'm talkin to you, Lawrie? If yer old man was still alive, he'd tan yer arse.

**Lawrie**    Keegan's got no backbone, Jimmy, this whole country's lost its spine.

**Jimmy**    Oh piss off

**Lawrie**    We ruled the world.

**Lee** (*approaching*)    Broth.

**Lawrie**    Go play wid yer monkey friends.

**Becks**    Ease up, Lawrie.

**Lawrie**    Did I ask yer for anything?

**Becks** (*scared*)    Nuh, mate, you didn't.

**Lawrie** *catches* **Barry***'s eye.*

**Lawrie**   You wanna have a pop? Well, come on then, black boy, show us how English you are.

**Lee**   Back off, Barry.

**Barry**   He challenged me.

**Lee**   He'll kill yer.

**Lawrie**   I'll have you, then those monkeys out there.

**Gina** *gets her baseball bat from behind the bar and waves it around.*

**Becks**   Whoa!

**Gina**   Not in my pub, you understand? Be told.

**Jason**   Yeah, Gina, watever you say.

**Phil**   I'm told.

**Alan**   Lawrie? (*Motions him to come over.*) Here!

**Lee**   Don't.

**Gina**   Leave him alone, Lee. He's a big boy.

**Lawrie** (*approaching*)   Why didn't you say anything?

**Alan**   Why won't you listen?

**Lawrie**   Cos I can't. Awright!

**Alan**   You won't even give yourself a chance. The smartarses want to write you off as a brainless wanker, and you're letting them.

**Lawrie**   Juss let me have 'em. I won't mess up, I ain't stupid like that kid in Reading.

**Alan**   What do you know about Reading?

**Lawrie**   Got it from Lee. If this kid got himself caught, then thass his lookout.

**Alan**   The kid's name was Brian.

**Lawrie**   You gonna let me?

**Alan**    You remind me of him. Short fuse, kept running off on his own.

**Lawrie**    Come on, Alan.

**Alan**    He wouldn't listen. And I don't have time for people who refuse to listen, Lawrence!

**Lawrie**    Well, I'm tired of waiting. I wanted him. He wanted me. They all want it. Ask any coon. Let's juss stop all this fuckin about, and get it on. Lass one standing at the final whistle, wins England.

**Alan**    You gotta trust me, my way is the way forward.

**Lawrie**    No wonder this Brian kid got pissed off with yer. I mean fer fuck's sake, Alan, d'yer really think those smartarses are gonna let us be as clever as them? I don't even want it.

**Glen** *is changing the loo paper in the Gents.* **Mark** *comes out of the next cubicle.*

**Mark**    You awright?

**Glen** *is getting frustrated as he cannot seem to get the finished loo roll off.*

**Mark**    Let me help.

**Glen**    No.

**Mark**    Don't be silly, there's nuttin to it.

**Glen**    Move.

**Glen** *shoves him, and as he does, a long kitchen knife drops from inside his jacket, on to the floor. He picks it quickly, but* **Mark** *has already seen it.*

**Mark**    Wat you doin wid that? Do you want me to go out and get yer mum, wat you doin wid that?

**Glen**    They fuck wid me, I'm gonna fuck wid them.

**Mark**    No, no that ain't the way, Glen.

**Glen**    You lot, you think yer so fuckin bad, I'll show you who's bad.

**Mark**    But this ain't the way. Duane and Tyrone yeah, they're juss boys. Not black boys, but juss boys. Stupid boys.

**Glen**    They're on us every day at school, all the white kids. Cos they think they're bad.

**Mark**    They're stupid boys, Glen.

**Glen**    You gonna move?

**Mark**    We are not all the same.

**Glen**    Move.

**Mark**    Juss gimme the knife.

**Mark** *moves to disarm him,* **Glen** *dodges* **Mark***, and stabs him repeatedly in the stomach.* **Mark** *drop to the floor.* **Glen** *cannot quite take in what he has done. He dashes out. Goes upstairs.*

**Gina**    You finished? Glen? Fine, ignore me why don't yer.

**Lawrie** *pops to the loo. He sees* **Mark***'s bleeding body and comes rushing out.*

**Lawrie**    We gotta go.

**Alan**    I don't waste time on losers, Lawrie, piss off.

**Lawrie**    Alan! We gotta go.

**Alan**    What have you done?

**Lawrie**    Nothing.

**Jason** (*comes running out of the loo*)    Oh shit!

**Gina**    Wat?

**Jason**    It's Mark.

**Barry**    Bruv? (*Sees* **Mark***.*) Mark!

**Lee**    Don't touch him.

**Barry**    Get off me.

**Lee**    Let me see, let me see.

**Barry**    Ambulance!

**Lee**    Barry, listen . . .

**Barry**    Get off me.

**Gina**    Christ!

**Lee**    Get out.

**Barry**    Help him.

**Lee**    Barry, he's dead, look at me, he's dead.

**Barry**    Who fuckin did it!

**Lee** *spots* **Phil** *and* **Becks** *trying to leave.*

**Lee**    Ware you going? You can't leave.

**Phil**    Oh, come on, mate.

**Lee**    No one leaves! Who was last in here?

**Lawrie** (*feels* **Alan**'s *stare*)    Wat?

**Lee**    Lawrie?

**Lawrie**    Oh yeah, here we go.

**Lee**    You were lass in the toilets.

**Lawrie**    It weren't me.

**Alan**    You bloody fool.

**Lawrie**    Alan, it weren't me, I saw him thass all.

**Barry** *runs at* **Lawrie**, *who holds him down, hitting him twice in the face.* **Lee** *pulls him off.*

**Lee**    Lawrie, enough, get off him.

**Lawrie**    I'm gonna line you up next to him.

**Lee**    Where's the knife, wat you do with it?

**Lawrie** *spits in his brother's face.*

**Lee** Lawrence Bishop. I am arrresting you on suspicion of murder, you do not have to say anything, but it may harm yer defence if you do not mention when questioned something you may rely on in court. (**Lawrie** *spits in his face again.*) Anything you do say will be given in evidence. You made me choose.

**Jason** This is fucked up.

**Becks** Let us go, Lee.

**Lee** No.

**Jimmy** *comes out, dragging* **Glen** *behind him.*

**Gina** Dad?

**Jimmy** Gina.

**Gina** Wat? Wat!

**Jimmy** *throws the bloodstained knife on to the bar.*

**Gina** No!

**Becks** Oh shit.

**Lee** Glen, come here.

**Gina** No, Glen!

**Lee** I said come here.

**Barry** It was you!

**Lee** Barry, juss back off, yeah.

**Barry** Don't you fuckin touch me!

**Glen** He's a black bastard, they all are.

**Gina** Shut up.

**Jimmy** Jesus.

**Gina** Hard enuff for yu now, Dad?

**Jimmy**    Gina?

**Alan**    Rivers of blood.

**Barry**    Yu shut yer mout, I'll kill yer. I'll kill all of yer. Come on, come on! Who wants me, come on! Yer fuckin  white cunts, all of yer! All of yer. Cunts! Come on! Yer white cunts.

**Lee**    Barry?

**Barry**    No.

*He wipes the paint off his face.*

No! No. (**Lee** *approaches*.) Fuck off. Get away from me.

**Lawrie**    Monkey lover.

**Jason** (*peers through window*)    Oh shit, they're only coming back.

**Phil**    Who?

**Jason**    Fuckin blacks.

**Lawrie**    No point playin games, Alan.

**Alan**    I don't know you.

**Lawrie**    No matter what, it'll come to this.

*Sound of police sirens approaching.*

**Lee**    Barry?

**Barry**    No.

**Lee** (*to* **Barry**)    Don't lose yerself.

**Kwame Kwei-Armah**

# Fix Up

**Kwame Kwei-Armah** won the Peggy Ramsay award for his first play, *Bitter Herb* (1998), which was subsequently put on by the Bristol Old Vic, where he also became Writer-in-Residence. He followed this up with the musical *Blues Brother, Soul Sister* which toured the UK in 2001. He co-wrote the musical *Big Nose* (an adaptation of *Cyrano de Bergerac*) which was performed at the Belgrade Theatre, Coventry in 1999. In 2003 the National Theatre produced the critically acclaimed *Elmina's Kitchen* for which in 2004 he won the *Evening Standard* Charles Wintour Award for Most Promising Playwright, and was nominated for a Laurence Olivier Award for Best New Play 2003. *Elmina's Kitchen* has since been produced and aired on Radio 3 and BBC4. His next two plays, *Fix Up* and *Statement of Regret*, were produced by the National Theatre in 2004 and 2007. He directed his play, *Let There Be Love*, when it premiered at the Tricycle Theatre, London, in 2008. He received an honorary doctorate from the Open University in 2008. His latest play was *Seize the Day* (Tricycle Theatre, 2009, part of their Not Black and White season).

*Fix Up* was first presented in the Cottesloe auditorium of the National Theatre, London, on 16 December 2004. The cast was as follows:

| | |
|---|---|
| **Brother Kiyi** | Jeffery Kissoon |
| **Carl** | Mo Sesay |
| **Kwesi** | Steve Toussaint |
| **Norma** | Claire Benedict |
| **Alice** | Nina Sosanya |

*Director*   Angus Jackson
*Designer*   Bunny Christie
*Lighting Designer*   Neil Austin
*Music*   Neil McArthur
*Sound Designer*   Gareth Fry

**Characters**

**Brother Kiyi** (*pronounced 'Key'*), *an old fifty-five, with greying unkempt locks. Owner of the Fix Up bookstore.*

**Carl**, *thirty-five. A local care-in-the-community delivery boy.*

**Kwesi**, *thirty-two. A militant black activist who uses a room upstairs in the shop.*

**Norma**, *fifty. Kiyi's long-time best friend.*

**Alice**, *thirty-four. A beautiful but troubled visitor to the store.*

**Non-Present Characters**

**Marcus Garvey**, *Jamaican-born leader of the UNIA back-to-Africa movement in America, early 1920s. Seen as the godfather of Black nationalism.*

**James Baldwin**, *celebrated outspoken New York novelist, essay writer and playwright.*

**Claude McKay**, *celebrated poet of the 'Harlem Renaissance'.*

## Scene One

*Fix Up bookstore.*

*It's Thursday, late afternoon in early October – Black History month. Outside is well cold! We are in 'Fix Up', a small, old-school, 'Black conscious' bookstore. The place is much too small to hold the many shelves and bookcases that jam and squeeze up next to each other. However, although at first sight the shop looks chaotic, with no subject labels or even indicators, to the trained eye it is perfectly arranged. Starting at the shelf closest to the door each subject is in alphabetical order, subdivided by genre, again in alphabetical order, followed by the authors, again in painstaking alphabetical order. Sitting nobly on each and every bookshelf, almost as closely stacked together as the books, are African statues and carvings of giraffes, busts of great leaders, perfectly formed couples entwined, Ashanti stools, sculptured walking sticks, etc. Various Kentes and African cloths are hung on what little wall space there is left. Hanging from the ceiling in a less ordered fashion are a few dusty-looking male and female African outfits. Written over the door and above* **Brother Kiyi***'s till enclosure is a sign reading* 'closing down sale'. *It is well old and dusty. On the floor, however, is a big black bin. The sign above that reads:* 'help keep us open – any donation welcome'.

*Playing a little too loudly is a speech by the early Black leader Marcus Garvey. It is an old 1920s recording. As with all recordings of that day it's slightly speeded up, but through the hiss we can hear the words clearly enough. Although his Jamaican accent is clear, we can hear Marcus is over-articulating in a 'Trumanesque' style.*

**Carl***, thirty-five, happy by nature, enters through the front door. He is a care-in-the-community patient.*

**Carl**   Owiiii, 'cuse us, mate, you sell rat-poison in here?

**Brother Kiyi** *is still out of sight, but we hear his anger. He has a refined but noticeable West Indian accent.* **Carl** *hides behind a shelf.*

**Brother Kiyi**   No! I do not sell rat-poison. Rat-poison is sold in the shop three doors down on the left. You'll find it behind the Halal meat refrigerator and to the right of the 'well cheap airfares to the subcontinent' counter.

*Now standing,* **Brother Kiyi** *can't see the hidden* **Carl**. **Brother Kiyi** *is dressed in an African-shaped Kente shirt on top of a thick woolly polo-neck with jeans. He has very long, greying locks. They are not hanging but twirled on top of his head almost like a turban.*

**Brother Kiyi**   Hello! Hello!

**Carl** *is still hidden.*

**Carl** (*using cockney accent*)   No, I was definitely told the Fix Up bookstore sold a whole load of rat-poison . . .

**Brother Kiyi**   What? . . .

**Carl**   Filling de yout' dem hea, hea, head, wid rubbish!

**Brother Kiyi**   You see you? When is stupidness you talking you don't have no stammer dough!

**Carl**   I love it! You get so *ig, ignorant* when your vex.

**Brother Kiyi**   Ignorant? How many times do I have to tell you, I am not ignorant! Ignorant is when you are not aware, I, on the contrary *am* aware –

**Carl**   – of the rightful place I hold in hi, hi, history –

**Brother Kiyi**   – because unlike the overwhelming majority of my people –

**Carl**   – I read –

**Brother Kiyi**   – digest and make manifest –

**Carl**   – the greatness of our heritage.

**Brother Kiyi** (*a positive acclamation*)   Iiiiiitchsss!

**Carl**   Wish I never said it now!

**Brother Kiyi**   Oh dash!

*He runs back to his desk, picks up the phone.*

Hello, hello, yes! I'm terribly sorry, I've found it now . . .
The order reference number is . . .

*He stands with an very old-fashioned telephone in his hands.* **Carl** *is looking at the books.*

**Brother Kiyi**    WA 23767. Brother Kiyi, Fix Up bookstore, Tottenham N15. No, Brother is not my Christian name! The name on the order sheet should simply say . . . You know what? I have been waiting three weeks for what should have been here within ten days! Have you ever faced a crowd that's waiting for their history to arrive? . . . No, it has not been delivered!

**Carl** *has wheeled his trolley into view. He tries to point to the boxes on it, but can't catch* **Brother Kiyi***'s eye.*

**Brother Kiyi**    My friend, I am the only person that works here.

**Carl** *waves this time. Still no attention is being given to him.*

**Brother Kiyi**    If a parcel from DHL had been delivered today . . .

*We can see that the boxes have 'DHL' written all over them.*

**Carl** *starts to point to the boxes in an over-the-top manner.*

**Brother Kiyi**    It could only have been delivered to me!

**Carl** (*shouts*)    Brother Kiyi!

**Brother Kiyi**    Excuse me. (*Barks.*) What?

**Carl**    Are these dem?

**Brother Kiyi** *looks at the logo blazoned all over the books. He goes back to the phone.*

**Brother Kiyi**    Madam, I may have to call you back!

*He puts down the phone.*

Carl. What are you doing with my delivery of . . . (*He calms himself.*) With my delivery?

**Carl**   The brother was unloading his van, and that's my job innit? Delivery! I saw it was for you, signed for it and brought them in. Bloody stinking parking warden was just about to give the man a ticket, you know? Delivering, you know, and was still gonna ticket him, you know.

**Brother Kiyi**   I figure I know, Carl.

**Carl**   Shotters for them.

**Brother Kiyi** *looks up sharply.*

**Brother Kiyi**   I don't believe he deserves to get shot for doing his job.

**Carl**   You've changed your tune. When they introduced the red lines you said they were murdering you and dem deserve death!

**Brother Kiyi**   Well, that was . . .

**Carl**   When Mr Mustafar bought the freehold you said fire pon the weak hearts that didn't back you up . . . and when . . .

**Brother Kiyi**   Yes, I get the message . . . (*Changes the subject to get out of it.*) That still no excuse for you to not tell me they reach!

**Carl**   I tried to, but you know what you're like when you're focused on one ting. You shut out the rest of the world.

**Brother Kiyi** *comes swiftly towards the boxes. He approaches them with reverence.*

**Brother Kiyi**   That's cos man is only suppose to do one ting at a time.

**Carl**   What you talking about? When I'm with my gal, I does be stroking (*hip actions*) and feeling. (*Tuning in a radio for the breast action.*) It feels perfectly natural to be doing those two tings at the same time!

**Brother Kiyi**   You never stutter when you're talking nastiness. (*Indicates the boxes.*) Help me na!

*Enter* **Kwesi**, *thirty-two, good-looking.* **Brother Kiyi** *likes* **Kwesi**, *mainly because of his militant Black stance. He has a big box in his arms.*

*He makes his way to the back of the store almost as if he doesn't want to say hello to* **Brother Kiyi** *and* **Carl**.

**Brother Kiyi**    Tende Mwari, Brother Kwesi.

**Kwesi**    Tende Mwari.

**Brother Kiyi**    They reach, you know, they reach! History, my friend, reach!

**Kwesi**    Great!

**Brother Kiyi**    You've three friends upstairs waiting for you.

**Kwesi**    Thanks.

**Brother Kiyi**    Somalians? I don't know much about their history. What happen to Jamal, Eric and Ade?

**Kwesi** (*still trying to get away*)    . . . Need people around you with backbone, know what I'm saying?

**Brother Kiyi**    Know what you're saying? I am surrounded by the most spineless punks this town has ever seen!

**Kwesi**    That's Babylon. Later.

**Brother Kiyi** *looks at the box in his hands.*

**Brother Kiyi**    Big box?!

**Kwesi**    Computer from home.

*He leaves.*

**Carl** *notices the slave narratives.*

**Carl**    How much did they set you back?

**Brother Kiyi**    All I have . . . I feel like a *child* in a . . . (*Questioning his own lack of eloquence.*) Words, what are they, huh?!

*He pulls out another book from the box. Carefully opens it and looks through. He pulls another book from the box. He does this again and again.*

**Brother Kiyi**   You know what these are? Forget Booker T, forget Langston Hughes! These are the great voices of we past. Twenty-four volumes of truth!

**Carl** *decides to pick one up and read the title for himself. He struggles with the words.*

**Brother Kiyi**   Careful!

**Carl**   'Sla-slave nar-ra-tive . . . '

**Brother Kiyi**   That's right, 'narrative' . . .

**Carl**   'Collection of her Majes . . . '

**Brother Kiyi**   'Her Majesty's . . . '

**Carl**   'Colonial voices.'

**Brother Kiyi**   Well done!

**Carl**   Yeah! What's all that about then?

**Brother Kiyi**   In 1899 a group of social anthropologists went across the entire West Indies – British, French, Spanish, Dutch – and interviewed the last remaining beings that were enslaved. Two thousand three hundred Africans that were between the ages of five and twenty-five when slavery was abolished. Most of them old like 'so-um! But this is bondage, brother . . .

**Carl** *raises his eyebrows and smiles at the word 'bondage'.*

**Carl**   'Bondage', oh yeah?

**Brother Kiyi**   Come on now, don't be stupid.

**Carl***'s face returns to studious enquirer.*

**Brother Kiyi**   This is the institution that brought us here, Carl, spoken about, written down in their own words, their dialect. That's always been the problem with slavery, see

. . . We've been able to witness other people talking about *their* genocide, but ours, well ours has been confined to saccharine American sagas or puerile political statements by people who don't give a blast about we!

**Carl**    I don't know what the fuck you're talking about.

**Brother Kiyi** (*catches himself about to preach*)    At last, this is the human connection, Carl. Maybe if more of the youth could hear, see where they've come from, they'd have a little bit more respect for where they are.

**Carl**    Seen. Look, gotta go, all this deep talk is making me sick. Mr Dongal, from the Halal butcher's, wants me to run down to the abattoirs with him. First time. Neat, huh?

**Brother Kiyi**    We'll do your reading when you come back then.

**Carl** (*sings to himself as he leaves*)
    The main reason me like it from behind
    You can reach under me belly rub me clit same time!

*Enter* **Norma**.

**Norma**    What nastiness is that?

**Carl**    Sorry, Aunty Norma.

**Norma**    Stop that 'aunty' ting. People will think we is family.

**Carl**    But we are family! The African family. What Marcus say, every black man is an African, innit, Brother Kiyi?

**Brother Kiyi**    Exactly, Carl.

**Norma**    I'm not related to no crack addict!

**Brother Kiyi**    Norma!

**Carl**    Former! . . .

**Norma**    Hard love, Kiyi, hard love.

**Carl**    Later.

*He exits.*

**Norma**    Every time I see that boy on the street is a next white woman he chasing. You don't see the amount of half-caste pickney ah run de street already.

**Brother Kiyi** *ignores her.*

**Brother Kiyi**    Um ha!

**Norma**    So they reach?

**Brother Kiyi**    Yeah man.

**Norma**    Good, good.

**Brother Kiyi** *undoes his locks and shakes them out.* **Norma** *looks at* **Brother Kiyi**'s *hair.*

**Norma**    Boy, don't shake that ting at me. One sum'ting I don't like, that Rasta ting you have on you head.

**Brother Kiyi**    And that alien hair you have on your head is better? It don't have nothing to do with no Rasta . . .

**Norma**    I don't care about you symbol of rebellion stupidness. You should have dropped that gaol nonsense years ago. You wash it?

**Brother Kiyi**    Yes, Norma, is wash me wash me head. You happy now?

**Norma**    Na man vex me vex. I sit down in front the television nice and comfortable, ready to watch me dog dem run, when the husband come in a start to harangue me soul.

**Brother Kiyi**    What he want?

**Norma**    Sex innit! No, hard yard food. He want me to run out the road to buy some cowfoot and pig trotters. I know you doesn't like me to buy from dem people next door, but Dongal and dem is the only place man could find a decent home food. Not one of dem black shop close to me have anything to make old West Indians happy.

**Brother Kiyi**   That they don't sell that kinda slave food is what makes this West Indian happy.

**Norma**   My grandfather use to eat cowfoot and there was nothin' slave about him! Except maybe him name.

**Brother Kiyi**   Which was what?

**Norma**   George de Third!

**Norma** *goes round to the desk and carefully pulls out a draughts board. The pieces are still on it.*

**Norma**   You looking damn thin you know, boy! You use all you corn to pay Mustafar he money innit?

**Brother Kiyi** *doesn't reply, just smiles slightly.*

**Norma**   I making a broth tonight, come over na?

**Brother Kiyi**   Thanks, but I'll pass on the swine!

**Norma** *plays back* **Brother Kiyi***'s reaction to the money question.*

**Norma**   You have paid him, haven't you?

**Brother Kiyi**   Abraham's always use to give me a month or two bligh! Why should I pay as soon as Mustafar ask for it?

**Norma**   Because Abraham's doesn't own the place any more. Mustafar does.

**Brother Kiyi**   What's wrong with our people, eh, Norma? The Jewish man come here and buy up the place, then a next immigrant come and buy it off him. Leapfrogging the West Indian. What was wrong wid we, eh?

**Norma**   A black landlord would ah let you off you rent?

**Brother Kiyi**   That's not the point.

**Norma**   You owe the man he rent, pay you rent.

**Brother Kiyi**   I can't. I spend all me money.

**Norma**   On woman?

**Brother Kiyi** (*pointing to bookshelves*)    What need do I have of a woman when I have Morrison, Macmillan and Walker?

**Norma**    Dem don't bring you cocoa in bed or bury you when you dead. Woman is the only excuse I'll accept. But you've spent it on the books innit? You promised me you wouldn't do that. You promised.

**Brother Kiyi**    Oh Norma, I couldn't resist it.

**Norma**    You know what? Talking to you is only going to get my diabetes up. I have time for three moves.

**Brother Kiyi** (*referring to unpacking books*)    Norma, I'm doing something important!

**Norma**    That's right, losing. It's time me beat you, Ras – I mean it's time for me to take my victory! I can smell it.

**Brother Kiyi**    What nonsense you talking . . .

**Norma**    Don't be hiding behind no books. When is licks time, it's licks time.

**Brother Kiyi**    Come, three moves and that's it.

**Norma**    Is my move innit!

**Brother Kiyi** *pulls a piece of paper from the shelf.*

**Brother Kiyi**    Whose signature is this?

**Norma**    Mine.

**Brother Kiyi**    And what does it say?

**Norma**    Kiyi has the next move.

**Brother Kiyi**    Thank you.

*He looks over the board slowly.*

You see, nothin' like the power of de pen, girl. (*He moves.*)

**Norma**    How much of dem book you get?

**Brother Kiyi**    You back on that? Three set a eight.

**Norma**    Three sets of eight! (*She moves.*)

**Brother Kiyi**    And another two sets are on order, when I get a little money.

**Norma**    You don't have money for food, and you ordering two sets ah books?

**Brother Kiyi**    I'm forced to believe that we can survive whatever we must survive. But the future of the Negro in this country is precisely as bright or as dark as the future of the country. Jimmy Baldwin, 1963. (*He moves.*)

**Norma**    I bet James wasn't bloody hungry when he wrote that. (*She moves.*) King me, you bitch!

**Brother Kiyi**    For a woman of the cloth your language is very colourful.

**Norma**    Don't try dem dirty tactics to put me off. Watch you moves, not my language.

**Brother Kiyi**    Oh, of that you can be sure. (*He moves.*)

**Norma** *realises that her king has been blocked in.*

**Norma**    Ahhhh, man. How you could block in me king so?

**Brother Kiyi**    By watching the game.

**Norma**    Rah, last move. (*She moves.*) Scamp. Deal wid dat!

**Brother Kiyi**    Ummm.

**Norma**    Haaaa. You see!

*She starts to sing a church song.*

Victory is mine, victory is mine, victory today is mine. (*She switches back to serious speech.*) I *have* to go.

**Brother Kiyi**    Eh! Sign the paper.

**Norma**    Sign it for me na! You know me handwriting not too good.

**Brother Kiyi**    You too damn lie. Is challenge you want to challenge me when you come back. Sign the ting!

**Norma**    Alright. (*She writes it down.*) Brother Kiyi has the next move.

**Brother Kiyi**    Date!

**Norma**    15th October.

**Brother Kiyi**    Iiiiech!

*She signs. Just before she gets to the door, she takes a tenner out of her purse and gives it to* **Brother Kiyi**.

**Brother Kiyi**    Na man it's alright. I'm alright. Seriously.

**Norma**    Shut you mouth and take the ting.

**Brother Kiyi**    You *could* do me a favour though?

**Norma**    What?

**Brother Kiyi** *takes a letter out of the chest of drawers.*

**Brother Kiyi**    Just got this letter and I don't fully understand it. Could you ask you daughter to look over it for me?

**Norma**    Thought Beverly does your legal tings?

**Brother Kiyi**    She's got a lot of work on at the moment. I don't want to burden her.

**Norma**    You mean you owe her too much? No big ting. I go give Paulette when she come over this evening. I love you yuh na, brother, but (*points to the books*) you too stubborn for your own good.

**Brother Kiyi**    Where are we without hope?! Say hello to Bernie. And tell him stop eat de master cast-offs!

**Norma**    I'll tell him that when you cut you nasty locks!

**Brother Kiyi** *looks through another book. Suddenly he springs up and begins to search for a space to place the books. After much* *deliberation he decides to take down a row of modern black love stories.*

*He takes down the books and, carefully brushing down the bookshelf, places the new ones in their place, in a prominent place in the shop. He stops reading.*

*Enter* **Alice**, *thirty-four, mixed race.* **Brother Kiyi** *pulls the book back up as if reading again, but he is not. He is slightly taken by her attractiveness.*

**Alice**   Hi.

*He does not reply. She moves a little closer, tries again.*

**Alice**   Hello?

*He looks up from the book and smiles a little smile.*

**Brother Kiyi**   Tende Mwari.

**Alice**   What does that mean?

**Brother Kiyi**   Well, in the ancient language of Kwaswahili, it is the greeting that one villager would give to the other.

**Alice**   Right, that bit I get, but what does it mean?

**Brother Kiyi**   As you know, translations are always notoriously inaccurate . . .

**Alice**   . . . but?

**Brother Kiyi**   Roughly translated it means, 'Hello' . . .

**Alice**   And I say in return? . . .

**Brother Kiyi**   It's very difficult, I wouldn't worry yourself about it!

**Alice**   Right.

*He returns to the book. She returns to looking at the bookshelves.*

It's Black History month, isn't it?

**Brother Kiyi**   Indeed it is.

**Alice**   Must be a good time for business eh? Bet everyone like me comes in looking for something that will broaden their understanding of, well, black history. What do you recommend?

**Brother Kiyi**   Well, young lady . . .

**Alice**   I don't know about the young, according to my mother at thirty I should have been married at least once, and had my one-point-six children years ago.

**Brother Kiyi**   Your mother's from where?

**Alice**   Oh, um, she's English, from up north.

**Brother Kiyi**   Oh.

**Alice**   Why do you ask?

**Brother Kiyi**   It's a very Caribbean thing to say, that's all. My mother had me when she was twenty-seven and I'm the last of six.

**Alice**   Wow, what age did you start?

**Brother Kiyi**   Me? I don't have any children. To the profound disappoint of my mother.

**Alice**   I'm sorry.

**Brother Kiyi**   Nothing to be sorry about. I chose to over-share.

*But he returns to his book and she to the shelves. He turns the Marcus Garvey tape back on. Marcus is in full-throttle mode. It is passionate oration, and we hear the wild audience response.* **Alice** *tries to break the silence.*

**Alice**   Who is that speaking?

**Brother Kiyi** (*turning it down a tad*)   The Honourable Marcus Garvey.

**Alice**   Wow, I'll have one of those please.

**Brother Kiyi**    The cassette is my own personal property, but if you go to the other aisle on the fifth shelf you'll see many of his books.

*She does.*

**Alice**    Are his books any good?

**Brother Kiyi**    Well, er, I seem to think so!

**Alice**    Great! Then I'll buy 'em!

**Brother Kiyi**    There are a few! You might want to buy one to start off with.

**Alice**    Actually I don't so much as read but have one of those photographic memories. I kind of scan it and it goes in.

*She picks up two books and goes to the counter.*

I'll have these two. Thank you.

**Brother Kiyi**    Good.

*He methodically puts the books in a brown bag, writes the sales in a little black book and hands the bag to her.*

**Brother Kiyi**    That will be £31.90 please.

*She hands him her card.*

Sorry, we don't have the facility to process cards. Cash or cheques only. But cash is always best.

**Alice**    Good thing I bought my cheque book out with me.

*She writes it out while he watches. She hands him the cheque and the card.*

**Brother Kiyi** *looks at the signature for a while.*

**Brother Kiyi**    Do you have any other form of identification on you?

**Alice**    Why?

**Brother Kiyi**    The signature on the cheque is, well, it's a little different.

**Alice**    Let me see. Well, it doesn't look that different to me. Maybe it's a little untidy but I always write fast when I'm nervous.

**Brother Kiyi**    What do you have to be nervous about?

**Alice**    I didn't actually mean nervous, I meant excited.

**Brother Kiyi** *stares at her blankly.*

**Alice**    *New books!*

**Brother Kiyi**    I see.

**Alice**    Here's my driver's licence. Picture's a bit old but, hey, same chick.

*He looks at it for a while, then holds the books out so that she can take them from his hand. She doesn't.*

**Brother Kiyi**    Sorry about that, but one has to be careful.

**Alice**    One?

**Brother Kiyi**    Yes.

**Alice**    Thank you. By the way, I don't know about *Kwa*swahili but in *real* Swahili one responds to 'Hello' with 'Habari Yako'.

**Brother Kiyi**    Is that so? How do you know that?

**Alice**    I had an East African boyfriend. Once.

**Brother Kiyi**    Thank you for telling me that.

**Alice**    It's OK. I wanted to over-share.

*He waits for her to open the door.*

**Brother Kiyi**    *Safi*. That is also real Swahili.

*She turns around, slightly embarrassed, and then leaves.*

**Brother Kiyi** *turns Marcus back up and starts to read his slave narrative again.*

*Fade out.*

**Scene Two**

*Fix Up bookstore. The following day.*

**Brother Kiyi** *is sitting reading the slave narratives. Enter* **Norma**.

**Brother Kiyi**    Hey girl.

**Norma**    Don't 'hey girl' me, you stubborn old fool!

**Brother Kiyi**    What I do you now?

**Norma**    The letter you asked me daughter Paulette to look at.

**Brother Kiyi**    Yeah?

**Norma**    What don't you understand about if you don't pay your rent within twenty-one days Mustafar is going to send in the bailiffs?

**Brother Kiyi**    I understand it all. What I want to find out is what I can do about it.

**Norma**    You phone Beverly, get her to inform them you going to pay!

**Brother Kiyi**    Ah, Beverly's great but she don't have the stamina I require for this battle.

**Norma**    You mean she has grown tired ah you?

**Brother Kiyi**    What Paulette say?

**Norma**    That you need to pay! Like today! You know what the problem is? You think the world is waiting on you, Kiyi! While you're sitting in here being obstinate, Mustafar is moving forwards. Why weren't you at the town hall last night?

**Brother Kiyi**    I was busy.

**Norma**    My backside you were busy! All the other leaseholders were there!

**Brother Kiyi**    I don't go anywhere dem punk rockers will be. If I see them I might just lose me temper and . . . If they'd have stood by me in the first place none of this would have been happening!

**Norma**    That is history, Kiyi.

**Brother Kiyi**    No my friend, *his story* are the fables of his winnings. (*Points to slave narrative books.*) This is history. Anyway, it wasn't telling me anything I didn't know already.

**Norma**    Oh, so you know that he planning to turn the places above you into luxury flats? What do you think is gonna happen next?

**Brother Kiyi**    They'll pretty up the front, give me a new sign.

**Norma**    Which parent you think gonna loan dem child money to buy flat on top of an extreme Black bookshop? He has to get you out.

**Brother Kiyi**    Norma, me know all of that. Me even know he plan to replace my bookstore with shop that sells black hair products.

**Norma**    How do you know that?

**Brother Kiyi**    Two people came in here yesterday to measure up!

**Norma**    To measure up?

**Brother Kiyi**    Yes. But he's messing with the wrong guy. I'm gonna talk to my MP. I'm gonna start a petition, speak to all the local black celebrities . . .

**Norma**    I wouldn't count on them if I were you.

**Brother Kiyi**    You can't replace history with hair gel.

**Norma**    Kiyi, our MP was there. Smiling. Agreeing. Saying thank you. The only good ting about that meeting is that they asked me to talk. Dem requested that a community woman like myself make comment on dem plans.

**Brother Kiyi**    What you say?

**Norma**    I said I was outraged.

**Brother Kiyi**    And?

**Norma**    If you were bloody well there you'd have known what I said! We can't mek dem run roughshod over us like that man. Anyway, I went to the doctor this morning and you know what he tell me?

**Brother Kiyi**    You diabetes getting worse?

**Norma**    Me diabetes getting worse. This ting go take me to me premature grave.

**Brother Kiyi**    Hey girl, don't talk stupidness!

**Norma**    Listen, when me reach de Fadder gate, I want to be able to look he in the eye and say, 'Lord, I did do something down there!' (*Beat.*) So I went to the bank. There was three grand in it. Here's two. Pay the man.

**Brother Kiyi**    *Don't be stupid!*

**Norma**    *Take it.* I understand where you coming from, man, but you can't fight this from where you are, Kiyi. You need help. We need to keep the shop open. Now take this, pay the man. Pay me back when you can.

**Brother Kiyi**    Norma, you know that's not possible. Listen to me good. If I pay the man his money now, he's gonna expect it on time every quarter. My business doesn't run like that!

**Norma**    And neither does his!

**Brother Kiyi**    I always square up by end of year! What's wrong wid dat?

**Norma**   It's unreasonable, Kiyi.

**Brother Kiyi**   And so is the offer of your savings. I can't take it.

**Norma**   Kiyi, though I don't agree with all you stupidness, you love Black. And all of my life I have been taught to fear it, hate it. That ain't right! Take the money. Please.

*She forces the envelope into* **Brother Kiyi***'s hand.*

**Brother Kiyi**   Don't think that go stop me whipping you backside at draughts!

**Norma**   Phone him now. Tell them you coming!

**Brother Kiyi**   Now?

**Norma**   Now.

**Brother Kiyi** *picks up the phone.*

**Brother Kiyi** (*with smile*)   Just cos you give me little money you think you could boss me around? (*Serious switch.*) Hello, put me through to Mr Mustafar please . . . Who's calling? His nemesis . . . No, that's not all one word . . . Thank you . . . Mustafar, Kiyi here. You think you catch me, innit? Well you lie. I coming with you money . . . How about three? I think I can just about make that. Cool.

*He slams down the phone.* **Norma** *smiles.*

*Enter* **Kwesi**. **Brother Kiyi** *puts the envelope of money away.*

**Brother Kiyi**   Tende Mwari, Brother Kwesi.

**Kwesi** (*not reciprocating* **Brother Kiyi***'s joyous tone*)   Tende Mwari, Sister Norma.

*The slave narratives catch* **Kwesi***'s eye. He stops to look.*

**Norma**   Kwesi!

*She exits to the basement.*

**Brother Kiyi**   So, how's the revolution today?

**Kwesi**    Fine, my brother.

*He is about to walk past* **Brother Kiyi** *to the room upstairs when* **Brother Kiyi** *stops him.*

**Brother Kiyi**    Hey, I just read that Michael Jackson has been a signed-up member of the Nation of Islam for ten years?

**Kwesi**    How can you have the most prominent manifestation of Black self-hate as a member of a militant Black organisation? Char! Michael should have been shot the moment he bleached his skin.

**Brother Kiyi**    So what happen? A brother can't look a little forgiveness?

**Kwesi**    Can you forgive slavery? Can the European repent for that? Only thing this world understands, Kiyi, power. Till we have that, no matter what's up there (*pointing to head*), we're all just joking it.

**Brother Kiyi**    Good talk, Kwesi, but make sure your words don't take you where they shouldn't. Jail life na nice.

**Kwesi**    For real.

*He makes to go.*

**Brother Kiyi** (*grabbing the opportunity*)    Brother Kwesi, I tried to go into the room upstairs yesterday, but the door was locked.

**Kwesi**    Yeah, that's right. Sorry, I forgot to tell you. But it's OK, I've got the key.

**Brother Kiyi**    There's never been a key for that lock!

**Kwesi**    Oh, at last week's meeting we . . . we changed the locks. The new computers and that. I'm sorry, we should have informed you, but with all this march and all it must have slipped my mind.

**Brother Kiyi**    Right.

**Kwesi**    I'll do a copy and get it right to you?

**Brother Kiyi**   Fine.

*Enter* **Carl**.

**Carl**   Brother Kiyi, I ain't got but five minutes so we need to hit it straight away.

**Kwesi**   Hey, Brother Carl, are you coming on the march?

**Carl**   I'm not your brother, and which march is that?

**Kwesi**   The Reparations for Slavery march.

**Carl**   No, I don't think so.

**Kwesi**   You, a recipient of state brutality, can't find one hour out of your day to march for our people's right to be repaid! That's why our race is going nowhere. I'm upstairs, Kiyi.

*He exits.*

**Carl**   Why is he always so angry?

**Brother Kiyi**   He's a serious young man.

**Carl**   Do you reckon his face is vex like that when he's doing it?

**Carl** *demonstrates sex doggy-style with a vexed face just as* **Norma** *enters from downstairs.*

**Carl**   Huh! Huh! Huh! Take it, baby! Sorry, Aunty Norma. But it ain't natural, is it?

**Norma**   You want me to come with you at three?

**Brother Kiyi**   Na, man. I cool.

**Norma**   Alright, I gone. Later, dutty boy!

*She exits.*

*Enter* **Alice**, *who crosses with* **Norma** *at the door. She has her headphones on. She smiles and starts to look at a bookshelf.* **Carl** *decides to stay.*

**Carl**    What you saying, sister?

*He walks up to* **Alice**.

**Alice**    Pardon?

**Carl**    Are you one of those reparation-marching, hard-faced, straight-talking conscious types?

**Alice**    I don't think so!

**Carl**    I knew it. I could see you were different from your hair! I'm Carl.

**Alice**    Alice.

**Carl**    Come on, Brother Kiyi, let's get down to it. I haven't got long! (*Showing off.*) Excuse us. Brother teaches me to read. See, I ain't one of those ignorant niggers.

**Brother Kiyi** (*referring to 'niggers'*)    Carl!

**Carl**    Sorry – Nubians, that's afraid of edgedumacation.

**Alice**    I see.

**Alice** *moves to the back of the shop. Puts her headphones back on as politely as possible.*

**Brother Kiyi** *pulls out a book from beneath his counter.*

**Brother Kiyi**    Alright, where were we? Tell you what, try this today. You may struggle a little, but well!

*He goes to the shelf and pulls out a book of* Selected Poems. *He finds a poem and hands the book to* **Carl**.

**Carl**    What is it?

**Brother Kiyi**    Just read.

**Carl**    'If We Must Die.'

'If we must die, let it not be like hogs,
Hunted and penned in an ingl . . . '

**Brother Kiyi**    Inglor . . .

**Carl**

'. . . rious spot,
While round us bark the mad and hungry dogs – '

(*Stops reading.*) What does that 'inglorious' mean?

**Brother Kiyi**    I'll explain after. Carry on.

**Carl**

'Making their mock at our ac-curs-èd lot.' (*He exhales.*)

**Brother Kiyi**    Well done.

**Carl**

'If we must die, O let us nobly die,
So that our precious – '

(*Pleased with himself for recognising.*) That's that word from *Lord of the Rings* innit? (*Does impression.*) 'My precious.' (*To* **Alice**.) You know there's an actor from *The Bill* who lives right up the road dere, Brian something or other, he knows the guy that played Gollum, you know?

**Brother Kiyi**    I see. Carry on with the poem, Carl.

**Carl**    Where was I? Oh yeah. (*He looks at* **Alice**.)

'O, kinsmen! We must meet the common foe!
Though far outnumbered, let us show us brave,
And for their thousand blows deal one death blow!
What though before us lies the open grave?
Like men we'll face the murderous cowardly pack,
Pressed to the wall, dying but fighting back.'

*Enter* **Kwesi** *from upstairs, who has heard the last few lines. He gently giggles aloud at* **Carl***'s reading. He clocks* **Alice** *and likes what he sees but does not show it, much.*

**Brother Kiyi** *cuts his eye at* **Kwesi**.

**Alice**    Who was that?

**Brother Kiyi**    Claude MacKay.

**Carl**'s *mobile rings – the theme tune to* Batman. **Carl** *looks at the number and recognises it.*

**Carl**    Oh my gosh, Brother Kiyi, I gotta run, Mister Dongal done waiting for me. I liked that poem dough. Explain it to me tomorrow?

**Brother Kiyi**    Tomorrow!

*As he walks past* **Alice** *he smiles.*

**Carl** (*about* **Alice** *as he exits, malapropism of course*)    Inglorious!

**Brother Kiyi** *returns the books to the correct shelves.*

**Alice**    That's very good.

**Brother Kiyi**    What?

**Alice**    What you do. Reading and that.

**Brother Kiyi**    Care of the community! That is what they meant, wasn't it?

**Alice**    *In* the commu . . . Speaking of care, I came in today because I wanted to challenge the way you treated me yesterday. Like a common criminal.

**Brother Kiyi**    Criminal?

**Alice**    At least that's how I felt, and I wanted to let you know that in fact I am a teacher of much repute. I am a woman that should be respected.

**Brother Kiyi**    I have no doubts that you are. I apologised yesterday, and I will do so again if you wish.

**Alice**    You didn't actually.

**Brother Kiyi**    Didn't what?

**Alice**    You didn't apologise.

**Brother Kiyi**    I distinctly remember saying, 'I'm sorry, but one cannot be too careful.'

**Alice**   Not to split hairs, but that was apologising for having to do it. It wasn't an apology to me.

**Brother Kiyi**   What today is? Break-me-balls day?

**Alice**   Sorry?

**Brother Kiyi**   What is it you want, young lady? I'm very busy.

**Alice**   For a start, don't you think if you are introducing him to poetry, which I do think is great, maybe you should choose a less sexist poet?

**Brother Kiyi**   Less what?

**Alice**   A poet that doesn't exclude women from participating in 'the struggle'.

**Brother Kiyi**   It is Claude, 'the father of the Harlem Renaissance, the poet quoted by Winston Churchill to the British soldiers before the Battle of Britain', MacKay we are taking about here, isn't it?

**Alice**   Is it because I'm a woman you use that condescending tone with me?

**Brother Kiyi**   I'm not using a condescending tone with you.

**Alice**   Yes, you are! You're talking to me like I'm some 'stupid girl' that doesn't know what she's talking about.

**Brother Kiyi**   Well, I don't think you do actually . . .

**Alice**   Well, I beg to differ.

**Brother Kiyi**   Young lady, you are unknown to me. Why are you raising your voice?

*She pauses for a second and gathers herself.*

**Alice**   I tend to get passionate about what goes into the minds of those we are responsible for. I'm sorry.

**Brother Kiyi**   OK, please explain why Claude MacKay is sexist?

**Alice**    I don't actually know very much about Claude MacKay. I meant the poem sounded sexist.

**Brother Kiyi**    Lord have mercy!

**Alice**    The phrase 'If we must die', that's a call to participation.

**Brother Kiyi**    Right . . .

**Alice**    The phrase 'O kinsmen!' makes that call specific: the poem's would-be warriors are men. What about women? He only talks about the race by imagining the aspirations of men.

**Brother Kiyi**    Rasclaat!

**Alice**    No, not rasclaat or however you pronounce it – the contest for humanity in the poem is fought exclusively by men.

**Kwesi** *enters.*

**Kwesi**    Yes, it is.

**Alice** *turns and looks at* **Kwesi**.

**Alice**    Exactly.

**Kwesi**    And what's wrong with that?

**Alice**    Sorry?

**Kwesi**    What's wrong with that assertion? Battles are fought by men. Not women, not girls, but men.

**Alice**    I think you'll find that if you look at the number of active service people in the Gulf wars, Kosovo, Afghanistan, you'll see that the number of women . . .

**Kwesi**    . . . is vastly below the number of men. You guys can't have it both ways, you know?

**Alice**    What *guys* are we talking about here?

**Kwesi**   Women! One minute you're the saviour of mankind due to the size of your humanity and now you're the sword-bearers that defend the nation? Which way do you want it?

**Alice** (*taken aback*)   Wow. I don't know you, sir, but I would say that's a rather archaic viewpoint for such a – (*chooses her words carefully*) modern-looking man.

**Kwesi**   Books and covers.

**Alice**   Evidently!

**Kwesi** *exits upstairs. There's a moment's silence.* **Alice** *switches.*

**Alice**   What a great place. How many bookstores can you go into and have heated debates like that?

**Brother Kiyi**   That *was* my dream.

**Alice**   Who is that guy?

**Brother Kiyi**   Kwesi, my militant-in-residence. Head of the All-Black African Party. They meet in the room upstairs. (*Suddenly becoming suspicious.*) Why?

**Alice**   No reason. (*With passion.*) What a hateful man. That's why people don't go out with black men. (*She stops herself.*) I finished *The Philosophies of Marcus Garvey* last night.

**Brother Kiyi**   You did?

**Alice**   Yes.

**Brother Kiyi**   What about the other one?

**Alice**   No, I haven't started reading that.

**Brother Kiyi**   Why?

**Alice**   I kind of wanted to discuss the *Philosophies* book with someone first.

**Brother Kiyi**   I see.

**Alice**   But I don't really know anyone that is familiar with the works of Marcus Garvey.

**Brother Kiyi**    Right.

**Alice**    I mean, don't you think he's a little racist?

**Brother Kiyi**    Here we go again!

**Alice**    No, I mean he comes over to me as a, yeah, a black racist.

**Brother Kiyi**    You're a teacher, you say?

**Alice**    Yes, I am.

**Brother Kiyi**    What do you teach?

**Alice**    English and – and History.

**Brother Kiyi**    Just over there you'll find a dictionary – could you pass it to me, please.

*She does.*

Racist, what does it say here in this *Oxford Dictionary*. 'Racism – a feeling of superiority from one race to another.' Now I would argue, not today, because I'm tired, that we are certainly not economically superior, and I would say, due to the collective lack of knowledge of ourselves and our constant desire to imitate, impersonate and duplicate everything Caucasian, nor are we in a psychological position of superiority. Hence by that definition, we cannot be racist.

**Alice**    Why are you tired?

**Brother Kiyi**    I'm fine.

**Alice**    Cos I'm brown, everybody expects me to somehow know everything black. And I'm like, 'Hey, how am I suppose to know what . . . raaasclaat means, I'm from Somerset.'

**Brother Kiyi**    OK!

**Alice**    People down here are so fortunate to have a resource like this.

**Brother Kiyi**   You don't miss the water till the well runs dry . . .

*The phone rings.*

Tende Mwari . . . Yes, Brother Peter . . . I see. Have you spoken to our beloved local MP? . . . OK, his surgery days are . . . Yes . . . Monday, Town Hall, Martin Luther King Room. Saturday morning at the Steve Biko Library . . . No, you just turn up. If you'd like I have a book here somewhere on the working of . . . Yes, it will inform you of your rights! . . . Send your son to pick it up. Four o'clock? . . . Yes I'll be here. Tende Mwari.

**Brother Kiyi** *puts down the phone and gets up to search for the book. He has to squeeze past* **Alice** *to get there.*

**Brother Kiyi**   Excuse me.

**Alice** *is quite taken by the smell of his locks.*

**Alice**   What do you put in your hair?

**Brother Kiyi**   Um, Oil of Olay.

*Beat.*

**Alice**   Do you do that for everyone?

**Brother Kiyi**   What?

**Alice**   Advise them and then bam, sell 'em a book?

**Brother Kiyi**   I don't sell the books. I loan them.

**Alice**   Loan them? Do you get them back? . . .

**Brother Kiyi**   Most times . . .

**Alice**   In sellable condition? . . .

**Brother Kiyi**   Sometimes . . .

**Alice**   How many books do you sell a week?

**Brother Kiyi**   Why do you ask?

**Alice**    Curious? How many books did you loan last week?

**Brother Kiyi**    About twelve.

**Alice**    Any come back?

**Brother Kiyi**    They will.

**Alice**    You have a record of the books you loaned out, right?

**Brother Kiyi**    What is the problem here? I loan books. If I didn't they wouldn't be read.

**Alice**    What do you mean by that?

**Brother Kiyi**    I mean . . . (*Decides to share.*) Do you know what my best-seller has been for the last year? Apart from my Afrocentric cards, that is – you know, black mum kissing black dad. West Indian grandmother in big hat playing with a cat – um, the best-seller was *Shotter's Revenge*, and, oh, *Black Love*.

**Alice**    What's wrong with that? Who couldn't do with a bit of black love right now?

**Brother Kiyi**    What is wrong with that? I have on these shelves Van Sertima's *Africa, Cradle of Civilisation*! Chancellor Williams's *Destruction of Black Civilisation*, Peterson's *The Middle Passage*, Williams's *Capitalism and Slavery*. I've books on the Dogons, the Ashantis, the, the pyramids of ancient Zimbabwe, and what do they buy? Nonsensical nonsense about men with nine-packs doing in the sauna with black female executives. What is that, I ask you?

**Alice**    Six-packs!

**Brother Kiyi**    What?

**Alice**    No one has a nine-pack.

**Brother Kiyi**    I don't care what pack them have! That is nonsense reading when we face the things we face today. You know, you were the first person in an age to buy, well, to buy a book of substance. In fact . . . (*He checks the sales book.*) Yes, here it is! December of last year. One copy of *The Isis Papers* by Dr Cress Welsing. And that customer wasn't even black!

**Alice**   She was white?

**Brother Kiyi**   No, she was mixed.

**Alice**   I believe the term is now 'person of dual heritage'.

**Brother Kiyi**   I'm sure it is.

**Alice**   Shouldn't you be up-to-date on that sort of stuff? Being a leader of your community an' all!

**Brother Kiyi**   I suppose I should, if in fact I were a leader.

**Alice**   Why aren't you?

**Brother Kiyi**   A leader or up-to-date?

**Alice**   Both?

**Brother Kiyi**   You ask a lot of questions.

**Alice**   I need a lot of answers. Always have.

**Brother Kiyi**   Answers to what? You a policewoman?

**Alice**   No, I am not . . . Denied histories are fascinating to me.

**Brother Kiyi**   I wish that more of my community thought like that.

**Alice**   Maybe they do and just haven't told you.

*He suddenly remembers and stands.*

**Brother Kiyi**   Sugar, what time is it now?

**Alice**   Have I kept you?

**Brother Kiyi**   Kwesi! Kwesi!

**Kwesi**   Yo!

**Brother Kiyi**    Come and hold the store for me, please. Got to run out the road.

**Kwesi**    I'll be down in a second.

**Brother Kiyi**    I've got to go *now*!

**Kwesi**    OK, go, I'll be down in a minute.

**Brother Kiyi** *grabs his coat, checks that the envelope is secure and heads to the door.*

**Brother Kiyi**    You don't have to leave, you can, you know, look around still? There's a chair there.

*She runs up to him and hugs him passionately. Almost girl-like, but she's a woman.* **Brother Kiyi** *doesn't quite know how to deal with that much affection.*

**Brother Kiyi** *shouts up the stairs.*

**Brother Kiyi**    Kwesi! Kwesi!

**Kwesi**    I'm coming, I'm coming.

**Brother Kiyi** *strokes his hair. Then exits.*

**Alice** *walks around the shop looking at things more freely now that she is by herself.*

*She sees the slave narratives.*

*She goes to the desk and looks around. She looks though the contents and then under the counter. She stays there for a little while. Then takes a slave narrative. She decides to read.*

*The lights reduce to a spotlight on her. We are in her head. She takes on the voice of the story-teller.*

**Alice**    'Mary Gould, Grand Anse Estate, Grenada. One day Masser Reynolds come back from Barbados wid one high yellow gal he just buy. They say she was real pretty but I can hardly remember. But he never put she to live wid the other niggers, no, he buil' she a special little house away from the quarters down by the river which run at the back ah de plantation. Every negroes know Masser take a black woman quick as he did a white and took any on his place that he wanted and he took them often. But most his pickney dem born on the place looked like niggers. But not all. Once, two of his yella children went up to the big house where Dr Reynolds full-breed child was playing in their dolls' house and told them that they want to play in the dolls' house too. The story go that one of the Doctor full breed-child say, "Sorry, this is for white children only." The reply I'm told went, "We ain't no niggers, cos we got the same daddy you has, and he comes to see us every day with gifts and wonderful clothes and such." Well, Mrs Reynolds was at the window heard the white niggers saying, "He is our daddy cos we call him daddy when he comes to see our mammy." That evening that yella gal get whipped for almost three hours. And within one year all her children had been sold away. No sir, it don't pay to be pretty and yella.'

*The lights snap on as* **Kwesi** *rests his hands on* **Alice**'s *shoulders. She jumps.*

**Alice**   Ohhhh.

**Kwesi**   Did I scare you?

**Alice**   Yes, you did, actually. What are you doing over my shoulder?

**Kwesi**   You were breathing heavily.

**Alice**   I was reading!

**Kwesi**   Do you always breathe like that when you read?

**Alice**   I mouth the words as well!

**Kwesi**   You into that stuff?

**Alice**   Families?

**Kwesi**   Slavery! Old Kiyi here is addicted to that shit.

**Alice**   Aren't all you political types?

**Kwesi**   Hell, no. I only look forward, sister.

**Alice**   Sounds rather disrespectful to Brother Kiyi!

**Kwesi**   No it's not. He's cool. Big expert on all things slavery. Which is good for me cos I don't have to go to no Yanks when I wanna know something. I hate going to those Yanks. Been in the belly of the beast too long.

**Alice**   What does that mean?

**Kwesi**   It affects you, you know? Being around too much white folk. I seen the bluest of blackest men get too much exposure, bam, they lose their rhythm. Put on a James Brown tune and they start doing the Charleston to ras!

**Alice**   Isn't there an ointment you can get to mitigate that?

**Kwesi**   What?

**Alice**   Over-exposure to white folk?!

**Kwesi**   Ohhhh, somebody's getting touchy!

**Alice**   I'm not getting touchy.

**Kwesi**   Yes, you are. I say the word 'white folk' and you get all arms!

**Alice**   Two words, actually. Arms?

**Kwesi**   Vex! Wanna fight?

**Alice**   I don't want to fight you!

**Kwesi**   Why not? It's half your people, innit, that I'm cussing!

**Alice**   Half my p . . . ? You're trying to provoke me. Why?

**Kwesi**   You look like the type that likes to be provoked?

**Alice**   Well, Mr Kwesa . . .

**Kwesi**   Kwesi, Kwes-i, not -ah.

**Alice**   Sorry. It doesn't exactly roll off my half-tongue.

**Kwesi**  Very good. If you were 'fuller', I could quite like you.

**Alice**  Is that of body or of race?

**Kwesi**  Both.

**Alice**  If you're gonna come on to me at least engage on a higher level than that.

**Kwesi** *is slightly taken aback.*

**Kwesi**  I wasn't trying to come on to you.

**Alice**  Is that so?

**Kwesi**  I don't do your type!

**Alice**  My . . . And what is my type exactly?

**Kwesi**  West Indians. You guys are weak.

**Alice**  Yanks, West Indians, mixed. And there was I thinking it was because I'm from Somerset.

**Kwesi**  You're funny. I like you.

**Alice**  All of me or half?

**Kwesi**  Depends what side of you you're showing me. Let me tell you something. I don't trust you type of people. I see you coming in here trying to be down, so when the white man thinks he's choosing one of us you're there shouting, 'Hey, I'm black.' But you ain't.

**Alice**  Well, you're nothing if not clear, Kwesi.

**Kwesi**  Nothing, if not clear.

*He exits up the stairs.*

*Lights down.*

## Scene Three

*Fix Up bookstore. Day.*

**Brother Kiyi** *is in joyous mood. He runs over to the cassette recorder and throws in another tape. It gives out a very percussive rhythm made up of hand-claps and foot-stomps He starts to sing an old slave work-chant. It's a call and response.* **Brother Kiyi** *is calling, the recording responding. The lead line sounds like a blues refrain. He begins to dance with it. The dance is as if he is picking cotton from the ground and then cutting cane with two cutlasses.*

*Enter* **Norma**. **Brother Kiyi** *stops dancing for a moment, then continues.*

**Norma**   Boy, what you so happy about?

**Brother Kiyi**   You like the rhythm, girl?

**Norma**   I would, if it wasn't so blasted loud!

**Brother Kiyi**   What you say?

**Norma**   Turn that blasted ting down. You give Mustafar he money?

**Brother Kiyi**   When I hand it him he shit! All he could do was open he mouth so. (*Imitates jaw dropping.*) You know who was in the office? The same boys he selling it to. Oh God, it was sweet. Thank you, gal.

**Norma**   Good.

*She gets the draughts. They sit down to play.* **Brother Kiyi** *suddenly catches sight of her hair. She is wearing a very long and glamorous wig. It stops just beneath her shoulders.*

**Brother Kiyi**   Hey, gal! A next-animal ting you have on you head. It still alive? . . .

**Norma**   Don't be feisty. It's hundred-per-cent human!

**Brother Kiyi**   Human? . . .

**Norma**   Yes . . .

**Brother Kiyi**   As oppose to what? . . .

**Norma**   Horse!

**Brother Kiyi**   So you will spend your hard-earned money on hair dem chop from a horse?

**Norma**   I told you it's not no horse hair, it's hundred-per-cent Chinese . . .

**Brother Kiyi**   Chinese? . . .

**Norma**   Kiyi! Make we concentrate on the game.

**Brother Kiyi** *moves.*

**Norma**   Kiyi, you does need any special qualification to go into politics? (*She moves.*)

**Brother Kiyi**   Apart from a great capacity for wickedness. No. (*He moves.*) Why?

**Norma**   I feel community-connected. At the meeting the other night, and when me stand up, you know how they introduce me? 'Madam Norma, a woman who knows this community like no other.' You know how great that mek me feel? The head of the council calling me madam! The only time I get call madam previous to dat in me life is when they come to arrest me husband. (*She moves.*)

**Brother Kiyi**   What that have to do wid your Chinese wig, Norma?

**Norma**   If you gonna stand for election you have to look glamorous, don't it?

**Brother Kiyi**   Election of what? (*He moves.*)

**Norma**   I don't know. I had this dream last night that I was on me window ledge and all below me was darkness and me feel like me was going to fall off but me say no, and before me know it me just start to fly fly fly.

**Brother Kiyi**   What you think that mean?

**Norma**   I don't know. (*She moves.*) But I wake up and the first ting that jump in me mind is 'Norma stand for election'.

**Brother Kiyi**   You need an agent? Let me find you one na!

**Norma**   I told you I was just thinking.

**Brother Kiyi**   Norma, you don't even like politics.

**Norma**   I don't understand it, Kiyi! But before me dead, I'd like to understand something, something from the inside. That's why me and you generation fail, boy, we didn't engage.

**Brother Kiyi** *moves.*

**Norma**   Oh sugar mugar. How you see that move, dread?

**Brother Kiyi**   By watching the game.

**Norma**   How long you going to carry on so? No customers, no life . . .

**Brother Kiyi**   Norma, it's not going to stay so! Na man, I can smell it in the air. (*Beat.*) You see that young girl that does come in here, right . . .

**Norma**   The half-caste gal?

**Brother Kiyi**   Different, you know, dread. Angry, political, albeit about woman tings but still fantastic anger. I does sit down and talk to that girl and I does say to meself wooooy, where does that rage come from in these apathetic times? Then the wind whisper in me ears, 'Ah my time again.' That's why I know it's coming.

*Enter* **Alice**. *They turn around and look at her.*

**Alice**   What?

**Brother Kiyi**   Nothing.

**Norma** *looks at him. The women look at each other.*

**Norma** (*to* **Brother Kiyi**, *looking at his crutch*)   You sure it's the wind?

**Alice**    How are you today?

**Brother Kiyi**    Good. Very good. You?

**Alice**    Oh, OK! I . . .

*She stops herself, taking a quick glance at* **Norma**. **Brother Kiyi** *very subtly follows her eyes.* **Norma** *detects a vibe.*

**Norma**    Kiyi, I gone!

**Brother Kiyi**    OK, girl. Hail up Bernie.

**Norma**    Will do!

*She leaves.*

**Brother Kiyi**    What were you saying?

**Alice**    Oh, I didn't mean to . . .

**Brother Kiyi**    No no no no, Norma was just leaving.

**Alice**    I was just going to share that I got a call from my boyfriend this morning! Nothing earth-shattering.

*His heart sinks, but he doesn't let it show.*

**Brother Kiyi**    Boyfriend?

**Alice**    Well, ex.

**Brother Kiyi**    What did he want?

**Alice**    He wanted me to come back to him.

**Brother Kiyi**    Do you want to?

**Alice**    He's no good for me. It's time I either had wild abandoned sex with whoever I want, whenever I want, or settled down to have a family.

**Brother Kiyi**    Can't you do both with him?

**Alice**    He's married. In fact his daughter and I are roughly the same age. I know what you're thinking . . .

**Brother Kiyi**    . . . I don't think you do!

**Alice**    I mean, guys my age are great for sex and that, but, well . . . I need more. I love him, but, ahhh, I'm confused. I don't know what to think. What do you think?

**Brother Kiyi**    You should do. (*He doesn't quite know how to respond.*)

**Alice**    My father always use to warn me, 'What men say and what they really mean are often two different things.' If I were your child what would you tell me to do?

**Brother Kiyi**    Stick with the older man. Only joking . . .

*Enter* **Carl** *in a rush.*

**Carl**    Brother Kiyi, Brother Kiyi. What's up wid your phone, man?

**Brother Kiyi**    Calm down. What's the matter, Carl?

**Carl**    Beverly's been trying to get hold of you! She needs you to go to see her. Good ting I was passing with Dongal!

**Brother Kiyi**    See me for what?

**Carl**    She's gonna tell me that innit? But her face looked deadly! Dongal said it's because Mustafar's about to take back the shop.

**Brother Kiyi**    That's impossible . . . Alright, alright. Come and sit the shop for me. (*To* **Alice**.) Excuse me a moment, yeah?

**Alice**    Of course. Are you OK?

**Brother Kiyi**    Some people feel they playing with a boy! Well, they go see. Yes, it's all fine. Little while, yeah?

**Carl**    Yeah. Everything's safe wid me!

**Brother Kiyi** *pauses and looks at* **Carl** *for a beat before leaving.*

**Carl** *stands a fair distance from* **Alice**. *He's kinda smiling at her.*

**Carl**    Oh well.

**Alice**   What?

**Carl**   Nothing. Just oh well! Here we are. (*Sings.*) 'Just the two of us.'

**Alice**   Is . . . is Kiyi going to be OK?

**Carl**   Ah yeah, man, he's use to fighting. You don't see the locks? Lion of Judah! . . . They ain't taking nothing from him, dread. This place is too good for anyone to take away. It's great here, don't you think?

**Alice**   Yes.

**Carl**   It's a real tribute to Kiyi. Different people coming and going. I mean, look at you. You've come in an' caught the bug, right, like the rest of us?

**Alice**   What bug is that?

**Carl**   Culture. Nothing like knowing your roots!

*He starts to reggae DJ.*

> Me love me roots and culture, murderer,
> How black people dem a suffer – murderer!

(*A little embarrassed.*) It's an old Shabba Ranks tune. It must be great, being you.

**Alice**   Wow, where did that come from?

**Carl**   Yeah, you like must have the best of two worlds innit? Like you got the black beauty bit and you got the white money bit. Hoorah!

**Alice**   Hoorah!

**Carl**   Roots, you know, connection! I use to want to be white till I met Kiyi. Now I'm blue black brother. You couldn't make me white if you tried!

**Alice**   You think people try?

**Carl**   People try anything in this day and age you know! (*Pause.*) Is your hair easy to maintain?

**Alice**    Um, yes, I suppose.

**Carl**    Though I don't wanna be white, that's what I'd like. The mixed flowy type of hair. Girls like that, don't they? It's so beautiful.

**Alice**    I think your hair is fine. It's like mine!

**Carl**    You're just saying that to sweet me. You don't have to do that! Look, I'm gonna go do some reading. So, um, feel free to do what you want. Sure Kiyi won't mind.

**Alice**    Yeah, he said it was OK.

**Carl**    Good.

*He moves across to the desk and takes out a book. He sings to himself:*

'From the very first time I set my eyes on you girl,
My heart said follow through,
But I know that I'm way down on your line.
But the waiting deal is fine.'

**Alice**    Carl, what kind of man is Kiyi?

**Carl**    How do you mean?

**Alice**    What kind of man? Is he kind? Loving?

**Carl**    Mannn, he's got the biggest heart in the world, dread. Everything I am today I owe to Kiyi.

**Alice**    Is that so?

**Carl**    Yeah. I was sleeping on the street, everybody else walked over me, but he bent down, pulled me up, took me to his home and fed me. Not a lot of people would do that! Not in this day and age.

**Alice**    He took you to his home?

**Carl**    Yeah!

**Alice**    What did his wife say?

**Carl**    Kiyi ain't got no wife.

**Alice**    His woman, then . . .

**Carl**    You're not getting me. Kiyi's got his books and that's all he needs, bar probably a likkle bit of Norma!

**Alice**    Oh, he and Norma are . . . ?

**Carl**    Naa naaa. I put that over wrong. I'm always doing that! Norma's like a man to Kiyi! They like blokes, buddies and shit, stuff.

**Alice**    Stuff?

**Carl**    Yeah, between you and me, Kiyi did little time with Norma's husband and they looked after him when he came out. He never forgets a favour.

**Alice**    How long ago was that?

**Carl** (*sensing he's talked too much*)    Dunno. Got to take my hat off to him, though, I don't know how a brother goes that long without some grit . . . some . . . some . . .

**Alice**    Some what?

**Carl**    You know . . .

**Alice** (*playing*)    No.

**Carl**    Some, ha . . . !

**Alice**    Sex?

**Carl**    Exactly, that's the one. I didn't want to be rude.

**Alice**    Sex isn't a rude word, Carl.

**Carl**    I know, it's just not the kinda utterance you want to use in front of a lady, is it?

**Alice** (*laughs*)    You are so cute.

**Carl**    Thanks. So are you.

**Alice**   Does he ever talk about the old days – you know, his youth, his mother and stuff?

**Carl**   Naaaa. Not to me.

**Alice**   But at his house he must have pictures up and that?

**Carl**   No. He keeps all that stuff here.

*Enter* **Kwesi**. *He clocks* **Alice**.

**Kwesi**   You still here, girl?

**Alice** *gets up and starts to walk out.* **Carl** *is vexed.* **Kwesi**'s *just broken his vibe.*

**Alice**   I'll see you later, Carl.

**Alice** *leaves.*

**Carl**   She's pretty innit?

**Kwesi**   She alright. (*Referring to the box he has left.*) No, it's alright.

**Carl** *walks up to* **Kwesi** *and attempts to take the box from him.*

**Carl**   Hey, my job is delivery. That's what I do.

*He pulls the box.*

**Kwesi**   Carl, I said it's OK.

**Carl**   Your car's gonna get a ticket. Let me take the box. What's the problem?

**Kwesi**   I said it's alright.

*In a sudden burst of temper* **Carl** *rips the box out of* **Kwesi**'s *hands. It falls on the floor and bursts open. Lots of hair products spill on to the floor.*

**Carl**   Keep your fucking boxes then!

**Kwesi**   Are you out your fucking mind?

**Carl**   Sorry, sorry. I just like things to be clear, you know what I am saying? Know what I'm doing, know where I am?

*He gets down to put the stuff back in the box. He notices the hair products.*

**Kwesi**   Move. Move.

**Carl** (*picks up a bottle*)   Oh shit, I haven't seen one of these in ages. Gerry Curl Max. (*Fake-sprays it on his hair.*) 'Makes your hair wavyyyy.' (*Advert voice.*)

**Kwesi**   Give it back! Give it to me!

**Carl**   What you doing with hair products, Kwesi? You boys don't like that shit? (*Impersonates.*) 'Making your hair like white folk!'

**Kwesi**   Don't worry about it.

**Carl**   Just looking forward to seeing you with a perm! It's gonna suit you, trust me!

**Kwesi** *kisses his teeth and exits.* **Carl** *pulls out a hair leaflet he took from the box. He starts to read it. He looks perturbed.*

*Lights down.*

### Scene Four

*Fix Up bookstore. One hour later.*

*Lights come up slowly.* **Kwesi** *is in* **Brother Kiyi**'s *chair with his feet on the desk. He is on his mobile.*

**Kwesi**   Ha! Na, man, the boy's too stupid to put all that together. You're kidding! . . . How much? . . . Niggers, man! We can't afford that! . . . Tell him he's fixing up, not bloody rebuilding! . . .

*Enter* **Brother Kiyi**. *He looks upset.*

**Kwesi**   Look, gotta go. Yeah, yeah. Tendai Mwari.

*He gets off the phone and out of* **Brother Kiyi**'s *chair.*

**Brother Kiyi**    Hope you ain't planning on fixing up nothing in here?

**Kwesi**    Um, what do you mean?

**Brother Kiyi**    What you fixing up?

**Kwesi**    Um, some stats and stuff we just got from America. Trying to get a professional on the job. You know, for the new classes. Did you know the global buying power of black America ranks eleventh in the world? That's just below Spain and above India, you know? Some serious money Nubians be spending.

**Brother Kiyi**    How much they spend on education?

**Kwesi**    Good question, I don't know . . . But check this out. How much are we spending on cosmetics a year? Thirty-five million in this country alone, dread. I mean, come on, it don't take Pythagoras to work out why other people be getting rich off our backs, does it? That's why I always be telling you, Kiyi, I love this shop but niggers ain't ready!

**Brother Kiyi** *doesn't answer.*

**Kwesi**    You OK?

**Brother Kiyi**    I don't know about no niggers, looks like it was me that weren't ready. It's all over, Kwesi, game's over. I no longer have the shop, him take the money for back rent, I thought the option to extend the lease was with me. It's not.

**Kwesi**    I see.

**Brother Kiyi**    I mean, maybe I should have heeded your advice, opened this place up. Sold Jamaican videos and bashment-sound tapes and home food in the corner but . . . (*Loses it for a bit.*) This is a place of learning, Kwesi! Not a come-one come-all supermarket, but a sanctuary, a place away from the madness. Away from the pain.

**Kwesi** *doesn't know what to say. He feels for him.*

**Kwesi**  He's a businessman, Kiyi, what else is he gonna do? Me, I blame the people around here that have ignored what this is. That walk past safe in the knowledge that it's here but put nothing in. What you gonna go and put yourself in trouble for? For them? For those that buy one book a year?

**Brother Kiyi**  The road to freedom is seldom walked by the multitude.

**Kwesi**  It's not being walked by anyone right now, Kiyi. You got to take emotion out of this. You couldn't afford to run the shop because the people didn't support you. That's it. There's a lesson in that for all of us. A lesson for me.

**Brother Kiyi**  What is that?

**Kwesi**  Sometimes you got to do stuff in this world that ain't nice. But if you think it's right, you got to do it. That's what my Somalian brothers been showing me. They ain't wrong.

*His mobile rings. He glances at the text.*

I need to talk to you, Kiyi, not now cos I got to run, but you gonna be around later?

**Brother Kiyi**  Where else I go be?

**Kwesi**  Alright. I'll see you in while.

**Kwesi** *turns to leave.*

**Brother Kiyi**  Kwesi.

**Kwesi**  Yeah . . .

**Brother Kiyi**  You're a good brother!

**Kwesi** *turns and leaves.*

**Brother Kiyi** *begins to sob, silently at first. Slowly and quietly we hear his sobs.*

*Gently, barely audibly at first, he begins to hear the voices from the books. Passages, statements, prose and poetry all blend.*

*After a few beats he snaps out of it, inhales and then forcefully*
*exhales the air to pull himself together. He returns to his desk, gets*
*out the key to the chest of drawers, opens it pulls out an old-looking*
*box. He removes the photo album that is inside.*

*He stares at the first few pictures before drifting off into a state of*
*great sadness.*

*Enter* **Carl**.

**Carl**   Hey, Brother Kiyi, you OK?

**Brother Kiyi**   Yeah, man, course I'm OK.

**Carl**   How did the Beverly meeting go?

**Brother Kiyi**   Fine, fine. She just wanted to talk to me
about future plans and tings.

**Carl**   Tings?

**Brother Kiyi**   You know, expansion.

**Carl**   Right. So the shop's cool?

**Brother Kiyi**   Yeah man. Safe as it's ever been.

**Carl**   Seen. Wanna cup of tea or something?

**Brother Kiyi**   No.

**Carl**   Hear what! I wanna do something right.

**Brother Kiyi**   Alright.

**Carl**   I wanna bust a move on Alice.

**Brother Kiyi**   What?

**Carl**   Not bust a move exactly. I wanna ask her out.

**Brother Kiyi**   Um?

**Carl**   Truth is I just need to talk to someone and you like
a dad to me. Plus I ain't got no mates but that's wholly
secondary.

**Brother Kiyi** (*stunned*)   Carl . . . have I missed . . . do you
know if she feels anything for you?

**Carl**   Yeah, man. I *know* she feels something for me, Kiyi. I
feel it in bloodstream. Shit that powerful don't just happen
one way, it just don't . . .

**Brother Kiyi**   Maybe you've misread.

**Carl**   I can't misread what's in my heart, Kiyi.

**Brother Kiyi**   I don't doubt that you feel for her . . .

**Carl**   I don't feel, I know.

**Brother Kiyi**   . . . Look before you step to *any* woman – you
got to make sure that it is something they would like, that
you're compatible, that . . .

**Carl**   You think that I'm not good enough for her? Am I too
dark for her or something?

**Brother Kiyi**   Oh Carl, come on. That's not what I meant!

**Carl**   Yes it is! I'm alright for all those other girls round
here but Alice, noooo!

**Brother Kiyi**   Carl, calm down! Count to ten, come on,
slowly! One . . .

**Carl**   I'm not a crack addict any more, Kiyi. I mean, you're
treating me like the enemy and you don't understand, you
ain't looking. What's happening with the shop, Kiyi?

**Brother Kiyi**   Nothing's happening with the shop, Carl,
everything's going to be fine.

**Carl**   You're lying to me. Why does everybody lie to me all
of the time? I'm not a fool, I'm not an idiot.

**Brother Kiyi**   I didn't say you were, Carl. I was saying . . .

**Carl**   You're telling me everything gonna be alright. When
I know that everything is fucked!

**Brother Kiyi**   Carl, calm down!

**Carl**    I won't fucking calm down, Kiyi, this is serious. I'm trying to tell you something and you won't hear me. Kwesi's going to take over your shop, Kiyi.

**Brother Kiyi**    Ah, Carl, don't be ridiculous.

**Carl**    I'm not being ridiculous. Look . . . here's the order thingy. Now I could be wrong, you know, maybe I read it wrong, I've done that before, but . . . where the fuck is it?

**Brother Kiyi**    Carl.

**Carl**    I'll find it in a minute, just wait a second. I put it . . .

*He looks for the hair product order form.*

**Brother Kiyi**    Carl, come on. Kwesi! How you gonna be going there? Are you mad?

**Carl**    What did you call me? You see. You see. Do you have any idea how hard it is for me to tell you anything about Kwesi? About your fucking darling upstairs.

**Brother Kiyi**    Carl, look, I'm sorry if I . . .

**Carl**    I don't give a bombo about you're sorry, you think I'd just make that up? I may have done some bad things but I ain't the killer here.

**Brother Kiyi**    I'm trying to protect you.

**Carl**    That's what they use to say in da madhouse before them inject me, in the court house before them send me down, and in my mum's house before she box me in me mouth! You hurt me, Kiyi, you done fucked up.

**Brother Kiyi**    Carl!

**Carl** *walks out of the door just as* **Alice** *comes in. They nearly collide.*

**Alice**    Hi Carl . . .

**Carl**    Don't touch me.

*He exits.*

**Alice**   What's the matter with Carl?

**Brother Kiyi**   Nothing. We um, just had a little . . . You know, families do that, right. Alice, I've had a really hard day, I'm about to lock up.

**Alice**   I've never seen you upset before. I only came to return this. (*She pulls a slave narrative from her bag.*) I borrowed it earlier.

**Brother Kiyi**   You did?

**Alice**   Didn't think you'd mind, you lend books all of the time, don't you?

**Brother Kiyi**   Not those, I don't.

**Alice**   Why not those?

**Brother Kiyi**   Because they're really not supposed to leave the store. Why would you do that without asking me?

**Alice**   I'm sorry if I took your book without permission, but I've never seen, read anything like this before, I couldn't put it down . . . I read a story about this woman whose children wanted to play in the dolls' house of their brother and sister, and the children got sold and the mother got whipped, and she was mixed race like me . . .

**Brother Kiyi**   I know the one . . .

**Alice**   . . . and I've found this other story, listen to this!

*She reads to* **Brother Kiyi**.

**Alice**   'When me mudder see that Mr Reynolds had come to collect me to sell with the other ten or so pickney, she fell to her knees and begged him to spare me. When she seed that it weren't no good, she simply stood up and asked Him to ask whoever it was dat buyed me, to raise me for God. I was too young to understand what was going on, but now I understand. I never seed my modder again all my living days.' (*Beat.*) I was given away and I tried to imagine the pain of this mother, what this mother felt, this parent felt, but I just simply couldn't.

**Brother Kiyi**    Given away?

**Alice**    Adopted. Yeah! Can you imagine the pain of this parent?

**Brother Kiyi**    No!

**Alice**    The pain of that child when she realised she would never see her mother again? Can you imagine?

**Brother Kiyi**    Have you met your . . . birth parents?

**Alice**    My father yes, mother no.

**Brother Kiyi**    How come?

**Alice**    He was easier to find.

**Brother Kiyi**    I see. I'm sorry.

**Alice**    Oh there's nothing to be sorry about. My real mum and dad were . . . Actually, you know what? There is a book over there that I wish was out when I was kid. Caring for black hair. I didn't know you could wear your hair other than in two bunches until I was seventeen.

**Brother Kiyi**    This shop, Alice, will soon be, it will soon be a centre of excellence for black hair products. Run by two very nice-looking Turkish guys. They don't have a great grasp of English at the moment, but I'm sure they've enough to know the difference between Afro sheen and Dyke 'n' Dryden. It's not a problem, in fact I feel rather good that in the first months of trading no doubt more black folk will have passed through here than I'd have seen in my whole fifteen years! What is a problem is that I must start anew, afresh. Again. I can handle that, except, maybe, the last time I did that I had a lot to leave behind. However, today you have added power to my depleted strength. You're an angel and I thank you.

**Alice** *just stares at him. Suddenly she bursts into tears and runs out of the store.*

**Brother Kiyi** *doesn't know how to react to this.*

**Norma,** *who had entered near the end of their conversation and overheard 'angel', walks forward as* **Alice** *runs out past her.*

**Norma**    What you and that gal have, Kiyi?

**Brother Kiyi**    We don't have nothing.

**Norma**    So what, she just up and bawl so? Is mad, she mad?

**Brother Kiyi**    I don't know!

**Norma**    Woman don't just bust cye water so!

**Brother Kiyi**    Not all woman is hard like you, you know, Norma!

**Norma**    Indeed.

**Brother Kiyi**    That sounded worse than I meant it to.

**Norma**    No, it's OK.

*Beat.*

**Brother Kiyi** *starts to busy himself tidying the books.*

**Norma**    What you doing?

**Brother Kiyi**    I was about to call you, actually.

**Norma**    Really? So what was you going to call me to say?

**Brother Kiyi**    I . . . I . . .

**Norma**    Boy, something really must a bite you, dread. Cleaning up? Can't open your mouth. What?!

**Brother Kiyi**    Norma, Bernie vex you or something?

**Norma**    No. Bernie don't vex me. Is you making a fool of youself that's vexating me soul.

**Brother Kiyi**    Me?

**Norma**    Yes, you! One little mix-up girl breeze in here and is turning you head stupid?

**Brother Kiyi**   What you talking about?

**Norma**   You don't know that girl, Kiyi, and you be laughing up like a fool, talking to her as if you and she is companion.

**Brother Kiyi**   Norma, I converse with the girl, she's bright, what is the problem?

**Norma**   Oh, she's bright, is she? What else is there about this gal that you know for two minutes?

**Brother Kiyi**   Norma . . .

**Norma**   No, don't 'Norma' me. Tell me what else she is that makes you talk *shit* you should be keeping to youself? Or to you people them that has been here, with you, since morning?

**Brother Kiyi**   I don't know what's going on here, Norma, but it should stop. Right now.

**Norma**   Why? Why should it stop? It's the first real conversation we've had in a lifetime.

**Brother Kiyi**   That's not true, we talk all the time.

**Norma**   About what you want to talk about. When was the last time you told me something new? Something you've never said before. Something about you? About your hinterland?

**Brother Kiyi**   Norma, what you trying to say here?

**Norma**   How can that rasclaat girl that just reach be your angel, Kiyi?

*He is taken aback for a second.*

**Brother Kiyi**   I didn't mean . . .

**Norma**   Then what did you mean? Because words are everything and you wanna be careful about what you say because people might hear it and believe it.

**Brother Kiyi**   All I was trying to say was that . . .

**Norma**   That what?

**Brother Kiyi**　That I appreciate her being here.

**Norma**　And what about me, Kiyi? When was the last time you said you appreciate me, Kiyi?

**Brother Kiyi**　I say that all the time, what you want me to say that for?

**Norma**　Because sometimes a woman needs to hear it. But of course I'm hard Norma, I don't need to hear nothing.

**Brother Kiyi**　I appreciate you, Norma, there. You OK now?

**Norma**　Don't patronise me.

**Brother Kiyi**　Well, I don't know what you want, Norma, because I was simply expressing . . . Look, the licks I've been taking, I was simply expressing I'm pleased someone young wants . . . wants to engage. That's what this place was built for, Norma. It's what it is . . .

**Norma**　Well, maybe we give too much attention to the young . . . That young girl is playing you, Kiyi . . .

**Brother Kiyi**　What is there to play, Norma? I have nothing . . .

**Norma**　That's the problem – you don't see what you have. You have us, you have your shop.

**Brother Kiyi**　I don't have the shop any more, Norma! It's gone. I squander you money, OK?

**Norma**　I know. The whole of the street know.

**Brother Kiyi**　I'm sorry. I was waiting for you to come, I was going to call . . . But I plan to go out and . . . I'm going to get you money for you, Norma, it might take a little longer than I thought, but . . .

**Norma**　So that's it, then?

**Brother Kiyi**　Look so.

**Norma**    Not the shop, me and you? If you don't have here when am I going to see you?

**Brother Kiyi**    Come to my yard, I'll come to yours.

**Norma**    When was the last time you came by my house, Kiyi?

**Brother Kiyi**    Um, I came . . .

**Norma**    You know the last time you come? When the car knock me down and I was lay up in me bed for six weeks . . .

**Brother Kiyi**    Well, there you go then.

**Norma**    That was three years ago. That's not coming to see your friend. You only came because you thought I was going to dead. When last you just pick up yourself and say you'll come by me?

**Brother Kiyi**    I don't like other people's houses . . .

**Norma**    I is 'other people'?

**Brother Kiyi**    No, but . . .

**Norma**    But what . . . ?

**Brother Kiyi**    Family homes are for families, alright?

**Norma**    What shit is that?

**Brother Kiyi**    It's not shit, OK. Now I'm gonna get your money by hook or by crook.

**Norma** *turns to walk out but stops.*

**Norma**    Give me little satisfaction, Kiyi. When I come back me and you going to see Mustafar. Together.

**Brother Kiyi**    It's not going to do no good, Norma.

**Norma**    Did you hear me? If me have to lose ting never let it be said that I didn't fight. Good.

*She leaves.*

*Lights down.*

## Scene Five

*Fix Up bookstore. The next day, early morning.*

*There's a knock on the front door of the store. It's* **Alice***. She knocks three or four times before* **Kwesi** *eventually goes to the door.*

**Kwesi**   Kiyi's out.

**Alice**   Cool, I'll wait for him.

**Kwesi**   He didn't tell me to let anyone in.

**Alice**   Oh come on, Kwesi, open the door, it's cold out here.

**Kwesi**   Let me get the keys. (*He opens the shop door.*) New hairstyle. Nice.

**Alice**   Thank you for noticing.

**Kwesi**   Any problems, I'm upstairs.

**Alice**   As usual.

**Kwesi**   As usual!

**Alice**   Would be nice sometimes to converse!

**Kwesi**   Yeah, it would, wouldn't it?

**Kwesi** *goes upstairs.*

**Alice** *takes the key to the chest of drawers from the desk. She opens the drawer and removes the box.*

*The box slips and falls to the ground, making a loud sound. She picks it up after looking to see if* **Kwesi** *is coming.*

*She takes the box to the desk and opens it. She pulls out the old photo album.* **Alice** *is a little surprised. She holds it in her hands, but doesn't open it for a moment. She checks over her shoulder that no one is around, and nervously places it on the table.*

*If we could hear her heart beating it would be dangerously fast.*

*As she sits, the lights dim slightly until she is in a spotlight. She opens the photo album and turns to the first page. She gasps, covers her mouth with her hand as if trying to keep in what wants to come gushing out, and stares at the picture.*

*She turns to the next page and, without trying, tears begin to fall. She quickly turns to the next page, and the next, and lands on one that instantly makes her clench her teeth, cover both her eyes and silently moan.*

*Suddenly the lights snap back up. A hand lands on her shoulder. She jumps up.*

**Alice**   Ahhh! What the hell are you doing?

*She slams the album shut behind her, almost hiding it.*

**Kwesi**   I heard a bang.

**Alice**   Haven't I told you before about creeping up on me?

**Kwesi**   I wasn't creeping up on you.

**Alice**   Of course you were.

**Kwesi**   Easy na! Calm down. I wasn't.

**Alice**   Don't tell me what to do! . . .

**Kwesi**   I'm not *telling* you anything . . .

**Alice**   Yes, you are!

*He attempts to grab her.*

**Kwesi**   Listen . . .

**Alice**   Get off.

*She starts to hit him in his chest.*

Get off me . . .

*He holds her tighter to calm her down.*

**Kwesi**   I don't know about mans where you come from, but don't be shouting up at me.

**Alice**   Why, what you gonna do, hit me? I'm use to that . . .

**Kwesi**   Don't be stupid, what am I going to hit you for?

**Alice**   Then what? What? Whatever you're gonna do, do it!

*She begins to sob.* **Kwesi** *doesn't know what to do.*

*Still in his arms, she turns away.*

**Kwesi** *starts to look at the desk. It must be something she was reading. He sees the photo album.*

**Alice** *kisses him deep. Unsure of what is going on, he half-kisses her back.*

*The kissing becomes more intense.* **Alice** *starts to undo his shirt. He is a little surprised but allows her to do it, then she begins to undo his trousers.*

**Kwesi**   What are you? . . .

*She puts her finger to his lips.*

**Alice**   Ssshhhhh!

*She starts to kiss him. He takes her by the hand as if to lead her upstairs. She pulls him back into the desk.*

**Alice**   No. I want you here.

*They kiss.*

**Kwesi**   Upstairs.

*He takes her by the hand and leads her upstairs. She follows, still staring back at the photo album. As they reach the stairs she kisses him.*

*Silence.*

*After a few beats* **Carl** *appears from behind a bookcase.*

*The anger rises. He runs over to a bookshelf and throws loads of books off.*

*As he is throwing the books all over the place a bare-chested* **Kwesi** *comes running down the stairs. He sees* **Carl** *wrecking the joint.*

**Kwesi** Carl! What the fuck are you doing? What you doing?

**Carl** No. What are you doing, Kwesi?

**Kwesi** What?

**Carl** Who's upstairs with you?

**Kwesi** What you talking about?

**Carl** I said who's upstairs with you, Kwesi?

**Kwesi** No one.

**Carl** Is Alice up there?

**Kwesi** I don't know what you're talking about, but I figure you're losing your mind.

**Carl** But you don't even like her, Kwesi?

**Kwesi** Don't worry about what I like, you need to be . . .

**Carl** *makes to go upstairs.* **Kwesi** *blocks him.*

**Kwesi** Where you going?

**Carl** Get out my way! I need to talk to her.

**Kwesi** You ain't got no business up there . . .

**Carl** Yes, I have. This place still belongs to Kiyi, you know.

**Kwesi** But right now that's my space.

**Carl** Then why couldn't you settle with that? Why you gotta have everything, Kwesi?

**Kwesi** Carl, I'm not going to tell you again.

**Carl** *makes to head upstairs again.*

**Kwesi** Carl, didn't you hear me?

*He pushes him back.*

**Carl** I wanna see if she's alright. (*Shouts.*) Alice . . . Alice, it's alright, I'm coming. I'm coming to save you. I'm coming.

*He runs towards* **Kwesi**. **Kwesi** *tries to grab him. They struggle.*

**Kwesi**   I . . . told . . . you . . . to . . . calm . . . the . . . fuck down.

*Eventually they land on the floor.*

**Carl**   Ahhhh, why you got to take everything? Ahhhh!

**Kwesi**   Calm down, Carl.

**Carl** (*screams*)   Touch me again and I'll kill you. You – you stolen from me, you're stealing from Kiyi . . .

**Kwesi**   I didn't steal nothing from no one.

**Carl**   Yes, you did. It's not no Turkish boys taking over the store, it's you. You and your Somalians. How could you do that to Kiyi? After all he's done for you!

**Kwesi**   Kiyi ain't done nothing for me. What Kiyi does he does for himself. Is it my fault he can't run his affairs? I made him default?

**Carl**   You bastard!

*He runs at him again. They struggle.*

*Enter* **Brother Kiyi** *and* **Norma**, *unseen by the boys.*

**Brother Kiyi**   What the . . . What's happening . . . ?

*He runs over to the boys and tries to separate them.*

Boys, what the hell is going on? . . . Boys, stop this!

**Norma**   What the arse!

**Carl**   I told you it was him, Kiyi – him! I told you!

**Brother Kiyi**   Carl!

**Carl**   Tell him who's taking over the shop on Monday, Kwesi. Who's got boxes and boxes of curl juice sitting upstairs? You're a thief!

**Brother Kiyi**   Carl, calm down.

**Carl**   Will you listen to me for once! I've seen the boxes of perm juice. Ask him, Kiyi, ask the ginal!

**Brother Kiyi**   Listen, Kwesi, tell this boy that . . .

**Brother Kiyi** *looks at* **Kwesi**. *He sees the truth in his eyes.*

*Beat.*

**Kwesi** (*makes the decision to go front foot softly*)   People don't – want – books. They wanna party, and look good, have the latest hairstyles, and nails and tattoos. That's where niggers be at, Kiyi. They ain't spending shit in here. Why should the other man take our money? That's why we powerless, cos we ain't where the money at.

**Brother Kiyi**   It ain't about money!

**Kwesi**   That's why you're on your knees picking up books people don't wanna buy, innit? Where's the respect in that?

**Brother Kiyi**   Selling Afro-sheen gonna get you respect?

**Kwesi**   It's gonna get me into the position that when you want to renew your lease you come to me! Five years from now, Afro-sheen gonna buy us a next store and a next store and a next. Before you know it we got all of this place! If we don't do it, Kiyi, the man next door's gonna. I've been trying to tell you . . .

**Alice** *enters. She is still slightly dishevelled.* **Brother Kiyi** *looks at the topless* **Kwesi**.

**Brother Kiyi** *glances at* **Norma**. *She stares at him. He looks away, embarrassed. No one knows what to do or say.*

**Alice** *stands by the desk.*

**Brother Kiyi** *sees the photo album. As he picks it up,* **Alice** *places her hand on it.*

**Alice**   Are these pictures . . . ?

**Brother Kiyi**   Private.

**Alice**   Is that so?

**Alice** *opens the album and points to the picture on the first page. It's of a six-month-old baby girl.*

**Alice**   What a cute baby! Who is this? (*A little more intense.*) Who is this, right here? The one with the ribbons and the silly dress? Aren't you going to answer me?

**Norma**   Kiyi, don't take this, don't let the young girl talk to you so!

**Brother Kiyi**   Norma, let we talk later, na?

**Norma**   I'm not leaving you!

**Alice** *produces a picture and shows* **Brother Kiyi** *the photo album.*

**Alice**   You see this? This is the only picture I have of me as a child. Cheeks are a bit bigger, but hey! They look a lot alike, don't they? So I ask again, I wanna know who this is in the album?

**Brother Kiyi**   You already know, there's no need for me to . . .

**Alice**   Yes, there is a need! I need you to say, Alice, this is you. This is the child I gave away, this is the child I had and then couldn't be bothered or be arsed to look after so I dumped into some children's home to fend for herself, away from anything or anybody that cared, away from anyone that looked or sounded like her, away from all that is kin and natural and safe and you're a fucking fraud, Peter Allan, whatever you call yourself now, fucking Brother Kiyi. You're a fraud just like your fake fucking bookstore.

**Brother Kiyi**   It's not fake!

**Alice**   Look. You're more concerned about your stupid shop than you are about me, standing here before you, begging to be named, recognised.

**Brother Kiyi**   You're not begging to be recognised. You know who you are!

**Alice**    I do, do I?

**Brother Kiyi**    Yes, otherwise you wouldn't have come here to play with me, to test me.

**Alice**    I came to find out why I look the way I do, why I cross my legs when I'm afraid. And what did I find? A sad old man who pretends to love but hates everything around him.

**Brother Kiyi**    I do not hate. Disappointed, maybe. Hurt, possibly, but I don't hate. I love my community. I built this for my community.

**Alice**    You're making me want to throw up! What do you know about love? You leave your child to rot, to be raised by the very people you are educating your community against, and you talk about love? What did you build for me?

**Brother Kiyi**    I'm not educating my people against anybody, I'm teaching them to love themselves.

**Alice**    I AM YOUR CHILD!

**Brother Kiyi**    You know that's exactly what your mother would do to me. Twist me up. Lose her temper and start to scream and I wouldn't know what to do. It's her spirit in you come to haunt me, innit? You come to haunt me, Chantella?

**Alice**    My name is Alice!

**Brother Kiyi**    Your mother named you Chantella.

**Alice**    How did she even lay with a beast like you? You forced her, didn't you?

**Brother Kiyi**    What the fuck are you talking about? What do you know about your mother? You don't know nothin'! You don't know what she took to be with me, what shit I took just walking down the street, just fucking being with her. What do you know? What do you know? What does your blasted generation know? Do you have people spitting at you in the street? Do you have shit smeared on your windows? Do you have the pressure that makes you strike at the ones you love?

**Alice**    I don't know because you won't tell me!

**Brother Kiyi**    What do you want me to say? What do you want me to say?

**Alice**    I want to know why I don't have a mother!

**Brother Kiyi**    Of course you have a mother.

**Alice**    Why I don't have a mother that's here?

**Brother Kiyi**    I don't know – isn't your mother down there in Somerset or wherever you come from?

**Alice**    No. I don't have a mother, and I want one!

**Brother Kiyi**    Well, you can't, because I killed her, alright? Is that what you want me to say? Is that what you want? I – killed – her! I didn't mean to but I did, alright? I'm sorry. There! I've said it.

*As if all the energy has been drained from her, she stands and simply stares at* **Brother Kiyi**. *All his energy has suddenly gone as well.*

**Brother Kiyi** *looks between* **Alice** *and* **Norma**. *Although she had just worked it out,* **Norma** *has never heard* **Brother Kiyi** *say that before.*

**Norma**    Kiyi.

**Alice** *exits.*

*Silence.*

*Eventually* **Kwesi** *attempts to speak.*

**Kwesi**    I . . .

**Brother Kiyi**    Shhhhh! Please!

**Kwesi**    I didn't know she was your daughter.

**Brother Kiyi** *stares at him. He leaves.*

*Lights down.*

**Scene Six**

*Fix Up bookstore. Saturday evening.*

*The shelves of the bookstore are half-empty.*

**Brother Kiyi** *is sitting in the middle of the store. He is both physically and mentally in a world of his own.*

*Slowly he starts to chop off his locks. When all are gone, he runs his hands through what remains of his hair. His hands eventually fall on his face. He screams.*

**Brother Kiyi**    Ahhhhhhh!

**Norma** *re-enters the shop.*

**Norma**    You OK?

**Brother Kiyi**    Yes. Fine.

**Norma**    Well, everything done. Bernie waiting to go. What we can't fit in your garage we'll put in the shed. You coming?

**Brother Kiyi**    No, I'll walk if that's alright.

**Norma** *stares at* **Brother Kiyi**.

**Brother Kiyi**    What?

**Norma**    What do I do with all that I have learnt from you, Kiyi. If even *you* peddle lies, who can I trust?

**Brother Kiyi**    I don't know, Sister Norma.

**Norma**    I go see you.

**Brother Kiyi**    Yes.

*She leaves.*

*He begins to sing the blues slave chant 'Adam' to himself. Very slowly, void of emotion.*

**Brother Kiyi**    Ohhhhhh Eve, where is Adam. Ohhhhhhh Eve, Adam's in the garden picking up leaves.

*Enter* **Alice**.

**Brother Kiyi** (*without looking at her*)   An old slave chant from the Deep South. I would offer you something to read but I don't expect you will be staying here that long?

**Alice**   No.

**Brother Kiyi**   I like that. No more questions. Statements are clean, you know where you stand with statements, don't you? You weren't abandoned, you were taken.

*Silence.*

*She doesn't answer. After a few beats he realises that it is pointless trying to explain.*

*He picks up the photo album and brings it to her.*

*She opens it and looks at the picture of her mother.*

**Brother Kiyi** *stares at her, confirming the truth that she does look like her mother.*

*She puts the photo album to her chest.*

**Brother Kiyi**   I built this to shut out the cries. Of you.

**Alice** *takes that in.* **Brother Kiyi** *stands up, looks deep into* **Alice***'s eyes and walks out.*

**Alice** *is left alone in the store still clutching the photo album.*

*The lights go down.*

**Bola Agbaje**

# Gone Too Far!

**Bola Agbaje** was a member of the Young Writers' Programme at the Royal Court Theatre and her first play, *Gone Too Far!*, premiered there in February 2007. The production won a 2008 Olivier Award for Outstanding Achievement in an Affiliate Theatre before transferring to the Royal Court Theatre Downstairs in July 2007. Her other plays for theatre include: *Sorry Seems to be the Hardest Word* (Royal Court Tent at Latitude, 2007); *Reap What You Sow* (Young Vic, 2007); *Rivers Run Deep* (Hampstead Theatre, 2007); *Off the Endz* (Rough Cuts, Royal Court, 2008); *Legend of Moremi* (Theatre Royal, Stratford, 2008); *Good Neighbours* (Talawa Unzipped at the Young Vic, 2008) and *Detaining Justice* (Tricycle Theatre, 2009, part of their *Not Black and White* season). She is currently Pearson Playwright in Residence for Paines Plough and is adapting *Gone Too Far!* into a full-length screenplay for the UK Film Council and Poisson Rouge Pictures.

*Gone Too Far!* was first presented at the Royal Court Jerwood Theatre Upstairs, London, on 2 February 2007. The cast was as follows:

| | |
|---|---|
| **Armani** | Zawe Ashton |
| **Yemi** | Tobi Bakare |
| **Old Lady** | Maria Charles |
| **Razer** | Ashley Chin |
| **Policeman 2** | Phillip Edgerley |
| **Shop Keeper/Policeman 1** | Munir Khairdin |
| **Ikudayisi** | Tunji Lucas |
| **Flamer** | Ricci McLeod |
| **Mum/Paris** | Bunmi Mojekwu |
| **Blazer** | Marcus Onilude |

*Director*   Bijan Sheibani
*Designer*   James Cotterill
*Lighting Designer*   Nicki Brown
*Sound Designer*   Emma Laxton
*Choreographer*   Aline David

## Characters

**Yemi**, *sixteen, black, stubborn, short-tempered, does not understand or speak Yoruba, good-looking*

**Ikudayisi**, *eighteen, black, has an African accent which he changes to a fake American one when he is around other people, apart from Yemi; he speaks Yoruba*

**Mum**, *has an African accent and speaks Yoruba*

**Shopkeeper**, *Muslim Bangladeshi with an accent, wears a headscarf*

**Armani**, *fifteen, mixed race, speaks fast, with an attitude*

**Paris**, *sixteen, dark-skinned, pretty, very calm, with a soft-spoken voice*

**Old Lady**, *old and frail*

**Razer**, *seventeen, good-looking, dresses well*

**Flamer**, *seventeen, light-skinned, good-looking, wears the latest fashion, everything brand new*

**Blazer**, *eighteen, black, tall, well built; his presence shows he is not someone to mess with*

**Police Officers 1** *and* **2**, *white, cockney accents*

## Scene One

*It is mid-afternoon and we are in* **Yemi**'s *bedroom. It is a small room which is suitable for one but is clearly occupied by two. A single bed with a duvet cover on it and a mattress on the floor with only the sheets take up most of the space. There are suitcases on the floor, opened with clothes hanging out from them, a mixture of traditional African and casual attire. There is a small TV on the floor with a PS2 attached to it.*

**Ikudayisi** *is squatting up and down, pulling his ears. He is performing some sort of punishment; he has been doing it for a while and looks tired, but does not stop. He is wearing jeans and a T-shirt, which represent a fashion trend a few months behind the current times.* **Yemi**, *on the other hand, is kneeling down on the floor playing on his PlayStation; he is better dressed than* **Ikudayisi** *and is up to fashion in the clothing department. He has on the latest hoodie and a fresh pair of white trainers. He does not pay any attention to* **Ikudayisi** *behind him, who tries to glance over his shoulder every time he squats.* **Yemi** *is engrossed in his game.*

**Ikudayisi**   Can I play when you finish?

**Yemi** *does not respond.*

**Ikudayisi**   Oh, don't go that way-oh!

**Yemi** *looks round and cuts his eye at him.*

**Ikudayisi**   Is it games you are supposed to be doing or your punishment?

**Yemi** *remains silent.*

**Ikudayisi**   It's not fair-oh!

**Yemi** *still remains silent and continues to focus on his games.*

**Ikudayisi**   If you don't start doing your own I will tell Mum.

**Yemi**   LEAVE ME!

**Mum** *shouts from offstage.*

**Mum** (*off*)   Yemi. Is that your voice I'm hearing? Ahh ahh. Is that what I told you to be doing?

**Yemi** *jumps up from his game and begins his punishment.*

**Yemi**   It wasn't me, Mum!

**Mum** (*off*)   You better not be playing games up there. If I catch you . . . Ah! You will not know yourself-oh!

**Yemi**   I'm not doing anything.

*He starts to pack the games away quickly, and goes back to squatting like* **Ikudayisi**. **Mum** *continues her rant from offstage; she is moving around so the volume goes up and down.*

**Mum** (*off*)   You these children, you these children, you are trying to kill me but I won't let you. Before I go from this earth I will show you pepper. People are always telling me I am lucky to have big boys like you. They don't know-oh, they don't know. You don't do nothing for me. You don't cook, you don't clean. All you do is give me problems. If I have to come up that stairs today . . .

*The phone rings and she answers in a very English voice.*

Hello. Oh yes, yes. Don't worry, I will be bringing it tomorrow . . .

*Her voice trails off.*

**Yemi**   You're such an idiot.

**Ikudayisi**   What level was you on?

**Yemi**   Don't talk to me, man.

**Ikudayisi**   Did you save it?

**Yemi**   Stop talking to me.

*They continue their punishment in silence,* **Yemi** *struggling more than* **Ikudayisi**.

**Ikudayisi**   Do you know the punishment you are doing, it is not the one she told you to do.

**Yemi**   Don't talk to me, man. Can't you just shut your mouth?

**Mum** (*off*)   Ah ah! Yemi, Oluyemi, is that you again. Do you want me to come up there today? If I have to walk up these stairs . . .

**Yemi** *moves to the floor to continue his punishment – left hand stretched out, with his right leg up in the air and his right hand behind his back.*

**Mum** (*off*)   . . . you will not like the side of me that you will see.

**Yemi**   It wasn't me, Mum, it was him that keeps on talking – he is tryna get me in trouble.

**Ikudayisi**   *Ma, mi o se nkon kon* – [Mum, I'm not doing anything – ]

**Mum** (*off*)   IKUDAYISI!

**Ikudayisi**   Yes, Ma?

**Mum** (*off*)   *Wa bi baiyi.* [Come here.]

**Ikudayisi**   *Ma, mi o se nkon kon.* [Mum, I'm not doing anything.]

**Mum** (*off*)   *A bi ori ko pe ni?* [Is your head not correct?]

**Ikudayisi**   *Mon bo, Ma.* [I'm coming, Mum.]

**Yemi**   GOOD!

**Ikudayisi** *exits.*

**Yemi** *continues to do his punishment, but only for a little while. He looks at the door, waits for a sound and, when he does not hear anything, goes back to his computer game. As he is about to start playing,* **Mum** *calls him again.*

**Mum** (*off*)   YEMI OLUYEMI!

**Yemi** *jumps back to his punishment position.*

**Yemi**    Yes, Mum! Whatever he said he is lying. I'm still doing it. He is just tryna get me in trouble.

**Mum** (*off*)    Yemi, Yemi, I said come here.

**Yemi**    Mum, yeah, you told me do something, I'm doing it.

**Mum** (*off*)    Are you OK? Ah ah, nonsense. Is it me that you are talking to like dat? If I have to come up that stairs –

**Yemi**    AHHHH, MAN!

**Yemi** *leaves the room as* **Ikudayisi** *returns and barges into him on the way out.* **Mum** *is still ranting and raving.* **Ikudayisi** *picks up* **Yemi**'s *computer game and starts playing.*

**Mum** (*off*)    – you have no respect. It not your fault, it not your fault. It's my own, I have spoilt you too much. When I should have taken you to Nigeria, to boarding school, I let you stay here and now look at you.

**Yemi** *and* **Mum** *continue their conversation offstage while* **Ikudayisi** *plays on the computer game, listening.*

**Yemi**    Yes, Mum.

**Mum**    You and your brother go to the shop for me.

**Yemi**    What? Why can't Dayisi go alone?

**Mum**    Don't start that nonsense with me. Don't start.

**Yemi**    But Mum, why don't he go?

**Mum**    He does not know de way.

**Yemi**    The shop is only round the corner.

**Mum**    You are going with your brother and that is final.

**Yemi**    But Mum, man!

**Mum**    Who are you calling man? Shut up, shut up your mouth. You listen up and you listen well. When I tell you to do something you do it. Don't ask me no silly questions. He is going to the shop with you and I don't want no trouble.

*She shouts for* **Ikudayisi**.

**Mum**    Ikudayisi! Ikudayisi!

**Ikudayisi**    Ma?

**Mum**    *Mo fe ki ewo ati Yemi lo si shop fumi.* [I want you and Yemi to go to the shop for me.]

**Ikudayisi**    Yes, Ma.

*He starts putting on his shoes, but then sees some Nike Air trainers in a box on* **Yemi**'s *side of the room and picks them up. He puts on the trainers and start profiling in front of a mirror.*

**Ikudayisi** (*to himself*)    Hey, fine boy. Cool guy!

*He does a bit of breakdancing.* **Yemi** *and* **Mum** *continue to talk offstage.*

**Yemi**    MUM! I don't want him to go with me. I will go by myself.

**Mum**    Yemi, don't start-oh, don't start. Do you think I'm stupid, do you think I'm stupid? When I send you by yourself, you will just go and galavant on the street. I said he is going with you. He is going! Always you, always you, giving me problems. I'm too young to die-oh. You better go and buy me milk now, and you better come back quick quick.

**Yemi**    OK!

**Mum**    It is always you. Always you giving me high blood pressure. I will kill you before you kill me. I will kill you!

**Yemi**    OK, OK! I'm going.

*Blackout.*

**Scene Two**

**Yemi** *and* **Ikudayisi** *walk out onto the estate. It is run-down, with graffiti all over the walls. It is the scene of a typical south London estate with rows of flats. The shop is at the far end of the stage and the* **Shopkeeper** *is outside putting up a newspaper stand. There is Islamic music playing loudly from inside the shop and he is singing along to it. He is wearing an England shirt and a headscarf. There are also England flags hanging all around the shop. He immediately notices the boys and hovers around the door watching them closely.* **Yemi** *has his hood over his head.*

**Ikudayisi**   How much did she give you?

**Yemi**   Don't talk to me.

**Ikudayisi**   If there is money left I want to buy chocolate.

**Yemi** *ignores him and bops ahead towards the shop. As soon as they get to the door, the* **Shopkeeper** *stands in the way.* **Yemi** *tries to walk past him, but he refuses to move away from the door.*

**Yemi**   Scuse, boss.

*The* **Shopkeeper** *clears his throat and points to the hood.*

**Shopkeeper**   No hoods.

**Yemi**   Uhhh.

*He attempts to get past again but fails.*

Can you move out of the way?

**Shopkeeper**   Sorry, no hoods.

**Yemi**   I wanna buy something dough.

**Shopkeeper**   I said no hoods allowed.

**Yemi**   And who are you?

**Shopkeeper**   My shop, my rule.

**Yemi**   Come out the way, I need to buy somink.

**Shopkeeper**   Take off hood and you can enter.

**Yemi**   This ain't Tesco, you nah.

**Ikudayisi**   Yo bro, why don't you just take off the hood, man, it will save a lotta trouble.

**Shopkeeper**   Yes, listen to friend.

**Yemi**, *stunned by the accent, turns and looks at* **Ikudayisi**, *puzzled.*

**Yemi** (*to* **Shopkeeper**)   Be quiet. (*To* **Ikudayisi**.) What's with the accent?

**Ikudayisi**   What accent, man?

**Yemi**   That one! You need to lauw dat, man, cos it don't sound good. We're not in America, we're in England!

*He looks down and sees his trainers on* **Ikudayisi**.

**Yemi**   What are you doing with my trainers on?

**Ikudayisi**   I'm borrowing them. Don't you think it looks nice on me?

**Yemi**   No, it don't suit you.

**Ikudayisi**   You know I look fine, fine.

**Yemi**   Look, yeah, what have I told you bout taking my stuff?

**Ikudayisi**   What's your problem? You can have it back when we get home.

**Yemi**   Just *don't* touch my stuff. Goss, man, do I need to start putting a padlock on my shit?

*Bored by the conversation, the* **Shopkeeper** *starts to go inside, and* **Yemi** *tries to follow. The* **Shopkeeper** *puts his hand in* **Yemi**'s *face to stop him.*

**Shopkeeper**   Still have hood.

**Yemi**   I ain't ere to teef nothing. I just need to buy somink. So *move*, man!

**Shopkeeper**   I don't want trouble.

**Yemi**   And no one ain't looking for trouble, boss. Just let me in.

**Shopkeeper**   Please, I don't want to call police.

**Yemi**   What! You're making me mad now. Why are you talking bout police for? We only here to buy something, you get me?

**Ikudayisi**   He doesn't get you, he not moving.

**Yemi**   Shut up! I'm not talking to you! Just stand over there, man.

**Ikudayisi** *moves to the side and watches* **Yemi**.

**Yemi**   Boss, stop the long ting and let me in.

**Shopkeeper**   Take off hood.

**Yemi**   Just move!

**Shopkeeper**   Please, no trouble.

**Yemi**   Don't you know nothing about human rights? You of all people should understand where I'm coming from – being a Muslim and dat.

**Shopkeeper**   Are you Muslim?

**Ikudayisi**   No, he is not-oh.

**Yemi** (*to* **Ikudayisi**)   You eediate, I said no one ain't talking to you. Just be quiet. (*To* **Shopkeeper**.) No I'm not a Muslim. But you're Muslim, innit?

**Shopkeeper**   Yes.

**Yemi**   See, that's what I'm saying, we're the same peoples.

**Shopkeeper**   I no black, I Bangladeshi.

**Yemi**   I know you're Indian –

**Shopkeeper**   Bangladeshi.

**Yemi**    Don't get it twisted, blud. Man, oh man, don't care where you're from. What I'm saying is I *know* you feel oppressed and dat when mans tell you, you can't wear your head ting in certain places. It the same like me! Bare people going around thinking you're gonna do dem something when all *we* wanna do is get on with our life. I understand you, blud!

**Shopkeeper**    Then no hood.

**Yemi**    You're not getting what – Hold up. (*To* **Ikudayisi**.) Listen to the music this guy is tryna play.

**Ikudayisi**    It nice.

*He mimics the song and tries to sing along.*

**Yemi**    Shut up, man. It's not nice. (*To* **Shopkeeper**.) How do we know it isn't some Islamic chant that you're playing?

**Shopkeeper**    It's prayer music.

**Yemi**    You only saying that cos we don't understand it. Furthermore, how do I know it ain't a bomb factory you got back there? That why you ain't tryna let me in.

**Shopkeeper**    I NO BOMBER, I NO SUPPORT TERRORIST!

*He moves towards* **Yemi***, waving his hands in his face.*

**Shopkeeper**    I LOVE THIS COUNTRY. I NO TERRORIST. NO BOMB IN MY SHOP, NO BOMB IN MY SHOP.

**Yemi**    Don't start coming nears me now, you might try blow me up –

**Shopkeeper**    You mutta mutta, you lie, no bomb in my shop –

**Yemi**    Look at the way you acting. You see, you see, that's why you of all people shouldn't judge, cos you're not liking it when you're getting judged.

**Shopkeeper**   I NO EVER SAY BAD THING ABOUT ENGLAND.

**Yemi**   Calm down, man, I was just making a point. Just cos I got a hood on my head don't mean I'm tryna rob nobody. Same ways *I know* just cos you're Indian don't mean you're a BOMBER!

**Shopkeeper**   I TELL YOU ALREADY I NO BOMBER! I PROUD TO BE ENGLISH. NO TROUBLE, NO TROUBLE. SHOP CLOSE, SHOP CLOSE.

*The* **Shopkeeper** *goes inside and closes the door.* **Yemi** *tries to open the door but it is locked.*

**Yemi**   Let me in! Don't you understand English? I was just making a point.

**Shopkeeper** (*from behind the door*)   Go away! I will call police now. You trouble.

**Yemi** *begins kicking on the door.*

**Yemi**   That's what I can't stand bout you Indians! Smelling of curry, coming over here, taking up all the corner shops, and man can't buy nothing. What da fuck you got a shop for if you're not tryna sell nothing? Call the police, call the police, I ain't doing nothing.

**Ikudayisi**   This is stupid, let's just go.

**Yemi**   I ain't going nowhere. Let the police come. (*To* **Shopkeeper**.) YOU HEAR ME? CALL THE POLICE. What can they do me for? It's more like they'll come and search up your shop. I just need to tell them you got a bomb in there. I bet *you* get arrested before I do!

*The* **Shopkeeper** *has now turned off his Islamic music and is playing the England World Cup song: 'Three Lions on the Shirt'.*

**Ikudayisi**   Let's just go, it not worth it at all, you are just scaring him.

**Yemi**    Scaring him? I should be scared of *him*. He is strange man!

**Ikudayisi**    It's not worth it.

**Yemi**    And what would you know? You wasn't even here on July the seventh when *his* people blew up bare heads last year.

**Ikudayisi**    What has that got to do with you wearing your hood in the shop? And you are lying – I heard about the July story. Not all Indian people are the same, and one of them was even black. Look at you, you should not judge like that.

**Yemi**    You're so backwards! Don't you know nothing at all? That how they look at us. Dem people are racist, they don't like black people, and I don't like dem either.

**Ikudayisi**    It's not cos you are black that he shut the door.

**Yemi**    You have a lot to learn.

**Ikudayisi**    I don't need to learn rubbish. You have to pick your battles well. Taking your hood off is nothing. You could have put it back on when we have finished.

**Yemi**    Shut up!

*He pushes past* **Ikudayisi** *and starts banging and kicking the door.*

**Yemi**    Let me in, you bloody Paki. You're going on like I ain't got money. I got bare dough.

**Ikudayisi**    He is not going to open de door when you are acting like a baboon.

**Yemi** *stops and turns to* **Ikudayisi**.

**Yemi**    Baboon! You're one to talk. You da one who lived in da jungle.

**Ikudayisi**    Your head is not correct.

**Yemi** *tries to punch* **Ikudayisi** *but misses.*

**Ikudayisi**    You are foolish, you don't know yourself.

**Yemi**   You eediate, you so dumb. I wish you would just go back to where you belong. You get on my nerves.

**Ikudayisi**   I am here to stay so you better digest it well well.

**Yemi**   Why don't you just piss off and die?

**Yemi** *pushes* **Ikudayisi**, *who falls to the ground.*

**Ikudayisi**   OK, I'll go home.

*He turns to leave and* **Yemi** *stops him.*

**Yemi**   NAH NAH NAH, you can't.

**Ikudayisi**   Now you want me to stay eh, ehh? Why?

**Yemi**   I'm sorry innit, I didn't mean it.

**Ikudayisi**   You meant it. Oh, you are evil! I'm going back home. Let the police come and catch you here.

**Yemi**   I'm not going to beg you, you nah.

**Ikudayisi**   I don't care. You are crazy.

**Yemi** *stands in his way.*

**Yemi**   Use your head. If you go home without the milk, *we* will get in trouble.

**Ikudayisi**   NO! *You* will get in trouble. I will just tell her you are misbehaving.

**Yemi**   And *I* will tell her you tried to steal somink.

**Ikudayisi**   That's a lie! You are the one causing trouble outside here. I was not part of it, I never did anything.

**Yemi**   SO! But how will she know dat?

**Ikudayisi**   Cos it a lie.

**Yemi**   Who has she known longer? Trust me, blud, don't test me.

*Blackout.*

**Scene Three**

**Ikudayisi** *and* **Yemi** *have now walked to a different part of the estate.*

**Ikudayisi**    We have been walking for long-oh.

**Yemi**    Stop your complaining.

**Ikudayisi**    So, how far are we going to go before we go back home?

**Yemi**    She said not to come back without the milk. What about *dat*, don't you understand?

**Ikudayisi**    But all the shops are closed.

**Yemi**    You always point out the obvious, innit. Indian shops are always open on a bank holiday in this country. They are money-orientated people, they will do anything for money.

**Ikudayisi**    What, like the other shopkeeper did? Have you forgotten he didn't care if you had money, he didn't want you in his shop.

**Yemi**    No! It was *me* who didn't want to go into *his* shop.

**Ikudayisi**    Your memory is short.

**Yemi**    Whatever.

**Ikudayisi**    So where is this other shop? I'm tired! We have been walking, walking, and I cannot see de shop. I don't want to walk no more, I want to go back home.

*He sits down.*

**Yemi**    I don't know what you are complaining bout. Don't you have to walk miles in Nigeria to get water? And now you're in England you going on like you can't even walk. We haven't even gone far. That's the problem with you people straight from the bush, you get to this country and want bare luxuries. What, you think, a horse and carriage is gonna come and carry you around? I was raised in these ends so I know where I'm going.

*He starts walking but* **Ikudayisi** *remains seated.*

**Yemi**   GET UP! You know how Mum stays, so why do you act all dumb? If we go back empty-handed, what do you think she will do?

**Ikudayisi**   I don't care. You are de one dat is scared of punishment.

**Yemi**   I'm not scared.

**Ikudayisi**   So let's go back home then ah ah now.

**Yemi**   No. We've been stuck inside da house for a week and now we are out, you want to go back in. Are you mad? You GO! I'm not going till I get this stuff, and if that means going to bare different shops, I'm going.

**Ikudayisi** (*looking around*)   It's only now you are saying I should go. Do I know where to go? We have been walking, walking, walking . . .

**Yemi**   Boy! If you don't know the way – I guess you got to stay den, innit!

**Ikudayisi**   *Ah ah koda now.* [That is not good.]

**Yemi**   WHAT DID YOU SAY?

**Ikudayisi** *starts laughing.*

**Yemi**   I SAID, WHAT DID YOU SAY?

**Ikudayisi**   You are Nigerian, you should know.

**Yemi**   What are you talking about? You know I don't understand.

**Ikudayisi**   It's not my problem.

**Yemi**   I hate it when you speak dat language.

**Ikudayisi**   Why, are you ashamed of being Nigerian? You can't change what you are.

**Yemi**   I'm not. I SAID I'M NOT!

*Offstage there is giggling, then two girls come onstage.* **Yemi** *notices them and runs up to them.*

**Yemi**   What's up, Armani, Paris?

**Paris**   Hi, Yemi.

**Yemi**   You're look Chung today, Paris.

**Paris**   Thanks!

**Yemi**   So where you lovely ladies going?

**Paris**   Nowhere, we were just about –

**Armani**   None of your business.

*Pause.*

**Yemi**   So, Paris, when are we gonna link up?

**Armani**   She's not! (*To* **Paris**.) Come, man, let's go.

**Paris**   I can talk for myself, you nah.

**Armani**   Why would you . . . ?

**Ikudayisi** *has bopped up to* **Yemi** *and is profiling behind his shoulder. He looks at the girls in admiration.*

**Ikudayisi** (*in a dodgy American accent*)   Yo, Yemi, you're not gonna introduce me to your friends?

**Armani**   Whoo's dis?

**Yemi** *shrugs* **Ikudayisi** *off.*

**Yemi**   I don't know him.

**Ikudayisi**   Ah ah . . . Oluyemi Adewale, so you are going to pretend we are not bruddas?

**Paris**   You got a brother? I never knew dat.

**Yemi**   No, he's my brother, but not my –

**Armani**   I never knew you was African.

**Paris**   You don't look African.

**Ikudayisi**    I don't look African?

*The girls laugh.*

**Armani**    No, *you* look African. Yemi don't look African.

**Ikudayisi**    *Ori e o pe.* [Your head is not correct.]

**Armani**    Wat did he say?

**Yemi**    I don't know, I don't speak dat language. What does an African look like? What is it you're tryna say?

**Armani**    You come from his country – what did he say?

**Yemi**    What does an *African* look like?

**Armani**    That's not what he said.

**Yemi**    No, *I* said what does an African look like.

**Armani**    I don't care!

**Yemi**    Well, I do. What does one look like?

**Armani**    An African, innit. Now what did he say?

**Paris** *nudges* **Armani**.

**Paris**    Lauw it, Armani.

**Yemi**    Nah, tell her to say what she mean.

**Paris**    She doesn't mean nothing.

**Yemi**    Let Armani speak.

**Paris**    It's just –

**Armani**    *Forget* it, man, I was only saying you don't look African, innit. What your problem? It's a compliment.

**Yemi**    *Compliment?*

**Armani**    You should be happy you don't look like dem. Be grateful you don't have big lips and big nose.

**Yemi**    What?

**Paris**    Armani!

**Armani**    It the truth, why am I going to sugar-coat it for?
You're lucky you're not black black.

**Ikudayisi**    All of us are black. We are all from Africa-oh.

**Armani**    Nah, later, I'm from *yard*, bruv.

**Ikudayisi** (*laughing*)    D' backyard? (*To* **Yemi**.) *Werre.*
[Crazy.]

*He continues laughing.*

**Armani**    What did he say now?

**Yemi**    What is wrong with having big lips?

*He begins to feel his lips.*

**Armani**    Why you covering up for him for? Dat's not what
he said.

**Yemi**    I told you before, I don't speak dat language.

**Ikudayisi**    *Omo iranu koti e mo kun ko.* [Stupid girl, don't
even know nothing.]

*He laughs again.*

**Armani**    But *you're* African –

**Yemi**    I was *born* here!

**Paris**    He is laughing hard dough. Seriously, Yemi, what
did he say?

**Yemi**    I don't know.

**Ikudayisi** (*to* **Yemi**)    Backyard. *Omo jaku jaku.* [This silly
girl.]

**Armani**    Yemi, are you tryna take da piss?

*She moves towards* **Yemi**.

**Yemi**    Back up, man. I ain't the one saying or doing
anything, he's the one speaking. Speak to him.

**Armani** *moves still closer to* **Yemi**.

**Yemi**   You're starting to get on my nerves now. Just duss –

**Armani**   Are you taking the piss?

**Ikudayisi**   *Omo girl e omo jaku jaku.* [This silly girl.] *Oti so ro so ro ju.* [She talks too much.] *Werre.* [Crazy.]

**Armani**   Listen, Adebabatunde, or watever your name is, yeah, we are in England so tell ya people to speak fucking English if they got something to say.

**Yemi**   IS THE WORDS EVEN COMING OUT OF MY MOUTH? I TOLD YOU I DON'T SPEAK THAT LANGUAGE. GET OUT MY FACE.

**Armani**   AND WHAT YOU GONNA DO, YOU AFRICAN BUBU?

**Yemi** *(starts squaring up into her face)*   Who da fuck you talking to like that?

**Armani**   I'm talking to *you!*

**Yemi**   You better watch your mouth, yeah.

**Armani**   What what what, what are you gonna do?

**Yemi**   Just watch your mouth.

**Paris**   Yous lot, man . . .

**Ikudayisi**   Please, let's not fight –

**Armani**   Nah, later, man, chatting like he gonna do something. Make him come and do something. (*To* **Yemi**.) If you're gonna do something, do something, innit.

**Yemi**   Move. I ain't got time for you.

*He turns to leave.*

**Armani**   See, you're just a pussy, all you African people dem are. Jus go home and eat your jelly and rice.

**Yemi**   WHAT?

**Armani**    What, you got problem understanding English now? (*She puts on an African accent.*) EH EH, do I need to speak in your language –

**Yemi** *goes for* **Armani** *and pokes her in the head.* **Paris** *tries to stop him and gets pushed to the ground.*

**Paris**    No, don't . . .

**Armani**    AHH . . .

**Ikudayisi**    No no no, Yemi, you cannot hit a lady. (*To* **Paris**.) Yo, mammy, you OK?

**Paris**    Yeah, I'm cool.

**Armani**    Oh my God, oh my God, you just touch me, you just touch me! Nah nah, I ain't having dat.

*She tries to go for* **Yemi** *but* **Ikudayisi** *holds her back.*

**Ikudayisi** (*to* **Armani**)    Yo princess, you gotta calm down.

**Armani**    Don't touch me, don't touch me! Move, man, don't come near me.

**Ikudayisi**    Let's go, Yemi.

**Yemi**    Shut up, man. (*To* **Armani**.) You started this. I ain't going nowhere.

**Armani**    Just watch, yeah, fink sey you can touch mi and get away with it. Watch wen my man hears bout this, you think you're gonna be alive? My man gonna have you up, he is gonna slash you up. You think you're a bad now, yeah, yeah, yeah. Watch, yeah, watch.

**Yemi**    I'm watching.

**Paris**    Please, you two –

**Armani**    Is it, is it. Mans don't lay their hands on me and live to see the next day, you know. People like you get taken and buried where no one can't find you. Even your mum's gonna be searching for your body, she not even gonna know where to look, yeah, yeah.

**Yemi**   Ohhh, *gangsta* now, is it?

**Armani**   I ain't tryna be gangsta, I'm just telling you how it is. You made the worst mistake of your life today, the worst mistake. This is the beginning, blud, this is the beginning. Living on this estate is gonna be the hell from today. Everywhere you go you're gonna have to watch your back. You see, you see, you forget, yeah, I know bare people on these ends. Once everyone knows what you tried to do today, what, you're done for. You better pack your bags and go back to Africa now.

**Yemi**   SHUT YOUR MOUTH. SHUT UP AND DUSS. GO GET YOUR MAN. THINK MANS LIKE ME IS SHOOK?

**Paris**   Yemi, please –

**Armani**   Nah, don't beg babatunde for nothing, let him talk, cos everything he is saying now my man's gonna hear bout it. (*To* **Yemi**.) Just watch you, bubu.

**Yemi** *goes for* **Armani** *again.*

*Blackout.*

### Scene Four

**Yemi** and **Ikudayisi** *have moved to another part of the estate.* **Yemi** *is sitting down with his legs up on a bench and his bum on the top half. He is still very angry about his run-in with* **Armani**. **Ikudayisi** *watches him and when he registers that* **Yemi** *is not moving he too sits down on the bench.*

**Ikudayisi**   Yemi, next time you should not hit a woman-oh.

**Yemi**   She's not a woman, she's a yout.

**Ikudayisi**   You should try and talk it out.

**Yemi**   You saw her – I didn't even get a word in. She is always running up her mouth. And for the record, I never hit her, I only *revered* her. And if it wasn't for you this wouldn't have happened in the first place.

**Ikudayisi**   I didn't do anything.

**Yemi**   You were talking in that language that nobody *understands*! I told you already I didn't like it – see what you started.

**Ikudayisi**   She was talking nonsense.

**Yemi**   She is *such* an idiot.

*Pause.*

And so is her man too, bout she saying she gonna get him on to me. Make him come, I'm ready for him, blud. I'm not afraid of no one.

**Ikudayisi**   Just calm down. Don't go looking for trouble.

**Yemi**   I ain't looking for no trouble. All I'm saying is, if it comes I'm ready! Come, man, get up – we ain't got time to sit down.

**Ikudayisi**   But . . . you . . . please let's just stay here for a minute, all that punishment I have been doing today has hurt my legs. I am tired-oh.

**Yemi**   So? So am I.

**Ikudayisi**   So let's rest. What is the big hurry?

**Yemi**   Look at the time. It getting late.

**Ikudayisi**   I don't have a watch.

**Yemi**   Like that should stop you – can't you just look at the sun and know the time?

**Ikudayisi**   Ah ah, Yemi, what *nonsense* are you talking? You are so ignorant! *Ki lo she e?* [What is wrong with you?]

**Yemi**   Why do you always mix English with Nigerian?

**Ikudayisi**    It's not called Nigerian – the language is Yoruba.

**Yemi**    I don't care what it is.

**Ikudayisi**    *Kini problem e?* [What is your problem?]

**Yemi**    You don't listen. See, that what I mean. Don't you know when you speak nobody round here understand a word you're saying.

**Ikudayisi**    You can learn if you want.

**Yemi**    Dat's long.

*Pause.*

**Ikudayisi**    What was that jelly and rice she was talking about?

**Yemi**    Who?

**Ikudayisi**    Dat girl.

**Yemi**    Oh, dat idiot. She was tryna say *jollof rice*, innit.

**Ikudayisi**    How can jollof rice be jelly?

**Yemi**    Exactly!

**Ikudayisi**    *Omo jaku jaku.* [Silly girl.]

**Yemi** (*laughs*)    That word is funny. Dat's what you called her innit? Did you see her face when you said that?

**Ikudayisi**    Of course now, she looked like this.

*He mimics* **Armani***'s face and they both laugh.*

**Yemi**    What was the other word you used?

**Ikudayisi**    Which one? I used a lot.

**Yemi**    That word beginning with 'w'.

**Ikudayisi**    Oh, *werre.*

**Yemi**   Yeah, dat one is funny too. I heard Mum saying that on the phone a few times. What does it mean?

**Ikudayisi**   It means crazy.

**Yemi**   For real. How do you say it?

**Ikudayisi**   *Werre*.

**Yemi**   *Warrri*.

**Ikudayisi**   No, *way* as in 'way' and *ray* as in 'ray'.

**Yemi**   *Way-ray*.

**Ikudayisi**   Yes, that's close.

**Yemi**   I guess that word is alright. Teach me ano – Nah, forget it, man.

**Ikudayisi**   Stop fighting it – you want to learn Yoruba.

**Yemi**   I don't.

**Ikudayisi**   It's easy.

**Yemi**   No man, I don't want to know.

**Ikudayisi**   Why?

**Yemi**   What is the point? When in Rome do as the Roman.

**Ikudayisi**   What do you mean?

**Yemi**   Meaning, what is the point of learning to speak *your* language when I don't even live in *that* country. We are in England. I only need to know how to speak English.

**Ikudayisi**   It's a nice language.

**Yemi**   No, it's not, it's not like it's Spanish or anything – now *dat's* a sexy language, I'll learn dat *any day*.

**Ikudayisi**   Yoruba is sexy too. Back home when I use it on the girl Kai! They come running, and I have to beat them away with a stick.

*He moves towards* **Yemi** *and demonstrates.*

**Ikudayisi**  Come here and let me show you. *Omo ge ki lo ruko e?* [Sexy girl, what's your name?]

**Yemi**  Move, you batty man.

**Ikudayisi**  Stop your shakara. Don't try and fight it. Yoruba can hypnotise you. When it does, there is nothing you can do. Come here, stop trying to resist it. *Omo ge, omo ge.* [Sexy girls, sexy girls.]

**Yemi**  Move, I'm not convinced. There is nothing sexy bout the language.

**Ikudayisi**  It bad-oh.

**Yemi**  What's bad?

**Ikudayisi**  That you are not embracing your culture. What does Mum say when you talk like this?

**Yemi**  She don't say nothing. She don't care bout speaking African either.

**Ikudayisi**  Ah ah, that not true, she speaks *Yoruba* all the time.

**Yemi**  No, she only started when you came. Before, she was forever speaking English. I never knew she could even speak in that language. Don't you hear, when she is on the phone she acts more English than me?

**Ikudayisi**  Come here, let me teach you Yoruba. Try it – *omo ge, omo ge.*

**Yemi**  Get lost!

**Ikudayisi**  You can use it on dat girl's friend. I saw da way you were looking at her, your mouth touch the floor.

**Yemi**  Shut up! Move, man.

**Ikudayisi**  I know you have never kissed a girl –

**Yemi**  What?

*An* **Old Lady** *enters with some shopping bags. She is halfway across when she notices* **Yemi** *and* **Ikudayisi**. *She stops in her tracks and contemplates turning back, but is too afraid to move.*

**Ikudayisi**    Before, you can use Yoruba on her, she will lie down at your feet, treat you like a king!

**Yemi**    See, that's why I can't stand you, you're going on like you know everything bout me – you don't know shit.

**Ikudayisi**    I'm only playing. I know you have kissed plenty of girls.

**Yemi**    Shut up, man! You don't know nothing about me . . . You going like –

**Ikudayisi** *notices the* **Old Lady** *now and jumps off the bench.*

**Ikudayisi**    Ma, sorry, don't you want to sit down?

**Yemi**    Ahhhhhh –

*He rolls his eyes, takes out his phone and starts playing with it.*

**Old Lady**    No no no no. I'm OK!

**Ikudayisi**    I can see you are tired – please come and sit down.

*The* **Old Lady** *stays still, scared.*

**Ikudayisi** (*to* **Yemi**)    Move now.

**Yemi**    What? NO! What for?

**Ikudayisi**    For this lady – she needs to sit down.

**Yemi**    What is wrong wid you?

**Old Lady**    I'm not looking for trouble. (*To* **Ikudayisi**.) I'm OK, I just wanna go home.

**Yemi**    Exactly. Let her go.

**Ikudayisi**    No, it's not OK. (*To* **Yemi**.) You're going to have to move your feet.

**Yemi**   She don't need a seat.

**Ikudayisi**   Yemi, where is your manners?

*He snatches* **Yemi**'s *phone and the* **Old Lady**, *frightened, drops her shopping.* **Ikudayisi** *goes to help.*

**Yemi**   Give it back.

**Old Lady**   Please don't touch me – I told you, I'm not looking for trouble.

**Yemi**   Give me the phone back – the battery low.

**Ikudayisi**   Ma, let me help you.

*The* **Old Lady** *starts edging backwards, raising her voice.*

**Old Lady**   Stay away! Stay away.

**Yemi** (*to* **Ikudayisi**)   What wrong with you?

**Old Lady**   Please . . .

**Ikudayisi**   I'm only helping.

**Old Lady**   Please, I just wanna go home.

**Yemi**   Go.

**Ikudayisi**   We can't let her go – her bags have broken.

*He tries to help her gather up the things that have fallen on the ground.*

**Old Lady**   OH GOD!

**Yemi**   Are you blind? She don't want you to come near her.

**Old Lady**   I know what you're trying to do, you can take it.

**Yemi**   What you talking about?

**Old Lady**   Anything, have anything.

**Yemi**   Oh my dayz, see what I'm saying?

**Old Lady**   Please, please, I just wanna go home.

**Yemi**   DAYISI, JUST MOVE AWAY FROM HER!

**Old Lady**   Have it, have it, anything you want.

**Ikudayisi** *moves away from the bag.*

**Yemi**   Stop making noise, man, no one is near you.

**Ikudayisi**   Ma, I'm sorry, I only trying to help.

**Old Lady**   Stay away from me! STAY AWAY!

*She picks up her bag but is too frightened to move.*

**Yemi**   Go, blud!

*The* **Old Lady** *scurries off the stage.*

**Yemi** (*to* **Ikudayisi**)   You're so dumb.

**Ikudayisi**   What are you talking about? You shouldn't talk so harsh to her – she is not your mate.

**Yemi**   What?

*Blackout.*


## Scene Five

*It is late afternoon, around five o'clock.* **Razer**, **Flamer**, **Armani** *and* **Paris** *are hanging around on another part of the estate, drinking and making noise.*

**Armani**   . . . and then he tried to get rude, can you believe it? He put his hand on me, you nah.

**Paris**   To be fair, he only revered you in the head.

**Armani**   So what, he's your man now.

**Paris**   NO!

**Armani**   You meant to have my back.

**Paris**   I'm just saying what happened.

**Armani**   You calling me a liar?

**Paris**   No . . .

**Armani**   So what you saying?

**Paris**   Nothing, forget it.

**Armani**   Nah man, I'm not forgetting it. You been like this all day. Say what you got to say, Paris, say what you got to say.

**Paris**   Nothing.

**Armani**   It better be.

**Paris**   What better be?

**Armani**   I'm just saying, innit. You're meant be my friend. And friends always have each other's backs, no matter what. Know whose side you're on.

**Razer**   Stop talking to her like dat – Paris is your girl, man.

**Flamer**   She's always got your back.

**Armani**   Not today she didn't. Anyway, back to the story . . .

*A big boy with a hood start is slowly walking towards them.*

**Paris**   I wonder who that is.

**Armani**   ERHH UM! Hello!

**Flamer** *and* **Razer** *ignore* **Armani**, *turn round and draw out their knives.*

**Paris**   What is wrong with you? What's that for? Put them away.

**Flamer**   Mans can't be too careful on the ends. We can't let our guards down just cos we are home.

*The figure is still walking towards them suspiciously.*

Mans better identify themselves before they reach any closer, you know.

**Blazer**   What's up, my youth?

*Everyone recognises the voice immediately and lets their guard down, except* **Armani** *who kisses her teeth.*

**Razer** *and* **Flamer** *burst into the song and start dancing. They put their knives away.*

**Razer** *and* **Flamer**    Who you calling my yout, my yout?

**Armani**    I'm not anyone yout but my mother's.

**Blazer**    Shut up.

**Armani** *kisses her teeth and rolls her eyes.* (*To* **Razer** *and* **Flamer**.) You should have seen you mans' faces, you were shook.

**Flamer**    Nah man, we were prepared.

**Flamer** *shows* **Blazer** *his knife.*

**Blazer**    Nice, nice, it's good to see you mans are following rule number one.

**Razer**    Yep! You always got to watch your back –

**Flamer**    – cos your enemies are always closer than you think.

**Blazer**    Ahhh, my youts are learning fast.

*He nudges* **Flamer** *and* **Razer**.

**Armani**    Oh please, you ain't teaching anyone anything worthwhile.

**Blazer**    Every time I see you, you always got something to say. I am the preacher on these ends, so you better listen.

**Paris**    Preacher! You're funny.

**Armani**    He is not funny, Paris!

**Blazer**    Whatever. (*To* **Flamer** *and* **Razer**.) So what's popping, my soldiers?

**Flamer**    Nothing – Armani was just telling us bout her run-in wid Yemi.

**Blazer**   Which Yemi?

**Paris**   The one who lives on Farnborough Way –

**Armani**   Oh yeah, before we got rudely interrupted. As I was saying, *dat babatunde*, yeah –

**Blazer** (*to* **Flamer**)   I thought you said Yemi?

**Flamer**   Yeah –

**Armani**   Excuse me, I'm talking now –

**Blazer**   Hold on. Armani, are you trying to take da piss?

**Armani**   As I was saying –

**Blazer**   What, *all* African are called *babatunde*, yeah?

**Razer**   Blud, she ain't saying dat.

**Blazer**   So, what she tryna say? Cos I swear Flamer said she was talking bout Yemi and now she calling him *babatunde*!

**Flamer**   It's just a figure of speech.

**Blazer**   Nah, it's rude. (*To* **Armani**.) When you're in my presence you got to speak properly. If you talking bout Yemi, call him Yemi. If not –

**Armani**   Oh my God, yeah, why are you longing everything out? I just want to finish my story.

**Blazer**   Nah!

**Armani**   But I'm talking.

**Blazer**   No, I'm talking now. Listen and understand. If you talking bout a specific person say their name.

**Armani**   Cha, man, I'll do whatever I wanna do.

**Blazer** *moves towards* **Armani** *and stands really close to her face.*

**Blazer**   No, you do as I say. You're talking bout Yemi, his name is Yemi.

*Unafraid of his presence,* **Armani** *moves away and continues talking.*

**Armani**   His name can be called Kunta Kinte for all I care. I don't give a shit.

**Blazer**   You need a lesson in history then, cos Kunta Kinte is from Gambia.

**Armani**   I don't care, I don't care. I wasn't even talking to you in the first place. I know all history I need to know, you ain't got to teach me anything new. All I need to know is, I'm from yard!

**Blazer**   I've seen your mum – she's *white*!

**Armani**   So my dad is black.

**Blazer**   And?

**Armani**   And he is Jamaican. So dat makes me Jamaican.

**Blazer**   Have you *even* seen him? Probably don't even know what he looks like.

**Razer**   Lauw it, blud, you don't have to bring her dad into this.

**Blazer** (*to* **Armani**)   I've never even seen you set foot outside this estate, let alone go to another country, so how can you say you're Jamaican? Do you have a passport? Do you even know what a passport looks like?

**Flamer**   Blazer, man, it's not called for.

**Blazer**   Nah, blud, she's too rude and needs to learn her place. If her mum doesn't know how to teach her bout respect, I'll teach her. (*To* **Armani**.) When someone older is talking to you, you keep your mouth shut. Speak only when spoken to. Know your place. Respect your elders.

**Armani**   You're not even related to me.

**Blazer**   SHUT UP! I said speak *only* when you're spoken to.

**Armani**   What are you talking about? You *are* speaking to me.

**Blazer** (*to* **Razer**)   Tell your girl to mind out, you know.

**Armani**   I should mind out, I should mind out. (*To* **Razer**.) You not gonna say nothing? Look how I've been quiet when this boy been shouting at me. When are you going to step in?

**Razer**   He's only playing. (*To* **Blazer**.) Ain't you, Blazer?

**Blazer**   Blud, I'm not! Your girl needs to mind out.

*They sit in awkward silence.*

**Paris** (*to* **Blazer**)   I thought Kunta Kinte was a made-up name.

**Blazer**   Nah, he was real.

**Paris**   How do you know that?

**Blazer**   Cos I read. (*Staring at* **Armani**.) Unlike some people. And does anyone have a problem with dat?

**Razer**   Lauw it, blud, man, this is not a history class.

**Flamer**   Yeah, let's just keep the peace.

**Blazer**   So what, *you two* got a problem with me?

**Razer**   Course not, blud, you know I'm easy. I don't want no trouble, innit. We're one big fam out ere.

**Flamer**   Yeah, man, just take it easy.

**Armani**   He ain't my family.

**Razer**   Armani!

**Armani**   Look, yeah, I don't know why you lot are begging it with him for. (*To* **Blazer**.) You wasn't even invited to this conversation, *Blazer*!

**Blazer** *stares at* **Armani** *and* **Razer** *jumps in.*

**Razer**    Armani, man, please.

**Armani**    Why can't I talk? No, I'll speak when I want to.

**Razer**    Just lauw it, man. Sometimes you really need to know when to keep your mouth shut.

**Armani**    What, like you?

**Razer**    We were having a good time before.

**Armani**    And am I the one who was spoiling it?

**Razer**    Ahhhh, man.

**Armani**    I don't know what you making noise for. I swear you people forgot this is a free country. And in a free country people can talk freely. We are not in no third world. I can do what I want. I ain't afraid of no one.

**Razer**    ARMANI!

**Flamer** *and* **Paris** *start laughing at* **Armani** *and* **Razer** *arguing.* **Blazer** *gets up to leave.*

**Flamer**    You gone already?

**Blazer**    Yeah, man, this is too childish for me. And before I do something I might regret –

*He looks long and hard at* **Armani**.

– it's best I'm off. When you mans are done here meet me up at frontline. There is something I need you two to work on.

**Flamer**    Yeah, fam.

**Blazer**    One.

*He nudges the boys.*

See you later.

**Paris**    Yeah, see you later.

**Blazer** *exits.*

**Armani** *looks at* **Paris** *and gives her a dirty look.*

**Armani**   I hate him, you nah.

**Razer**   He can ruin the mood sometimes.

**Flamer**   So can your girl, you know.

**Flamer**, **Razer** *and* **Paris** *start laughing*.

**Paris**   I like Blazer, I think he is cool.

**Armani**   Yeah, you would.

**Flamer**   Nah, she right, most times he is alright. But he likes to talk a lot. We all know it shit, but it don't matter. When he talks just let him talk, innit.

**Armani**   Why? He not my dad. I'm not gonna shut *my* mouth cos he's around. He don't control me. No one does.

**Flamer**   But you ain't got to stir things up.

**Armani**   Stop sitting on the fence and defending him. You don't have to worry, your *boss* is gone, he can't hear me. You can now tell the truth bout what you really feel, speak your mind. You won't get arrest for it, you know. This is a *free* country.

**Flamer**   That's your problem, Armani, you don't listen. Didn't you hear me? I'm agreeing with you, and he ain't my boss.

**Armani**   You could have fooled me. When he comes around you lot start shaking.

**Razer**   Not me.

*He nudges* **Flamer**.

**Armani**   Whatever! He rules you too. Cos you chat different bout him when it just me and you. Den when he is in your face you're nuff quiet like a likkle biatch! I'm surprise you ain't following him around on a leash.

**Razer**   It's not like dat man – shut up.

**Paris**  I think he chats nuff sense. He is cool with me. He got a nice way about him, I love the way he proud bout where he from.

**Armani**  What, like being so fucking proud to be African but then calling himself Blazer? I bet you don't even know what his real name is.

**Razer** *laughs.*

**Razer**  She's right you nah. I can't remember his real name. Do you, Flamer?

**Flamer**  Yeah, course I know.

**Armani**  What is it?

**Flamer**  It's one long ass-funky name like Oluade . . . Oluwaye . . . ahhh, I can't remember it.

**Paris**  Why does dat matter doe? He may not like people *knowing* his real name. Most people never know how to pronounce African names properly anyway. It probably frustrates him. Anyways, Blazer is only his street name. (*To* **Razer** *and* **Flamer**.) Not dat many people know yous lot names either, do dey?

**Armani**  You're so stupid – that's not the reason.

**Paris**  What the reason, then?

**Armani**  *He is ashamed!*

**Paris**  He's not, he always talking bout Africa. How can he be ashamed?

**Armani**  *So* why doesn't *he* hang around his people den? Everyone *I* see him with is West Indian.

**Paris**  Dat don't mean nothing.

**Armani**  Look, Paris, yeah, you're always sticking up for dem people. I told you once already today – know your sides! You forget back in da days they sold us off as slaves, you nah.

**Flamer**   I ain't no slave. My nan told me she was invited to this country, you get me?

**Razer**   Yeah, same here, fam.

**Flamer** *and* **Razer**   WINDRUSH!

*They nudge each other.*

**Armani**   You two are so dumb. We are all slaves, all of us from the West Indies. Dat why I don't like African, cos they sold us off to da white man, and den stayed in Africa living as kings and queens, while all my ancestors had to work hard.

**Razer**, **Flamer** *and* **Paris**   WHAT?!

**Armani**   Nah, blud, I'm not happy with dat and I'm not having it either. You can go around loving off your African people but I stick with my own.

**Paris**   You have it so messed up. Everything you're saying don't make no sense. It doesn't even go like dat and furthermore you're half white . . . so . . . do you hate white people as well?

**Armani**   No, eh, my mum's white, *hello*!

**Paris**   You're not making any sense, Armani. You can't just be one-sided. How can you hate African people but not the white people who were also involved in slavery?

**Armani**   Cos slavery started in Africa.

**Paris**   But white people *went* to Africa and took them from their land.

**Armani**   So, what, *you* love African but hate white people now?

**Paris**   I didn't say dat.

**Armani**   Well *that's* what I'm hearing.

**Paris**   No, that's what you want to hear. You're not getting my point.

**Armani**    Yeah I am, yeah I am, it's all coming out now.

**Paris**    You're still not understanding me –

**Armani**    I'm getting exactly what you're tryna say.

**Paris**    You're not.

**Armani**    Yes, I am. It's all coming to light now. Now I understand the way that you been acting towards me. I'm so stupid, I should have seen it before.

**Paris**    What are you talking bout?

**Armani**    You're a *racist*, Paris.

**Paris**    What?

**Razer**    No she's not, man.

**Flamer**    She is far from racist – Paris is the nicest person we know.

**Armani**    Yes she is, YES SHE IS – she said it with her own mouth.

**Paris**    Said what? I never said anything.

**Armani**    Oh my God, you're a liar too.

**Paris** (*to* **Razer** *and* **Flamer**)    You two woz here. Did I say I hate white people?

**Flamer** *and* **Razer**    No.

**Armani**    I don't care, you can't backtrack now, I know you're a racist.

**Paris**    But if I'm racist you're racist too, then.

**Armani**    No, far from it.

**Paris**    Yes, you are. Hating African is *just as* racist as hating white people. So if you're calling me a racist, you're racist too.

**Armani**    That's not even the same.

**Paris**   Why – is it one rule for you and another for me? You can't have it your way *all the time*, Armani.

**Armani**   At least I know why you don't like me now.

**Razer**   How can she not like you? You been friends for years.

**Armani**   That's just a cover-up.

**Paris**   You really don't know what you are talking bout.

**Armani**   Yeah, I do. Things like this happen all the time. That's why I hate being friends with girls.

**Paris**   But I've never had a problem with you before *or* now.

**Armani**   I know where this hatred comes from anyway. It's jealousy.

**Paris**   What are you talking bout *now*?

**Armani**   Dark-skinned girls always have problems with light-skinned girls.

**Flamer**   Ahhh, come on.

**Armani**   It's the truth. All dark-skinned girls are like dat, they are forever hating –

**Flamer**   Paris is not like dat – why would she hate, she pretty herself –

**Armani**   They forget us light-skinned girl are not to blame, you nah. We don't get to pick our parents.

**Paris**   First I'm a racist and now I am hater. Make up your mind, Armani.

**Armani**   Ask Razer – he knows what I'm talking bout.

**Razer**   What?

**Paris**   What's she talking bout, Razer?

**Razer**   Don't get me involved in dis.

**Paris**  What, Razer, you think I hate light-skinned girls?

**Razer**  I've never said dat.

**Armani**  Don't lie now.

**Razer**  I'm not, don't get me involved in yout madness.

**Paris**  Well, everything you say is wrong. I haven't got any problems and never had one either.

**Armani**  You're such a liar. At least everyone here gets to know it now.

**Paris**  Stop talking rubbish, Armani.

**Armani**  I'm not, it's the truth!

**Paris**  It's not me that tryna be something dat I'm not.

**Armani**  What you saying?

**Paris**  Exactly what I just said!

**Flamer**  Take it easy, girls.

**Paris**  Nah! I'm fed up of being quiet. If you want me to get everything out in the open, *I'll* be real with you.

**Flamer**  Paris, lauw it, it's not worth it.

**Razer**  Girls, man, you're meant to be friends.

**Paris**  No, I'm fed up of this. It's my time to speak now.

**Armani**  Speak then – ain't no one holding you back.

**Paris**  I think it's *you* with the big problem.

**Razer**  Keep the peace, man, keep the peace.

**Paris**  But it not your fault cos *all* mixed-raced girls are confused.

**Flamer**  Paris!

**Paris**  I said girls.

**Armani**  Nah, later. Not me.

**Paris**    Especially you! You don't know what to identify yourself with. Should you be on the white side, should you be on the black side – *you don't know.* You try and act like you're blacker dan anybody else, but then you contradict yourself cos you go on like it's a bad thing for me to look black, or anyone else at that. I've always been cool with myself and even cooler wid you. When other *light-skinned* girls have chatted shit bout you, I've been the one to defend your ass. But I'm the hater – cos I'm dark-skinned! You just don't get it. You are *so* confused!

**Flamer**    Ooohhh, see what you started, Armani. I bet you thought Paris never had no mouth.

**Armani**    Oh my God, you're so funny – is that what you think?

**Paris**    No, it what I know. You forget sometimes how long I've known you and what you *used* to be like. How would you know about the black-hair shops if I didn't take you there? Cos your *mum* never knew what to do with your hair. You were walking around with a picky Afro *until the day I met you*! I've still got pictures in my house! I'm the one who still braids your hair! And who taught you about the dance moves that they did in Jamaica, cos Blazer's right – you ain't never been there, or anywhere else apart from *here*. And furthermore, I been to your yard and the *only* food your mum showed you how to cook was beans on toast! Remember – I introduced you to rice and peas. So don't get it twisted!

**Flamer**    You got told!

**Armani**    WHAT? SHUT UP! She is such a liar. She never taught me nothink. Come say that to my face. COME SAY THAT TO MY FACE.

**Armani** *tries to go for* **Paris** *but* **Razer** *and* **Flamer** *hold her back.* **Paris** *stands her ground.*

**Paris**   If it's a lie why you acting all mad for? It shouldn't be bothering you. You should just be cool. You're the big bad Armani. You're always right – right?

**Armani**   How can you try and say you taught me bout hair? Look at my hair and look at yours. (*To* **Razer**.) Look, Razer, look.

**Paris**   *So*, as I said, it's my influence.

**Razer** *and* **Flamer** *start laughing.*

**Armani**   What, come say that to my face.

**Paris**   I am. The truth hurts, doesn't it?

*Blackout.*


## Scene Six

**Yemi** *is on another side of the estate,* **Ikudayisi** *is offstage, trying to catch up with him and calling his name.* **Yemi** *does not respond and goes and sits down on a wall, playing with his phone.*

**Ikudayisi** (*off*)   Yemi, Yemi, Yemi!

*He comes onstage and is shocked to see* **Yemi** *sitting down. He walks over to him.*

**Ikudayisi**   So is this where you have been all this time?

**Yemi** *ignores him.*

**Ikudayisi**   So, did you not hear me calling your name?

**Yemi** *still ignores him.*

**Ikudayisi**   Yemi! Can you not hear me asking you questions?

**Yemi**   JUST LEAVE ME ALONE.

**Ikudayisi**   No – what is your problem?

**Yemi**   AHHH, MAN!

**Ikudayisi**    Are you having some kind of breakdown?

**Yemi**    JUST LEAVE ME ALONE, leave me alone.

**Ikudayisi**    No, we need to talk about what happened before. You shouldn't have talked to that old lady like dat.

**Yemi**    What, are you dizzy?

**Ikudayisi**    She is as old as our grandmother and you were rude.

**Yemi**    She was *scared* of you! Why can't you just go away?

**Ikudayisi**    No, I'm your brother, I'm here to stay.

**Yemi**    Why did you have to come? Why couldn't you just stay in Nigeria. Ever since you come . . . I liked it how it was!

**Ikudayisi**    Why are you being like this?

**Yemi**    Why can't you just go away?

**Ikudayisi**    No, I'm here to stay. I couldn't wait to come, just to see you. To see my younger brother and this is de way you are treating me. If this was Nigeria –

**Yemi**    This is not Nigeria. Why do you think you could just come over here and take over?

**Ikudayisi**    I'M NOT TRYING TO TAKE OVER. I just want to be a part of your life.

**Yemi**    You come here and act the way you do, and think . . . and think . . . everyone should just accept that. All these stupid things you keep on doing like speaking in that language and trying to be friendly to everyone does not work here. People don't want you to be nice to them. YOU NEED TO UNDERSTAND THIS IS NOT NIGERIA, things are different here.

**Ikudayisi**    What do you mean?

**Yemi**    You can't do what you do there, *here*.

**Ikudayisi**    I can't be friendly?

**Yemi**   NO, you can't! This country is not like dat. People will look at you like you are crazy. You just need to mind your own business. Don't watch no one else.

**Ikudayisi**   That's nonsense. You are lost.

**Yemi**   NO, you're lost. You think being the way you are is cool. It's not! You're a joke. People in this country laugh at people like you – they find your look and your accent funny. They think you're a joke. But you can't *even* see dat.

**Ikudayisi**   That's nonsense. Since I have been here people have been nice to me – it's you that has been having problems.

**Yemi**   Are you stupid? You almost gave an old lady a heart attack. She thought you were robbing her.

**Ikudayisi**   What?

**Yemi**   If you stopped living in la-la land for once, you would see that. Stop being stupid and look around you.

**Ikudayisi**   You this silly boy. See what? What is there to see? You are not thinking straight. Your mind-set needs to change.

**Yemi**   You're the one who needs to change, not me! Stop all the 'we are the world' shit you keep on doing, and understand that in order to get along on this estate, in this country, you need to stop being you, Dayisi!

**Ikudayisi**   I can't change – being a Nigerian is what I am.

**Yemi**   I can't help you then, cos you're never gonna fit in.

**Ikudayisi**   That's a lie. I fit it well, I get on with everyone.

**Yemi**   Look! Take some good advice: you're not going to get far how you are right now – trust me, I know this.

**Ikudayisi**   You are strange-oh, you talk too much rubbish.

**Yemi**   No, I'm chatting sense and it best you listen to me, cos –

**Ikudayisi**   No, you listen to me. You are trying to educate someone who is already educated. I know who I am and what I stand for. I will not change for anyone. Ahhh, you disappoint me-oh, I didn't know your problem run so deep.

**Yemi**   You're buzzing. I ain't got time for this.

*He turns to walk away.*

**Ikudayisi**   Dat's your problem – you don't want to face up to nothing. You talk so much nonsense, but the minute someone else has something to say, you want to go.

**Yemi**   Shut up, man. What would you know? You don't even know me, man. What! WHAT! You been here two months and you think you can tell me bout me. I don't expect you to understand coming from a backward country.

**Ikudayisi**   Take that back! Nigeria is not backward.

**Yemi**   Uhhh, yes it is. Don't get it twisted, blud, just cos I ain't been there don't mean I ain't heard the stories. Duh! Mum's always talking bout you lot not always having electricity. How can you tell me dat not backward?

**Ikudayisi**   You don't understand . . . It's only when Nepa [*Nigerian Electricity Board*] takes the light. We have generators.

**Yemi**   But the lights are not on 24/7, are they? I bet you ain't even got traffic lights – how can you, with no electricity? Is there even cars in Africa? Do you even have houses?

**Ikudayisi**   You dis one who has never set foot in Nigeria and is now talking like you discovered it. You are de one that is backward and confused, talking bad about your mother homeland like that. Be careful God does not strike you now.

**Yemi**   Shut up. I don't even know why you getting offended for. You don't live there any more, you couldn't wait to come here. So everything you're saying is rubbish. Work on changing yourself and leave me out of it.

**Ikudayisi**    No, I'm proud of who I am.

*He sings.*

> Green white green on my chest,
> I'm proud to be a Nigerian!
> Green white green on my chest,
> I'm proud to be a Nigerian!

**Yemi**    Oh my dayz!

**Ikudayisi**
> Green white green on my chest,
> I'm proud to be a Nigerian!

**Yemi**    Do you not see how stupid you look?

**Ikudayisi**
> Green white green on my chest,
> I'm proud to be a Nigerian!

*He falls to his knees with his hands in the air.*

> Proud to be a Nigerian,
> Proud to be a Nigerian,
> Proud – to – be – a – Ni-ge-ri-an,
> Proud – to – be – a – Ni-ge-ri-an!

**Yemi**    But then you put on a fake American accent when you talking to other people.

**Ikudayisi** *stops singing.*

**Ikudayisi**    That is just my accent, it is always changing.

**Yemi**    No. (*He mimics **Ikudayisi**'s accent.*) This is your accent. (*He mimics **Ikudayisi**'s fake American accent.*) And this is you when you're trying to be American. They are two different accents.

**Ikudayisi**    I'm still proud to be Nigerian.

**Yemi**    You're telling me I'm lost, but what bout you? You can stand here all day going on bout how proud you are, but the truth is in your action, not just your word.

**Ikudayisi**   Jo, leave me.

**Yemi**   Ohh, did I hit a raw nerve? Don't worry – as I said, your accent a joke, everyone understands why you want to get rid. It's no big ting. No one ain't gonna hate you if you change – I've already told you, I think you need to!

**Ikudayisi**   You are so young, you don't understand anything at all. I was once like you. As I keep on saying, I just wish you went to Nigeria. The way you are talking you will see –

**Yemi**   I don't *wanna* go there.

**Ikudayisi**   That's your problem, and why I personally feel sorry for you. You are telling me I need to change, but I'm not the one with the problem, it's you. You are a lost puppy. One minute you feel you don't fit in here because people are racist but then you don't want to be a Nigerian. Then you want to be left alone, but you complain you have no friend. Do you know who you are, Yemi?

**Yemi**   Yes, I'm a free person.

**Ikudayisi**   Nobody is free-oh.

**Yemi**   You might not be, but I am.

**Ikudayisi**   How can you be free when you deny your own heritage? You don't like your name, you are ashamed of your language. If you are *so* free you won't care what people think about Nigerian and you will just be what you are.

**Yemi**   Do you think I care what people think? It's not other people that make me hate Nigeria, it's Nigeria that makes me hate it.

**Ikudayisi**   *But you have never been there.* How can you judge? Nigeria is a nice place.

**Yemi**   Forget it, man. You're not going to make me change my mind overnight. Let's go.

**Ikudayisi**   No, ah ah.

**Yemi**  I don't give a shit bout Nigeria. Why can't you just leave it?

**Ikudayisi**  YOU NEED TO LEARN TO RESPECT IT! What are you going to teach your children?

**Yemi**  THAT THEY ARE FREE LIKE ME.

**Ikudayisi**  And when they want to know about their family?

**Yemi**  This is long, man, lauw da chat.

**Ikudayisi**  No. Will you even give your kids Yoruba names?

**Yemi**  I don't care.

**Ikudayisi**  WELL, YOU SHOULD!

**Yemi**  Why? Why should I? I'm not you, I'm my own person. Stop trying to force your views on me. I'm sick of this. I just wanna be me. Don't wanna be no one else. Let me be me. Why do you care what I think?

**Ikudayisi**  You *really* don't understand. Despite all its problem, Nigeria is a great place. YOU HAVE TO BE PROUD OF WHERE YOU ARE FROM.

**Yemi**  If it's so great, why do you *all* wanna come here?

**Ikudayisi** *remains silent.*

**Yemi**  *Exactly!* No matter how bad this country is, I bet it better than there!

**Ikudayisi**  *Ironi yen.* [A lie.]

**Yemi** *cuts his eye at* **Ikudayisi** *and kisses his teeth.*

**Ikudayisi**  I don't understand you at all. If people saw us now they would not even know we are from the same mother. We are brothers, and you act like we are from different countries, different worlds.

**Yemi**  We are.

*Blackout.*

## Scene Seven

*It is early evening, and* **Yemi** *and* **Ikudayisi** *are still out on the estate. They have finally got the milk and are heading home. They have been to a chicken-and-chips shop, too, and are eating on the way.*

**Yemi** *spots* **Blazer** *and pushes* **Ikudayisi** *behind him so it looks like they are not walking together. He quickens his pace and tries to act cool.*

**Blazer**    What's up, blud?

**Yemi**    I'm cool, man.

**Ikudayisi** (*in dodgy American accent*)    Yeah, what's poppin?

**Yemi**    AHHH, MAN!

*He gives* **Ikudayisi** *a dirty look.* **Blazer** *laughs.*

**Blazer**    Who is dis?

**Yemi**    Erm . . .

**Ikudayisi** (*dodgy American accent*)    His older brother.

**Blazer**    I never knew you had a brother.

**Yemi**    I wish I never.

**Blazer**    What?

**Yemi**    Long story – he just come from Nigeria.

**Blazer** (*to* **Ikudayisi**)    *Ba wo ni.* [Hi.]

**Yemi**    What?

**Ikudayisi** (*goes to nudge* **Blazer**)    Fellow Nigerian, how now?

**Yemi**    You're Nigerian? I thought –

**Blazer**    Course I'm Nigerian – one hundred per cent. (*To* **Ikudayisi**.) *Se en gbadun ilu oyinbo?* [Are you enjoying England?]

**Ikudayisi**    *Ko bad now.* [Not bad.]

**Yemi**    What you two saying?

**Blazer**    Don't you understand Yoruba?

**Yemi**    No.

**Ikudayisi**    *Ko gbo nkan nkan.* [He doesn't understand anything.]

**Blazer** (*to* **Ikudayisi**)    Why ain't you teaching him?

**Ikudayisi**    I've tried-oh.

**Yemi**    Tried what?

**Ikudayisi**    To teach you Yoruba. (*To* **Blazer**.) But he said he don't give a shit about Nigeria, he telling me I need to change, forget about my heritage, be *free* like him.

**Blazer** (*to* **Yemi**)    Did you say dat?

**Yemi**    Nah, I never.

**Ikudayisi**    *Iro ti fo ori e.* [Lies are filled in his head.]

**Blazer** *laughs.*

**Yemi**    What did he say?

**Blazer**    Dat's why you need to learn to speak Yoruba, you nah.

**Yemi**    Uhhh.

**Blazer**    So dat you know what people are saying bout you.

**Yemi**    True dat, true dat. I never thought of it like dat.

**Ikudayisi**    What! True what? (*To* **Blazer**.) Before he was saying dat he don't want to have anything to do with Nigeria. He was talking nonsense, saying dat he is free, dat we are from different worlds.

**Yemi**    So? He tries to act like he is American.

**Blazer**    You *both* got something to learn.

**Ikudayisi**   I'm one hundred per cent proud of being Nigerian.

**Yemi**   Ehh, you think you're American.

**Blazer** (*to* **Ikudayisi**)   Blud, what is that all about?

**Ikudayisi**   When I put on the accent I'm only playing. I know who I am and where I'm from.

**Blazer**   Good, cos that LA Lagos shit pisses me off.

**Yemi**   Me too.

**Ikudayisi**   Me too what? You still don't know yourself.

**Yemi**   Shut up, man, you're chatting shit.

**Blazer**   Don't talk to your brother like dat, man. I swear he said he is older than you.

**Yemi**   So?

**Blazer**   So you need to learn to respect him, you nah. You can't go around talking to him like that. That's what makes us different.

**Yemi**   What does?

**Blazer**   Respect.

**Yemi**   From who?

**Blazer**   Da West Indians.

**Yemi**   See, that what I was trying to tell Dayisi bout us being different –

**Ikudayisi**   You were not talking about respect, you were talking rubbish.

**Yemi**   No I wasn't, I was saying –

**Blazer**   You two should know this already. Respect is something you shouldn't play wid. My mum taught me that years ago.

*He begins to sing.*

Money, power, respect is what you need in life.

**Yemi** *joins in.*

**Yemi**
Money, power, respect is the key to life.
You see in life, it's your given right.

**Blazer**   See, you know the song.

**Yemi**   Course, blud!

**Blazer**   Every word is the truth, mate.

*Pause.*

You see me, yeah, on the street I get bare respect, but don't get it twisted, it never came easy. I had to earn that shit. From when I learnt at home to show my family respect I came out on the road and showed mans respect. It like a chain reaction. You give respect to get respect, you get me?

**Yemi**   Yeah, man, I understand.

**Ikudayisi**   Hey-oh. God is listening to my prayers. (*To* **Yemi**.) You need more friends like this-oh.

**Yemi**   Shut –

**Blazer**   Yemi! I thought you understood. Come on, man, you couldn't have just forgotten what I *just* said.

**Yemi**   Sorry.

**Blazer**   It's important for you to respect him, man. He your older brother.

**Yemi**   I'm gonna try.

**Blazer**   It's not bout trying, you got to. He gonna show you tings no one can teach you.

**Yemi**   Nah, blud, *I'm* da one that teaching him tings.

**Ikudayisi**   It's a lie.

**Blazer**    If you were in Nigeria you would be calling him uncle, you nah.

**Yemi**    What?

**Ikudayisi**    It's true-oh.

**Yemi**    I'm not sure bout dat one – he is not my uncle, he is my brother.

**Ikudayisi**    You should even be bowing down to me.

**Yemi**    Please!

**Blazer**    He right. Even *now* I don't call my sister by her name and she is only two years older than me. I call her auntie.

**Yemi**    Even in the street?

**Blazer**    The streets, at home, everywhere. *Blud*, I don't play when it comes to being respectful, you nah.

**Yemi**    Don't you care what people think?

**Blazer**    Fuck what people think. You think I care? What da fuck can they try say to me? I'll have up any mans if they try to disrespect my tradition.

*Pause.*

You see me, yeah. I ain't ashamed of nothing.

*Pause.*

When I was younger, people used to take the piss out of me cos I had an accent. And it used to get me *mad*, but I never used to say nothing. But then one day I had enough and every man who tried to take the piss – got knocked out. Straight!

**Yemi**    I remember hearing your fight stories, but I never knew the reasons behind it. You kept it real, blud.

**Blazer**    So what, you think now people will try take the piss with me now?

**Yemi**   No.

**Blazer**   Exactly. It's not going to happen. They can say what they want behind my back, but to my face, mans have to be careful what they say. And that's the way I like it. Gone are da days when mans take the piss out of this African! Cos I run this estate now. And you know, I know they don't like it. But what can they do? The roles have reversed now.

**Yemi**   Rahh, I like it! I like it.

**Blazer**   I'm not saying to you, go around testing people. You just need to learn how to stand your ground, but keep it real at the same time. It's not a bad thing to be African. Be proud to be different.

**Yemi**   I will man . . . I mean, I am.

**Blazer**   Make sure you start to learn Yoruba from your brother.

**Yemi**   Yeah, course.

**Blazer** (*to* **Ikudayisi**)   Make sure you teach him.

**Ikudayisi**   *Mo gbo.* [I understand.]

**Blazer** (*to* **Yemi**)   Even if you want, blud, come round to mines, I will teach you. It's easy once you get started. (*To* **Ikudayisi**.) And make sure you don't put on that fake accent again.

**Ikudayisi** (*in dodgy American accent*)   No problem.

**Blazer**   Oi.

**Ikudayisi**   I told you, it was joke I'm playing, I'm playing –

**Blazer** (*to* **Yemi**)   What's your full name?

**Yemi**   Oluyemi Adewale.

**Blazer**   Do you know what it means?

**Yemi**   Nah.

**Ikudayisi**    I know.

**Yemi**    Tell me.

**Blazer**    Don't tell him. Let him find it out himself – it would be a good lesson for him. That's your first assignment.

**Yemi**    Why? What does it mean?

**Blazer**    It's your mission. You need to investigate it yourself.

**Yemi**    OK.

*Pause.*

**Blazer**    So what's this I'm hearing bout some mad run-in with Armani?

**Yemi**    How do you know? . . . I never done nothing to her – is that why you come to chat to me?

**Blazer**    No, calm down, Yemi man, it's a question.

**Yemi**    Oh, she is just a fool who talks too much.

**Blazer**    You don't got to say that twice.

**Yemi**    So how did you know about my run-in with her?

**Blazer**    I heard her telling Razer.

**Yemi**    So, what, he's proper looking for me now? Man ready for war, you nah?

**Blazer**    Nah, blud, calm down. They weren't even paying attention to her anyways.

**Yemi**    *Dey*?

**Blazer**    You know, Razer and Flamer are always together.

**Yemi**    So dey must be looking for me den.

**Blazer**    Nah, man, don't worry.

**Yemi**    I'm not. I telling you, I'm ready for dem mans if they wanna start something.

**Blazer**    Calm down. So for the last ten minutes you ain't heard a word I said.

**Yemi**    I did – you said to stand your ground.

**Blazer**    When needed!

*Pause.*

Dem youth are my soldier, man. They can't make any movement without my say so. I don't want you to get into no madness. I will talk to dem if you want.

**Yemi**    If mans come, I just know to be prepared, innit.

**Blazer**    Stop talking like dat, man. You got to pick your battles wise, you know. Look, I'm having a word with dem. You're too young to be getting into madness.

**Yemi**    Nah, it cool.

**Blazer**    Seriously, I don't mind to chat to dem. Us Nigerians need to stick together. (*To* **Ikudayisi**.) Innit.

**Ikudayisi**    Of course now.

**Yemi**    It cool.

**Blazer**    OK. But don't do nothing stupid. One.

*He nudges* **Yemi** *and* **Ikudayisi** *and exits.*

**Ikudayisi**    I like him-oh.

**Yemi** *stares after* **Blazer**.

**Ikudayisi**    I said dat I think he is a cool guy.

**Yemi** *still ignores him.*

**Ikudayisi**    YEMI, are you listening?

**Yemi**    WHAT?

**Ikudayisi**    Your friend, he is a cool guy.

**Yemi**    Yeah, he is alright.

**Ikudayisi**    What wrong now?

**Yemi**    Nothing. I can't believe he is Nigerian. I can see it now but I never saw it before.

*Pause.*

Do you know, that the first time he has ever proper stopped and chat to me? Usually it's just hi and bye.

**Ikudayisi**    And so?

**Yemi**    Don't you think it's strange with all that been happening today?

**Ikudayisi**    Stop over-analysing everything. Did you not hear a word he was saying?

**Yemi** *is still looking into the distance.*

**Ikudayisi**    Yemi, you are reading too much into it.

**Yemi** *is still silent.*

**Ikudayisi**    Snap out of it.

**Ikudayisi** *clicks his fingers in front of* **Yemi***'s face.*

**Yemi**    What does my name mean?

**Ikudayisi**    Now you want to learn.

**Yemi**    Stop being silly, just tell me.

**Ikudayisi**    Give me a hundred pound, and I'll tell you.

**Yemi**    Yeah, right! Just tell me, man.

**Ikudayisi**    OK, fifty pounds.

**Yemi**    This is why you get on my nerves.

**Ikudayisi**    OK, OK . . . it means 'God suit you'.

**Yemi**    'God suits me'! That's crap, man.

**Ikudayisi**    No, I mean, it hard to change it from Yoruba to English. It is better in Yoruba. Oluyemi is a big name.

**Yemi**   Whatever. Why did he go on like it was important for me to find out? What was he talking bout I need to know what it mean? That don't mean shit.

**Ikudayisi**   Nigerians believes names hold power.

**Yemi**   Why?

**Ikudayisi**   Cos they think that people will live up to it, they have special meaning.

**Yemi**   What does your name mean?

**Ikudayisi**   'Death spared me'.

**Yemi**   WHAT?! I should have got that name.

**Ikudayisi**   I came first.

**Yemi**   But that type of name don't suit you. You ain't no warrior. It suits a fighter like me!

**Ikudayisi**   Dat not what it means.

**Yemi**   What does it mean then, if it's not a warrior name?

**Ikudayisi**   It means that when Mum was having me she may have had some complications – you know, cos she had me young, and death spared me. I survived!

**Yemi**   *I don't care*, I should have had that name.

**Ikudayisi**   Look at you – now you want a Nigerian name. Anyway, I'm happy-oh.
   Green white green on my chest,
   You're proud to be a Nigerian.

**Ikudayisi** *starts to sing his song and notices* **Yemi** *bounces his head.*

**Ikudayisi**   Eh, eh, so now you are proud.

**Yemi** *pushes* **Ikudayisi**.

**Yemi**   Move. Shut up, man!

*They begin to play-fight and* **Yemi** *gets* **Ikudayisi** *in a head lock.*

**Yemi**   You may be older than me, but I'm stronger. See, that why I should have had your name.

**Ikudayisi**   Let go of me.

**Yemi**   Who's your daddy?

**Ikudayisi**   Olakunle Adewale.

**Yemi**   No, you fool, say I'm your dad.

**Ikudayisi**   No.

**Yemi**   Say it and I'll let go.

**Ikudayisi**   No.

**Yemi**   Who's your dad?

**Ikudayisi**   You are squeezing my neck. I can't breathe.

**Yemi**   Say I'm your dad and I'll let go.

**Ikudayisi**   I can't breathe!

*Two* **Police Officers** *come onto the estate.*

**Police Officer 1**   Oi, can I have word with you?

**Yemi** *lets go of* **Ikudayisi** *as* **Police Officer 1** *walks up to him.* **Ikudayisi** *begins rubbing his neck.*

**Ikudayisi** (*to* **Yemi**)   You play too ruff, you dey hurt my neck-oh.

**Police Officer 2** (*to* **Ikudayisi**)   You OK, son?

**Yemi**   Course he alright.

**Police Officer 2**   You will get your chance to speak in a minute, mate.

**Yemi**   We were just playing.

**Police Officer 2**   That's what they all say.

**Yemi**   What's that suppose to mean?

**Police Officer 1**   Watch your mouth, lad!

**Yemi**   What?

**Ikudayisi**   It's true, we were just playing.

**Police Officer 2** *moves* **Ikudayisi** *away from* **Yemi**.

**Police Officer 2** (*to* **Ikudayisi**)   Don't worry. We're here now, you ain't got to be scared anymore. Are you OK?

**Ikudayisi**   I'm OK . . .

**Yemi**   I told you we were just playing.

**Police Officer 2**   And I said *that's* what they all say.

**Yemi**   Are you buzzing, blud? What's your beef?

**Police Officer 2**   Who do you think you're talking to? I ain't your pal or your mate. Does it look like we are from the same blood? Show some respect and talk properly.

**Yemi** *heads to confront* **Police Officer 2** *but* **Police Officer 1** *gets in the way and they both crowd over him.*

**Yemi**   Man is speaking English.

**Police Officer 2**   You're not a man, you're still a boy.

**Police Officer 1** (*to* **Yemi**)   So where you heading off to now?

**Yemi** *remains silent.*

**Police Officer 1**   You deaf, *boy*? I'm asking you a question.

**Yemi** *still remains silent.*

**Police Officer 1** (*holds* **Yemi**'s *face*) I said, *where* are you going?

**Yemi**   NOWHERE. I ain't got to speak to you if I don't want to.

**Police Officer 1**   Do you wanna be answering these questions at a police station? If not, start talking.

**Yemi**   Is there something you're looking for?

**Police Officer 2**   Is there something *you're* tryna hide?

**Yemi**   You got time on your hands. I know my right. Why don't you go and fight real crime.

**Police Officer 1**   Black-on-black violence *is* a crime.

**Police Officer 2** *laughs.*

**Ikudayisi**   Please, what's the problem, sir?

**Police Officer 1**   We're just trying to find out what the problem is here, son.

**Yemi**   There is no problem – we were playing. Mans like you is just tryna harass us.

**Police Officer 2** (*to* **Police Officer 1**)   You understand what he saying?

**Police Officer 1**   Kids find it so hard to speak English nowadays.

**Police Officer 2**   All that seems to come out their mouths is bumba clat this, bumba clat that, and innit man, yeah man.

**Police Officer 1**   Such a disgrace. Schools really ain't teaching them anything.

**Police Officer 2**   I think I should start up my own school.

**Police Officer 1**   Oh yeah, what would you call it?

**Yemi**   You two are nuts. Let's go, Dayisi.

**Yemi** *begins to walk around them and* **Police Officer 2** *grabs his hand.*

**Yemi**   Let go of my hand.

**Police Officer 1**   We have not finished here.

**Yemi**   Man, best let go.

**Police Officer 1**   *Oohh,* is that a threat?

**Police Officer 2**    Sounds like one to me. You getting ready to assault a police officer?

**Yemi**    You don't know me – when I make a threat, *you will know*!

**Police Officer 2**    Oohh, I think the Yardie is getting mad.

**Police Officer 1** (*in a dodgy Jamaican accent*)    Bumba clat, we may need some backup, man, up in de place.

**Police Officer 2**    And request for the drug squad.

**Police Officer 1** (*in a dodgy Jamaican accent*)    SO man may start shooting up de place, he na care, him gangsta.

*The two* **Police Officers** *begin to laugh at their own jokes while* **Yemi** *still struggles.*

**Yemi**    Shows how much you know. I'm not even Jamaican. I'm Nigerian.

**Police Officer 1**    Stop being silly, you're not from Africa, he is.

**Ikudayisi**    We're both Nigerian.

**Police Officer 2**    He don't act African. He lied to you, son, he is a Jamaican.

**Yemi**    Yeah, I am Nigerian.

**Police Officer 2**    Let me see your passport.

**Police Officer 1**    You mean his photocopy?

**Yemi** (*to* **Ikudayisi**)    You hearing this now. I told you they treat you different when you are black.

**Ikudayisi**    Yemi, shh.

**Yemi**    What? Why should I be quiet, you blind?

**Ikudayisi**    Please, sir, we are just coming from de shop.

**Police Officer 1**    Don't worry, we know how to deal with him. We handle situations like this on a daily basis.

**Yemi** *still struggles with* **Police Officer 2** *but his grip on him gets tighter.*

**Yemi**   Stop tryna take the fucking piss.

**Police Officer 2**   Watch your language, son.

**Yemi**   I ain't your son.

**Police Officer 2**   Glad you ain't. If I had a child I'd teach him to have a lot more respect than you.

**Yemi**   Look – what do you want?

**Police Officer 1**   For you to show some manners and respect.

**Yemi**   But I'm not even doing nothing.

**Police Officer 2**   You're causing a scene.

**Yemi**   You're the one's who is *harassing* me. Touching me for no reason. You know you ain't got nothing on us. (*He gets free. To* **Ikudayisi**.) Let's go!

**Police Officer 2**   He is not going anywhere with you.

**Yemi** *attempts to grab* **Ikudayisi**'s *hand.* **Police Officer 1** *holds him back again.*

**Yemi**   STOP TRYNA FUCKING TOUCH ME UP. YOU BATTY MAN!

**Police Officer 1**   Ohh, bad mistake!

*He starts to bring out the handcuffs.*

**Ikudayisi**   Please, sir, he doesn't mean it.

**Police Officer 2**   Just stand over here, son.

**Yemi**   You can't hold me against my will.

**Police Officer 1**   We can if we suspect you being under the influence.

**Yemi**   Under the influence of what?

**Police Officers 1** *and* **2**    Cannabis.

**Yemi**    Dat's how I know you're chatting shit. Can you even smell anything on me?

**Ikudayisi**    Sir, please, how much do you want.

*He begins searching in his pockets.*

**Yemi** (*to* **Ikudayisi**)    Dayisi, are you mad, you don't got to pay for nothing.

**Ikudayisi**    How much do you want? I will go and get it and you can let him go.

**Yemi**    Stop talking!

**Police Officer 2** (*to* **Ikudayisi**)    Son, we're not corrupt officers, we don't take bribes – just sorting out this little dispute for you, OK?

**Ikudayisi**    Please, we don't want trouble.

**Police Officer 2** (*to* **Ikudayisi**)    Don't worry, it's not you that's causing the problems. (*He gets out his notebook. To* **Yemi**.) We will try this again. What is your name?

**Yemi**    I really ain't got time for this. Arrest me, innit.

**Police Officer 1**    Well, disturbing the peace is a big offence.

**Yemi**    Disturbing the peace, disturbing the peace – you're disturbing *my* peace. You came up to me with nothing to say, nothing! Just tryna force me to get mad. TO GET MAD SO I WILL DO SOMETHING, SO YOU CAN DO ME FOR SOMINK. That's how I know you people are corrupt. When you should be out doing something constructive. You're bugging me cos I'm black.

**Police Officer 1**    Don't try and use the race card here, boy, and keep your voice down.

**Police Officer 2**    There is nothing racist about us, stop tryna make a scene.

**Yemi**   You're stopping me from going home.

**Police Officer 1**   Home?

**Police Officer 2**   If you were willing to say that in the first place, of course we would have let you go home. Go on then.

**Yemi**   What?

**Ikudayisi**   We are sorry, sir.

**Yemi**   SHUT UP, DAYISI, WHAT YOU SAYING SORRY FOR? These mans are taking us for dickhead. Are you blind?

**Yemi** *goes to push him and the* **Police Officers** *hold him back.*

**Yemi**   The only reason they acting nice now is cos there are bare people around, looking at them, knowing they are being racist!

**Police Officer 1**   Oi, leave him alone.

**Police Officer 2** (*to onlookers*)   This is why, people, we're here. Just looking out for *his* best interest. (*To* **Ikudayisi**.) We wouldn't want anything to happen to you whilst you're in this country.

**Ikudayisi**   Uh?

**Yemi** (*to* **Ikudayisi**)   This is what I've been telling you all day, all day, but you never wanted to listen to me. What did I tell you bout this country?

**Police Officer 2**   Stop causing a scene.

**Yemi**   Nah, people need to hear what's going on.

**Police Officer 1**   Stop trying to be a smart alec.

**Yemi** (*begins shouting while being held*)   The only reason why these mans are holding me is cos I'm black. I ain't done nothing and they tryna arrest me.

*A message comes in on the police radio about a more important case.*

I'm being harassed, I'm being harassed!

**Police Officer 2**    Today's your lucky day, son.

**Yemi** *and* **Ikudayisi** *start to move, but get stopped again.*

**Police Officer 1**    No, you go that way and we will help him out.

**Yemi**    But we live *that* way.

**Police Officer 2**    There is still a chance of you getting arrested.

**Ikudayisi**    Please, he is my brother, sir.

**Police Officer 1**    You don't have to *pretend*, son, he won't trouble you again.

**Yemi** *kisses his teeth and heads off to the right. The* **Police Officers** *stay and watch till he goes offstage.*

**Police Officer 1**    Off you go then.

**Ikudayisi**    But –

**Police Officer 2**    Don't worry, son, we got you covered.

*The* **Police Officers** *stay and watch as* **Ikudayisi** *walks off to the left. He glances backwards once or twice, but the* **Police Officers** *stand their ground till he is out of sight.*

*Blackout.*


**Scene Eight**

*On the other side of the estate,* **Razer** *and* **Armani** *are walking down the street.* **Razer** *has his arms around* **Armani**.

**Razer**    You need to be more nicer to your friend, you nah.

**Armani**    Uh.

**Razer**    Paris, man, she is the only friend you got.

**Armani**    What? Whose side are you on? You saw the way she tried to speak to me.

**Razer**    Ah, don't worry. You two will be talking by the end of tonight.

**Armani**    I won't. She gets on my nerves and I'll let her know dat. I'm not fake – if I don't like someone I make dem know.

**Razer**    She's cool, man. How come she ain't got a boyfriend?

**Armani**    Cos she ugly.

**Razer**    Stop being silly. I'm tryna be serious.

**Armani**    Why are you interested for?

**Razer**    I'm not, it's for Flamer.

**Armani**    So let Flamer find out for himself. I'm never talking to her again.

**Razer**    You kinda messed up his flow.

**Armani**    How?

**Razer**    By making her storm off.

**Armani**    He needs to forget bout dat then.

**Razer**    Why?

**Armani**    Cos she tried to take me for an eediate, and I ain't no fool, and we are no longer friends.

**Razer** *lets go of* **Armani**.

**Razer**    You're so childish.

**Armani**    No, I'm just real.

**Razer**    No, you're just silly.

**Armani**    I don't know why you care. She is frigid, man. Anyways, Flamer don't stand a chance.

**Razer**    You're a hater, do you know that, Armani?

**Armani**    *No,* I'm not.

**Razer**   You are.

**Armani**   WHY ARE YOU SO FOCUSED ON TALKING BOUT PARIS FOR?

**Razer**   Forget it. Sometimes you get on my nerves. Man can't even have a civilised conversation with you without you running up your mouth.

**Armani**   I'm sorry. It's just today been a mad day. Everyone is trying to have a go at me. This is suppose to be a free country and people are not even allowing me to speak my mind.

**Razer**   Don't take it out on me.

**Armani**   Paris never even had my back.

**Razer**   You told this story already.

**Armani**   And you're my man, so don't you think you should have stood up for me when that dickhead African Blazer was shouting at me?

**Razer**   If you kept quiet Blazer would have left you.

**Armani**   And even when Paris tried to tell all those lies you never even said anything.

**Razer**   Aaaah, man.

**Armani**   Its true, dough – you could have said something.

**Razer**   Armani, you started most of these argument. What do you expect me to say?

*Pause.*

**Armani**   You gonna sort that Yemi out den?

**Razer**   Why?

**Armani**   Because these Africans are forgetting their place and you need to show him.

**Razer**    I'm not involved in this African war ting you're tryna start.

**Armani**    But he tried to attack me.

**Razer**    So? You tryna say you never done nothing to provoke him?

**Armani**    No – you know Africans are animals, man. He just went mad on me. He hit me in the head and he called you a dickhead, saying you can't do shit to him. You can't let him get away wid dat.

**Razer**    I'm not troubling nobody. If I get in trouble one more time I'm getting locked down, and I ain't going jail for no chick.

**Armani**    But –

**Razer**    Listen! I told you I'm not getting locked down for stupidness. Didn't you hear anything I said before? No chick gonna be the reason I get locked up, including you, Armani.

**Armani**    Then maybe you shouldn't be my man. I need a man who can look after me, one who is not afraid.

**Razer**    Go then.

**Armani**    A man is supposed to look out for his girl – he is meant to protect her no matter what.

**Razer**    I said, go then. Go fine a man better dan me.

**Armani**    That's why I should have gone out with Flamer. He's is not afraid of no one.

**Razer**    FUCK OFF!

**Armani**    You don't have to be so rude. What's your problem?

**Razer**    WHAT IS YOURS? You giving me a headache, man. I'm telling you to stop talking and all you do is talk. Can't you just be quiet for once, man? That's what gets you into trouble – your mouth. And you want me to get involved in your bullshit. I only fight battles that worth fighting. I'm tryna make changes and you're tryna force me to go down the wrong road.

**Armani**    Are you on your period or something?

**Razer**    Piss off, man.

**Razer** *puts up his hood and walks off, leaving* **Armani** *speechless.*

*Blackout.*


### Scene Nine

*It is now around eight in the evening, and* **Flamer** *is walking on the estate by himself when* **Ikudayisi** *runs onstage.*

**Ikudayisi**    YEMI, YEMI, WHERE ARE YOU NOW?

*He bumps into* **Flamer**.

**Flamer**    You idiot.

**Ikudayisi**    I'm sorry-oh, I didn't see you.

**Flamer**    So, what, I'm too black now?

**Ikudayisi**    Don't be stupid.

**Flamer**    You calling me stupid?

**Ikudayisi**    No, you don't understand. I'm saying how can I not see you, you are not that black.

**Flamer** *looks down at his trainers and sees one has a mark on it.*

**Flamer**    Look at my trainer, blud. Are you on a hype ting?

**Ikudayisi**    I'm sorry.

**Flamer**    What, is *that* all you're gonna say?

**Ikudayisi**    What do you want me to say now? It was only an accident. I didn't mean it.

**Flamer**    So what you gonna do about it then?

**Ikudayisi**   What do you want me to do? You can go home and clean it.

**Flamer**   Blud, do you think I'm a dickhead?

**Ikudayisi**   Please, I don' have time for this, I have to look for my brother.

**Ikudayisi** *start to walk off but* **Flamer** *catches hold of him.*

**Flamer**   Did I say we have finish?

**Ikudayisi**   What is wrong with today-oh? Why is everyone stopping people from walking? All I want to do is go home. I have said I'm sorry. What else do you want me to do?

**Flamer**   Sorry ain't gonna pay for it. I want my fifty pound!

**Ikudayisi**   Fifty pound for dis dirty trainer. Kayi! I don't have that kind of money-oh.

**Flamer**   Is this man dizzy? You steps on my foot and now you're tryna take me for an eediate. Are you buzzing?

**Ikudayisi**   I beg your pardon? I don't understand what you just said.

**Flamer**   What? All of a sudden you don't understand English now? Man better start understanding what I'm saying.

**Flamer** *brings out a knife.*

**Ikudayisi**   Ahhh, ARMED ROBBER! (*He raises his hands in the air.*) Be careful-oh. *Jo ma pa me! Ma pa me-oh!* [Don't kill me.]

**Flamer**   Speak English.

**Ikudayisi**   I don't have anything on me – please don't kill me.

**Flamer**   I'm not playing around! Give me my money.

**Ikudayisi**   I beg-oh. I don't have no money with me.

**Flamer**    Empty out your pockets.

**Ikudayisi**    Ah ah, now you don't believe me. Why will I lie? Look, I live on this estate. Give me your trainer and I will go and wash it for you now.

**Flamer**    I have never seen you round here before, so don't take me for an eediate. Empty your pocket.

**Ikudayisi** *empties out his pockets.*

**Flamer**    Where is your phone?

**Ikudayisi**    I don't have one.

**Flamer**    You ain't got a phone? What type of . . . ?

*He looks* **Ikudayisi** *up and down from head to toe.*

**Flamer**    Take off your trainers.

**Ikudayisi**    Ah, ah, I can't give you the trainers, I said I will clean your shoe for you.

**Flamer**    I said, take off the trainers.

**Ikudayisi**    It's not mine. Please, it's my brother's.

**Flamer**    Take off the fucking trainer, now.

**Ikudayisi**    Please, I didn't mean to step on your trainer. It was an accident, ah ah –

**Flamer** *moves closer to* **Ikudayisi** *with the knife.* **Ikudayisi** *quickly takes off the trainers.*

**Ikudayisi**    What is happening to this country? Why are you behaving like dis?

**Yemi** *enters and sees what is happening. He shouts over.*

**Yemi**    Oi!

**Flamer** *takes the trainers and runs.* **Yemi** *runs over to* **Ikudayisi**.

**Yemi**    Why you letting people push you around? This is what I mean bout you need to change.

**Ikudayisi**    Just leave me. *Awon olori buruku.* [These horrible people.]

**Yemi**    What happen, man?

**Ikudayisi**    This London *babanla problem lo wa fumi.* [This London is nothing but trouble for me.]

**Yemi**    I don't have time for this – what happen?

*Pause.*

Where is your – I mean *my* trainers?

**Ikudayisi**    He took it now.

**Yemi**    You got *jacked*!

**Ikudayisi**    No!

**Yemi**    So what happened?

**Ikudayisi**    I stepped on his trainer –

**Yemi**    You let someone take your trainers and you never even fought back? What the hell is wrong with you? See, see, I thought everyone was nice to you! You just made a man take you for an eediate and you couldn't do nothing.

**Ikudayisi**    I tried now.

**Yemi**    Tried! Tried! I swear in African you train with lion.

**Ikudayisi**    Yemi, don't start that . . . In Nigeria people die over things like this all the time-oh. I value my life. He had a knife.

**Yemi**    So?

**Ikudayisi**    What did you want me to do?

**Yemi**    NOT TO GET ROBBED!

**Ikudayisi**    I said he had a knife.

**Yemi**    If that was me, I would fight him same way. Do you think I care? You just made a man take you for an eediate and you didn't do nothing? And you were saying I don't know what I'm talking bout. I DON'T KNOW WHAT I'M TALKING ABOUT! Do you *now* see what this country is like? Do you see?

**Ikudayisi**    Where were you, eh?

**Yemi**    What! You tryna switch this on me? Was you not there when the police told me to walk? If you had any sense you would have followed me, instead of just standing around with them.

**Ikudayisi**    They told me to wait.

**Yemi**    Why did you listen?

**Ikudayisi**    Why didn't you stay?

**Yemi**    So is it my fault? You're a big boy and you got rob – I would never let that happen to me.

**Ikudayisi**    It wasn't my fault, it wasn't my fault. I beg him not to take it, he didn't listen. I'm not going to get killed because of trainer.

**Yemi**    You pussy.

**Ikudayisi**    I don't like this country. *Babalan* [enormous] problem.

**Armani** *enters, looking for* **Razer**.

**Armani**    Razer, where are you? RAZER!

*She sees* **Yemi**, *cuts her eye at him, then quickly runs off the other way.*

**Yemi**    Come on, let's go.

**Ikudayisi**    Where are you going to go?

**Yemi**    I'm going to settle this once and for all.

**Ikudayisi**    I don't have shoes on.

**Yemi**    We are going after the shoes.

**Ikudayisi**   You don't know where it is.

**Yemi**   Do you think it a coincidence that that girl is looking for her man in the same place you got robbed? Open your eyes.

**Ikudayisi**   Who?

**Yemi**   Armani. You blind? Did you not just see her come round da corner?

**Ikudayisi**   I don't want trouble. Let's just go home. We already have the milk. Mum will be worried.

**Yemi**   In this country you ain't got to look for trouble before it finds you. Can you not see dat? If you don't go for what is yours, they will always think you're a dickhead. If you don't stand your ground.

**Ikudayisi**   Who?

**Yemi**   Dem. That crew, it was dat Armani chick that told dem to come for you. We need to show them that they can't take us for eediate.

**Ikudayisi**   Please, let's just go home.

**Yemi**   Didn't you hear what Blazer was saying before?

**Ikudayisi**   Oh, please, eh, I don't like this.

**Yemi**   He said, yeah, we have to demand respect. I'm going to teach you how to stand your ground.

**Ikudayisi**   Listen to me, Yemi, I'm standing my ground now. Going after somebody who has a weapon is not good-oh. Yemi, I don't want to be a part of this. Let's go home.

**Yemi**   I ain't going nowhere till I sort this out. I have let this go on for too many years now. Mans ain't gonna take me for a dickhead *no more*!

**Ikudayisi**   Forget about years ago. You have to learn to choose your battle. There are more important things to fight over. Believe me.

**Yemi**    *Yes*, and this is one of them.

**Ikudayisi**    No, it's not – please, look, this is why you need to go to Nigeria and see. Things like this is small, small.

**Yemi**    Shut up! *Shut up!* Now is not the time to start talking your Nigerian shit.

**Ikudayisi**    Then what is it you are going to fight for? You are running to go and prove a point, but you don't know what point you are making.

**Yemi**    I'm doing this for me. I'm gonna make people know who I am.

**Ikudayisi**    Please, Yemi, this is not a good idea.

**Yemi**    Move out my way, Dayisi.

**Ikudayisi**    No, I can't let you do this. You have been telling me all day I need to change, but now it's time for you to stop and think. You make me laugh, you go on like your life is so hard. Believe me, you have it easy. Once you stop thinking dat the whole world has declared war on you, you will see how great your life is.

**Yemi**    Why don't you care about the fact that you just got robbed?

**Ikudayisi**    I told, I told you, it's not important. Do you think I have never had to make choices? I told you I was once like you. Is it the first time I got robbed? *No!* In Nigeria it happens all the time – even the police have robbed in broad daylight. I used to put up a fight but I told you, you soon realise thing like this is not important. As long as I'm alive, I'm happy. Friends in Nigeria have died over nonsense like this. I want to enjoy my life – those are the changes I have made. Don't waste your life away like this.

**Yemi**    Move. You ain't got to follow me. You can go off home.

**Ikudayisi** *tries to hold him back.*

**Yemi**   Get off me. This is going to be sorted with or without you!

*Blackout.*


**Scene Ten**

**Armani** *has caught up with* **Razer** *and they are walking together when* **Yemi** *comes round the corner, followed by* **Ikudayisi**.

**Yemi**   Oi, RAZER! Yeah, you, I'm talking to you. Give me my shit back.

**Razer** (*looks stunned*)   What? (*To* **Armani**.) What's he talking bout?

**Armani**   Move, you dickhead, who do you think you're talking to like that?

**Ikudayisi**   It wasn't him.

**Yemi**   Blud, why are you tryna take man for a dickhead?

**Razer**   What? What's wrong wid you people?

**Yemi**   I want it back now.

**Armani**   Are you crazy? Go talk your gibberish elsewhere, man.

**Yemi**   You think it is a coincidence my brother got robbed five minutes ago and then the only people I see on road – is you two?

**Razer**   Your brother?

**Yemi**   Yes, my brother. Don't think I'm stupid. You messed with the wrong person now.

**Razer**   Shut up, man. Move.

**Armani**   YEAH, DUSS.

**Yemi** (*to* **Armani**)   You shut up.

**Armani**    That's what I'm saying, Razer. Look, he is tryna get rude. Put him in his place. You see I wasn't lying. Look how he is acting like an animal.

**Razer**    Blud, just go home. I'm not in the mood.

**Razer** *tries to walk off but* **Yemi** *holds him back.*

**Ikudayisi**    Yemi, I told you it wasn't him.

**Yemi**    Only mans like him like to take advantage of people who can't defend themselves.

**Armani**    Be quiet, you bubo.

**Yemi**    I will knock you out.

**Ikudayisi**    *Omo girl e.* [Oh this girl.] Shut up your mouth.

**Armani**    SPEAK ENGLISH.

**Razer** *moves towards* **Ikudayisi**.

**Razer**    Don't talk to my girl like dat.

**Yemi**    He will talk to her any way he wants. Don't try to take him for an eediate and think he will sit down bout it. Give me my shit back.

**Razer**    Blud, don't get rude.

**Yemi**    What, you think you can pick on him cos he is African, but you can't deal with me?

**Razer**    I'm being nice – go home.

**Yemi**    Give me my tings and I'll go.

**Armani**    Razer, you're good, why don't you just thump him in his mouth, maybe then he will start making sense.

**Yemi** *moves close to* **Armani**.

**Yemi**    Thump who?

**Ikudayisi**    Yemi, leave her, it's not worth it at all. (*To* **Razer**.) We don't want trouble.

**Razer**   He seems to be asking it for it dough. You need to speak to your brother, cos I don't know what he is talking about.

**Ikudayisi** *tries to move* **Yemi**.

**Yemi**   DON'T TOUCH ME! I'm doing this for you. If you let people treat you like shit they will walk over you all your life.

**Ikudayisi**   Stop lying to yourself – I have already told you I'm not asking for this.

**Yemi** *pushes* **Ikudayisi** *and moves to* **Razer**.

**Yemi**   I just want my tings back.

**Razer**   Don't try and start something you can't finish.

**Yemi**   What dat suppose to mean?

**Razer**   This is da last time I'm going to tell you to go home. Don't try and get too big for your boot. Lauw da hype ting.

**Yemi** (*moves real close to* **Razer**)   I'm not on no hype ting – I just want my FUCKING TRAINERS BACK!

**Armani** (*to* **Razer**)   Why are you letting him talk to you like dat? This boy is a waste, man. DO SOMETHING.

**Yemi** *goes for* **Razer** *and* **Razer** *pulls out a knife.*

**Razer**   LOOK, I TOLD YOU GO HOME. Why are you making me do this?

**Ikudayisi**   Oh God, oh . . .

**Razer**   I'm trying, yeah, I'm trying. I don't wanna do this.

**Yemi**   You're making me mad and I don't want to get mad.

**Razer**   I DON'T WANNA GET MAD EITHER. Now I've told you I don't know what you're talking bout. So leave. NOW!

**Ikudayisi**   Please put it down.

**Yemi** (*to* **Ikudayisi**)    Stop BEGGING PEOPLE. (*To* **Razer**.)
I ain't scared of you, bruv. If you're gonna wet me then wet
me. But I don't care, I'm not going anywhere till you people
understand I ain't a dickhead. I ain't a dickhead.

**Ikudayisi**    Please, let's go.

**Armani**    Just wet him up, man, he deserves it.

**Razer**    Shut up Armani, man.

*As* **Razer** *gets distracted* **Yemi** *goes for the knife. They get into a
scrap and* **Yemi** *gains control over it.*

**Yemi**    Who is bad now, who bad now?

**Ikudayisi**    Yemi, put it down, you going to hurt somebody.
It wasn't him.

**Armani**    Yeah, listen to your brother.

**Yemi**    BE QUIET. YOU'RE ALWAYS FUCKING
TALKING. Don't you know when to keep your mouth shut,
uh? You really think you're bad, innit.

**Armani**    No.

*He waves the knife at her.*

**Razer**    Yemi, I swear – put it down.

**Armani**    No, please!

**Yemi**    See, you're scared now. I thought you were a bad
girl. African this and African that. You're not better than
me now, are you? Carry on running your mouth, see if you
don't get wet.

**Ikudayisi**    Why can't you listen to me? I keep telling you –
what you are fighting for is not worth it.

**Yemi**    Don't you get it? I don't care. These lots go on like
they run this fucking estate. It about time people sees who
really runs this estate. These jams think they are better dan
us Africans. Dat we ain't shit. That's why they robbed you. It

something they do all the time. They treat Africans like they are beneath them. I AIN'T BENEATH NO ONE.

**Razer**    Look, I'm tryna stay out of trouble, I ain't robbed no one in time.

**Yemi**    Well, you messed with the wrong person.

**Ikudayisi**    I didn't come from Nigeria to be a part of this. We are all BLACK! WE ARE ALL BLACK AND YOU ARE ACTING LIKE WE ARE ALL DIVIDED! It needs to stop now. We need to stop this nonsense. Why are we always fighting each other? Why can't we just get along? I just want everyone to get along. Yemi, you tell me you are free, be free to make the right choice. Don't go down the wrong road. It's your choice, make the right choice. GIVE ME THE KNIFE.

**Ikudayisi** *goes for the knife and struggles with* **Yemi**. *In the process the knife falls and* **Razer** *picks it up again.*

**Yemi** (*to* **Ikudayisi**)    Why do I bother listening to you – look what you done.

**Ikudayisi**    He doesn't want no trouble, he is going – leave him.

**Razer** *starts to walk.* **Yemi** *grabs him.* **Ikudayisi** *tries to stop him and as he gets in between his arm gets cut by the knife.*

**Ikudayisi**    Ahhhh!

*He falls to the ground.*

**Yemi**    IKU, IKU!

*He grabs* **Ikudayisi** *and holds him.*

**Armani**    Razer, look what you done, look what you done.

**Razer**    I didn't mean to, it was just in my hand. It wasn't my fault, it wasn't my fault. Ah fuck man! Yemi, it wasn't my fault.

*Blackout.*

**Scene Eleven**

*Two weeks later.* **Yemi** *and* **Ikudayisi** *are in their bedroom.*
**Ikudayisi** *is in traditional African attire and is struggling to put
on his hat because his arm is in a sling.* **Yemi** *is putting the agbada
over his head and is profiling in front of the mirror.*

**Mum** (*offstage, shouting*)    You two children, what is taking
you so long? We were supposed to be at the party from
seven o'clock. Look at the time now.

**Ikudayisi** *and* **Yemi**    I'M WAITING FOR HIM!

*They point at each other, look and begin laughing.*

**Mum** (*off*)    People already think I don't have any control of
you, that I leave you to gallivant and act like animals. What
are they going to be thinking when we show up late, eh? . . .
People always tell me that I'm –

**Ikudayisi**    LUCKY TO HAVE BIG BOYS!

**Yemi**    We are coming, Mum.

**Mum** (*off*)    I'M ONLY GIVING YOU TEN MORE
MINUTES!

**Ikudayisi** (*turns to* **Yemi**)    You're waiting for me? I've been
ready for an hour now and I'm the one that is handicap.

**Yemi**    Stop rinsing that line, it's played out now.

**Ikudayisi**    I know, I know, I just like making you feel
guilty.

**Yemi**    Badmind.

**Ikudayisi**    I will never forget the look on your face that day
when you thought I died.

**Yemi**    It wasn't funny, you nah. My heart skipped a beat.

**Ikudayisi**    And that Razer, I've never seen two boys cry as
much as you two.

**Yemi**   Why do you have to keep on telling the story like that?

**Ikudayisi**   Cos that is how it happened. Iku, Iku, don't die, don't die.

**Yemi** *punches him in the arm.*

**Ikudayisi**   Ow.

**Yemi**   Oh shit, oh shit. I'm sorry, I'm sorry.

**Ikudayisi** (*starts laughing*)   You are so gullible. At least I know you really love me.

**Yemi**   Shut up.

**Ikudayisi**   Come on, say it, you love me.

**Yemi**   Leave me.

**Ikudayisi**   Not until you say you love me.

**Yemi**   No! Stop acting gay.

**Ikudayisi**   Just say it.

**Yemi**   No.

**Ikudayisi**   I can't hear you.

**Yemi**   Cos I never said it.

**Ikudayisi**   Why are you being so –

**Mum** (*off*)   YOU THESE CHILDREN, I HAVE BEEN NICE TO YOU SINCE THAT DAY – OH, BUT I WILL STOP BEING NICE IF YOU DON'T LISTEN.

**Ikudayisi**   *Mon bo, Ma.* [I'm coming, Mum.] (*To* **Yemi**.) Just hurry up before she starts breathing fire and smoke comes out her nose.

**Yemi**   Yeah, OK.

**Ikudayisi** *turns to leave.*

**Yemi**   Ikudayisi.

**Ikudayisi**   Yeah?

**Yemi**   You have forgiven me, right?

**Ikudayisi**   For what?

*He turns to leave again.*

**Yemi**   Dayisi.

**Ikudayisi**   Yes?

**Yemi**   I'm sorry.

**Ikudayisi**   I know, I guess you now know what's important, right?

**Yemi**   Yeah, yeah I do.

**Ikudayisi** *goes to give* **Yemi** *a hug.*

**Ikudayisi**   Don't beat yourself up, we're brothers.

**Yemi**   Yeah, brothers.

**Ikudayisi** *exits.*

**Yemi** *picks up a basketball cap but then decides on the traditional hat. As he starts to put on his shoes he changes his mind and goes for his trainers. Once he has them on he stands in front of the mirror and checks himself out.*

**Yemi**   Yeah, I look heavy, man.

*He begins singing and dancing around the room.*

> Green white green on my chest,
> I'm proud to be a Nigerian!
> Green white green on my chest,
> I'm proud to be a Nigerian!
> Proud to be a Ni-ge-ri-an!
> Proud to be a Ni-ge-ri-an!

Lightning Source UK Ltd.
Milton Keynes UK
UKHW020211060720
366086UK00008B/266